packet

Soviet Military Thinking

Soviet Military Thinking

Edited by

DEREK LEEBAERT

Center for Science and International Affairs,
Harvard University

London
GEORGE ALLEN & UNWIN
Boston   Sydney

First published in 1981

GEORGE ALLEN & UNWIN LTD
40 Museum Street, London WC1A 1LU

British Library Cataloguing in Publication Data

Soviet military thinking.
  1. Russia – Military policy
  I. Leebaert, Derek
  355'.0335'47   UA770

  ISBN 0-04-355014-2
  ISBN 0-04-355016-9 pbk

Set in 11 on 12 point Times by Computape (Pickering) Ltd
and printed in Great Britain
by Mackays of Chatham

Contents

Preface

The study of military thought has focused traditionally on how military ideas are created, and how they are conveyed from one society, culture or institution to another. In studying any specific state, questions about doctrine tend to be clouded by definitional and methodological controversies. This is especially true when discussing the Soviet enigma. What does the range of verbal evidence called military doctrine tell us about Soviet goals and intentions, planning and force structures, estimations and expectations of relations with rival states? Official writings need to be juxtaposed with Soviet defense programs and international policies in order to clarify the opponent's preconceptions about the uses of force. Understanding the Soviet perspective is especially important at a time of increasing uncertainty about the future of East–West relations.

There has been a search for new intellectual moorings in approaching the political and military problems of coexisting with the Soviet Union. This has been brought about in part by enhanced Soviet military capacity, as well as by what some see as qualitatively new developments in Soviet international behavior. Faced with this troubling unfolding of events, the West is still wrestling with such fundamental philosophical questions as whether the Soviet Union is or is not less well-intentioned than we would wish it to be.

Irrespective of any degree of malevolence attributed to the Soviet Union, it is probable that within the near future, East–West relations will undergo further strain. A period of turning inward is likely to characterize the Soviet leadership succession. One disturbing problem for the West is whether such introspection will be accompanied by quiescent or by military behavior abroad in light of the intractable problems that the Soviets have to face at home.

Parallels have been drawn between the early years of the cold war and the late 1970s, given the low state of East–West relations and a perceived seizure of initiative by various revolutionary movements backed by the Soviet Union. But there was a great difference in the military potential of the superpowers in these two eras. Preponderance in nearly all sectors of military capability made it less important then than today for Western defense analysts to comprehend the Soviet Union, and to be acquainted thoroughly with the thinking of their counterparts. The Soviets have not been so remiss.

In the late 1940s, writings by Arendt, Kennan, Morganthau, Niebuhr, and others, were crucial to the development of a consensus within the United States on American policy toward the Soviet Union. Despite ambiguities and claims of misinterpretation, these works provided both a base and a sense of consistency to political analysis. But those in the West who can now authoritatively address questions of Soviet military affairs are relatively few. Scholars in Soviet area studies generally focus on other matters without coming to grips with political-military issues. Strategic analysts, on the other hand, have an unfortunate tendency to deal for the most part with relatively narrow technical matters. There is a need to examine thoroughly Soviet military thinking and to create a wider and more incisive literature on its origins, contents and implications.

The motivation for writing *Soviet Military Thinking* was felt nearly three years ago. The foreign policy quarterly, *International Security*, had commissioned several provocative essays that addressed the uncertainties of Soviet defense planning and intentions. At about the same time, the directors of Harvard University's Center for International Affairs, Russian Research Center, and Program (now Center) for Science and International Affairs sponsored a seminar series concerning Soviet military doctrine. The results of both of these efforts were curious. Authors of journal articles or of seminar papers had largely studied the same Soviet writings. Each had a considerable degree of expertise in defense analysis, having demonstrated previously an incisive understanding of the military balance and its evolution. Yet their conclusions and prognoses of these analysts were not only different, but occasionally contradictory.

Marked disagreements over fundamentals still exist in this book as well. Whether or not the Soviet leadership believes that a balance of mutual retaliatory capability should be maintained is a key part of the ongoing US national defense debate, a controversy that is reflected in these chapters as well as by discussion about such purported policy changes as Presidential Directive 59. Assumptions about the Soviet interpretation of deterrence then influence Western strategic building programs, budgets, arms control negotiations and alliance relationships.

On the conventional level, there is considerable doubt about the character of any Soviet attack on Western Europe. The United States, as its army field manuals show, plans for a linear, attrition-oriented engagement in which the cumulative effect of firepower is depended on to destroy enemy targets. This makes it convenient to then use only simple mathematical relationships in which wartime uncertainties are confined to technical unknowns. The image of a cumbersome, slow-to-mobilize opponent is at odds with von Mellenthin, among many others, who visualized that 'the air fleets and tank armies of the Soviet Union will throw themselves upon us with a velocity and fury far eclipsing any Blitzkrieg of World War II'.

Whether von Mellenthin's fears are borne out by actual Soviet force planning and capacity remains uncertain. The dilemma is that on both the strategic and non-strategic levels, Western defense decisions are based largely on suppositions about Soviet military thinking. Weighing the East–West balance is not as simple as would be indicated by Friedrich Engels's dictum that military superiority depends upon technology. Misunderstandings of Soviet thinking, along with an excessive reliance on technology, can lead to defense planning that overemphasizes the management principles of microeconomics while neglecting the operational dimension of war.

An *ad hoc* work group was established to study the many facets of Soviet military thinking. Its purpose was to produce individual chapters on some of the most vexing topics in defense studies: the contrast of superpower strategic theory, the status and origins of Soviet nuclear planning, the continuing expansion of Gorshkov's navy, Moscow's weapons procurement policies, and the exercising and utility of Soviet conventional forces. The assumption was that these subjects could be studied in both a scholarly and policy-oriented fashion, one that would not give in to the frequently apocalyptic tone of the defense debate. The collaborative approach was essential in my judgment, since it brought to bear the thoughts of different experts on specific research problems with which each was especially familiar.

The book's purpose is not to draw lessons, nor to offer policy prescriptions. The reader will even discover in several instances that the authors' conclusions are less than complementary. There are three general observations, however, that can be derived from this study. They emphasize the superpower strategic relationship which for a generation has dominated the field of security studies.

The first observation is that the Soviets believe that, if there is war with the USA, it will be or will very soon become nuclear. The second is that they argue, that given this belief, it is only sound military planning to be the one to initiate the nuclear exchange when war approaches. The third concerns US decision-makers. In light of these perceptions, there is a need to disrupt any Soviet calculation of the advantages seen in being the first to go nuclear. It is necessary to reduce the pay-off of pre-emption to the lowest extent possible.

Soviet Military Thinking does not evaluate the policy recommendations that are a part of the ongoing strategic debate in the West. Will the Soviets continue to be deterred, if they can count only on destroying those strategic assets that the USA has long regarded as susceptible to a first strike? Or will the vulnerability of US ICBMs tempt pre-emption as a superpower crisis mounts? Questions such as these often have more in common with theology than with strategy. But the overall debate needs to be based on more than a casual acquaintance with the Soviet perspective.

The 1980s will be a decade of special uncertainty for Western political and military planners. Few are preoccupied with a bolt-out-of-the-blue attack. Instead, there are new problems such as those that could arise from a non-SALT environment. One can argue that a different strategic world with ballistic missile defenses and mobile ICBMs may be a safer one, but it would also be a world with exceedingly complicated military assessments. With or without further constraints on strategic systems, the history of the nuclear age shows that no weapon will retain its invulnerability for ever. Comforting assumptions of Western leads in military technology, of control of sea lines of communication, and of secure second-strike capabilities are also slipping into the past.

The following chapters each offer different views and approaches. This may be the best illustration of the topic's special complexities, as well as the most thorough way to confront the analytical challenges ahead.

Derek Leebaert
Cambridge, Massachusetts
1981

Acknowledgements

A book written by several authors has a unique development. Problems of criticism, coordination and logistics compound the already-challenging tasks of analysis. Therefore, the advice and encouragement of people not formally a part of the work group are especially important. Our purpose during the past year has been to address with originality and dispassion the exceedingly controversial topic of Soviet military thinking. To the extent that we have succeeded, we would like to thank specifically those associates who have also contributed to this study.

Melissa Healy, Assistant Managing Editor of *International Security*, and a member of the professional staff of Harvard's Center for Science and International Affairs, performed as a true Stakhanovite throughout the preparation of this book. Her substantive and editorial skills were, quite simply, indispensable. We would also like to thank the Directors of the Center, notably Albert Carnesale, for assisting this project in ways too numerous to catalogue. Michael Mandelbaum, a friend and Harvard colleague, offered that special combination of wit and judgment that is essential in sustaining any extended collaborative process. In addition, two other academic colleagues, Professors Stephen Meyer of MIT and Catherine Kelleher of the National War College were especially most forthcoming in sharing advice and criticism.

The benefits of unique perspective and authoritative debate were provided by Elizabeth Bancroft, Onno Leebaert, M. E. Lewis, Richard Pipes, Dimitri Simes, Lord Saint Brides and Anne Day Thacher. Their expertise in contending with a variety of international political problems, in addition to those of security studies, was a constant source of instruction.

The authors believe it essential to emphasize that we alone are responsible for the analysis and opinions that follow. It may seem obvious to record this, but we do so because of the many affiliations reflected in this collective effort. Arguments do not represent the positions of any of the academic or governmental offices with which the authors are affiliated.

PART ONE

The International Setting

1

The Context of Soviet Military Thinking

DEREK LEEBAERT

This chapter discusses the role of military power in the political processes, traditions and international behavior of the USSR. Soviet military doctrine cannot be discussed *in vacuo*. As is true of foreign policy intentions, doctrine is not static. Like intentions, it is influenced by the capabilities of the armed forces. Amid all of the controversies in the West about Soviet military affairs, two points are agreed upon. The first is that the military balance has shifted in Moscow's favor. The second is that military power has a unique significance in the deliberations of the Politburo. Disputes over all other problems of analysis are a matter of degree. The purpose here is to highlight the implications of the ways in which the balance has changed, and to examine the array of issues that are raised by the Soviet emphasis on military capacities.

Soviet poet Yevgeny Yevtushenko wrote a popular song of which the title, the first and the last lines all asked, 'Do the Russians want a war?' Of course his answer is that they do not, with the immense sufferings of World War II given as the reason for a profound Russian yearning for peace. Trying to answer this question beyond the world of song, however, is not as simple as whether one side or the other wants war. Neither does. War, after all, is not physically started by the aggressor, but only by the defender who chooses to resist. In any period of high international tension one state cannot count altogether on the rational calculation of its opponent.

It is necessary to examine more problematical questions about war to avoid the miscalculations that can both bring it about, and that can result in some form of defeat should deterrence fail. Why is it now especially important to examine Soviet military thinking? How should one approach the analytical difficulties involved? Finally, can the issues that emerge from such a study assist Western policy-makers?

The USSR has achieved superpower status largely by virtue of its military capabilities, being relatively deficient in other indicators of national power. Reviewing Soviet military writings as well as weaponry, can help explain how the Soviets see their armed forces as an adjunct to foreign policies. It can also help clarify the views of Soviet military and government officials concerning the uses of force. Such understanding is especially important, if there appears to be a convergence of Soviet leadership predispositions with articulated military doctrine. An increasingly accepted view in the West is that the Soviets are heading toward what they believe is a nuclear war-winning capability. At a minimum, enhanced Soviet strategic forces are seen as a backdrop for a profound growth in Soviet strength. Some perceive a disturbing congruence of doctrine and military acquisitions in the direction of military superiority.

These developments come at a time when, in the absence of SALT, the future of the superpower strategic relationship is especially unclear. Both the USA and the USSR have adhered to the freeze of the SALT I Interim Agreement. Only the USSR reaches the ceiling of SALT II. Uncertainty for the West is compounded, since it does not share the USSR's benefit of studying the Russian equivalent of the publicly disseminated US five-year defense plans. In addition, the acknowledgement of nuclear parity and the continuing turmoil in South Asia have focused renewed attention on Soviet naval and conventional forces. The uses and potential of the Soviet military will be central to international relations of the 1980s. There is more than an academic need to explore Moscow's views on the utility, circumstances and precedents surrounding military power.

Why Soviet Military Thinking is Now Being Studied

During the past decade, a presumed political relaxation created the impression that the intensity of the military rivalry had been moderated. Unsurprisingly, this did not last. Regional instabilities have brought renewed attention to the military arena. There are new opportunities for expanded Soviet influence around the Persian Gulf, in East Asia, and elsewhere. Should the USSR exploit these opportunities, it is less likely than in the past that ensuing conciliatory overtures to the West will be sufficient to ease increasing antagonisms. The USA may today be on the threshold of foreign policy decisions as far-reaching as those made early in the cold war. The sea-change in US foreign policies during the first months of 1980 reflected the extent of the decline in relations between East and West. For the USA, a more realistic view of the Soviet system and Soviet foreign policies emerged. In both capitals there exists a widening gap in the perception of international events.

Postwar debates concerning the mechanics of Western defense have been remarkably redundant. This results not so much from the intellectual impoverishment of the analysts, as it does from the fact that so much of the debate consists of only contrasting opinions. But specific historical cases can be useful for both the lessons they provide, and for their help in creating a data base for examining current security dilemmas.

Thirty years ago, for example, the USA embarked on a re-assessment of Western defense that, in the sense of urgency and peril, is not dissimilar from today's political-military stock-taking. Some have concluded that knowledge of the events of the 1950s can help sensitize US decision-makers to many of the persisting requirements of their national security policies.[1] A series of reversals abroad and perception of an increasing diminution of the US world power position led to the seminal 1949–50 strategic appraisal known as NSC 68. In its assumption of a delicately poised balance of power and in its definition of US national security interests in terms of foreign threats, this product of the State-Defense Policy Review Group laid the foundation for a generation of US policy decisions.

An historical debate continues about both the construction of NSC 68, and about the preconceptions of its architects.[2] But regardless of the document's correctness, it has a familiar ring. Above all, it emphasized a burgeoning Soviet military capacity counterposed by both inadequate Western defense spending and by less than coherent security policies. The assumptions made in NSC 68 about Soviet military intentions, and the recommendations presented for meeting them, helped establish the course for two decades of East–West competition. The decisions taken today may not be as pivitol as were those of 1950. But at this time of reassessment, the need for dispassionate and careful analysis is especially important.

Richard Lowenthal warned in 1978 that major Soviet decisions might soon be prepared in a situation in which the Soviets have the impression that they have nothing to hope and nothing to fear from the USA or, indeed, from the West in general.[3] Decisions in Moscow can now be made against a substantially, and from its perspective, favorably revised military balance compared to fifteen years ago. It is uncertain how dangerous to the West will be the political advantages that result.

One explanation for the current impasse in superpower relations is that by the end of the 1970s, the Soviets were very much in a situation of having little to hope and little to fear. The potential benefits from détente were not as large as either side had expected. Moscow may have anticipated that SALT II would be defeated. And the failure of trade to grow as assumed can be seen as another example for a Soviet loss of hope in any returns stemming from improved relations with the USA. Closer ties with China, the NATO agreement to modernize theater nuclear forces, the US decision to proceed with the MX ICBM, and the increase in Alliance defense budgets, could together have convinced the Soviets that there were not many more adverse paths that the West could follow. The Soviets see US hostility on one hand, and relative impotence on the other. They believe that Washington has a nostalgic and unrealistic view of the world, but at the same time it is unwilling to pay the real price for its imperial design.

There has been no need for the Soviet Union to observe recent Western reactions passively. The Brezhnev era has given it the economic base for a sustained arms competition with the West. Whereas Stalin was preoccupied with military development as the exclusive product of an improved economy, ensuing leaderships strove for a more comprehensive rivalry. Nevertheless, the Soviet military remains the only sector that is globally competitive. In foreign trade, for example, the size of Soviet arms transfers as a percentage of total exports shows the importance given to military means in an effort to gain international influence.[4]

The magnitude of Soviet military spending and construction only partially explains the trends in the superpower military relationship. The existing balance is the result of two processes: the US diversion of enormous defense resources into the Vietnam War, and the simultaneous balanced incremental growth of Soviet defense spending. An estimated 250 billion US defense dollars were sacrificed in Southeast Asia. Considering that over 50 percent of the defense budget goes into personnel and maintenance, these dollars in Vietnam were the equivalent of many years' worth of defense investment.

The resultant cuts in real US defense spending amounted to some 20 percent of outlays during 1971–6. The USSR, however, proceeded with a gradual but consistent expansion of strategic and conventional forces. In part through this continuing program, the Soviets were able to compensate for the more concerted US strategic spending during the 1960s that ranged from 14 to 28 billion yearly in FY 80 constant dollars, with US ICBMs increasing from 200 in 1962 to the current number of 1,054 in 1967. Soviet forces now reflect the cumulative result of a real increase in defense spending by the Central Intelligence Agency to be estimated 3–4 percent per annum over the last twenty years.[5] The crossover point in comparative spending was reached in the early 1970s and the line continues upward for the USSR. The Soviets have also devoted greater percentages of their total expenditures to research and development. But given the ambiguities in spending estimates, attention should be directed to how these moneys have actually affected Soviet forces.

Heightened controversy about Western defense priorities has occurred against the backdrop of what former Secretary of Defense Donald Rumsfeld called 'a dynamic, deteriorated, still deteriorating strategic situation'.[6] On the other hand, a presumed strategic deadlock is nothing new. Alistair Buchan already believed in 1958 that such a deadlock was fundamentally unbreakable.[7] But current anxiety in the West stems from the counterforce potential of Soviet land-based missiles, as well as from a significant increase in Moscow's capability for dispatching power through improved air and sea lift.

In the fall of 1962, presidential adviser John McCloy invited First Deputy Foreign Minister V. V. Kuznetsov to his farm in Connecticut. The US Second Fleet had imposed a blockade and American nuclear forces had been on a Defcon 2 alert only several weeks earlier during the Cuban missile crisis. The ratio of opposing forces had been clearly unfavorable to the USSR. As the two men negotiated the details of the withdrawal of the Soviet MRBMs and IRBMs, Kuznetsov summed up the crisis to McCloy in a remark also attributed later to Khrushchev: 'We will not let you do this to us again.'[8]

The outcome of those thirteen days was not just the result of a military equation. Nor should the events be seen as a *deus ex machina* for subsequent Soviet military acquisitions. (Lead times in naval building, for example, indicate that decisions to procure recent generations of ships could not have been initiated immediately after Cuba.) But Kuznetsov's remark was correct in capturing one important lesson for the Soviets. It was also correct in forecasting that the missile crisis would be the last time that the USA could apply such overwhelming nuclear and conventional superiority. Since then, Soviet weapons development has belied Secretary McNamara's assurance in 1965 that 'the Soviets have decided that they have lost the quantitative' strategic arms race and 'are not seeking to engage us in that contest'.[9]

McNamara was soon proven incorrect, and today's trends in

the strategic balance are the consequence of having taken such assertions seriously. Intelligence estimates then said that the Soviets were unlikely to exceed substantially the US number of ICBM launchers. When the Soviets did outpace the USA, it was argued that they would not try for a capability to fight, and in some fashion, win a nuclear war.[10] By 1980, the new US National Intelligence Estimate, NIE-1138-79, indicated that at the end of the decade, the USSR could have approximately 14,000 highly accurate warheads mounted on its land-based missile force.[11] These trends have markedly changed academic as well as government assessments of Soviet intentions, and of Soviet military thinking.[12]

Former Secretary of Defense Harold Brown's observations during the first year of the Carter administration that 'we have a certain amount of catching up to do in some areas', helped minimize the adverse trend in military capability, one that probably warrants more concern with the US conventional than with the nuclear forces.[13] Obviously, the USA has substantially augmented its own forces over the past fifteen years. The Soviets, for their part, note that it was the USA that first deployed MIRVed warheads and that for the moment it is the USA that has a greater absolute number of warheads, even if the ratio of warheads to ICBMs is in the Soviet favor. But the US acquisition process has not been as dramatic, nor as concentrated, as that of the Soviets. During these years, the Soviet forces were improved as follows:

- an addition of about 1 million in military manpower;
- a fivefold increase in the number of strategic delivery vehicles, and an expansion of the number of warheads these vehicles can carry by a factor of 11;
- a deployment of five new types of ICBMs, three new SLBMs, MIRV warheads for both, and a quintupling of ICBM accuracy;
- the beginning of a modernization program for the Soviet medium-range peripheral attack forces, including the SS-20 and the Backfire bomber;
- the addition of some twenty-five divisions to the Soviet Ground Forces, the deployment of new tanks, new armored fighting vehicles, new self-propelled artillery, new chemical warfare systems, new attack helicopters, new air defense systems and tactical missiles, and the provision of about 1,000 more front-line combat aircraft to the structure of Frontal Aviation, which is also being modernized.

The balance is susceptible to a variety of interpretations. But only recently has the official and unofficial US defense community agreed that there is a great similarity between Soviet weapon acquisitions and the Soviet military literature's long-standing emphasis on operational strategic competence in all its dimensions. This emphasis has been directed toward whatever potential there may be for victory. The challenge to every tenet of strategic stability as defined in the West raises questions not only about future Soviet foreign defense policies, but also about Moscow's conception of war. There is a fundamental tension between strategic war-fighting capability and nuclear stability.

The Analytical Difficulties

Thucydides first recorded the ambiguities of distinguishing between offensive and defensive preparedness. Such difficulties are evident in studying the Soviet military. For example, a technically effective counterforce capability against fixed US ICBMs is unsurprisingly claimed by Moscow as being defensive. Regardless of whether or not one accepts this claim, an opponent's stated intentions can hardly be taken as immutable.

Force effectiveness itself is exceedingly difficult to quantify, the numerical comparisons portray only a rough perceived balance. The advent of versatile technologies such as the cruise missile, as well as the relative imponderables of command/control/communications effectiveness, wartime alliance cohesion, and other factors, add to the complexities of comparing superpower capabilities.

American analysts have often cited US technological superiority as offsetting continuing Soviet deployments. They point to Soviet difficulties with microchips and with submarine technologies as explanations for Moscow's development of a high throw-weight ICBM force. Whether or not this reason for the Soviet force structure is correct, any US qualitative advantage is hardly guaranteed. For example, the Carter administration was shocked in December 1977 by the high test accuracy of the Soviet SS-18 heavy ICBM, later calling such technological success a 'betrayal'.[14] Similar Western underestimates preceded the speed and technical ability with which the Soviets have been bringing their petroleum reserves to fruition. The lesson is that US complacency over the qualitative deficiencies of the Soviet command economy, one that has to buy an entire truck plant from the West, will not long compensate for quantitative shifts in the military balance.

The dominant Western prognoses through most of the 1970s about Soviet military trends have been proven wrong. Once-fashionable beliefs about the Soviet definitions of parity and deterrence are now, at the least, exceedingly controversial. There is a need to focus on specific research problems that have so far made accurate military and political assessments elusive.

Determining the Extent of the Soviet Effort

There are those, among them the chairman of the Joint Chiefs of Staff, who see a Soviet military expansion reminiscent of German rearmament in the 1930s.[15] Others, such as Congressman Les Aspin, offer a radically different view.[16] Each draws inferences, reasonably enough, about Soviet intentions from his interpretation of trends in military capability. Marx wrote that a nation's military spending is like throwing its capital into the water. Moscow hardly seems to agree. No matter whether one accepts the views of the JCS chairman or of the congressman on the intensity of the Soviet build-up, the totality of military trends is going against the USA.

Ten years ago on the eve of détente, the 24th Party Congress decided to shift the focus away from heavy and defense industries toward more consumer goods. This decision has remained largely a commitment on paper. The USSR has been able to avert a guns-or-butter decision during the arms build-up of the last fifteen years through steady economic growth. But the Soviet economy has reached a point where a simple trade-off no longer characterizes the relationship between the two. An economy constrained by declining rates of growth in the 1980s could demand sacrifices in both sectors. Given current spending patterns, an optimistic Western analysis might conclude that this slower economic growth could lead to an abatement of military developments. An economic slowdown would certainly make it more difficult to sustain newly accelerated weapon programs. Acquiring guns gets more difficult for the USSR in the 1980s, regardless of any changes in emphasis on butter.

Soviet economic difficulties should not be exaggerated. But an unbridled superpower arms race is at least not economically in Moscow's interest. There has historically been a positive correlation between Soviet economic growth and increases in military spending, resulting in a military share of GNP that is roughly 12–14 percent, according to the CIA.[17] The overall growth rate of the Soviet economy is likely to decline in the 1980s, and this diminished rate of growth may be reflected in commensurate decreases in the growth rate of military sending.[18] None the less, based upon the record of the past, military expenditures should continue to increase in absolute terms, albeit more slowly in line with the modest expansion of the economy. An increase in Soviet military expenditures at a ratio similar to that of the 1970s should be able to continue for the forseeable future without significantly disrupting economic programs or social stability.[19]

The conclusion can be reached that the USSR's newly acquired position of military strength will endure in this decade despite greater Western efforts to increase defense spending. But projections of Soviet military budgets remain essentially speculative, complicated in part by the uncertain effects of increasing energy shortages, the decline of the productivity factor and rises in consumer demand.

The valuation of personnel and high-technology equipment will continue to obscure precise assessments of Soviet spending, and of the degree of the Soviet economy's inbalance.[20] For example, the CIA estimates about the extent of the Soviet sacrifice for military capability have recently been both changed and challenged. The different meaning of prices in market and planned economies makes military spending an uncertain factor in comparing forces.

Some understanding of spending levels, however, is important, since they serve as an index of commitment and as a measure of the opportunity costs that a nation accepts in pursuing its military goals. Fluctuations in Soviet defense spending as well as constraints on the Soviet economy are variables to be studied in analyses of military doctrine or arms race behaviour. But concern with the causes, consequences and likely trends in Moscow's defense outlays has more often been addressed ideologically rather than empirically.

What is more important in discussions of Soviet military thinking than the volume of defense spending is the question of where the moneys are directed. This can have important implications for determining the degree of threat that the opponent presents. For example, Soviet investment during the early 1960s in what was labeled 'airpower' was construed falsely as adding substantially to offensive capacity. This was not the case, and in fact such spending was directed chiefly toward air defense.

Sensitivity to the relation between spending and capability, as well as a high level of disaggregation in looking at weapon acquisitions, is central to a meaningful contrast of opposing forces. The analyst also has to gauge how much strain is being placed on the Soviet economy, and then determine how this affects his own prognoses. He must recognize the pitfalls in assessing forces and budgets, precision becoming increasingly important as the opponent grows more technically and industrially proficient.

Intentions and Capabilities

The Western analyst has to depend in large part on his interpretation of Soviet intentions in making his policy recommendations. He cannot focus exclusively on spending levels and capabilities. This would be too ready a justification for worst-case planning, with all the drawbacks of over-reaction and wasted expenditure that that suggests. What occurs is the classic analytical dilemma of how heavily to weight the opponent's statements, beliefs and fixations. John Strachey confronted this problem nearly twenty years ago:

> It is a military maxim that in framing a country's defense policy, the capability alone, and never the intentions of other nations must be taken into account. But this is one of those maxims which however dutifully are preached in the staff colleges, can never be adhered to in the cabinet rooms.[21]

The study of intentions, or the importance of considering what an opponent is saying as well as what he is doing, is not without operational significance. It could be argued, for example, that had Washington paid more attention during the past decade to stated Soviet objectives of nuclear superiority, the USA would not be in its current military predicament.

This argument, however, is a *post hoc* rationalization for the defense budgets of the early 1970s, which declined consistently in real terms, but for reasons other than just an underestimation of Soviet building programs. The USA is actually experiencing the results of a self-inflicted restraint. But if Soviet intentions are seen as indicating a probability of war, US defense spending could be increased substantially and without severe economic dislocation. Recall the US debate in early 1950 over a 15 percent rise in the defense budget. This evaporated after 25 June as a 300 percent increase was achieved. The character as well as the magnitude of defense preparations are reflections of judgments about the likelihood of war, and other needs for military power of various kinds. Most recently, reassessment of Soviet intentions resulted in the supplement to the FY 1981 Defense Department budget, despite vigorous denials of this cause and effect by the then Secretary of Defense.

Two airpower examples illustrate the dangers of studying only capabilities or intentions. Looking at the former exclusively, Soviet planners in the 1950s invested approximately 10 billion rubles in building an air defense against the new US B-52 bomber. The B-52 was known as capable of high-altitude attack. The Soviet investment became largely wasted once the modernized bomber became intended for below-radar penetration. Twenty years later, dwelling largely on intentions, US SALT negotiators agreed that the Backfire bomber, with a longer range than many B-52s, would be excluded from Soviet strategic force totals if it was only based in certain areas. This is an arms control agreement that is unique in depending upon the opponent's good faith in not using weapons that have been purportedly deployed for other purposes.

Policy recommendations founded entirely on opinions of enemy intentions are as fraught with peril as are those resting just on capabilities. But besides the volatility of intentions, their study is a far more esoteric, subjective, and fault-prone exercise than that of capabilities. An over-reliance on capabilities or on intentions can be hazardous. There is a need for the analyst to strike a balance. Serious study has been given to Soviet military statements in so far as they complement and explain newly achieved capabilities.

In the 1960s and into the early 1970s, Soviet writings claiming the need for a strategic war-winning posture were overshadowed by US nuclear preponderance. Today, discussion of Soviet military thinking is especially important in light of incorrect assessments of the past and the Defense Department's acknowledgement that it finds Soviet doctrine 'murky'.[22]

The Status of Soviet Doctrine

It is against this background of international tension and military competition that the significance of Soviet doctrine is being debated. There is a need to go beyond either accepting Soviet military writings as blueprints of procedures and expectations, or dismissing them as not representative of civilian thinking. Just as precision is crucial in examining the strategic forces of the two superpowers, so too is it important to be clear about what is meant by doctrine.

At one pole are those Western analysts who claim that the Soviets mean what they say, and that current Soviet weapon programs reflect the conviction that a nuclear war can be fought and won. At the other are those who argue that military writings mainly support different purposes such as sustaining troop morale or satisfying ideological desiderata.[23] The latter group tends to believe that contrary to the impression given by much of the Soviet military literature, Moscow accepts mutual assured destruction, conceived in essentially the same way as it was once articulated by American academic theorists. The assumption here is that a nuclear balance is maintained by the common certainty that an opponent can inflict unacceptable damage after absorbing a first strike.

This simple dichotomy becomes obscured when analysts agree that the military literature means what it says, but who then emphasize different writings in making their competing arguments. The Soviet literature on military doctrine is not monolithic. These two poles are useful, however, for showing the breadth of the debate over Soviet military thinking, a correct answer concerning Soviet beliefs probably being somewhere in between.

The Soviets formally define their doctrine as 'the sum total of scientifically based views accepted by the country and its armed forces on the nature of contemporary wars that might be unleashed by the imperialists against the USSR, and the goals and missions of the armed forces in such a war, on the methods of waging it, and also on the demands which flow from such views, for the preparation of the country and the armed forces'.[24] The formation of doctrine for the USSR is an accretionary process, as for any other nation of its size and complexity. Among the formative internal sources of Soviet doctrine are the country's location, demographics, level of economic development, history and the nature of the political system. External sources include the nature of its involvement in the alliance systems, as well as the perception and evaluation of the opponent's capabilities and intentions.

In a precise encapsulation, Michael MccGwire uses 'doctrine' to cover the accumulated policies, practices, concepts and procedures (explicit as well as implicit) which combine to shape and to provide the framework for behavior at all levels of action, from strategic planning to weapon procurement and tactical operations.[25] Problems of definition and content nevertheless remain.

Soviet doctrine can be highly generalized and ambiguous. The Soviets draw distinctions between military art (the theory and practice of preparing and conducting military operations) and military science (the system of knowledge about the character and laws of war). The strategic, operations and tactical theory of military art forms part of military science. These distinctions may appear scholastic, but they arise frequently in discussions of Soviet military policy-making.

Influences that in the past have been cited to explain the peculiarities of Soviet doctrine include the military's institutional chauvinism, bureaucratic inefficiency, lags in the Russian learning curve about the implications of new weaponry, and even the effort to exploit US susceptibility to being strategically outmaneuvered. A copious literature of example and refutation surrounds each argument. Officially, as Benjamin Lambeth has explained, Soviet views on war and deterrence are a product of continuous refinement by theoreticians in the senior service academies, the main political administrations of the armed forces, and the main operations directorate of the General Staff.[26] The military-technical side of doctrine is affected by lead times and refinements in weapon systems, as well as by a broad reading of the views of the probable enemy. It deals with the methods of waging war, the organization of the armed forces, their technical equipment and their combat readiness. Final approval by party leadership follows the Defense Ministry's integration into finished doctrine of the criteria for peacetime weapon acquisitions and wartime force employment.

The political side of military doctrine, for its part, is shaped by the political and economic strategies of the Communist Party, by current developments in national science and technology, and to some extent, by the perception of global trends. Soviet theorists claim that the military-political component is the more decisive in the formulation of military doctrine. Western discussions of Soviet practice, however, are inevitably somewhat abstract. But the degree of imprecision can be reduced by juxtaposing more concrete types of evidence, such as weapon programs, against Soviet public pronouncements and writings.

Western analysts of Soviet military thinking resort to an array of Russian source material. They then engage in the academic swordplay of footnoting by citing the same generally available published references. Intellectual mysteries result, however, from the different and occasionally contradictory conclusions that they reach. Analysts ascribe varying levels of authority to these Russian writings, and the ensuing debates have something in common with those among students of the sixteenth-century Muscovite state.[27] There are controversies about the purpose and meaning of the respective literatures, while the reader himself is left to grant such writings their proper political significance.

It can be stated with as much certainty as is possible in discussing the Russian enigma that simple comparisons of Soviet military writings with those of senior US officials are seriously misleading. Several years ago, Nathan Leites used an apocryphal story to emphasize the difference in the way that US and Soviet military officers discussed war. He created a Defense Department bureaucrat, naming him John Jones, who wanted to get a classified report concerning damage limitation through nuclear pre-emption cleared for outside publication.[28] Jones duly presented the report to a review committee which squelched it, because of the report's inflammatory and preposterous conclusions. In his story, however, Leites used in the language of the report real quotations from Vice-Admiral V. V. Yakavlev's book, *The Soviet Navy.* The purpose of Leites's story was to show not only the different types of public writings condoned by the respective defense establishments, but also to determine a reader's reaction to such bellicose passages were they to have emanated from the office of the Joint Chiefs of Staff. Whereas the Western reader would be shocked by the excesses of any such JCS-sponsored writings, he has come to dismiss the extremeness of precisely the same statements made by a Russian officer.

The centerpiece of Soviet writings on military matters is Marshal V. D. Sokolovsky's *Military Strategy* (*Voennaya Strate-quiia*), first published in 1962 and updated in 1963 and 1968. In the West, it is among the most frequently cited books on these matters, which is not surprising for it was the first work of its kind since A. Svechin's *Strategy* was published in 1926. An abundance of military writings followed the 22nd Party Congress in 1961, with its rhetoric of de-Stalinization, and the flow continues. Expositions on doctrine, strategy and other facets of military science can be found throughout this literature. Nearly all is available in translation. For example, the seventeen volumes of the Officer's Library, written between 1965 and 1975 and developed for acquainting the officer 'with a knowledge of the fundamental changes which have taken place in recent years in military affairs', are now accessible in English and have received wide attention in the West.[29]

The official military-theoretical journal *Voennaya mysl'* is noteworthy and cited often, since as the organ of the Ministry of Defense, not the Main Political Administration, it is intended strictly for internal use. Therefore, it can be studied by the analyst with relatively little worry that it is aimed at less sophisticated mass military and lay Soviet readerships – or at non-Soviet audiences. (In 1968, then Minister of Defense Marshal Rodin Ya. Malinovsky noted that this journal is the main military-theoretical organ of the Ministry, and that 'it plays an important role in the working out of military-theoretical problems'.)[30] Some issues are now available to US analysts for open citation. But it is clandestinely acquired and only those available issues through 1973 are now declassified.

There are different Western views about how to interpret and apply such source materials. The approach of some analysts is to read and reread them, trying 'to understand the Soviet mind-set and isolate the basic principles that appear to dominate Soviet military thought'.[31] The underlying assumption of these analysts is that the Soviets adhere exactly to such writings. On the other hand, there is something like William Kaufmann's 'Ritz-Carlton theory'. He argues that if a Soviet analyst was isolated in this Boston hotel with nothing to read but US journals such as *Strategic Review* and *Orbis*, he would arrive at a view of his opponent's belligerency as disturbing as the view Western analysts would form from reading Soviet military periodicals. This theory, however, has been discredited by the evolution of the portfolio of Soviet nuclear weaponry.

The authority that the Western analyst attributes to Soviet military writings, naturally enough, shapes his ensuing conclusions about Soviet intentions. This is especially true in the Western debates about the role of war-fighting in Soviet nuclear planning. Already in 1959, General James Gavin described the work of Clausewitz as the Rosetta Stone to understanding Soviet military thinking, a metaphor that has been used many times since.[32] He among others argues that the Soviet conception of both nuclear and conventional force is intertwined with Clausewitz's proposition that war is the continuation of politics by other means, or that war is the continuation of policy with an admixture of other means.

Soviet writings clearly indicate that there are military provisions for the failure of nuclear deterrence. The leadership is not ready to acknowledge that such a failure means forgoing any political goals. It has no illusions about the catastrophic consequences of such a conflict, and it recognizes the possibility of war inherent in the dynamics of the international system. But the question is whether the Soviet consideration of war-fighting in the contingency of the failure of deterrence should be seen as aggressive or merely prudent. Paradoxically, those Western analysts who most emphasize this war-fighting aspect of Soviet military writings and programs run the risk of seeming to want it both ways. They see such trends towards a war-fighting capability as a destabilizing indication of Soviet aggressiveness; yet at the same time they want the USA to enhance its own counterforce options, pursuing out of prudence what could also be seen as a first-strike capability.

The Issues That Emerge

Several specific questions are raised while establishing an analytical framework for studying Soviet military thinking. They are implicit in all analyses of Soviet military thinking. To what extent are Soviet foreign policy objectives offensive? Is there a noticeable surplus of Soviet military capabilities over essential requirements for defense? In what ways and in what circumstances might greatly enhanced military capability lead Moscow to consider using it? What correlation if any has there been between Soviet assertiveness abroad and overall Soviet relative weakness or strength? Answers can be pursued by considering international events as well as the USSR's perception of its own security needs.

The Political Context

When one talks about superpower competition, there is the implicit consideration of a third element, the terrain of international relations on which the powers meet. In the early 1980s, the competitive aspects of the superpower relationship have come increasingly to the forefront.

Cooperative ventures such as expanded trade, arms control negotiations and scientific exchanges endured through the late 1970s largely as legacies of a détente once thought to be 'irreversible'.[33] Inevitable disappointments arose from the conceptual failure that was connected in both capitals to false assumptions. Each power had interpreted differently the 1972 Statement of Principles. Whereas Washington advertised it as a codification of a new era of improved relations, Moscow regarded the agreement as permitting continued struggle between states with different social systems, but without resort to war. Disagreement in the West over the causes of the demise of détente is another reason to try and reach a consensus about Soviet military arms.

The Soviets believe that current international discord is due to US displays of its inability to accept the new fact of global politics, that the USSR is a superpower and, as presumably in Afghanistan, will behave like one. An outward-looking leadership encourages such a world view. The intended comparison is with the

USA in the first two decades after World War II. Conflicts arise, however, in so far as this Soviet view has coincided with a constricted US definition of its own security interests. Today's calculus of Western security is complicated by dependence on Persian Gulf oil and by Soviet nuclear weaponry. The one point that is certain is that there is less margin for error than in the past for gauging the intentions and assessing the capabilities of the opponent.

New military instrumentalities complement Soviet foreign policy objectives, some of which are *status quo* oriented and others which are more clearly destabilizing and contrary to Western interests. *Status quo* objectives include global political equality with the USA, maintenance of the Soviet system in Eastern Europe, maintenance of at least the existing military balance, and maintenance of Soviet economic development, which includes commercial ties with the West. A further range of objectives are widely, if not universally, attributed to Moscow. Examples are Soviet efforts to obstruct increased Chinese strength and to impede Western relations with Peking, to extend Soviet influence into peripheral states, to loosen the commitment of the European allies to NATO, and to guarantee adequate energy supplies potentially by moving toward the Persian Gulf.[34]

The capabilities of the Soviet general-purpose naval forces are in the West seen in conjunction with many of these objectives. The navy has been improved with greater missile firepower, the addition of over fifty Backfire bombers with air-to-surface missiles for Soviet Naval Aviation (with two VTOL in commission and one under construction), a new and large ship for amphibious operations, a new deep-diving submarine, and seven new classes of cruisers. As with the successive generations of Soviet strategic missile forces, the enhanced navy makes earlier conclusions such as that 'the Soviets have not shown much restraint in their military defense decisions' appear inordinately sanguine.[35]

A discussion of any Soviet calculation of hope and fear in their foreign policy decisions would be speculative. Trying to determine the political effects of a changed military relationship can get into such ethereal matters as the diplomatic dividends obtained from a perceived edge in one or more indices of nuclear capability. US strategic-force planners may find such a calculation useful in their own decisions, but in academic circles, this philosophizing can quickly lead to the clash of opinions that characterize defense studies.[36]

Given in part the revised military balance, some have argued that the Soviet leadership decided to invade Afghanistan since 'they judged the correlation of military and political forces in their favor'.[37] This interpretation by Andrei Sakharov postulates Soviet military planning that cooly assesses and then acts on international trends. The invasion of Afghanistan, which has proven pivotal in redefining superpower relations, is not necessarily so simple. Soviet decision-makers only had to conclude that it was better to intervene than not to, rather than to believe that there would be a net gain regardless of the world correlation of forces. But irrespective of how one explains the particular decision involving Afghanistan, the unprecedented intervention outside of the Warsaw Pact underlines an increasingly assertive Soviet foreign policy that is backed by effective military capability.

The Soviet Security Dilemma

Moscow appears to see itself surrounded by a hostile coalition involving China, Western Europe, Japan and the USA. The paradox is that as the USSR becomes stronger economically and militarily, its sense of paranoia seems to increase.[38] One of the most compelling historical antecedents for the USSR is that of invasion. In the twelfth century it was the Mongols, and in the ensuing years came the Teutonic knights, the Tatars, the Turks, the French and the Germans. Even the USA is included in this litany, the Soviets recalling the intervention in northern Russia and Siberia as an early attempt to smother the Revolution.[39] This visceral preoccupation with invasion and encirclement continues, if one is to believe Soviet rationalizations for the invasion of Afghanistan, for maneuvering in Poland, or for deploying along the Chinese border.

During 1978–9, it can be argued, the Soviets felt themselves menaced by this quadruple entente. Global developments such as US-Japanese relations with China and NATO TNF modernization resonated with traditional Russian fears. And slanted reports from their own intelligence apparatus may have served 'even more to feed traditional Russian paranoia about anything foreign'.[40] As William Hyland noted presciently in fall 1979, the most obvious gap in this purported Western design was in what the British used to call the northern tier, Iran and Afghanistan.[41]

The feeling of encirclement, geographical vulnerabilities, and the fielding of mass forces, all underlie Soviet military thinking. The Soviets show a prevailing doubt about the completeness of their security. As Rome dealt with Antiochus, with Carthage, and with Mithradates, the Soviets assume a need to remove from their immediate periphery any opposition that appears to be getting too strong. There is a preoccupation that the West is 'preparing to cast socialism from the heights of world influence which it has won'.[42] Whether or not Soviet foreign and defense policies are driven by some internal Marxist dynamic, by the inherent behavior of an empire, or by a legitimate concern for national defense, the leadership pays little attention to apprehensions that their behavior generates abroad. The Soviet sense of security depends at a minimum on a corresponding insecurity among its opponents.

Forty-five years ago, Stalin warned that 'those who fall behind get beaten ... The history of old Russia is one unbroken record of the beatings she has suffered for falling behind, for her backwardness'.[43] A sentiment such as this stresses the criticality to the leadership of at least military equality with the West. When seen along with continuing military developments, this obsession with physical security can lead one to conclude that the USSR is striving for the ultimate insurance of some form of military superiority.

The concept of strategic culture has been used in discussing specific national approaches to military affairs, the argument being that unique solutions will be advanced for uniquely defined defense problems.[44] It is grounded in deep geopolitical and historical circumstances, and can offer insights into pathologies such as the self-image of a nation under siege. Exhibit A for this cultural interpretation is the USSR. Moscow's emphasis on military security can be tied to these centuries of national trauma. But one drawback of a strategic cultural explanation is that it is often used to imply primarily defensive motivations for Soviet international behavior. The sufferings from foreign invasion and the expansion of empire may be two sides of the same coin. But it is misleading to dramatize a Soviet preoccupation with frontier defense. It has been noted, after all, that 'a country does not become the largest state in the world, as Russia has been since the seventeenth century, merely by absorbing or repelling foreign invasions'.[45]

The greater throw-weight and higher MIRV capacities of Soviet strategic forces can be rationalized by sympathetic analysts citing the strategic culture concept. They presume a not necessarily malevolent Soviet affinity for size and quantity in defense planning. Lenin wrote that in numbers there is strength, and forty years ago, numbers indeed served Moscow well. As Hitler noted to his Panzer commander General Guderian: 'Had I known they had as many tanks as that, I'd have thought twice about attacking.'[46] But by then, it was too late. The question follows whether a tradition focusing on size and quantity translates well into the MIRV era, and whether this is a credible reason for current Soviet building programs.

Cultural explanations can be applied to specifically national approaches to war and, according to some analysts, can show the motivations behind military planning. Stanley Sienkiewicz and then Robert Legvold have advanced this view. The latter describes the Soviet preoccupation with only the operational concepts of war as a product of their military strategy. Whereas 'for the United States, deterrence is an explicit intellectual construction, invented by civilians and rooted in psychological or game theory', the Soviets reject the idea of a strategic doctrine and substitute instead military science, a preparedness to wage war successfully at all levels.[47] The distinction is not intended to imply bellicosity, but rather to emphasize the different conceptions of deterrence arising from different cultures.

It is clearly important in talking about managing escalation to understand this Soviet view of war. Mechanistic considerations alone cannot offer sufficient guidance in decisions about the use or threat of use of nuclear weapons in tactical operations. A failure to study Soviet military thinking and intentions can result in something like the so-called 'firebreak theory', in which the enemy is expected to cooperate by not initiating the use of nuclear weapons as a high level of violence steadily mounts. As Bernard Brodie argued in writing about such calibrations in warfare, there is a need to consider the hopes, fears and motivations of the enemy.[48] Knowing the capabilities of opponents simply gives the analyst the raw data on which to base his defense requirements.

Recognizing the Soviet security dilemma and understanding some of its cultural origins is academically respectable. Yet the question persists. Are the Soviets really seeking a war-winning capability? Some in the West believe that they take seriously the Leninist concept of a fight to the finish between two social systems, and are preparing for such a struggle. Others explain recent weapon acquisitions as the result of just an action–reaction model of superpower strategic force decisions intensified by Russian paranoia. As Strobe Talbott notes, 'there has never been anything more offensive than a Russian on the defensive'.[49] But how far should the West go in accommodating such fears, some so ingrained that even in the age of ICBMs, foreigners are prohibited from photographing train stations? The analyst himself has to determine the bounds of any legitimate Soviet defense preparedness.

Conclusion

The complexity of studying Soviet military thinking is apparent from the many influences, analytical approaches, and individual interpretations that surround the topic. It cannot be discussed both categorically and authoritatively. No single variable, such as verbal evidence or military hardware, can alone be used to explain Soviet doctrine. There is a special need to go beyond enumerating respective forces, an excessively quantitative approach tending to trivialize other influences on Soviet planning. The analyst has to look carefully at past Soviet military and foreign policies, cultural idiosyncrasies, leadership perceptions and general international trends.

Balanced analyses are as important as they are difficult to achieve. An understanding of the evolution of the superpower security relationship is helpful in reaching this end. Western debate about Soviet nuclear war-fighting capabilities is an example of a problem that can be clarified through an historical perspective. The theoretical acceptance of gradations of violence for political purposes is, after all, not unknown in US defense planning. NSC 68's expectation of 'conducting offensive operations to destroy vital elements of the Soviet war-making capacity' was an early integration of national objectives with military planning through the vital importance of a nuclear air offensive.[50] Today's concern about Soviet war-fighting intentions may be well-founded. But to avoid over-reaction, the opponent's counterforce capability should not be seen as unique or unprecedented. It is a common fallacy in any military competition to regard an enemy as more purposeful, innovative and competent than may be the case.

There is now a prevalent Western disinclination to prosecute successfully a nuclear war should deterrence fail. If one believes that the Soviets share this apparent view of the disutility of nuclear weapons, then there must be other reasons why Soviet military writings address the possibility of victory while the strategic forces seem designed along these lines. If, on the contrary, one believes that Einstein's observation remains correct – that the atomic age has changed everything but man's thinking – and that the Soviets regard a strategic exchange as essentially a more devastating variant of interstate conflict, then the statements about victory indeed indicate that winning in their view is a militarily possible task.

During the 1970s, many Western analysts have been more willing to express a degree of understanding for Soviet military statements and actions than any enthusiasm in countering them. But assumptions have changed due to prevailing military trends and Soviet foreign policies. There is now a greater tendency in the West to take Soviet nuclear as well as conventional military pretensions more seriously. The same writings and the same steady enhancement of military capability are being studied anew. A balanced analysis is complicated, however, when some in the West now credit nuclear weapons for influencing past crises in which they were not seen as instrumental at the time.

If one does not see the USSR as a moderate power searching for moderate military means, it is easier to believe that current and prospective acquisitions go considerably beyond even Soviet defensive needs. Such development far exceeds the Soviets post-World War II conception of security, one that required strongly defended frontiers and contiguous buffer zones. Moscow now explains the size of its forces by noting that it must include China, Western Europe and Japan, in addition to the USA when it assesses the risks of war. The irony is that Soviet vulnerability has increased steadily along with its capacity to inflict punishment.

The Western analyst has to decide how much to sympathize with the Soviet sense of beleaguerment. Russia had always sought to push back the encircling danger by enlarging its empire. A feeling of pervasive insecurity was reinforced by Marxism which, in its isolation, inherited the militarism of the czars. Now that the USSR is at least militarily equal to the other superpower, the question is open as to the extent to which it will be able to indulge its fears. A correlation between the increasing military strength of the USSR and its assertiveness abroad remains to be drawn. During the past fifteen years, however, the latitude of Soviet military actions that the West is able to tolerate has expanded steadily.

In the early 1980s, there is a re-creation of the basic East–West shift of the post-World War II era. The wisdom of accepting the USSR as an effective partner in world affairs has been challenged. There is concern in the West that now that the Soviets have achieved coequal military power, they will make territorial and political inroads as they have always intended. For the USA, a minimum real dollar increase of 100 percent in defense spending for the first half of the decade reflects the expectation of at least a determined weapons competition. Today, a country does not need to have a history of paranoia to feel insecure.

Notes: Chapter 1

1 Samuel F. Wells, Jr, 'Sounding the tocsin: NSC 68 and the Soviet threat', *International Security*, Fall, 1979, pp. 116–58.
2 See John Lewis Gaddis and Paul Nitze, 'NSC 68 and the Soviet threat reconsidered', *International Security*, Spring, 1980, pp. 164–75.
3 Richard Lowenthal, 'Dealing with Soviet global power', *Encounter*, June, 1978, p. 90.
4 *World Military Expenditures and Arms Transfers 1968–1977*, US Arms Control and Disarmament Agency, October 1979; Soviet arms exports between the years 1970–77 ranged from 25 to 12 percent of total exports, whereas for the USA the percentage ranged from a high of 7 to a low of 4 percent.
5 This estimate, to say the least, is highly controversial. The International Institute for Strategic Studies offers a concise introduction to the expenditure debate in *The Military Balance 1979–1980* (London: IISS, 1979), pp. 11-12; a strong refutation of the CIA estimates is in William T. Lee, *Soviet Defense Expenditures in an Era of SALT*, United States Strategic Institute Report 79-1, Washington, 1980. So far, no review essay exists that weighs the various arguments in this debate.
6 Statement of the Honorable Donald H. Rumsfeld, Armed Services Committee of the US Senate, 11 October, 1979.
7 Alistair Buchan, 'Their bomb and ours', *Encounter*, January, 1959, p. 12.
8 Charles Bohlen, *Witness to History* (New York: Norton, 1973), p. 496; also, the author's conversations with Mr McCloy.
9 'Interview with Robert McNamara', *U.S. News and World Report*, vol. 58, 12 April, 1965, p. 52.
10 Albert Wohlstetter first addressed these problems authoritatively in 'Is there a strategic arms race?', *Foreign Policy*, Summer, 1974; and 'Rivals, but no "race",' *Foreign Policy*, Fall, 1974. Also see 'The National Intelligence Estimates A-B team episode', *Report of the Senate Select Committee on Intelligence*, 16 February 1978: 'Separate views', p. 12.
11 Michael Getter and Robert Faiser, 'Intelligence estimate said to show need for SALT', *Washington Post*, 31 January, 1980.
12 Benjamin Lambeth, 'Deterrence in the MIRV era', *World Politics*, January, 1972; the conclusions about Soviet force development that this respected analyst reached in 1972 are notably more hopeful about the Soviet desire for parity than those which he has recently articulated. See, for example, his 'The political potential of Soviet equivalence', *International Security*, Fall, 1979.
13 Department of Defense, Annual Report, FY 1979, p. 6.
14 Comment by Undersecretary of Defense for Research and Development William Perry, Center for International Studies, Massachusetts Institute of Technology, 14 May, 1980.
15 General David Jones, as quoted in Edger Ulsamer, 'The Soviet juggernaut: racing faster than ever', *Air Force Magazine*, March, 1976, p. 57.
16 Congressman Les Aspin, 'What are the Russians up to?', *International Security*, Summer, 1978.
17 The CIA notes that, despite the poor performance of the economy, evidence indicates that Soviet defense spending will continue to increase at least through 1985 at or near the long-term rate of 4–5 percent. This means that the defense share of Soviet GNP, according to these estimates, could rise to as much as 15 percent by 1985; see Central Intelligence Agency, *The Soviet Economy in 1978–1979 and Prospects for 1980*, ER80-10328.
18 For a discussion on the relationship between consumer and military spending, see *The Soviet Economy in a Time of Change*, Joint Economic Committee, US Congress, Vol. 1, 10 October, 1979, and specifically the essay by Henry W. Schaefer, 'Soviet power and intentions: military-economic choices'.

19 For an incisive and comprehensive discussion of the 'politics of stringency', see Seweryn Bialer, *Stalin's Successors*, pt V (New York: Cambridge University Press, 1980).

20 See Franklyn D. Holzman, 'Are the Soviets really out-spending the U.S. on defense?', *International Security*, Spring, 1980, for one point of view on the continuing Soviet defense expenditure debate. Another is offered by Abraham Becker, in *The Soviet Economy in a Time of Change*, op. cit.

21 John Strachey, 'Communist intentions', *Partisan Review*, Spring, 1962, p. 215.

22 Department of Defense, Annual Report, FY 1981, p. 83.

23 Among those who appear most optimistic about 'victory' in a nuclear conflict are writers such as retired Rear Admiral V. V. Shelyag, whose professional expertise was in troop motivation. The role of ideology is summed up in such statements as 'not a single serviceman should remain outside the sphere of constant political influence'.

24 As cited in Benjamin Lambeth, *How To Think About Soviet Military Doctrine*, p-5939 (Santa Monica, Ca.: Rand Corporation, 1978), p. 4.

25 Michael MccGwire, 'Naval power and Soviet global strategy', *International Security*, Spring, 1979, p. 134.

26 *How to Think About Soviet Military Doctrine*, op. cit., p. 5.

27 In *Russian Political Culture* (US Department of State, Contract No. 1722-420119, 1976), Edward L. Keenan addresses the ceremonial literature of Muscovy: 'To the extent that political statements for the consumption of outsiders were made at all, they were intended to deceive, and in general to serve the purposes of the political system itself' (p. 47); modern scholars cite these texts at their peril in explaining Muscovy's 'official ideology'.

28 Nathan Leites, *Pretense, Wisdom and Folly in Current Soviet Words on Nuclear War: Glimpses of the Well Hidden* (WN-9085-ARPA, Rand Corporation), May 1975.

29 Colonel General N. A. Lomov (ed.), *Scientific-Technical Progress and the Revolution in Military Affairs* (A Soviet View), trans. US Air Force, Soviet Military Thought Series, No. 3 (Washington, DC, GPO, 1974), p. v.

30 'Fifty Years of Military Thought', *Voyennaya mysl'*, no. 6, June, 1968, p. 26, as discussed personally with Raymond Ghartoff.

31 Joseph D. Douglass, Jr, and Amoretta M. Hoeber, *Soviet Strategy for Nuclear War* (Stanford, Ca.: Hoover Institution Press, 1979), p. 5.

32 Lt General James M. Gavin, *War and Peace in the Space Age* (New York: Harper, 1958), p. 154.

33 *Pravda*, 22 June, 1973.

34 'Afghanistan's role in Soviet strategy', *Conflict Studies* monograph, David Rees, no. 118, May, 1980.

35 Department of Defense, Annual Report, FY 1981, p. 39.

36 Department of Defense, Annual Report, FY 1975.

37 *New York Times*, 3 January, 1980.

38 See Helmut Sonnenfeldt, 'The Soviet Challenge', in J. A. Pechman (ed.), *Setting National Priorities: Agenda for the Eighties* (Washington, DC: Brookings, 1980).

39 Nikolai V. Sivachev and Nikolai Yakoulev, *Russia and the United States* (Chicago: University of Chicago Press, 1979), trans., Olga Adler Titelbaum, pp. 51–62.

40 Characterized by former CIA Inspector-General Lyman B. Kirkpatrik, Jr, as quoted by Richard F. Staar, in Peter Duiganan and Alvin Rabashka (eds), *The United States in the 1980s* (Stanford, Ca.: Hoover Institution Press, 1980), p. 740.

41 W. G. Hyland, 'The Sino-Soviet security conflict: a search for new security strategies', *Strategic Review*, Fall, 1978.

42 As quoted in Timothy J. Colton, *Commissars, Commanders and Civilian Authority: The Structure of Soviet Military Politics* (Cambridge, Ma.: Harvard University Press, 1978), p. 200.

43 Speech of 4 February, 1931, delivered at 1st All-Union Conference of Leading Personnel of Soviet Industry: as cited in J. V. Stalin, *Problems of Leninism* (Peking: Foreign Language Press, 1976), p. 528.

44 See Jack L. Synder, *The Soviet Strategic Culture: Implications for Limited Nuclear Options*, R-2154-AF (Santa Monica, Ca.: Rand Corporation, September, 1977), for one of the first and most widely discussed analyses of this concept.

45 Richard Pipes, 'Militarism and the Soviet state', *Daedalus*, Fall, 1980, p. 2.

46 David Irving, *Hitler's War* (New York: Viking Press, 1977), p. 286.
47 Robert Legvold, 'Strategic doctrine and SALT: Soviet and American views', *Survival*, January–February, 1979, p. 8.
48 Bernard Brodie, *Escalation and the Nuclear Option*, RM-4544-PR (Santa Monica, Ca.: Rand Corporation, 1965).
49 Strobe Talbott, 'Whatever happened to détente?', *Time*, 23 June, 1980, p. 34.
50 NSC 68, *Foreign Relations of the United States: Vol. I* (pp. 234-92 for NSC 68 of 14 April, 1950).

2

Two Languages of War

ROBERT BATHURST

One of the elements of the Russian character to which it is most
difficult for the Westerner to adjust himself is the passion for
self-immolation.

Edmund Wilson

Inventing the Enemy

Tyutchev, the nineteenth-century Russian poet, is frequently
quoted with pride for his assertion that no foreigner could ever
understand his countrymen. (It is seldom mentioned that he also
thought that Russians could 'but dimly apprehend themselves'.)
Now we have Solzhenitsyn blaming us not only for not understanding Russians, but also for confusing them with the Soviets
whom we do not understand either.[1] If we consult other Euro-
peans, we are likely to hear charges about American naïveté; and
the Soviets accuse us of being mystical and ahistorical. There is
little doubt that America has invented a Soviet Union, as Edward
Luttwak[2] recently said, but anyone who remembers the almost
universal failure of the estimates of Nazi intentions (or Japanese)
in the World War II years will recall that inventing or not inventing an enemy has not exclusively been a problem of the contemporary American mind. But when the question is war, we cannot
be so dull-witted as not to ask ourselves, periodically, what we are
inventing.

The French anthropologist, Claude Levi-Strauss, found such
powers of invention even on the Vichy-ruled island of Martinique
in 1941. Although no fighting had occurred or was threatened,
the soldiers were in a state of panic. In their 'sick minds' they had
replaced Germany as the real enemy, which by its distance had
become invisible and abstract, with an imaginary enemy which
had the advantage of being close at hand, with America. 'They
needed,' explained Levi-Strauss, 'enemies on whom they could

vent their feelings of aggressiveness ...; they needed someone to blame'.[3]

But knowing whom to blame has not been a Soviet problem. Enemies are inherent in the language of Soviet politics and are one of the dynamics of Soviet society. Far from leading to the disintegration of social order and authority which Dostoevsky predicted in *The Devils*, this paranoid function of inventing enemies has been made one of the not inconsiderable organizing principles of the Soviet state, certainly of the military. The 'spies are everywhere' campaigns are a periodic feature of the Soviet press,[4] and induce the panic about war and enemies in which some of Soviet life is led.[5] The panic has its military uses. It reinforces the intense campaign for military readiness – a campaign to *repel* sudden attacks but equally useful for *launching* attacks – not only in the army garrison, but also in the towns and cities. The formula which Brezhnev repeated every year of détente – 'History teaches that while imperialism exists, the danger of new aggressive war remains'[6] – appears to be the cornerstone of Soviet policy which makes somehow reasonable the notion of CIA agents on streetcars in Alma Ata or leading rebel forces in Afghanistan. This theme, born in the conspiratorial world of the Russian leaders, was proclaimed by Lenin in 1902, when he warned, 'We are surrounded on all sides by enemies, and we have to advance almost constantly under their fire'.[7] It has become central to Soviet military thought and has been used as a weapon in the forced transformation of the Soviet state into a military-industrial complex, as Seweryn Bialer called it.[8]

Levi-Strauss's experience on Martinique serves to remind us, if we need it, that the language of war and the designation of enemies, are subject to factors other than reason, that preconceptions can be so strong that they mask a reality, elsewhere self-evident. Something of that sort must explain why President Carter does not understand that he is the automatic enemy of the Soviet state as the leader of the imperialist system and that the dialectics of history do not permit a non-coercive solution to the differences between socialism and capitalism. This position has been restated with little variation for sixty-three years. President Carter, in describing his honest confusion about attacks on him in the Soviet press and on the American position on SALT, made it quite clear that in trying to analyze Soviet politics, he ignored this most basic Marxist perception of the world:

I don't know how to explain the unfriendly rhetoric. I believe the

> Soviets perhaps have some political reasons . . . I don't know what those reasons are. And the public statements that the Soviets make attacking me personally or our nation's good faith are both erroneous and ill-advised. But what their reasons for it might be, I don't know.[9]

That the President failed to understand one of the most fundamental tenets of Leninism – that only through the destabilization of the world order as it exists can imperialism be overthrown – was made embarrassingly clear by a question which must have dumbfounded Soviet leaders. It was asked in the President's State of the Union Address of January 1980. Even after referring to the efforts of American diplomacy to stop Soviet aggression in the 1940s, 1950s, 1960s and 1970s, and calling the invasion of Afghanistan a 'radical and aggressive new step' for the 1980s, the President asked the remarkable question:

> Will it [the USSR] help promote a more stable international environment in which its own legitimate peaceful concerns can be pursued? Or will it continue to expand its military power far beyond its genuine security needs and use that power for colonial conquest?[10]

That the President could ask such a question shows a basic misconception about the Soviet use of violence, a misconception strengthened, perhaps, by the assumption that when we and the Soviets discuss war, we are talking about the same thing. Actually, we are not; what we are talking about is an overlapping of concepts that makes words convey meanings which they do not properly have.

When the USA discusses war, there are two primary meanings – strategic nuclear war and war in Europe – and many secondary ones related to various kinds of police and stabilizing actions. Because there is not a unity of views, in the Soviet sense, the action being discussed has to be understood in terms of who is speaking and the discipline he represents. However, as we shall see, this discussion of war often has certain unusual features: it does not include the traditional concept of victory; in some cases, it tries to orient itself toward universal application without specific enemies; and in certain kinds of battle – nuclear for one – it stops in mid-course while the battle is still on.

On the Soviet side, there is a similarity in the discussion of nuclear war and even war in Europe, but the discussion is overshadowed by the concept of the political beginning and political ending of war. Or as the new Soviet military encyclopedia states:

'The Soviet Union will regard a future world war, if the imperialists succeed in unleashing it, as a decisive confrontation between
two opposing world social systems.'[11] What the Soviets are talking
about when they talk about any war is the transformation of the
world order. The objective of the war, or hundreds of kinds of
wars which they think could occur, is not only geographical; it is
for the control of consciousness. On that most basic level, it
appears that the President among others, consistently tries to
invent some other war.

It is not surprising that the Soviet language of war differs vastly
from that of the West. It grew out of the experience of the
conquering Bolshevik Party which had absorbed the conspiratorial tactics of such predecessors as the People's Will – which
believed in bringing about strategic change through assassination
– and the nihilists. The slogan of one of the leaders, Pisarev, was
'everything that can be destroyed must be destroyed'. Its leaders
had to make 'the incredibly swift transition from wild violence to
the most delicate deceit'.[12]

Its world view, in contrast to that of the West which reads
history as the story of a progression toward stability, demands the
rewriting of history in order to stress every struggle and sees the
present and future as a series of conflicts with an inevitable
conclusion in a World War III or at the very least as the violent
defeat of the existing order. For internal stability, a Marxist-
Leninist Soviet Union was perceived by its leaders as requiring
external instability; the American President needed just the
opposite: external stability in order to achieve his internal needs.
Brezhnev put it clearly for the USSR. He would pursue 'a line in
international affairs which helps further to invigorate the worldwide anti-imperialist struggle, and to strengthen the fighting unity
of all its participants'.[13]

Thus, the Soviet language of war does not begin where the
American does, with a breach of legality, or end where it does
with a military defeat. It begins with the exacerbation of class
warfare (which emerges often as the warfare of political parties)
and ends with nothing less than the transformation of society. The
last Soviet battle does not take place when the missiles have
ceased to fly, but when the revolutionary executions against the
wall have stopped.

Western scholarship may be influenced into assuming a similarity of military thought by the frequent references in Soviet literature to Lenin's admiration for Clausewitz. The idea of stable
nation states with legal borders, balanced power and established
indentities is at the basis of Western military thought and is the

world that Clausewitz described. But it is not the basis of Soviet thought in which, as Lenin said, 'all borders in nature and society are conditional and mobile'.[14]

While the Soviet Union does undeniably operate also in the Clausewitzian mold – most dramatically at the time of the Molotov–Ribbentrop Pact which tried to stabilize power – its dominant orientation is toward the class nature of war. In that non-Clausewitzian language there are many voices: those of statesmen; those addressing workers; those addressing nationalities; those subverting established systems; those inciting guerrillas. The Soviet language of war is saturated with the problems of controlling people, in the attack, in the rear, in preparation for war and for sacrifice. It does not deal only in terms of the annihilation of enemies, but also with the control of those who remain.

The language of the USA, on the other hand, focuses not on people, as a Soviet critic observed, but on how to 'automate war and combat operations in order to avoid having to commit ground forces to action'.[15] Its language is that of punitive measures such as blockades, economic sanctions, escalating bombing, strategies meant to stabilize but not to transform the world order. They are, moreover, strategies which de-emphasize the role of manpower and increase the role of technology.

Whereas on every level, Soviet society is organized for struggle with a clearly defined victory, whether in the five-year plan or on the battlefield, the USA seems to have given up the idea of victory in war as in diplomacy. This kind of victory-less war, first in Korea, then in Viet Nam and now in NATO war plans, suggests that the battle is thought of as being with the technology of the opponent, as if defeating a war machine defeats as well the process that set it in motion.

Such an idea seems to be behind the strategy of attrition NATO has adopted in Europe. According to such a strategy, if the Soviets invade, NATO forces will stop them after a certain distance, 'the forward edge of battle'. (It is some measure of a sense of unreality about war that different NATO nations still have different concepts of where this 'forward edge of battle' is located and plan their major offensives separately.)

The lack of a notion of how to end the war with the Soviet state (the doctrine of massive retaliation, the strategy of the Dulles years, was a punishment, not a plan for political order) seems to apply as well to the smaller wars, the kinds which the Soviets promise we will face increasingly in the future as the imperialist system is further weakened.

Behind the idea of being able to fight these wars is the assumption that the right kind of equipment in the right quantity can win. That is a recurrence of the Naval War College idea of the early 1970s that the study of war can be abstracted from people. With such planning, armed forces tend to become transformed into enormous riot squads being sent to a neighborhood they don't know to fight an enemy difficult to recognize, an enemy with technological characteristics, but no human face.

Such an approach appears to lead military planners to overlook major strategic assets involving people. There is not, for example, a military policy of using the resource of the discontent in Eastern Europe, the Baltic states or other nationalities under Soviet domination where the desire for liberation could lead to an alteration in the correlation of forces. (The equivalent use of such a weapon by the Soviets is accepted as a diplomatic norm.)

Military policy must support national policy and that presents a dilemma to military planners. That the USA's enormous military might should have for its guiding policy nothing more far-sighted or original than the objective of Czar Alexander I at the Congress of Vienna, to uphold the ruling princes in power, is an irony of history. But the nature of war has changed vastly and weapons have become very specific. One cannot fight all wars with the same weapons, as Alexander I could do. Helicopters designed to operate over water cannot operate over sand; airplanes equipped for northern climates cannot lift the same weapons in the jungle; tanks designed for the plains of Europe are useless in monsoon mud. While the navy and air force can, with many limitations, think of themselves as a pragmatic reaction force freed, somewhat, from the local human condition,[16] the army cannot and if victory means being able to impose stability, then no one can.

War as an Abstraction

After the war in Viet Nam, there was a feeling in the Defense Department, not unlike President Carter's in the State of the Union Address, that the strong should not coerce the weak, that the language of war and enemies was immoral, distasteful and old-fashioned and that these subjects could be made more agreeable by being denationalized and universalized. Those were the years of SALT I and détente. In the new spirit, in 1972 the Naval War College in Newport eliminated all Soviet studies entirely from the curriculum. That made it very difficult to teach strategy and tactics on a modern level, since only the Soviet navy was an adversary comparable to our own. So great, however, was the desire not to identify an 'enemy' that fictitious foreign equipment was described (though few students were ignorant of its inspiration) for the purposes of classwork.

The study of tactics could be continued under these conditions, though with serious shortcomings. The study of strategy, however, at least as it related to the modern world, was nearly impossible. The solution developed by the naval strategy department was quite bizarre. After making a bow to Thucydides, it concentrated on the study of land warfare in Europe. Perhaps in order to support impartiality in international relations, it assigned Napoleon's campaigns in Central Europe but excluded the Russian battles, including the historic model for Stalingrad, the Battle at Borodino.

Of course, not recognizing the enemy on the battlefield had the concomitant in the curriculum of not recognizing the role of psychology, the interpretation of intelligence, national differences, the dynamics of Marxism–Leninism, Russian modes of thought, or the language of war. The language did reflect the American mood, however, at least for that time and place. The US concept was that war could be made moral by translating it, through its historical evolution, into some universal laws that would apply to all weapons and all nations. What was being proposed was a reduction of the idea of military violence to the study of its use in police-like action.

Although the army had just emerged from a defeat in Viet Nam resulting largely from an inadequate understanding (in Washington and Saigon) of psychological, ideological and national factors, like the navy, it also tried to teach war with impersonal enemies. A tactical handbook called *The Threat*, published in 1976, pictured Soviet tactics and equipment with all identifying data removed. It advised the soldier, with the European theater in mind, that 'to offset our enemy's numerical superiority, we must use superior tactics to defeat him'. All artillerymen were told to know 'the organization, equipment, doctrine and vulnerabilities of our potential enemies and be able to exploit them', although the army did not tell the artillerymen who those enemies were, the characteristics of their system or what they would be fighting for.[17] In *The Threat*, published in the year of the bicentennial of the American Revolution, men were told that they would be fighting to defend 'land areas'.[18] One general's explanation for needing to defend 'land areas' was that: 'The more fantastic become the vehicles of interstellar space, the more precious are the areas from which they are launched and the natural resources from which they are fabricated'.[19] Apparently, this was the new US language of war, devoid of ideals or patriotism, without political goals or military policy, appropriate for mercenaries, perhaps, but not a language to inspire self-sacrifice. It would surely have been more effective to read the soldiers excerpts from the *Gulag Archipelago*.

Soviet references to the enemy lack such indirectness. 'Hate the enemy' campaigns are a constant feature of the Soviet press. 'Hate' is widely described as 'the most important component part of the perseverance and heroism of the Soviet troops'.[20] And lest the Soviet populace forget the 'enemy's' identity, there is constant, specific analysis of American and NATO equipment and in the Soviet press, almost daily reference to the threats from imperialist (Soviets are taught to read, automatically, 'American') leaders, the CIA and German 'revenge-seekers'.

The Role of the Rear

The Soviet and American languages of war differ also in the way that they refer to the role of civilian sectors. In the US military literature, the rear, as it is called militarily, is hardly mentioned at all; in Soviet literature, it is hardly distinguished from the military sector. The importance of the rear has always been crucial in Soviet experience: it was the collapse of the rear that made the October Revolution a success; that the rear held in the civil war and in World War II allowed the Soviet regime to present itself as a miracle-working political force. In contrast, it was not until Viet Nam that Americans first experienced so forcefully the strategic importance of this problem of the front and the rear. That was when villages were discovered to be civilian by day but guerrilla bases by night, no matter how much energy and equipment was expended on their defense.

In Soviet military doctrine since the time of Frunze, in the 1920s, civilian resources have largely been merged with military resources, the military front becomes hardly distinguished from the civilian rear. Frunze's idea that 'wars pull into their orbit and decisively subordinate all sides of social existence and they affect all state and social interests, without exception' has not even been modified in Soviet military thought of the present.[21] Civilian life has been militarized to a degree that would have surprised even that most autocratic of czars, Nicholas I, who in thinking of his ideal, militarized state, said, 'I consider the entire of human life to be merely service, because everybody serves'.[22]

To make the rear aware that it, too, is on the front line, enormous attention is given to keeping alive memories of the last war. The message for the current generation is that it has an obligation to prepare for the same sacrifice as was made by the old revolutionaries and the Soviet population in World War II. That the front and rear were hardly distinguished, was made clear to the Soviet citizens in that war in which more than one-tenth of the population died. That Americans who have lost in all their wars since the American Revolution fewer than the Soviets lost during the siege of Leningrad alone have difficulty in understanding the implications for the present of that vast historical disaster, is not surprising.

In a manifestation of that war, a recent fashion is for brides to go directly from their wedding ceremony to leave their flowers at the memorial to the war dead. An attempt is made throughout the USSR to raise children in the spirit of self-sacrifice. In the curriculum of all grade schools are included stories of heroes such as Alexander Matrosov, who covered a machine-gun with his chest to save his comrades and of the twenty-eight Panfilovtsy, a squad of soldiers who died heroically stopping German tanks on the road to Moscow. In March 1980, on the front page of *Izvestia* was an announcement that Leonid Brezhnev, the President of the Presidium of the Supreme Soviet of the USSR, had awarded the small city of Dzerzhinsk the order of the Red Banner for Labor for its contribution to victory *in World War II* and for its work in the chemical industry. (The award curiously connects Dzerzhinsk's widely known military chemical industry with World War II. It appears that Dzerzhinsk's success is probably in the production of chemical weapons.)[23]

Claude Levi-Strauss would find this indicative of an atmosphere far more obsessed than the one he found on Martinique in 1941. Others, habitualized to the USSR, who, for example, no longer find it strange that one-sixth of the world's land surface is surrounded by barbed wire, might find this a reasonable response given Soviet norms and experience. However, the atmosphere specifically relates to education for violence, to the language and concept of war. It makes it a norm of Soviet life. What this implies is an enormous resource available to the military commander, one given major emphasis in Soviet military doctrine, while almost unrecognized in the US military literature.

The Method of War

The heavy emphasis on the psychological preparation of the

population for war raises questions about the different ways in which Soviets and Americans speak of fighting wars or of planning them.

It has been argued that American wealth and Russian poverty have caused the USA to approach war in very different ways.[24] General Eisenhower knew that. He said that Americans fought wars 'by inundation'.[25] The Soviets have also been aware of this. Colonel A. A. Sidorenko in describing the attack, contrasted the Soviet, and English, and American approaches:

> The characteristics of an attack by forces of the U.S. and England are: a prolonged preparation of the operation, massing of overwhelming superiority over the enemy in forces and equipment, especially in aviation (where there is a superiority of 10–20 times the enemy), detailed planning and an all-encompassing materiel and technical support.[26]

While it would undoubtedly be a mistake to emphasize Eisenhower's notion of 'inundation' unduly, there is no doubt that the term is helpful in directing attention to differences between the Soviet and American approaches. Just as the USSR's position of technological inferiority and geographical vulnerability has influenced the way that it has thought about war, so, it is reasonable to assume, has the USA's wealth and geographic isolation influenced its way. As a result, the Soviets put an enormous emphasis on people and how they can be used; the US emphasis is on technology, its invention and production, the means for inundation.

From an inferior force, the only possible military equalizer is psychology; that is, manipulating the enemy through such devices as deceit, surprise, sabotage, politics and the like. This was the kind of thing Stalin had in mind when he said: 'In order to pluck ... victory on the front, several spies somewhere on the army staff, or even divisional staff, capable of stealing the operational plan and giving it to the opponent is all that is necessary.'[27]

Without superiority of forces, the Soviet way of war had to avoid direct confrontation on the battlefield, using instead maneuver and encirclement with annihilation of enemy forces a necessary concomitant. (It could not be assumed that there would be the luxury of a second chance.) One had to fight as the Israelis and Vietnamese fought: not only was it necessary to know in advance which of the enemy's weapons could be defeated and precisely how, but survival in the first place depended upon accurate predictions of his behavior, on estimating his intentions, as the Soviets found in the Finnish War and the USA did in Viet

Nam. It meant the development of tactics for destroying the enemy from the rear, of using guerrillas and political parties and a vast network of agents.

Such a view of war influenced military decisions. The Soviet government had the largest submarine fleet in the world before World War II, although there was little use for it in shallow Soviet waters from the Western point of view. But, for the inferior force, submarines can be the perfect naval equalizer. They can be used to attack and run, for espionage, for surprise missions as well as to control an enemy whose strategy is to attack only after accumulating enormous supplies.

What emerges from comparing the two languages of war is that one culture which thinks of war as external to its normal pursuits cannot understand another in which war is, and has been for centuries, central to its existence. The former trivializes the seriousness of the other's intent and minimizes or ignores the anger of its rhetoric; the latter maximizes the danger and exaggerates the hostility. It is this incongruence which accounts more than any other for each side's incomprehension of the language of the other: for the Soviets to believe that imperialism does not reciprocate their institutionalized hate, and for Americans to understand that the violence with which the Soviet leaders speak may be objectively translated into military doctrine and hardware.

The Relativity of Capabilities

In military thought, there is unresolved debate about whether one should study more heavily the subject of capabilities, the specifics of the weapons and their destructiveness, or intentions, the way in which it is assumed the weapons will be used. The language of capabilities is, on balance, the language of the force with abundance of materiel; the language of intentions is the language of the force with less.

With its technological superiority which emphasized the diminished role of people, the USA concentrated on capabilities. At the Naval War College, with the new curriculum in 1972, not a single lecture on Soviet intentions (or US intentions either) was delivered by the staff. Only capabilities were discussed, but not Soviet capabilities. The discussion was about the capabilities of US weapons. Attention was not given to the weapons of other nationalities.

It would be inaccurate to assume that this reflected the idiosyncrasy of the military mind. There was a largely new teaching staff brought to the college by Admiral Stansfield Turner composed primarily of civilians from academia and private think-tanks. Although the president of the Naval War College was a naval officer, his closest advisers were civilians. What was being emphasized was the new abstractness of war in US thought, the notion that détente had reduced the need for strategic forces and that navies had to find new and practical missions. But it also showed a difference between the US and Soviet approaches to thinking about war. The Soviets emerging from a period of inferior capabilities naturally stressed intent, making surprise and the attack the central ideas of their new doctrine.

The notion of 'inundation', though undoubtedly an oversimplification, is at least helpful in explaining the way the two cultures imagine war in Europe. The American and NATO side has given up the advantage of surprise by renouncing attack and a counteroffensive in favor of a strategy of attrition. Attrition, stopping an attack and gradually eliminating enemy forces, requires a huge build-up of equipment and manpower, exceedingly accurate intelligence reporting, and remarkable powers of predicting intentions. The increase in capabilities is to be achieved by vast air and sea lifts to create stockpiles of men and materiel for the counterattack. That alone is fraught with problems and dangers given the accuracy, range and destructiveness of modern weapons. As for the psychological and human factors, however, there is little assurance of remarkable powers of prediction or understanding in the history of recent Soviet-American relations.

When General Eisenhower discussed the war in Europe with Marshal Zhukov, their opposite experiences were constantly being dramatized: it was the culture of inundation against that of scarcity. One problem they discussed was how to clear a minefield. General Eisenhower complained of the loss of time required to bring up the technical equipment necessary for such a task. Marshal Zhukov told him of a quicker solution. 'When we come to a mine field,' he said, 'our infantry attacks exactly as if it were not there'.[28]

The solution Marshal Zhukov advocated to clear a minefield had some historical precedent. It was the method of the Imperial Russian Army to clear the mines, first employed by the Turks to protect Pleven in 1877. There were also Death Battalions in the Imperial Army during World War I, manned primarily by volunteer officers and there were even women's battalions.[29]

One is tempted to generalize from the punishment battalions about the Soviet disregard for human life. (That there is a difference is amply documented in the *Gulag Archipelago*.) But the recognition of human capabilities and resources is also conditioned by the sense of the reality of the threat to survival. The solutions the Soviets have chosen when threatened in war have not relied upon what, in the West, would be considered a judicious expenditure of lives and equipment. Instead, they have tried to define the specific problem and to apply from what was available, the resources to solve it. While the conditions of modern war complicate that approach, Soviet experience suggests that there is not a historical precedent in battle for the same distinctions US military analysts see between chemical, nuclear and conventional wars. This is even more certain when one recalls that Soviet definitions of war are not determined by the weapons at all, but by the political consequences. During most of his adult life, President Carter has been hearing Soviet leaders say such things as: 'The full triumph of the socialist cause all over the world is inevitable. And we shall not spare ourselves in the fight for this triumph, for the happiness of the working people.'[30] But from his State of the Union speeches and press conferences, it is obvious that on some level President Carter does not perceive such statements as indicative of a totally different world view.

Such resistance to the recognition of contrary information among world leaders is not unprecedented. Stalin dismissed solid evidence of Hitler's intentions, as did many European leaders; President Franklin D. Roosevelt also had some cultural or psychological block which prevented him from understanding Stalin or from crediting information contrary to his instincts about the USSR.

Before going with Churchill to Teheran to meet Stalin, President Roosevelt explained how he would deal with the communist leader and, consequently, with the fate of millions. He explained it in a conversation (in the vastness of its implications worth quoting in some detail) later repeated by then ex-Ambassador William Bullitt, who had tried to dissuade him:

> Bill, I don't dispute your facts, they are accurate. I don't dispute the logic of your reasoning. I just have a hunch that Stalin is not that kind of a man. Harry [Hopkins, Roosevelt's emissary to Stalin] says he's not and that he doesn't want anything but security for his country, and I think that if I give him everything I possibly can and ask nothing from him in return, *noblesse oblige*, he won't try to annex anything and will work with me for a world of democracy and peace.[31]

Despite all its diversity, there is a striking line of continuity in

US political thought between this assessment by Roosevelt – which was being contradicted at the very time it was stated – and a similar statement made in 1978 and equally contradicted by the evidence. Although separated by forty-seven years, there remain the same kinds of preconceptions, the same appeals to reason, the avoidance of reference to ideology, a contradiction of the rules of elementary psychology and an avoidance of reference to Soviet history in the following statement by a high official of the State Department, a former scholar with access to the most sensitive of classified information:

> Being acknowledged as an equal justifies the Soviets: willingness to negotiate in SALT to their allies, to themselves, and to their own domestic hawks ... They no longer have to feel humiliated by the fact that they are inferior in certain areas. And being recognized as equal also reduces the importance of military posturing toward the outside world to maintain status and prestige.[32]

Both of these statements, besides reflecting the extreme subjectivism which the Soviets frequently charge is characteristic of US thought, also reflect patterns that constantly recur in our military and strategic literature: the attempt to personalize major movements of history; the assumption of reason in war and rationality in the speaker freeing him from his culture; and a reliance on facile psychological translations.

Unlike the dialectic, so useful in Soviet thought, American military analysis relies heavily on paired opposites: either/or, aggressive/defensive, strategy/tactics, nuclear/conventional, and so on. Here there is a preconception that one is either an equal or an enemy; if an equal then, apparently, it can be assumed that one follows the same goals.

Great Men or Great Ideas

The line of analysis of attempting to personalize relationships with the USSR – which sidesteps ideological implications – emerged at our first official diplomatic encounter with the new state, the accreditation of the first Soviet ambassador in the White House in 1933. Troyanovsky's speech, as reported in *Izvestia*, was entirely businesslike. President Roosevelt responded in a more personal mode. He told Troyanovsky how glad he was to receive as ambassador a man who was known and liked in Washington.[33] Although that was a small incident, it presaged a colossal one, for Roosevelt thought that if he could get Stalin to like him at

Teheran – and to do so he was willing to slight Churchill – he could induce the Soviet government to set aside nothing less than the aims of the Russian Revolution. The attempt to personalize was also apparent in Mrs Mautner's reference to the hawks in the Kremlin, as if the US idea of hawks would make any sense in Soviet terms.

These kinds of conceptions have important influence in US military analysis. For example, it was widely thought that the rise of the Soviet navy was the result of the personal success of its chief, Admiral Gorshkov. Those who were convinced by this argument were distracted from seeing the naval build-up as part of a larger strategy.[34]

Preconceptions about reason also affect our ability to predict military intentions. President Carter assumes that the Soviets want stability; Mrs Mautner assumed that the Soviet military build-up is only for 'posturing to the outside world'; both, in spite of the fact that Soviet military practice is quite the opposite. Many assumed that they agreed that nuclear war made no sense. Seaplan 2000 is a current military document reflecting such assumptions. It projects naval forces to the year 2000 without coping even with Soviet doctrine on nuclear war.[35]

A very good example of how the projection of a reasonable assumption about the military balance can affect military analysis is found in the naming of the Soviet helicopter carrier, the *Moskva*. A proper navy, from the Western, certainly the US, point of view, was organized around aircraft carriers because their mission was to control the seas, at least the sea lines of communication. It was assumed that the Soviet navy would see the problem that way, too, and that when it emerged from being an arm of the ground forces, it would start with an aircraft carrier. When the *Moskva* first appeared for sea trials in 1967, it was unlike any ship ever built. That made its classification difficult. (It also embarrassed the large number of analysts who habitually assumed that the Soviet military planners imitated the West.) The Soviets called it, and still do, a large antisubmarine cruiser. But the West needed it to be a carrier and called it that. The need was not only to support arguments that carriers were effective modern naval platforms, but also to support classifications that were traditional. To compare capabilities neatly between the Soviet navy and the US navy, one needs an essential equivalence. As the assessment of the Soviet navy turned almost entirely in terms of capabilities, and not on intentions, analysts naturally translated Soviet terms into Western categories. The effect of this translation was to mask, sometimes seriously, Soviet intentions. For example, calling the antisubmarine cruiser a carrier tended to divert attention from the very major efforts that the Soviets were making in antisubmarine warfare, efforts meant to cope with the detection of our ballistic missile submarines, an effort that, if successful, would change the strategic balance.

Many Western military minds are in the thrall of paired opposites: a strategy, a weapon, a war must be either this or that. The problems this causes would not be so serious if it were understood that the pairs arrange the data of the senses only in a relative way. But they seem to have a much more powerful channeling effect. For instance, the debate about whether the Soviets serve ideology or practical politics nearly always falls into these extremes, as if any human being can live outside of his history and culture, that is, outside of his ideology. More pointedly, the nuclear/conventional category appears to obscure the many other kinds of wars for which the Soviets plan. That seems to be the reasoning behind the former Chairman of the Joint Chiefs of Staff, General Brown's statement that 'In Angola and Ethiopa, they [the Soviets] have exploited crises, but in a way which has avoided direct confrontation between major powers'.[36] Referring to these wars, General Brown could not classify them, although they constituted threats to world stability not less significant, one would assume, than the invasion of Afghanistan. General Brown described Soviet aggression with the language of neutrality as 'when it has served their interests to do so, the Soviets have continued to seek involvement where there is political or social instability'. Here is an example of how language de-escalates strategy.

Another aspect of this polarity is that it appears to cause discussion of military problems to be centered around the strategic debate, neglecting the vast new array of lesser problems assaulting the military commander and failing to educate the public. Such problems as what infantry or ship formation is best if there is a 25 percent chance of a chemical attack are seldom explored, apparently because such an attack would fall into neither category of conventional or nuclear. It is even more alarming that there is almost no consideration of what to do after a nuclear exchange. American scenarios stop with the nuclear explosions. In that sense, our war plans end where the Soviet war plans begin. Although there will be armies in the field, the military operation is assumed to have stopped where the imagination did.

Finally, the either/or thought pattern damages our perception of Soviet military thought. The military problem is not either

Soviet or not Soviet. It is multinational, multiracial and multi-cultural. The USSR is an empire, a conglomerate of many building an international military force. In every possible way, it has been forewarning other nations that its notion of expansion is by way of uniting with other proletarian (political) parties, integrating with their armies in the style of the Warsaw Pact and then not letting go. This is what General Brown called 'involvement', but others think of as the Brezhnev doctrine.

In the same way that we familiarized the Soviet large anti-submarine cruiser by calling it a helicopter carrier, so we tend to familiarize Soviet military doctrine by thinking of it in terms of our strategy or tactics. However, in Soviet thought there is a category of *operations* inserted between strategy and tactics which changes everything. Operations are like the Inchon Landing, something on a very large scale, solving some important problem. Strategy is always about winning, and in that sense, emphasizes as do other Soviet approaches to war, the problem-solving war-fighting nature of the thought process.[37] However, what has happened in the last few years in Soviet military thought is the realization that with modern weapons and the speed of warfare, operations are able to solve strategic problems and even tactics can contribute to strategic solutions. The effect of this is to acknowledge a revolution in ground warfare and in strategic concepts as well. It further enlarges the incongruities of our two languages of war.

Trying Not to Repeat Past Wars

Soviet patterns of thought are no less definitional and, under Stalin, also led to a sterility of imagination. But there is, in the dialectic, the process by which they arrive at a military decision, a safeguard against refighting old wars.

As a system of thought, it was swept in with Marxism, but it seemed to suit the Russian mind, while serving the abstractions of German idealism. In some ways it is similar to the American paired opposites in that it sets up a thesis and then its antithesis. That might match President Carter's thesis, 'will the Soviets help the world to be stable', or (the President's concept of its opposite) 'will they pursue colonial power', the antithesis. The difference between Soviet thought and the US President's would probably be that he would be likely to stop after posing his question, the reflection of a basically static concept of the world. The Soviets, however, would not be able to stop there. Between the imperialist stability (the thesis) and the colonial instability (the antithesis) they would posit a struggle which would issue in a new synthesis (a socialist state). The dialectic, thus, matches the violence of Soviet politics: it never allows rest, it implies that the struggle is endless. It leads to a concept of fluid borders, fluid wars and ever-changing definitions. It suggests that parity, for instance, could not be a Soviet concept, for it implies stability in a system of thought which denies that possibility.

Of course, as the paired opposites mask Soviet concepts, so the dialectic distorts the West in Soviet eyes. There is no process for understanding what the Soviets refer to as the 'mysticism' of US concepts, its moral judgments, its search for equality, respect for sovereignty, and the like. It could not prepare them for the US response to the invasion of Afghanistan (for the Soviets, a perfectly dialectical decision), for it cannot deal with spontaneous outrage.

In Search of a Synthesis

Understanding another language always involves a reduction of its meaning and intensity. The process by which language is understood is translation, which in its search for equivalence, must necessarily force foreign structures into its own domestic shape. This is no less true of poetry than of war, if this chapter has been convincing. Translation is a rich ground for nurturing preconceptions and overlooking nuances. It can make dangers unforeseen or create threats out of nothing. But it is a problem that must be dealt with by strategists as well as by poets. Both must think new thoughts; but they must watch themselves as they think to be aware when they are reacting to their own preconceptions and not to the foreign thoughts at hand.

In translating Soviet experience and thought into comprehensible patterns, there are those who refer to Russian history as the key to understanding current strategy. For them, it is easier to understand the Soviet methods by noting continuities in Russian behavior through the decades. For these analysts, the lessons of the English visitor, Giles Fletcher – writing in 1591 on patterns of behavior by the Russian czar in conquering and controlling occupied lands – continue to be borne out in the Baltic and East European countries today. In administering his new territories, Fletcher described, the czar denuded them of goods, divided them into small parcels and appointed multiple authorities so that each would report on the other. He sent 'secrete messengers of speciall trust about him as intelligences, to prie and harken out what is doing'.[38]

For others, for military and diplomatic analysts who seldom have time in their two- and three-year rotations to become intimate with Russian and Soviet history, there is no time to grasp the emotional significance in Soviet society of the 20–30 million dead in World War II alone. They must deal *ahistorically*, translating current strategy into the more static and enduring language of ideology. For them, there is important evidence of continuity in Soviet (not Russian) strategic thought in the writings of the leading military theoretician, the old Bolshevik, Frunze, who is much quoted and followed to this day. In the business of consolidating power, Frunze uses a distinctly ideological idiom to draw a conclusion quite in keeping with Fletcher's observations:

> The Red General Staff will fulfill its mission only if it is able to rise above the nation-state point of view. We must think of ourselves as a potential nucleus, as a potential center of a broader Red General Staff. The mission of helping the proletariat of those countries which still do not know how to conquer the class enemies amidst themselves – to help them conquer these enemies – is placed on us.[39]

If the historical beacon of Giles Fletcher provided a thesis, and the ideological beacon of Frunze an antithesis, then it was Stalin who provided a synthesis, suggesting that both history and a contemporary Marxist-Leninist ideology live comfortably side by side in the Soviet mind. It is pertinent that those who made their careers under Stalin's leadership are still in power, and have only criticized the rigidity of his postwar military thought, but not the ideas themselves.

In making a politico-military analysis of his sixteenth-century predecessor, Ivan the Terrible, Stalin provided a kind of dialectic solution to the question of the relative force of history and ideology in Soviet international policy. At the same time, he stated a position that no translation can totally emasculate.

The situation was Stalin's discussion of Ivan's method of dealing with the nobles, the boyars, who were trying to share his power. The report of his opinion was as follows:

> And then Iosif Vissarionovich [Stalin] added humorously that 'Here, God interfered with Ivan: Grozny [Ivan the Terrible] liquidates one feudal family, one boyar line, and then for a whole year repents and prays forgiveness, whereas what he should have done was to act still more decisively!'[40]

In a succinct form, here is a model of the Soviet dialectics of war, neither ideology nor history working alone, but the one reinforcing the other. Stalin's vision, as is that of his contemporaries, was set on the end result, the transformation of society, not on individual guilt, reason or a natural evolution. The problem of the leader was to accumulate the power to make society fit that preconceived vision, whether that means destroying one noble family or five. The chapters that follow will show how these dialectical themes have been translated into a Soviet language of war.

Notes: Chapter 2

1 Alexander Solzhenitsyn, 'Misconceptions about Russia are a threat to America', *Foreign Affairs*, Spring, 1980, pp. 797–825.
2 Edward Luttwak, 'The American style of warfare and the military balance', *Survival*, March–April, 1979, pp. 57–60.
3 Claude Levi-Strauss, *Tristes Tropiques*, trans., John and Doreen Weightman (New York: Pocket Books, 1977), p. 16.
4 In one recent article in *Red Star*, the headlines announced that 'outsiders have found out the names of our classmates and that's no secret!' What caused the uproar was that two soldiers riding on a streetcar in Alma Ata had, in casual conversation, named some of their fellow students, thus revealing information to spies presumed to be collecting names on streetcars: P. Chernenko, 'Need for vigilance', *Red Star*, 6 January 1978, p. 4.
5 An insightful description was given by Mikhail A. Meerson, 'Jewish emigration in Russian perspective', *Vremya i my*, no. 4, 1979, p. 101.
6 Leonid Brezhnev, for example, made such references in speeches quoted in *Pravda*, 28 June 1972; 28 March 1973; 21 January 1974.
7 V. I. Lenin, 'What is to be done?', *Collected Works*, Vol. V (Moscow: Gosizdat, 1963) (42 vols), p. 355.
8 Lecture, Wellesley College, 2 April 1980.
9 *New York Times*, 14 July 1977, p. 10.
10 President Jimmy Carter, State of the Union Address, 23 January 1980, Current Policy No. 132, US Department of State, Washington, DC, p. 2.
11 B. I. Kuznetzov, 'Strategiya', *Soviet Military Encyclopedia*, Vol. II (Moscow: Voenizdat, 1977–9), p. 564.
12 Cited by George Kennan, *Memoirs: 1925–1950* (Boston, Ma.: Little, Brown, 1967), p. 523.
13 Leonid Brezhnev, 'Report of the CPSU Central Committee to the 24th Congress of the Communist Party of the Soviet Union', 30 March 1971, in *Reprints from the Soviet Press*, 14 May 1971, p. 27.
14 V. I. Lenin, *Complete Collected Works*, Vol. XXX (Moscow: Gosizdat, 1963), p. 5.
15 I. Grabovoy, 'In search of super-accurate weapons', *Krasnaya zvezda*, 6 August 1975.
16 See Stansfield Turner, 'Missions of the navy', *Naval War College Review*.
17 *The Threat* (TC 6-5-1), US Army Field Artillery School, Fort Sill, Oklahoma, 30 September 1976. This depersonalization of the enemy must have been also a function of the heavy emphasis on discussing an adversary's capabilities, with little attention given to his intentions, even when they were so obviously connected to the transforming goal of a Marxist state. As the period of fighting an 'anonymous enemy' began to moderate, however, capabilities continued to be emphasized. The nature of the men behind the capabilities was seldom discussed.
18 ibid.

19 William E. DePuy, '11 men, 1 mind', *Training for Combat*, (Fort Benning, Ga.: US Army Combat Training Board, 1974), p. A-3. This is a reprint of General DePuy's article which was first published in 1958. As the general commanded the training command and was one of the army's major influences in planning, the article is particularly significant.

20 Herbert Goldhamer, *The Soviet Soldier* (New York: Crane Russak, 1975), p. 224, citing *Aviatsiya i kosmonavtika* (July 1972), pp. 1–2.

21 M. V. Frunze, *Izbrannye proizvedenia*, Vol. II (Moscow: Voenizdat, 1957), Vol. 6.

22 N. Schilder, *Imperator Nikolai Pervyi: ego zhizn' i tsartsvovanie* (St Petersburg, 1903), Vol. I, p. 147, cited in Nicholas V. Riasumovsky, *Nicholas I and Official Nationality in Russia, 1825–1855* (Berkeley, Ca.: University of California Press, 1967), p. 1.

23 *Izvestia*, 28 March 1980, p. 1. It was this issue of *Izvestia*, incidentally, which initiated what was to become the anti-CIA pre-Olympic Games 'spies are everywhere' campaign. Much space was devoted to the discovery that there are microphones in the shape of tree stumps in the woods around Moscow.

24 Edward Luttwak, op. cit.

25 Dwight D. Eisenhower, *Crusade in Europe* (Garden City, NJ: Doubleday, 1948), p. 4.

26 A. A. Sidorenko, 'Nastuplenie', *Soviet Military Encyclopedia*, Vol. V, p. 520.

27 *Obshchaia taktika*, Vol. 1 (Moscow: Voenizdat, 1940), p. 380; cited in Raymond L. Garthoff, *Soviet Military Doctrine* (Glencoe, Il.: Free Press, 1953), p. 258. This quote was said to have been in a speech delivered to the Plenum of the Party Central Committee, 3 March 1937, but it was excised from the collected edition of Stalin's works. The speech, launching a new wave of terror and purges, was on the theme cited above of 'spies are everywhere'. In any case, the argument is totally consistent with Soviet practice or military experience anywhere.

28 Eisenhower, op. cit., p. 468; there were battalions for this purpose formed of undesirable elements in Soviet society and of those from the army being punished. Assignment to such a battalion was, of course, an extralegal death sentence.

29 Catherine Breshko-Breshkovsky, otherwise known as 'the Little Grandmother of the Revolution', proposed forming a women's death battalion in 1917. For the Imperial Death Battalion, reference is made in F. A. Golder, *Documents of Russian History, 1914–1917* (Gloucester, Ma.: Peter Smith, 1964), p. 430 and the women's battalion in A. S. Blackwell (ed.), *The Little Grandmother of the Russian Revolution* (Boston, Ma.: Little, Brown, 1919), p. 323.

30 Brezhnev, op. cit.

31 William C. Bullitt, 'How we won the war and lost the peace', *Life*, 30 August 1948, p. 94; as Bullitt's advice had been disregarded and his career curtailed, it is reasonable to question his account of this discussion. There was a confirmation, however, in Roosevelt's conversation with his Secretary of Labor, Frances Perkins, in her book, *The Roosevelt I Knew* (New York: Viking Press, 1946), p. 383, and in the transcripts of conversations between Harry Hopkins and Stalin in Robert E. Sherwood, *Roosevelt and Hopkins* (New York: Harper, 1946).

32 Martha C. Mautner, 'A closer look at Soviet capabilities', Institute of World Affairs, Racine, Wisconsin, 29 June 1978. Mrs Mautner was at the time the Chief of the Soviet Foreign Policy Division, US Department of State, Bureau for Intelligence and Research. The whole of Mrs Mautner's speech is in the same vein of almost total ethnocentric projection about how figures in the Kremlin must feel on the basis of her own feelings. It is very sobering reading, indeed.

33 *Izvestia*, 9 January 1934, p. 1.

34 'The missions of navy', *Naval War College Review*, March–April, 1974, pp. 2–18.

35 'Sea plan 2000', Selected Readings in Defense Economics and Decision Making: Non-Quantitative Factors, n.d., n.p., n.a. This plan was called 'the principal articulation of the Navy's vision of a future war [which] pictures a global contest between the United States and the Soviet Union in which nuclear weapons play no part': Linton F. Brooks, *Proceedings U.S. Naval Institute*, January, 1980, vol. 106, p. 29.

36 George S. Brown, 'United States military posture for FY 1979', Statement for the Congress, 20 January 1978, p. 4.

37 Robert Legvold discusses the confusion between our military doctrine and our idea of Soviet military strategy in an important article: 'Strategic "doctrine" and SALT:

Soviet and American views', *Survival*, January–February, 1979, p. 9.

38 Giles Fletcher, *Of the Russe Commonwealth* (Cambridge, Ma.: Harvard University Press, 1966), p. 65.

39 Frunze, ibid., p. 6.

40 S. M. Dubrovsky, 'Protiv idealizatsii deatel'nosti Ivana IV', *Voprosy istorii*, no. 8, 1956, p. 128.

3

Contrasts in American and Soviet Strategic Thought

FRITZ W. ERMARTH

For some time, Western observers have been troubled by Soviet strategic doctrine. Debate about US strategic security and SALT has widened awareness that Soviet thinking about strategy and nuclear war differs in significant ways from that of the USA. To the extent one should care about this – and that extent is a matter of debate – we do not like the way the Soviets seem to think. Prior to 1972, appreciation of differences between Soviet and US strategic thinking was limited to a small number of specialists. Those who held it a matter of high concern for policy were fewer still. Since that time, concern about the nature and consequences of these differences has spread in large measure as a result of worry about the Soviet strategic build-up and the continued failure to achieve SALT agreements that genuinely limit the strategic competition.

Heightened attention to the way the other side thinks about strategic nuclear power is timely and proper. The nature of the Soviet build-up and some of our own previous choices have denied us purely 'hardware solutions' to our strategic security problems that are independent of the other side's values and perceptions. Whatever one thinks about the manner in which we have negotiated SALT, it is desirable that management of the US-Soviet strategic relationship contain an explicit dialogue. That dialogue should include more attention to strategic concepts than we have seen in past SALT negotiations. Moreover, whatever the role of SALT in the future, the existence of 'rough parity' almost by definition means that we cannot limit strategic policy to contending merely with the opponent's forces. In the cause of stable deterrence, effective crisis management and, if need be, conducting war, we must thwart his strategy. This requires understanding the opponent's strategy better.

The Need to Understand Strategic Doctrine

Let us define 'strategic doctrine' as a set of operative beliefs and principles that in a significant way guide official behavior with respect to military research and development, weapons selection, deployment of forces, operational plans, arms control, etc. The essence of US doctrine is to deter central nuclear war at the lowest feasible levels of arms effort ('arms race stability') and strategic risk ('crisis stability') by presenting the credible threat of catastrophic damage to the enemy should deterrence fail. In the event deterrence should fail, this doctrine says it should be the aim and ability of US power to make the world assuredly miserable for the enemy. Making the world following the outbreak of nuclear war more tolerable for the USA, has been, at best, a lesser concern. Soviet strategic doctrine stipulates that Soviet strategic forces and plans should strive in all available ways to enhance the prospect that the USSR could survive as a nation and, in some politically and militarily meaningful way, defeat the main enemy should deterrence fail – and by this striving both help to prevent nuclear war and help the USSR attain other strategic and foreign policy goals.

These characterizations of US and Soviet strategic doctrine and the differences between them are important. Had US strategic policy been more sensitive to them over the last ten years, we might not find ourselves in so awkward a present situation. We would have been less sanguine than we were about prospects that the Soviets would settle for a strategic parity comfortable for both sides. We would not have believed as uncritically as we long did that the SALT process was progressing toward a mutually desired strategic stability based on already tacitly accepted, shared strategic principles.

It is, if anything, even more important that these asymmetries be fully appreciated today. They are a crucial starting point for strategic diagnosis and therapy. But they are only a starting point. What we call US and Soviet strategic doctrine is more complicated, qualified and contradictory than the above characterizations admit by themselves.

Comparative Strategic Doctrine

The following discussion is intended only to suggest some of the contrasts that exist between US and Soviet strategic thinking. The issues raised are not treated exhaustively, and the list itself is not exhaustive. Our appreciation of these matters is not adequate to the critical times in the US-Soviet strategic relationship we are facing. It would seem highly desirable to develop the intellectual discipline of comparative military doctrine, especially in the strategic nuclear sphere. Systematic comparative studies of strategic doctrine could serve to clarify what we think and how we ourselves differ on these matters, as well as to organize what we know about Soviet strategic thinking.

Although many have views on how both the USA and the USSR deal with strategic problems, there is in fact little systematic comparison of the conceptual and behavioral foundations of our respective strategic activity. In this area, more than other comparative inquiries into communist and non-communist politics, there are the obstacles of secrecy in the path of research. Perhaps as vital, neither government nor academic institutions appear to have cultivated many people with the required interdisciplinary skills and experience.

The most influential factor that has inhibited lucid comparisons of US and Soviet strategic thinking has been the long and uncritically held assumption that they had to be very similar, or at least converging. We have been quite insensitive to the possibility that two very different political systems could deal very differently with a common problem. We have presumed to understand the task of keeping the strategic peace on equitable and economical terms. As reasonable people the Soviets, too, would come to understand it our way.

Explaining this particular expression of our cultural self-centeredness is itself a fascinating field for speculation. It probably goes beyond the US habit of attributing our own views to others. It may result from the fact that postwar developments in US strategy were an institutional and intellectual offspring of the natural sciences that spawned modern weapons. Scientific truth is transnational, not culturally determined. But, unfortunately, strategy is more like *politics* than like science; cultural and historical conditions, not to mention national politics, condition strategy.

The next five to ten years of the US-Soviet strategic relationship will be characterized by mounting US anxieties about the adequacy of our deterrent forces and our strategic doctrine. It is now quite unlikely that the SALT process will substantially alleviate these anxieties. Even if a more promising state of affairs emerges, however, it is hard to see us managing it with calm and confidence unless we develop a more thorough appreciation of the differences between US and Soviet strategic thinking.

Things have progressed beyond the point where it is useful to have the three familiar schools of thought on Soviet doctrine arguing past each other: one saying, 'whatever they say, they think as we do'; the second insisting, 'whatever they say, it does not matter'; and the third contending, 'they think what they say, and are therefore out for superiority over us'.

Comparative studies of strategic doctrine should address systematically a series of questions:

- What are the central decisions about strategy, force posture and force employment or operations that each country's doctrine is supposed to resolve?
- What are the prevailing categories, concepts, beliefs and assertions that appear to constitute the body of strategic thought and doctrine in question?
- What are the hedges and qualifications introduced to modify the main theses of official thinking?
- What are the non-strategic, e.g. propagandistic, purposes that might motivate doctrinal pronouncements? Does the doctrinal system recognize a distinction between what ideally ought to be, and what practically is (a serious problem in the Soviet case)?
- In what actions, e.g. force posture, does apparent doctrine have practical effect? Where does it lie dormant?
- To what extent are doctrinal pronouncements the subject of or the guise for policy dispute?
- What perceptions does one side entertain as to the doctrinal system of the other side? With what effect?

Answering these questions for both the US and the USSR is admittedly no easy matter, especially in a highly politicized environment in which many participants have already made up their minds how they want the answers to come out with respect to assumed impact on US strategic policy. But we have the data to do a good deal better than we have to date.

US and Soviet Doctrine Contrasted

The Soviets provide definitions of doctrine (*doktrina*) and policy (*politika*) that state they are official principles guidance and instructions from the highest governing authorities to guide the building of the armed forces and their employment in war.

These definitions are narrower than our common usage. They

remind us that we do not have literal access to Soviet strategic doctrine through the most commonly available sources, i.e. Soviet military literature and various pronouncements of authoritative political and military figures. Our insight into Soviet strategic doctrine, as the Soviets define it, is derived by inference from such sources along with inferences from observed research and development and force procurement behavior, what we manage to learn about peacetime force operations and exercises, and occasional direct statements in more privileged settings, such as SALT, by varyingly persuasive spokesmen.

The value of all these sources is constrained by the limitations of our perceptive apparatus, technical and intellectual, and the fact that Soviet communications on strategic subjects serve many purposes other than conveying official policy, such as foreign and domestic propaganda. For all that, we have gained over the years a substantial degree of understanding of the content of Soviet strategic thinking, of the values, standards, objectives and calculations that underlie Soviet decisions. It is this total body of thinking, more akin to our notion of doctrine, and its bearing on action that are of concern here.

Where lack of access complicates understanding of Soviet strategic doctrine, an overabundance of data confuses understanding of the US side, a point that Soviets make with some justice when berated with the evils of Soviet secrecy. If, in the case of the USA, one is concerned about the body of thinking that underlies strategic action, it is clearly insufficient to rely on official statements or documents at any level of classification or authority. Such sources may, for one reason or another, not tell the whole story, or paper over serious differences of purpose behind some action.

One of the difficulties in determining the concepts or beliefs that underlie US strategic action is that strategic policy is a composite of behavior taking place in at least three distinguishable, but overlapping arenas. The smallest, most secretive, and least significant over the long-term, assuming deterrence does not fail, is the arena of operational or war planning. The second arena is that of system and force acquisition; it is much larger and more complex than the first. The most disorganized, largest, but most important for the longer-term course of US strategic behavior, is the arena of largely public debate over basic strategic principles and objectives. Its participants range from the most highly placed executive authorities to influential private elites, and occasionally the public at large. Strategy-making is a relatively democratic process in the USA.

To be sure, many areas of public policy-making can be assessed in terms of these overlapping circles of players and constituents. But the realm of US strategic policy may be unusual in the degree to which different rules, data, concerns and participants dominate the different arenas. These differences make it difficult to state with authority what US strategic policy is on an issue that cuts across the arenas. For example, *public US policy* in the past has stated a clear desire to avoid countersilo capabilities on grounds that they endanger strategic stability. The *weapons acquisition community* may, for a variety of reasons, simultaneously be seeking a weapons characteristic vital to countersilo capability, improved ballistic missile accuracy. As best they can with weapons available, meanwhile, *force operators* may be required by the logic of their task to target enemy missile silos as a high priority.

Despite these complexities, however, it is possible to generalize a body of policy concepts and values that govern US strategic behavior. There have been strong tendencies that dominate US strategic behavior in the areas of declaratory policy, force acquisition and arms control policy. Again, the case of US countersilo capabilities may be cited. Today, the USA lacks high-confidence, missile-delivered capabilities against Soviet missile silos. This is in part the result of technological choice, the early selection of small ICBMs and the deployment of low-yield MIRV weapons. It is also the result of Soviet efforts to improve silo hardness. But the main reason for this lack is that – until the decision to deploy the M-X – we have abided by a conscious judgment that a serious countersilo capability, because it was feared to threaten strategic stability, would be a bad thing for the USA to possess.

The situation is more straightforward, if secretive, on the Soviet side. Soviet strategic policy-making takes place in a far more vertical and closed system, capped by the Politburo's Defense Council. Expertise is monopolized by the military and a subset of the top political leadership long deeply involved in military matters. Although elites external to this group can bid for its scarce resources to some extent, they cannot seriously challenge its values and judgments. Matters of doctrine, force acquisition and war planning are much more intimately connected within this decision group than in the USA. Policy arguments are indeed possible. A series of Soviet debates on nuclear strategy appeared to take place from the mid-1950s to the late 1960s, although the issues and alternatives in these debates remain obscure.

These considerations make difficult, but not impossible, the comparative treatment of US and Soviet strategic beliefs and concepts. One may describe with some confidence how the two very different decision systems deal with certain concerns central to the strategic nuclear predicament of both sides. Much about US and Soviet strategic belief systems can be captured by exploring how they treat five central issues:(1) the consequences of an all-out strategic nuclear war; (2) the phenomenon of deterrence; (3) stability; (4) distinctions and relationships between intercontinental and regional strategic security concerns; and (5) strategic conflict limitation.

(a)   *Consequences of Nuclear War*

For a generation, the relevant elites of both the USA and USSR have agreed that an unlimited strategic nuclear war would be a disaster of immense proportions. Knowing the experiences of the peoples of the USSR with warfare in this century and with nuclear inferiority since 1945, one sometimes suspects that the human dimensions of such a catastrophe are more real to Russians, high and low, than to Americans, for whom the prospect is vague and unreal, if certainly forbidding.

For many years the prevailing US concept of nuclear war's consequences has been such as to preclude belief in any military or politically meaningful form of victory. Serious effort on the part of the state to enhance the prospect for national survival seemed quixotic, even dangerously misleading. Hence US relative disinterest in air defenses and civil defenses over the last fifteen years, and US genuine fear that ballistic missile defenses would be severely destabilizing. Growth of Soviet nuclear power has, until recently, reinforced this view of nuclear conflict among the majority of Americans. But even when the USA enjoyed massive superiority, when the USSR could inflict much less societal damage on the USA, and then only in a first strike (through the early 1960s), the awesome destructiveness of nuclear weapons had deprived actual war with these weapons of much of its strategic meaning for the USA.

The Soviet elite, however, has clung in the worst of times tenaciously to the belief that nuclear war cannot – indeed, must not – be deprived of strategic meaning, that is, some rational relationship to the interests of the state. It has insisted that, however awful, nuclear war must be something the state can survive and that some kind of meaningful victory is attainable in principle. As most are aware, this issue was debated in various ways at the beginning and end of the Khrushchev era, with

Khrushchev on both sides of the issue. But the regime has consistently decided that it must continue to believe in survival and victory of some form. Not to believe this would mean that the most basic processes of history, on which Soviet ideology and political legitimacy are founded, could be derailed by the technological works of man and the caprice of an historically doomed opponent. Moreover, as the defenders of doctrinal rectitude have continued to point out, failure to believe in the 'manageability' of nuclear disaster would lead to pacificism, defeatism and lassitude in the Soviet military effort. This should not be read as the triumph of an irrational or ideological will over objective science and common sense. From the Soviet point of view, nuclear war with a powerful USA has been a real and present danger. Should the state merely give up on its traditional responsibilities to defend itself and survive in that event? The Soviets' negative answer hardly strikes one as unreasonable. Their puzzlement, alternating between contemptuous and suspicious, over US insistence on a positive answer is not surprising.

In recent years the changing strategic balance has had the effect of strengthening rather than weakening the asymmetry of the two sides' convictions on this matter. Dubious when the USA enjoyed relative advantage, strategic victory and survival in nuclear conflict have become the more incredible to the US as the strategic power of the USSR has grown. For the USSR, however, the progress of arms and war survival programs (e.g. civil defense) has transformed what was in the past no more than an ideological imperative into a more plausible strategic potential. Soviet leaders may believe that, under favorable operational conditions, the USSR could win a central strategic war today. Notwithstanding strategic parity or essential equivalence of forces, however, they may also believe they could lose such a conflict under some conditions. The possibility that such seemingly antithetical beliefs could coexist simultaneously in Soviet doctrine is a feature of great importance examined further below.

(b) *Deterrence*

The concept of deterrence early became a central element of both US and Soviet strategic belief systems. For both sides, the concept had extended to regional dimensions, and a good deal of political content. There has, in short, been some functional similarity between the deterrence thinking of the two sides: restraint of hostile action across a spectrum of violence by the threat of severe punishment. Over time and with shifts in the overall military

balance, latent asymmetries of thinking have become more pro-
nounced. For the USA, strategic deterrence tended to become
the only meaningful objective of strategic nuclear forces, and it
threatened to become progressively decoupled from regional
security. For the Soviets, deterrence – or war prevention – was the
first, but not the only, and not the last, objective of strategy.
Deterrence also means to provide the military underpinnings of a
foreign policy that had both offensive and defensive goals. And it
was never counterposed against the ultimate objective of being
able to manage a nuclear war successfully should deterrence fail.
The Soviet concept of deterrence has evolved as the strategic
balance has improved for the USSR from primary emphasis on
defensive themes of war prevention and protection of prior political gains to more emphasis on themes that include the protection
of dynamic processes favoring Soviet international interests.
Repetition of the refrain that peace, détente and the progress of
'healthy forces' are a product of Soviet strategic power, among
other things, displays this evolution.

(c)   *Stability*

Strategic stability is a concept that is very difficult to treat in a
comparative manner because it is so vital to US strategic thinking, but hardly identifiable in Soviet doctrine. In US thinking,
strategic stability has meant a condition in which incentives
inherent in the arms balance to initiate the use of strategic nuclear
forces and, closely related, to acquire new or additional forces are
weak or absent. In an environment dominated by powerful offensive capabilities and comparatively vulnerable ultimate values,
i.e. cities and society, stability was thought to be achievable on the
basis of a contract of mutually vulnerable societies and survivable
offensive forces. Emphasis on force survivability followed, as did
relative lack of interest in counterforce and active and passive
defenses.

  Soviet failure to embrace these notions is sufficiently evident
not to require much elaboration. One may argue about Soviet
ability to overturn stability in US terms, but not about Soviet
disinclination to accept the idea as a governing principle of
strategic behavior. Soviet acceptance of the ABM agreement in
1972 is still frequently cited as testimony to some acceptance of
this principle. It is much more probable, however, that the
agreement was attractive to Moscow because superior US ABM
technology plus superior US ABM penetrating technology would
have given the US a major advantage during the mid to late

1970s. From their unilateral point of view, the Soviets saw the ABM agreement as stabilizing a process of strategic catchup against a serious risk of reversal. But it did not mean acceptance of the US stability principle.

The US has always been relatively sensitive to the potential of technology to jeopardize specific formulae for achieving stability, although it has been relatively slow to perceive the pace and extent to which comparative advantage has shifted from passive survivability to counterforce technologies. The Soviets have also been sensitive to destabilizing technologies. But they have tended to accept the destabilizing dynamism of technology as an intrinsic aspect of the strategic dialectic, the underlying engine of which is a political competition not susceptible to stabilization. For the Soviets, arms control negotiations are part of this competitive process. Such negotiations can help keep risks within bounds and also, by working on Western political processes, restrain Western competitiveness.

While rejecting US strategic stability notions as strategic norms, the Soviets do see certain constellations of weapons technology and forces as having an intrinsic stability, in that they make the acquisition of decisive military advantages very difficult. What they reject is the notion that, in the political and technical world as they see it, those constellations can be deliberately frozen and the strategic dimension thereby factored out of the East–West struggle permanently or for long periods.

(d) *Intercontinental and Regional Power*

Defining the boundary line between strategic and non-strategic forces has been a troubling feature of the US-Soviet strategic dialogue and of SALT from the beginning. It is one of diplomacy's minor ironies that forward capabilities that the US has long regarded as part of the general purpose forces (e.g. FBS), the US has been hard pressed to keep out of the negotiations. But peripheral strike forces the Soviets have systematically defined and managed as strategic have been very difficult to bring into the picture, until the TNF negotiations began.

Geography imparted an intercontinental meaning to the term strategic for the USA. The same geography dictated that, for the USSR, strategic concern began at the doorstep. Soviet concern about the military capabilities in the hands of and on the territory of its neighbors is genuine, although Soviet arguments for getting the US to legitimatize and pay for those concerns at SALT in terms of its own central force allowances have been a bit contrived. They are tantamount to penalizing the USA for having genuine friends and commitments to sovereign allies, while rewarding the USSR for conducting itself in a manner that has left it only vassals or opponents on its borders.

Underlying these definitional problems are more fundamental differences between US and Soviet doctrines on what is generally called 'coupling'. It has long been US policy to assure that US strategic nuclear forces are seen by the Soviets and NATO allies as tightly coupled to European security. Along with conventional and theater nuclear forces, US strategic nuclear forces constitute an element of the NATO 'triad'. The good health of the alliance and the viability of deterrence in Europe have been seen to require a very credible threat to engage US strategic nuclear forces once nuclear weapons come into play above the level of quite limited use. For more than twenty years NATO's official policy has had to struggle against doubts that this coupling could be credible in the absence of clear US strategic superiority. Yet the vocabulary we commonly employ itself tends to strain this linkage in that theater nuclear forces are distinguished from strategic. Ironically, the struggle to keep so-called Forward Based Systems out of SALT, because we could not find a good way to bring in comparable Soviet systems, tended to underline the distinction. In our thinking about the actual prosecution of a strategic conflict, once conflict at that level should begin we tend to forget about what might be the local outcome of the regional conflict that probably precipitated the strategic exchange.

The Soviets, on the other hand, appear to take a more comprehensive view of strategy and the strategic balance. Both in peacetime political competition and in the ultimate test of a central conflict, they tend to see all force elements as contributing to a unified strategic purpose, national survival and the elimination or containment of enemies on their periphery. The USSR tends to see intercontinental strike forces, and strategic forces more generally, as a means to help it win an all-out conflict in its most crucial theater, Europe. Both institutionally and operationally, Soviet intercontinental strike forces are an outgrowth and extension of forces initially developed to cover peripheral targets. Land combat forces, including conventional forces, are carefully trained and equipped to fight in nuclear conditions. In the last decade, the emergence of a hostile and potentially powerful China has more firmly riveted the 'rimland' of Eurasia into the Soviet strategic perspective.

Whatever the consequences of a central US-Soviet nuclear conflict for their respective homelands, Soviet strategy would aim at eliminating US power and influence on the Eurasian landmass. If, by virtue of its active and passive damage limitation measures, the USSR suffered measurably less damage than did the USA, and it managed to intimidate or destroy China as a military power, the resultant Soviet domination of Eurasia would represent the crucial element of 'strategic victory' in Soviet eyes. In any case, regional conflict outcomes seem not to lose their significance in Soviet strategy once intercontinental nuclear conflict begins.

(e) *Conflict Limitation*

Nuclear conflict limitation is a theme on which influential American opinion is divided. After much thought and argument, the Nixon administration adopted a more explicit endorsement of limited strategic nuclear options as a hedge against the failings of a strategy solely reliant on all-out war plans for deterrence or response in the event of deterrent failure. The Carter administration was initially doubtful about the value of limited nuclear options because it doubted the viability of nuclear conflict limitations, and also shared the fear of some critics that limited options could seem to make nuclear use more tolerable and therefore detract from deterrence. With the issuance of PD-59 in 1980, however, the Carter administration re-established the place of limited nuclear options and flexibility in US strategic doctrine.

Theories of nuclear conflict limitations entertained in the USA tend to rest on concepts of risk management and bargaining with the opponent. We are interested in limited options, because they are more credible than unlimited ones in response to limited provocation. Whether or not they can be controlled is uncertain; hence their credible availability enhances the risk faced by the initiator of conflict. Should conflict come about, then limited options might be used to change the risk, cost and benefit calculus of the opponent in the direction of some form of war termination. This would not be a sure thing, but it is judged better to have the limited options than not.

How the Soviets view the matter of nuclear conflict limitations is obscure. The least one can say is that they do not see it in the manner described above. From the early 1960s, since McNamara's famed Ann Arbor speech, Soviet propagandists have denounced limited nuclear war concepts as US contrivances to make nuclear weapons use more 'acceptable' and to rationalize the quest for counterforce advantages. They have replayed the criticism that such concepts weaken deterrence and cannot prevent nuclear war from becoming unlimited.

To some degree, Soviet propaganda on this theme can be suspected of intending to undermine US strategy innovations that detract from the political benefits of Soviet strategic force improvement. Given differences of view in the USA on this subject, moreover, the Soviets could hardly resist the temptation to fuel the US argument. There are several reasons why Soviet public pronouncements should not be taken as entirely reflecting the content of operative Soviet strategic thinking and planning for limited nuclear use. For one thing, qualified acceptance in Soviet doctrine and posture of a non-nuclear scenario, or at least a non-nuclear phase in theater conflict displays some Soviet willingness to embrace conflict limitation notions previously rejected. Soviet strategic and theater nuclear force modernization, in addition, have given Soviet operational planners a broader array of employment options than they had in the 1960s and may have imparted to them some confidence in Soviet ability to *enforce* conflict limitations. It is likely, therefore, that the Soviets do some contingency planning for various kinds of limited nuclear options at the theater and, perhaps, at the strategic level.

One may seriously doubt, however, that Soviet planners would approach the problem of contingency planning for limited nuclear options with the conceptual baggage their US counterparts carry. It would seem contrary to the style of Soviet doctrinal thinking to emphasize bargaining and risk management. Rather the presence of limited options in Soviet doctrine would seem likely to rest on more traditional military concepts of economizing on force use, controlling one's own actions and their consequences, reserving options, and leaving time to learn what actions are optional in the course of a campaign. The Soviet limited options planner would seem likely to approach his task with a more strictly unilateral set of concerns than his US counterpart.

In US thinking, limited nuclear options are seen as a means of bargaining for a stalemate. The Soviet style of strategic thinking would treat them as a means of maneuvering for a checkmate.

Methods of Assessing the Strategic Balance

Comparative study of US and Soviet strategic doctrine should give attention to a closely related matter: how we measure force balances and weigh their importance. Allusion has already been made to asymmetries between US and Soviet definitions of strategic forces, what should be counted in SALT, etc. This is by no means the heart of the matter. US and Soviet methodologies for measuring military strength appear to differ significantly.

Many misleading views about the way the Soviets measure and value military strength prevail; for example, that the Soviets have some atavistic devotion to mass and size. Mass they do believe in, because both experience and analysis show that mass counts. They can be quite choosy about size, however, as a look at their tank and fighter designs or ground force divisions reveals. Within the limits of their technological potential, they have been quite sensitive and in no way primitive in their thinking about quality/quantity tradeoffs.

Another widespread notion is that the Soviets have an unusual propensity for worst-case planning or military overinsurance. This is hard to demonstrate convincingly in Soviet behavior. The Soviet theory of war in central Europe, for example, is daring, not conservative. Despite much rhetoric on the danger of surprise and the need for high combat readiness, Soviet strategic planning has not accorded nearly the importance to 'bolt-from-the-blue' surprise attack that the USA has. This does not look like over-insurance.

The problem of measuring military strength goes more deeply to differing appreciations of the processes of conflict. US measures of the overall strategic balance tend to be of two general types. First, come the so-called static measures of delivery vehicles, weapons, megatonage and equivalent megatonage, throw-weight and, perhaps, some measure of hard-target kill potential (such as weapon numbers times a scaled yield factor divided by the square of Circular Error Probability). Comparisons of this type can display some interesting things about differing forces. But they say very little about how those forces, much less the nations that employ them, will fare in war. By themselves, static measures can be dangerously misleading.

We then move onto the second, or 'quasi-dynamic', class of measures. Here the analyst is out to capture the essential features of a 'real war' in terms general enough to allow parametric applications, frequent reiteration of the analysis with varying assumptions, and easy swamping of operational and technical details which he may not be able to quantify or of which he may be ignorant. Typically, certain gross attributes of the war 'scenario' will be determined, e.g. levels of alert, who strikes first, and very general targeting priorities. Then specified 'planning factor' performance characteristics are attributed to weapons. Because it is relatively easy, a more or less elaborate version of the ICBM duel is frequently conducted. The much more subtle and complicated, but crucial, engagement of air and sea-based forces is usually handled by gross asumption, e.g. n percent of bomber weapons get to target, all SSBNs at sea survive. Regional conflicts and forces are typically ignored. All C^3 systems are assumed to work as planned – otherwise the analysis would become hopelessly complicated and inconclusive. Finally, 'residuals' of surviving forces, fatality levels and industrial damage are totaled up. A popular variant is to run a countermilitary war in these terms, i.e. only against military targets, and then see whether residual forces are sufficient to inflict 'unacceptable damage' on cities. If so, then deterrence is intact according to some. Others point to grossly asymmetric levels of surviving forces favoring the Soviets to document an emerging strategic imbalance.

Most specialists agree and explicitly admit that this kind of analysis does not capture the known, much less the unknown, complexities, uncertainties, and fortuities of a real strategic nuclear conflict of any dimension. Such liturgical admissions are usually offered to gain absolution from their obvious consequence, namely, that the analysis in question could be, not illuminating, but quite wrong. However, more heroic analytic attempts at capturing the real complexity and operational detail of a major nuclear exchange are usually not made, because they are: (a) usually beyond the expertise of single analysts or small groups; (b) not readily susceptible to varied and parametric application; and (c) *still* laden by manifold uncertainties and unknowns that are very hard to quantify. Hence, they are very hard to apply to the tasks of assessing strategic force balances or the value of this or that force improvement. The more simplistic analysis is more convenient. The analyst can conduct it many times, and talk over his results with other analysts who do the same thing. The whole methodology thereby acquires a reality and persuasiveness of its own.

The influence of this kind of analysis in our strategic decision system has many explanations. It has sociological origins in the dominance of economists and engineers over soldiers in the conduct of our strategic affairs. It conforms with the needs of an open and argumentative policy process in which there are many and varied participants, from generals to graduate students. They need a common idiom that does not soak up too much computer time and can be unclassified. Finally, in part because of the first explanation cited, when it comes to nuclear strategy, we do not believe much in 'real' nuclear war anyway. We are after standards of sufficiency that are adequate and persuasive in a peacetime setting.

Two things about this style of strategic analysis merit stating in the context of this chapter. First, on the face of it, the value of simplistic, operationally insensitive methodologies is assuredly less in the present strategic environment than it was when the USA enjoyed massive superiority. Not only are weapons, force mixes and scenarios more complicated than these methodologies can properly illuminate, but the relative equality of the two sides going into a conflict makes operational subtleties and uncertainties all the more important for how they come out. Secondly, the Soviets do not appear to do their balance measuring in this manner.

One can gain a fair insight into the manner of Soviet force balance analysis from public sources, particularly Soviet military literature. Additional inferences can be drawn from the organization and professional composition of the Soviet defense decision system, and from some of the results of Soviet decisions. On the whole it appears that Soviet planners and force balance assessors are more sensitive than the US to the subtleties and uncertainties – what we sometimes call 'scenario dependencies' – of strategic conflict seen from a very operational perspective. The timing and scale of attack initiation, tactical deception and surprise, uncertainties about weapons effects, the actual character of operational plans and targeting, timely adjustment of plans to new information and, most important, the continued viability of command and control – these factors appear to loom large in Soviet calculations of conflict outcomes.

The important point, however, is a conceptual one: unlike the typical US planner, the Soviet planner does not appear to see the *force* balance prior to conflict as a kind of physical reification of the war outcome and, therefore, as a comprehensive measure of strategic potential by itself. Rather he seems to see the force balance, the 'correlation of military forces', as one input to a complex combat process which will be influenced by other factors of great significance, and the chief aim of which is a new, more favorable balance of forces. The sum of these factors is strategy – how and how well the war is fought – and strategy itself is a significant variable in the power equation to the Soviet planner.

As a generalization, then, the Soviet planner is very sensitive to operational details and uncertainties. Because these factors can swing widely, even wildly, in different directions, a second generalization about Soviet force analysis emerges: a given force balance in peacetime can yield widely varying outcomes to war depending on the details and uncertainties of combat. Some of these outcomes could be relatively good for the USSR, others relatively bad. The planner's task is to improve the going-in force balance, to be sure. But it is also to develop and pursue ways of waging war that tend to push the outcome reliably in favorable directions.

This kind of thinking occasions two very unpleasant features in Soviet military doctrine: a strong tendency to pre-empt in the use of main force and a determination to suppress the enemy's command and control system at all costs. The Soviets tend to see any decision to go to nuclear war as being imposed on them by a course of events that tells them 'war is coming', a situation they bungled memorably in June 1941. It makes no difference whose misbehavior started events on that course. Should they find themselves on it, their operational perspective on the factors that drive war outcomes places a high premium on seizing the initiative and imposing the maximum disruptive effects on the enemy's forces *and* war plans. By going first, and especially by disrupting the enemy's command and control, the highest likelihood of limiting damage and coming out of the war with intact forces and a surviving nation is achieved, virtually independent of the force balance.

This leads to a final generalization. We tend rather casually to assume that, when we talk about parity and 'essential equivalence', and the Soviets about 'equal security', we are talking about the same thing: functional strategic stability. We are not. The Soviets are talking about a going-in force balance in which they have an equal or better chance of winning a central war, if they can orchestrate the right scenario and take advantage of lucky breaks. It is the job of the high command to see that they can. If it fails to do so, the USSR could possibly lose the war. This is not stability in our terms.

This is not to argue that the Soviets do not foresee appalling destruction as the result of any strategic exchange under the best of conditions. In a crisis, Soviet leaders would probably take any tolerable and even costly exits from the risk of such a war. But their image of strategic crisis is one in which these exits are closing up, and the 'war is coming'. They see the ultimate task of strategy to be the provision of forces and options for pre-empting that situation. This then leads them to choose strategies that, from a US point of view, seem not particularly helpful in keeping the exits open, and even likely to close them off.

It is frequently argued – more frequently as we become more anxious about the emerging force balance – that the Soviets could not have confidence in launching a strategic attack and achieving the specific objectives that theoretical analysis might suggest to be possible, such as destruction of US Minuteman ICBMs. Particularly because they are highly sensitive to operational uncertainties they would not, in one of the more noteworthy phrases of the 1978 DOD posture statement, gamble national survival on a 'single cosmic throw of the dice'. This construction of the problem obscures the high likelihood that decisions to go to strategic war will be made under great pressure and in the face of severe perceived penalty if the decision is not made, but the war comes anyway. They are not likely to come about in a situation in which the choice is between an uncertain war and a comfortable peace. It also obscures the fact that the heavy weight of uncertainty will also rest on the shoulders of US decision-makers in a crisis.

Dangers of Misunderstanding

In sum, there are fundamental differences between the US and Soviet strategic thinking, both at the level of objectives and at the level of method. The existence of these differences and, even more, our failure to recognise them, have had dangerous consequences for the US-Soviet strategic relationship.

One such might be called the 'hawk's lament'. Failing to appreciate the character of Soviet strategic thinking in relation to US views, the US has underestimated the competitiveness of Soviet strategic policy and the need for competitive responsiveness on its own part. This has been evident in both its SALT and its strategic force modernization behavior since the late 1960s.

A second negative effect might be termed the 'dove's lament'. By projecting our views onto the Soviets, and failing to appreciate their real motives and perceptions, we have underestimated the difficulties of achieving genuine strategic stability through SALT and oversold the value of what we have achieved. This has, in turn, set us up for profound, perhaps even hysterical, disillusionment in the years ahead, in which the very idea of negotiated arms control could be politically discredited. If present strategic trends continue, it is not hard to imagine a future political environment in which it would be difficult to argue for arms control negotiations even of a very hard-nosed sort.

The third and most dangerous consequence of our misunderstanding of Soviet strategy involves excessive confidence in strategic stability. US strategic behavior, in its broadest sense, has encouraged the USSR to pursue more assertive foreign and military policies. This has, in turn, increased the probability of a major East–West confrontation, arising not necessarily by Soviet design, in which the USA must forcefully resist a Soviet advance or face a collapse of its global position, while the USSR cannot easily retreat or compromise because it has a newly acquired global power status to defend and the matter at issue could be vital. Such circumstances could easily arise in Southwest Asia or even in Europe. In such conditions, it is all too easy to imagine a 'war is coming' situation in which the abstract technical factors on which we rest our confidence in stability, such as expected levels of force survival and 'unacceptable damage', could crumble away. The strategic case for 'waiting to see what happens', for conceding the operational initiative to the other side – which is the essence of crisis stability – could look very weak. Each side could see the great operational virtues of pre-emption, be convinced that the other side sees them too, and be hourly more determined that the other side not have them. This, in any case, is too likely to be the Soviet way of perceiving things. Given the openness of US and NATO strategic decision processes as contrasted with Soviet secrecy, actual US ability to pre-empt is likely to be less than the Soviets', quite apart from the character of the force balance. Add to that the problem of a vulnerable Minuteman ICBM force plus our lately advertised C^1 vulnerabilities, and you have a potentially very nasty situation.

What we know about the nature of our own strategic thinking and that of the USSR is not at all comforting at this juncture. The Soviets approach the problem of managing strategic nuclear power with highly competitive and combative instincts. Some have argued that these instincts are largely fearful and defensive, others that they are avaricious and confident. My own reading of Russian and Soviet history is that they are all of the above, and for that, the more difficult to handle.

The USA and the USSR share two awesome problems in common, the management of industrial societies and the management of nuclear weapons. Despite much that is superficially common to our heritages, however, these two societies have fundamentally different political cultures that determine how they handle these problems. The stamp of a legal, commercial and democratic society is clearly seen in the way the USA has approached the task of managing nuclear security. Soviet styles of managing this problem bear the stamp of an imperial, bureaucratic and autocratic political tradition. While the USA has been willing to see safety in a compact of 'live and let live' under admittedly unpleasant conditions, the USSR operates from a political tradition that suspects the viability of such deals, and expects them, at best, to temporarily mark the progress of historically ordained forces to ascendancy.

It is not going to be easy to stabilize the strategic competition on this foundation of political traditions. If we understand the situation clearly, however, there should be grounds for optimism. Along with a very uncomfortable degree of competitiveness, Soviet strategic policy contains a strong element of professionalism and military rationalism with which we can do business in the interest of a common safety if we enhance those qualities in ourselves. The Soviets respect military power and they take warfare very seriously. When the propaganda is pared away, they sometimes wonder if we do. We can make a healthy contribution to our own future, and theirs, by rectifying this uncertainty.

PART TWO

The Strategic Question

4

Soviet Nuclear Doctrine and the Prospects for Strategic Arms Control

STANLEY SIENKIEWICZ

The euphoria in some quarters of the US strategic community following the SALT I accords was largely based upon the inference that Soviet acceptance of a virtual ABM ban signified fundamental agreement on strategic nuclear doctrine. Many concluded that this provided a hopeful basis for further collaboration in strategic nuclear arms control. Subsequent disillusionment has been triggered by the widespread disappointment with the SALT II agreements and the subsequent suspension of their Senate consideration in the wake of the Soviet occupation of Afghanistan. The continuing Soviet strategic build-up[1] during the protracted negotiations in SALT II and since has also contributed substantially to the growing doubts about the prospects of greater success in US-Soviet strategic arms control. On the one hand, the result has been a growing pessimism that divergent strategic doctrines preclude significant strategic accommodation.

On the other, some have argued that reconciliation of nuclear doctrine be placed first on the SALT agenda, as the necessary basis for further substantive agreement.[2] It is important to consider whether nuclear doctrine is as important as these two views imply with respect to the question of strategic nuclear arms control. There are structural and ideological barriers to an explicit reconciliation of nuclear doctrine and, barring the most thoroughgoing transformation of the Soviet system, these appear insurmountable. However, the question of whether there is a future for US-Soviet efforts to constrain strategic arms competition by negotiation appears to be more complex and dependent upon other factors. Thus, while nuclear doctrine is no doubt a central consideration, it is not the only consideration. This chapter, therefore, explores the evolution of US and Soviet nuclear doctrine in an attempt to develop conclusions about the relationship of that doctrine to the prospects for useful negotiation about constraints upon strategic weapons.

Until 1953, Soviet military thought, like all other significant aspects of Soviet life, was conditioned by a primitive Stalinist orthodoxy. In military thought, this orthodoxy did not extend much beyond the assertion of the decisiveness of Stalin's so-called permanently operating factors. There were: the stability of the rear; the morale of the armed forces, the quantity and quality of divisions; the equipment of the fighting forces; and the organizational abilities of the commanders.[3] Coupled with the asserted superiority of the Soviet social order, based upon the Marxist-Leninist science of society, these factors amounted to a theological assertion that the USSR would prevail in any future conflict. This recipe, expounded by the 'greatest military genius of modern times', precluded the possibility that other factors, such as nuclear weapons or the element of surprise, could affect the outcome of war. Not only was this a prescription for avoiding reassessment of the lessons of the Great Patriotic War (in which the 'surprise' had resulted from Stalin's personal obduracy), but it prevented any serious attempt to evaluate the impact of nuclear weapons upon Soviet security.

Despite the homily that armies seem always to be preparing to fight the last war, the military is fundamentally a pragmatic and empirically based profession, though to call it scientific might be to overstate the point. It is clear in retrospect that the Soviet military had chafed under the Stalinist orthodoxy, because it was grossly at variance with the postwar world. They had, after all, themselves endured the consequences of surprise in 1941 and could not easily swallow Stalin's assertion that the rapid German advance had been part of a carefully designed strategy to lure the enemy deep into Russia, as Kutuzov had done to Napoleon in 1812.[4] They were also well aware of the enormously destructive effects of thermonuclear weapons. Thus, the debates over military doctrine which emerged soon after Stalin's death were inevitable. That they became public is perhaps related to the weakening of control at the top produced by the power struggle between the Malenkov and Khrushchev factions. Reviewing these debates provides significant insight into the character of Soviet defense thinking in the nuclear age – an insight which has an important bearing on the future of the US-Soviet strategic dialogue. In fact, a review of these debates and their outcomes compared to the parallel debates in the USA helps to explain why military doctrines, particularly nuclear doctrines, are unlikely to converge.

The Evolution of Soviet Nuclear Doctrine

The classic studies of the post-Stalin military debates were produced at the Rand Corporation more than two decades ago by Herbert S. Dinerstein and Raymond L. Garthoff.[5] The most prominent issues in the debates were the inevitability of war[6] and the potential decisiveness of surprise attack. What can be inferred from the Rand reconstructions is that these issues were associated with two quite separate debates.

The question of the inevitability of war arose as a largely instrumental issue in the leadership struggle between the Malenkov and Khrushchev factions. Soon after Stalin's death, Malenkov and his associates began to argue that war between the capitalist states and the USSR was no longer inevitable.[7] This attempt at revising fundamental dogma was probably linked to Malenkov's effort to shift resources from military spending and the supporting heavy industry to consumer goods.[8] However, it also provided Khrushchev with a convenient opportunity to attack Malenkov. Malenkov's argument was not only revisionist (and therefore dangerous in so pervasively doctrinaire a political system), but also associated with a threat to reduce allocations to the military. Thus, Khrushchev gained a significant bureaucratic ally in his struggle for power.

The susbsequent history of this struggle is well known. By 1957 Malenkov and his associates were vanquished and Khrushchev was in full control. He then completed the shift toward the Malenkov position which he had already begun at the 20th Party Congress in 1956.[9] By the 21st Party Congress in 1961, he had established Malenkov's proposition that war was no longer 'fatalistically inevitable' as a tenet of official Soviet doctrine. It has not been repudiated to this day, though it is hardly mentioned by the Brezhnev regime.

Khrushchev also adopted the policy which Malenkov had associated with his view of the non-inevitability of war. He pressed for reallocation of resources from the defense to the domestic sectors, most prominently to agriculture. He advocated a one-third reduction in the Soviet armed forces[10] and he reduced naval surface ship construction.[11] In general, he argued the obsolescence of many elements of traditional military capability, and the primacy of nuclear missile forces.[12] More importantly for the argument that follows, Krushchev premised his view of the Soviet deterrent posture upon a secure capability to retaliate.[13]

The military, who had allied themselves with Khrushchev in opposition to Malenkov, may well have felt betrayed when faced with Khrushchev's attempts to cut defense spending and conventional forces in favor of the domestic sectors. They may even have felt perversely vindicated when the Cuban missile crisis demonstrated Soviet strategic and naval weaknesses. One might infer a continuing concern about the susceptibility of senior Soviet political leaders to the US ideas of sufficiency and deterrence; this might help explain the continuing intensity of some of the military literature on these subjects. For example:

> The premise of Marxism–Leninism on war as a continuation of policy by military means remains true in an atmosphere of fundamental changes in military matters. The attempt of certain bourgeois ideologists to prove that nuclear missile weapons leave war outside the framework of policy and that *nuclear war moves beyond the control of policy, ceases to be an instrument of policy* and does not constitute its continuation is theoretically incorrect and *politically reactionary.*[14] (emphasis added)

This is as clear a statement as one is likely to find that the position adopted by Khrushchev (and widely held in the West) is not only wrong, but revisionist according to Marxist strictures. His position was based upon the conclusion that nuclear war can escalate to levels of destruction beyond all sensible ends of policy, levels of destruction at which the victor is indistinguishable from the vanquished. If this is true and both sides gain such enormous capabilities for destruction, that position suggests, mutual deterrence may well be assured with little need for additional capabilities. In US strategic thought the prospect of this condition also raised open speculation about whether strategic nuclear retaliation could credibly deter limited aggression. In the Soviet debates this recognition took a somewhat different and more subtle form. In fact, the Soviet military seem to be trying to have it both ways, for it is commonly asserted that even very limited nuclear exchanges will inevitably escalate to all-out levels of destruction. Yet, Soviet doctrine continues to assert that massive strategic nuclear exchanges may be followed by a long and ultimately decisive 'conventional' war. This leads directly to requirements not only for substantial strategic nuclear forces, but for large and diverse conventional capabilities to fight a war – a war seemingly not much affected by the potential exchange of thousands of nuclear weapons. The solution to this paradox may be found in considering the different audiences to which such arguments may be addressed, as well as the different purposes which they may be intended to serve. The view set forth above can be read as intended for internal consumption (perhaps even for remaining strands of 'radical or modern'[15] thought within the armed forces themselves). It may be seen as shoring up the barriers against the kind of Malenkovian-Khrushchevian revisionism that has been associated with attempts to cut Soviet defense budgets. The argument on the inevitability of escalation, on the other hand, is more plausibly interpreted as intending to strengthen deterrence by persuading Americans that there is nothing to be gained from limited nuclear war strategies. We should also, of course, keep in mind the additional requirements of the Soviet defense posture, aimed at securing the fruits of World War II in Eastern Europe and maintaining adequate capabilities on other land borders of the Soviet state, most notably the long border with China.

One should not, therefore, conclude that the predominant motivation of the Soviet military is merely the pragmatic defense of their budgets. An important component may well be the sincere belief that the political leaders – who in the past have 'misunderstood' the requirements of military security – may mistakenly risk that security again. These analytically distinct motivations are unlikely to be clearly separated in the military mind.

This juxtaposition brings us to the debate among the professional military. It was concerned primarily with the potential decisiveness of surprise. By contrast to the debate reflecting the political struggle, this issue was not instrumental, but rather was substantively important in shaping the Soviet defense posture.

The Stalinist assertion of the dominance of the permanently operating factors ruled out the possibility that such so-called transitory factors as surprise could be decisive in war. Such a view obviously constrained practical efforts to improve the Soviet defense posture against surprise attack. Yet military planners were well acquainted with the destructive effects of nuclear weapons and the prospects for long-range delivery systems. They could easily extrapolate the effects of a large-scale nuclear surprise attack, and no doubt found it difficult to reconcile such calculations with the Stalinist proposition that surprise attack – even with such weapons – remained a relatively insignificant and merely transitory factor.

This debate was short and its resolution conclusive. The potential decisiveness of surprise attack in the nuclear age was clearly established. As then-Marshal of tank forces Rotmistrov concluded in 1955:

[Surprise attack in the nuclear age could] . . . cause the rapid *collapse of a government whose capacity to resist is low as a*

*consequence of radical faults in its social and economic structure
and also as a consequence of an unfavorable geographic position.*[16]
(emphasis added)

This quotation raises interesting questions in terms of the Aeso-
pian communication that characterizes Soviet public discourse.
They are worth pondering from today's perspective. Although
the debate was carried on in very general terms, the problem
which provoked it was the defense of the *Soviet Union* in the
nuclear age. Thus, one wonders what 'government' Rotmistrov
had in mind. It was the Soviet Union which was ringed by NATO
bases deploying nuclear-armed aircraft (though he could also
have been referring to small European countries within easy
range of the USSR). Certainly the geographic position of the
USA remained the least 'unfavorable'. What were the 'radical
faults in social and economic structure'? Were they inadequate
organization and regimentation of the population in an effective
civil defense program,[17] inadequate dispersal of industry, or
allocation of resources to heavy industry and to military
preparedness?

The issue of surprise attack, then, was clearly resolved. It could
decide the outcome of war in the nuclear age. The military were
now free to seek 'real world' solutions to the problem. Or were
they? The admission that a confident solution might be impossible could pose a serious doctrinal problem for the USSR. It
would undermine the Marxist prediction of the inevitable victory
of socialism. Thus, if too explicitly argued, it could be construed
as revisionism of a more fundamental kind. The Soviet political
system was imposed and has been maintained by force; it has
pursued its social goals by forcibly extracting enormous sacrifice
from its people. It has done so on the utopian premise that it was
consistent with and supportive of the inevitable course of history.
It would therefore carry substantial risk to openly admit that the
rationale for this history of suffering had been fundamentally
mistaken, that in fact the ultimate victory of socialism could be
prevented if Soviet deterrence failed and the capitalist powers
mounted a nuclear surprise attack.

From the start, therefore, the Soviet search for 'real world'
solutions to the security dilemma of the nuclear age was inhibited
by this Marxist-Leninist doctrinal context. It is a context which
makes very difficult any approach premised upon the open
admission that no confident defense capable of preserving at least
the appearance of inevitable Soviet victory can be erected.

The Soviet solution, therefore, had to be premised upon the

assertion that even were a surprise attack to be mounted, Soviet military power could still ensure victory. The obvious answer was to assert the capability to strike pre-emptively, and blunt the aggressor's attack. It was in fact the conclusion, to which this debate led many in the West, that a pre-emptive first-strike capability was precisely what the Soviets were after.[18]

The Soviet assertion that in countering a surprise attack, the Soviet armed forces will 'repel the attack successfully . . . deal the enemy counterblows, or even preemptive surprise blows of terrible destructive force'[19] has continued to be characteristic of the military literature on nuclear war. This assertion, however, creates difficulty with the other frequent assertion in Soviet literature that the USSR will not initiate war – that it will limit itself to pre-emptive rather than preventive attack.[20]

Defense Management and Military Solutions

Though in important respects pragmatic or empirical, the military profession is also characteristically conservative. This is a characteristic that might provoke deep suspicion of the idea that military security may be found in acknowledging the vulnerability of one's society to the principal adversary, and vice versa. The logical corollary is still worse. It is the idea that military security may be maintained by agreeing to cooperate with the adversary in maintaining that condition. This is not the idea of deterrence *per se*, for deterrence is a well-established concept in military thought. Historically, however, it has not been distinguished from defense. In the new doctrine emerging in the USA (one with which Khrushchev so dangerously flirted), security was not to be maintained by automatically seeking military-technical solutions to an adversary's threatening capabilities, but rather by maintaining largely punitive capabilities. In the traditional military view, if the enemy develops a capability to attack one's homeland with long-range forces, there is no doubt about the proper response: it is to devise ways to defend that homeland. Depending upon the nature of the technical problem, there is no principled distinction among active defense, passive defense and pre-emptively offensive capabilities. The distinctions are entirely pragmatic. If the problem is difficult and no single measure stands out in its effectiveness, then all are pursued.

It is important to understand the implications of this approach because of the current role of the Soviet military in all areas of national security management, especially as compared with the

USA. Both defense establishments may be seen as organizational pyramids, functionally differentiated and performing all the tasks necessary to the management of the national security apparatus. In the USSR, however, all aspects of this activity – from intelligence and analysis to the production and deployment of weapon systems – are almost entirely in the hands of the professional military.[21] Does this mean that major issues of resource allocation among defense and other sectors – or even within the defense establishment – are decided solely by the military? This is unlikely. What it does suggest is that they frame the defense problem and specify the range within which military solutions are to be sought. To argue that security in the nuclear age is to be found in agreeing to a posture of mutual vulnerability, therefore, is not only doctrinally risky, but at radical variance with all of the traditions and professional instincts of the Soviet military establishment; a military establishment which, at least since Khrushchev, has had a far greater role in shaping the Soviet military posture than has its counterpart in the USA. This is the basis for the central difference between the American and Soviet approaches to the problem of military security in the nuclear age. While there are important historical and national-psychological underpinnings for this fundamental difference between the US and Soviet approaches to national security, the argument put forth here is that the principal determinant of the Soviet response to the problem of security in the nuclear age was in fact that it was shaped by a professional military establishment.

But what is the role of ideology in the Soviet military? If the profession of arms is fundamentally a pragmatic business, it is likely to be as resistant to cumbersome Marxist-Leninist ideological impositions as it was to Stalinist dogma. Here lies the crux of the matter.

In a highly arbitrary yet pervasively ideological political system, perhaps the most dangerous error is the ideological one. The accusation of doctrinal deviation is more powerful than the accusation of stupidity or mistaken judgment. Whether or not one believes literally in relevant tenets of Marxism–Leninism, it is prudent in policy debate to avoid positions which can be attacked as doctrinally wrong. It is this phenomenon which probably inhibits Soviet policy debate rather than any widespread literal belief in the doctrinal orthodoxy. The inhibiting effect is indirect but hardly inconsiderable.

In the case of military doctrine, however, this effect may be somewhat less than in other areas of political life, and not only because of the pragmatic nature of the profession. The military is among the more autonomous of occupations despite the system of political controls created to ensure their reliability. The Soviet military by and large promote their own, probably up to quite senior levels, largely on the basis of traditional military criteria. It is in the military more than in any other pursuit in Soviet society that we find the most reliable, functioning system of promotion and tenure rules. Thus, the explanation for the Soviet solution to the problem of security in the nuclear age derives more from the fact that it is a solution devised by the *military* profession, and not that it was devised by the *Soviet* military profession.

The thoughtful military planner recognizes not only the extreme importance of his task, but also its pervasive uncertainty. No matter how carefully analyzed the problem and how well-designed the armed forces, the imponderables of warfare – morale, leadership and chance – may determine the outcome of battle. And it is the task of the peacetime military planner to predict the outcome of hypothetical wars. These conditions imply that the professional military cannot be satisfied short of un-ambiguous superiority over any combination of enemies. The notion of sufficiency or parity, on the other hand, is not merely an *American* invention. It is more importantly a *civilian* invention.[22]

Khrushchev's position on the primacy of strategic forces (thus the possibility of reductions in conventional forces) was not widely shared in the military,[23] and the apparent absence of severe resource constraints on military spending since 1964 largely precludes this point of view as a rationale in intramilitary resource allocation debates. All of the military services seem substantially to have engaged in the Soviet military build-up during the Brezhnev era. In fact, it seems likely that a bargain was struck in 1964 between the military and the Brezhnev faction which has permitted, among other things, across-the-board Soviet military growth ever since. It appears to have established both an unprecedented degree of independence for the military in the management of their own affairs and a significantly more prominent voice in the shaping of foreign policy.[24]

The accession of Dmitri Ustinov, a civilian defense manager to the post of Defense Minister, may well not alter this conclusion, since he appears not to have attempted the kind of pervasive 'civilianization' of the upper reaches of the defense establishment associated with Robert McNamara's tenure as Secretary of Defense in the USA.

In this light, the Soviet military build-up of the Brezhnev period appears natural. It is the fulfillment of the military planner's dream, the opportunity to hedge against virtually any important uncertainty. If it cannot yet confidently be ruled out that the West could successfully mount a surprise attack, then one continues to pursue all plausible measures to preclude it (i.e. civil defense, air defense, vigorous ABM research and development, and hard-target counterforce capabilities, though these latter are probably as much the descendant of technological necessities as of any conscious early choice to build big missiles). If there is still insufficient confidence in the state's security, then one must be prepared to fight conventionally after the strategic nuclear exchanges in order to occupy a relatively intact Europe or to defend against an opportunist China. The best overall deterrent, furthermore, is a sufficiently impressive across-the-board military capability to intimidate any possible combination of enemies.

It takes only a small leap of imagination – putting oneself in the shoes of the Soviet military planner – to produce a long list of worrisome contingencies, and thus requirements for military forces. Perhaps the worst case from his perspective is the two-front war against the Chinese hordes to the east and the capitalist industrial machine to the west. With decisive escalation deemed too risky in either case, recourse to strategic nuclear forces is deterred. Such a scenario may help explain the very large investment in Soviet war production capabilities in recent years.

The critical question about this Soviet military growth is not, however, its doctrinal rationale or its internal dynamic. Instead one should ask how the Soviet political masters may have viewed it, how they may seek to put it to use today, and what are the implications of all of this for the security planning and posture of the West. As an element of that security planning, there is also a need to consider the prospects for negotiated arms control arrangements.

Civilian Strategists and Strategies

The conclusion of the Soviet military debate – that surprise attack could be decisive – was almost, but not quite, the same formulation as that reached in the USA. American strategists agreed that surprise attack could be decisive in the nuclear age. Thus, the task of military policy was to make surprise attack infeasible. American strategists, however, concentrated on a particular kind of surprise attack, the so-called first-strike disarming attack in which the victim's capabilities for a substantial retaliatory strike would be destroyed. This emphasis arose from the fact that the US strategists went a logical step farther than their Soviet counterparts; this step may have been foreclosed to the Soviets by the strictures of Marxism–Leninism, and perhaps by the traditions of military problem-solving.

The Americans agreed that surprise attack could be decisive, because the immense destructiveness of thermonuclear weapons – combined with great numbers and modern, long-range delivery systems – produced a variety of attacks against which defense was at best problematic. The logical conclusion, therefore, was that deterrence would henceforth have to depend upon the reliable capability to strike second. It was the survival of these second-strike forces which became critical to enduring deterrence. The Soviet formulation and military posture have been based upon the opposite premise: that a defense must be erected, no matter what the cost. From these fundamentally differing conclusions have come the substantially different strategic nuclear force preferences and postures which we see today.

The American conclusion – that there is no defense against nuclear attack and that strategic deterrence must be premised upon reliable retaliation – in all likelihood, had to be imposed by civilian strategists; it is the point of departure from the traditional military perspective on deterrence and defense. For Soviet strategists, surprise attack with nuclear weapons could be decisive, because it could destroy the ability of the government to function and of their military forces to defend their state. Thus, it called for extraordinary efforts to reorder the society and government to endure such a war and to re-equip the armed forces to fight it. For the American strategists, surprise attack could be decisive if it could eliminate the victim's punitive capabilities. Thus, it led directly to the principal preoccupation in US strategic planning with the survivability and penetration capability of the US strategic forces.

American strategic thought thus shifted from preoccupation with military solutions (i.e. attempts to counter in a technical–military fashion any capabilities the adversary deployed which could conceivably be seen as threatening) to the unique civilian invention of deterrence as the peacetime manipulation of largely punitive threats. This is almost entirely unconnected to the problem of actually defending against nuclear attack.

The result of the US approach is obvious. If the problem of surprise attack has to do primarily with a fairly narrow band of capabilities threatening the adversary's second-strike forces, then we have *prima facie* a basis for limited superpower cooperation toward enhancing the security of both. They can cooperate, explicitly or tacitly, in managing force postures so as to minimize the threats posed to their respective second-strike capabilities, and the USA has of course always unilaterally adjusted its own forces to prevent the emergence of threats to its punitive capabilities. This is the basis of the US definition of stability, a definition not acknowledged by the USSR.

The three principles of US doctrine have been: the maintenance of secure second-strike forces; limited war forces, *to extend and enhance deterrence*;[25] and the avoidance of threats to Soviet second-strike forces. The implications for force postures and defense budgets have been intensely debated, but the principles have generally been accepted. Whereas the US answer to the military security problem has entailed an explicit distinction between deterrence and defense, the Soviet answer has not. The idea of pre-empting an American surprise attack is inherently a defensive idea predicated upon the traditional military solution. It continues to treat deterrence as a direct function of operational military capability.[26]

The implicit scenario for the Soviets requires successful anticipation of an imminent US 'surprise attack'. Thus, the strategic forces of the USA, assuming sufficient warning of the impending US attack, would be largely destroyed by a pre-emptive strike. Those US forces which survived Soviet pre-emption and were actually launched, would be met by the massive Soviet air defenses, and greatly degraded. Those, finally, which succeeded in delivering their weapons to their targets would have attacked a population organized and, to the degree feasible, protected by a vigorous civil defense program and an economy and political control structure also organized to cope with such an attack. Combining such across-the-board capabilities with a strong emphasis upon offensive action[27] wherever possible, has been the Soviet solution to the problem of military security in the nuclear age.

Concern that such a posture was, in fact, feasible was more appropriate in a period when the strategic delivery capabilities resided exclusively in aircraft. There was a real prospect of pre-emptive capability against soft, slow bomber forces deployed on small numbers of airfields – particularly if they were in Europe or elsewhere on the Soviet periphery. Extensive air defenses could be expected to substantially degrade surviving bomber forces attempting to retaliate, and the still-limited nuclear weapon stockpiles of the 1950s made such a doctrine far more plausible than is possible today.

It is likely that the early Soviet deployment of medium and

intermediate-range ballistic missiles targeted against the NATO bases on which US strategic forces were deployed was the outgrowth of this kind of perspective. Unfortunately for the Soviets, the US strategic forces were in the process of being withdrawn to the continental United States, as increasing range in follow-on aircraft permitted.[28] This, in turn, helped to stimulate increased Soviet efforts to deploy intercontinental-range ballistic missiles. The deployment of MRBMs and IRBMs proceeded, since NATO bases continued to deploy nuclear capable aircraft.[29]

Conditions are, of course, far different today. Given the dominance of ballistic missile delivery systems of virtually constant readiness (a large proportion of which remain highly survivable aboard ballistic missile submarines), and the absence of effective antiballistic missile systems, a large nuclear attack cannot be effectively blunted. The US strategic literature recognized this prospect clearly by the end of the 1950s. Yet Soviet doctrinal literature on nuclear war still does not concede this point, for to do so could create both the ideological problem for Marxism–Leninism referred to above, and risk another Khrushchevian attempt to cut the defense budget. It would be similarly difficult to agree in SALT with the US formulation of the surprise attack problem. This would mean implicitly agreeing that there is no defense against strategic nuclear attack, that such an attack could in fact halt or reverse the 'inevitable' course of history, and that the only solution lies in the essentially 'non-military' approach devised by the Americans – the relationship of mutual assured destruction (MAD). Such a position means that once the security of second-strike forces is assured – and this might be achieved cooperatively – there is a *prima facie* basis for arguing that little if anything more is necessary in the way of military forces. This argument supports a policy of 'sufficiency' – uniquely a product of civilian defense strategists or political leaders. The Soviet formulation, by contrast, is a prescription for relatively unrestrained defense spending[30] following the traditional military approach to national defense.

It is unnecessary to impute purely budget-protecting motives to those who resist the US deterrence model whether they are Soviet marshals or American 'hawks'. Rather, one might impute a belief that such a posture is simply too risky, and cite the consequences of the Cuban missile crisis in support. Whatever the mixture of motivations, such 'operational' views are more likely to arise in the military – hence the significance of the role of the Soviet military in the management of Soviet defense. By contrast, US nuclear strategic ideas were developed almost exclusively by the 'civilian strategists'.[31] The power of their ideas came to dominate both the scholarly strategic community and, under Secretary of Defense McNamara, the top levels of the national security establishment in the USA. Civilian dominance has remained and, if anything, grown in US security planning – a crucial difference between the USA and the USSR. The 'operational' perspective, however, has enjoyed a substantial resurgence in the USA in recent years, as growth in Soviet military capabilities has again led US strategic analysts to explore a variety of limited nuclear war scenarios; ideas such as 'escalation ladders' and 'escalation dominance' become involved.

Nuclear Doctrine and the Future of SALT

Two important factors have largely determined the evolution of Soviet nuclear doctrine. One is the sometimes inhibiting effect of the Marxist-Leninist doctrinal context within which all Soviet intellectual activity occurs. The other is the strong influence produced by the exclusive authority of the Soviet military over virtually all military activity below the major Politburo-level choices. The doctrinal inhibition raises obstacles to any strategic concept that would require a logical admission that the ultimate victory of socialism is not inevitable. This would remain true even were a civilian strategic establishment to arise advocating such a concept. The dominant formative influence, however, has been the pre-eminence of the professional military in all spheres of military and strategic thought, coupled with the political decision to grant them substantial and long-term real growth in the allocation of Soviet resources. Thus, for Soviet nuclear doctrine to become more like that of the USA would require a class of strategic thinkers substantially freed of both traditional professional military perspectives and Marxist-Leninist constraints, as well as the political power to impose the change upon a highly resistant system.

The absence of such conditions has resulted in a fundamental difference between US and Soviet strategic theory. Soviet doctrine does not dismiss deterrence. On the contrary, most of the open military literature seems preoccupied with enhancing it. It is a theory of deterrence, however, which is substantially at variance with the US formulation. As a result of the difference, Soviet doctrine denies the US formulation of stability – the absence of threats to each side's punitive capabilities – but rather defines it, when it does, more generally and self-servingly as the absence of any significant innovation or new deployment above what is described as parity. This is not a sign of inability to comprehend the US strategic analysis. More likely, it is an inability and perhaps unwillingness to exit from the corner into which their doctrinal evolution has pointed them. The Soviet military almost certainly recognize the dangers posed by US developments which threaten the survivability of Soviet second-strike forces; this is evident in their doctrinal writing and in their deployments. To acknowledge that such developments are especially threatening however, would be to admit the validity of the US strategic concept, and perhaps more important, to concede an important bargaining advantage in SALT. For it is *Soviet* ICBM forces which pose the earliest threat to the survivability of a major US strategic force component. And it is these ICBM forces which have been the major SALT concern of the USA since the ABM treaty was signed. It is also the USSR which maintains large investments in other 'damage-limiting' capabilities, such as air and civil defense programs. The only practical Soviet position, therefore, has been to deny the US formulation of the strategic arms problem, while bargaining in entirely pragmatic terms.

Soviet nuclear doctrine has been the basis for the development of Soviet strategic forces which today appear to pose precisely the threat which their public doctrinal debates of the 1950s made clear they would like to pose. The large throw-weight of Soviet ICBMs lends itself to an early threat to the US Minuteman force. Yet we must keep in mind that this has been the major Soviet strategic program for two decades. In addition, large ICBMs have turned out to be the vehicle for catching the USA in one of the major measures of strategic competence, multiple independently targetable re-entry vehicles. To concede the validity of the US theories of deterrence stability thus sacrifices the argument against the central US theme in SALT (i.e. that constraints upon threats to the survivability of each side's retaliatory capabilities ought to be the central focus). This concession would have a major impact upon the most important Soviet strategic modernization programs, and none of consequence upon US programs, for the near term.

Seeking doctrinal convergence as a formal goal in SALT thus seems impractical at best.[32] But does this fundamental irreconcilability warrant the pessimism in some Western strategic circles about the prospects of any progress in SALT? The answer is a qualified no. First, the Soviets have shown themselves able to reach SALT agreements at variance with their military doctrine. The obvious example is the ABM treaty. Secondly, the USA may find arrangements desirable which do not visibly conflict with the prescriptions of Soviet doctrine (though they may conflict with military judgments about what is prudent). Here, a variety of lesser measures may prove marginally useful. High ceilings on weapon numbers would be roughly compatible with Soviet doctrine, as would a variety of constraints ensuring the effectiveness of warning and verification systems. In the longer run and perhaps not so much longer, given the age of the current leadership, the USSR may again have a leader like Khrushchev who is more amenable to US ideas about deterrence and sufficiency, and more interested in shifting resources into non-military investment, particularly given the magnitude of the economic and energy problems looming on the Soviet horizon for the 1980s. This is not a prospect that we should, of course, depend upon, but one we ought to keep in mind as we consider how we might try to manage US-Soviet relations over the coming decade.

How are we to deal with SALT in the absence of doctrinal convergence? Here the ABM treaty is instructive. The ban on ABM systems embodied in SALT I is consistent with the US view of the nuclear problem and its solution. Observance of the treaty precludes any hope of effective defense against major ballistic missile attack. In fact, there was some euphoria in the US arms control community when it was signed, as many concluded that it signalled Soviet acceptance of the US strategic view. Disillusionment eventually replaced excessive euphoria (although more pragmatic satisfaction with the concrete consequences remains justified). The alternative explanation for Soviet agreement on ABM is that they were in technological difficulty, and could not rule out the possibility that US ABM research might lead to a competent deployed system.[33] The ABM treaty, thus, was a straightforward bargain – pay the Americans their price to get them to stop something which might eventually prove worrisome.

This interpretation of doctrinal convergence could testify to a Soviet understanding of – and perhaps even some tacit agreement with – the US formulation, perhaps more convincing than an open Soviet announcement would have been. Why else would they pay any price at all to halt a 'purely defensive' US program, if they did not perceive that it might eventually affect their deterrent? Though their deterrent is not formally and primarily premised upon a second-strike capability, they have never successfully elaborated a convincing case that pre-emption might actually work with contemporary forces. In any case, they have worked hard to attain an unquestioned capability for major strategic attack upon the USA, whether pre-emptively, preventively, or in a *de facto* second strike.

It is not, in fact, necessary to assume any sort of common interest to justify continued strategic arms negotiation, merely to remain open-minded about the possibility that we can achieve limits upon Soviet strategic forces which we find useful at a price which we are prepared to pay. It would be self-defeating to rule out that possibility in advance.

This is the key to long-run progress in SALT – pragmatic case by case bargaining. It will not be found in some chimeric search for a formal common understanding on strategic principles. The USA is, in any case, more interested in Soviet strategic behavior – in what forces they do or do not deploy in answer to US attempts to influence those choices. We are unlikely to influence Soviet choices by asserting our good intentions or by demonstrating conclusively the flawless logic of US theories. This game is played with sticks and carrots, threats (necessarily subtle and as private as possible) and incentives. For the necessary chips with which to play, we should expect to pay a price, and therefore seek to accumulate and maintain sufficient amounts of the appropriate currency.[34]

Notes: Chapter 4

1 The dimensions of the build-up or continuing emphasis – civil defense, air defense, hard-target counterforce capability – lack only one element – ABM of a comprehensive damage-limiting posture, a posture based upon a different view of deterrence and nuclear strategy than has shaped the US strategic forces in the nuclear age.
2 See, for example, Alton Frye, 'Strategic restraint, mutual and assured', *Foreign Policy*, Summer, 1977.
3 Cited in Herbert S. Dinerstein, *War and the Soviet Union*, (Santa Monica, Ca.: Rand Corporation), p. 33.
4 Described in Bernard Brodie, *War and Politics* (New York: Macmillan, 1973), pp. 443–5.
5 Herbert S. Dinerstein, op. cit.; Raymond L. Garthoff, *Soviet Strategy in the Nuclear Age* (NY: Praeger, 1958, 1962); *The Soviet Image of Future War* (Washington, DC: Public Affairs Press, 1959).
6 Lenin held that as capitalism–imperialism declined, the capitalists would war among themselves and ultimately against socialism. This would be the vehicle for the ultimate victory of the socialist camp. Stalin's formulation remained consistent with this view; Dinerstein, op. cit., p. 66.
7 Adam B. Ulam, *The Rivals* (New York: Viking, 1971), p. 219.
8 ibid., p. 221.
9 'When he amended the Leninist thesis of "inevitable war",' Thomas W. Wolfe, *Soviet Strategy at the Crossroads* (Cambridge, Ma.: Harvard University Press, 1964), p. 2.
10 Arnold L. Horelick, 'The strategic mind-set of the Soviet military', *Problems of Communism*, March–April, 1977; Wolfe, op. cit., p. 31.
11 George E. Hudson, 'Soviet naval doctrine and Soviet politics, 1953–1975', *World Politics*, October, 1976.

12 Wolfe, op. cit., p. 31; Garthoff, Introduction to V. D. Sokolovsky, *Military Strategy: Soviet Doctrine and Concepts* (New York: Praeger, 1963) (US air force translation), pp. viii–ix.
13 ibid.
14 From *Kommunist vooruzhennykh sil (Communist of the Armed Forces)*, November, 1975, cited by Foy D. Kohler in Foreword to Leon Goure, *War Survival in Soviet Strategy* (Coral Gables, Fl.: Center for Advanced International Studies, University of Miami, 1976).
15 Garthoff, Introduction to Sokolovsky, op. cit., p. ix.
16 Marshal of Tank Forces P. Rotmistrov, 'On the role of surprise in contemporary war', *Voennaia mysl'*, February, 1955, cited in Dinerstein, op. cit., p. 186.
17 It is worth noting that this was also a period of concern and debate over civil defense in the American defense community. See, for example, Klaus Knorr, 'Passive air defense for the United States', in William W. Kaufmann (ed.), *Military Policy and National Security* (Princeton, NJ: Princeton University Press, 1956); *Deterrence and Survival in the Nuclear Age* ('Report to the President by the Security Resources Panel of the Office of Defense Mobilization Science Advisory Committee', the so-called Gaither Report), 1957, declassified 1973.
18 Dinerstein, op. cit., pp. 200–8.
19 Rotmistrov, op. cit., cited in Dinerstein, p. 187.
20 Bernard Brodie, among others, discussed this issue with great insight; see particularly ch. 7 of *Strategy in the Missile Age* (Princeton, NJ: Princeton University Press, 1959). The Soviets themselves were not insensitive to the difficulty, as Dinerstein's analysis makes clear; see ch. 6, particularly p. 188.
21 The Western consensus on this point is strong; see, for example, Horelick, op. cit., p. 81; John Erickson, 'Soviet military capabilities', *Current History*, October, 1976, p. 97; Thomas W. Wolfe, *Military Power and Soviet Policy*, Rand Paper P-5388, March, 1975, pp. 15–18; William R. Van Cleave, 'Soviet doctrine and strategy', in Lawrence L. Whetton (ed.), *The Future of Soviet Military Power* (New York: Crane, Russak, 1976); etc. This is a consensus supported by unpublished remarks at a seminar at the Massachusetts Institute of Technology, 15 April, 1977, by Dr Mikhail Milstein (Lt General retired) of the Institute for the Study of the USA and Canada Studies. Richard Pipes, however, implies some difference of view: 'Soviet military planning is carried out under the close supervision of the country's highest political body, the Politburo'. If my inference is correct, it would be interesting to see the evidence for this assertion. See Pipes, 'Why the Soviet Union thinks it could fight and win a nuclear war', *Commentary*, July, 1977, p. 27.
22 Coincidentally, this point was also emphasized by, perhaps, the most prominent of the US civilian strategists; see Bernard Brodie, 'The development of nuclear strategy', *International Security*, vol. 2, no. 4, Spring, 1978, p. 67.
23 In professional military circles, this issue arose in a debate about whether the next war would be a short decisive nuclear war or whether it could also be long and conventional. The answer, of course, would shape the force structure and the result was a predictably military compromise. It could be either. Thus, a requirement for both kinds of forces; see, for example, Sokolovsky, *op cit*., pp. 194–204.
24 At least one scholar discerns a growing visibility to the military establishment in all spheres of Soviet life, though he seems to conclude that rather than a potential problem for the party or the political leadership, this is the result of a choice explicitly made by that political leadership; see William E. Odom, 'Who controls whom in Moscow', *Foreign Policy*, Summer, 1975; and his 'Militarization of society', *Problems of Communism*, September–October, 1976; Pipes, op. cit., p. 29, would take Odom's judgment much further.
25 Both sides maintain a variety of limited war forces. It is the difference in rationales which is suggestive. For the Soviets, such forces are obviously needed to fight the possible long war, occupy territory and defend against similar capabilities possessed by the adversary. For the USA, the rationale is almost always that such forces enhance the *credibility* of an extended deterrent, first, and only secondarily, that they might be needed to fight the Soviets at various limited war levels.
26 Van Cleave, for example, agrees, but seems to prefer the Soviet view on this point; op. cit., p. 48.

27 One of the lessons the Soviet military appears to have drawn from World War II, and perhaps from Soviet and Russian history more broadly, is the importance, whenever attacked, of going over to the offensive as rapidly and decisively as possible. See, for example, A. A. Sidorenko, *The Offensive* (Moscow, 1970); translated and published under the auspices of the US air force, 1974.

28 Another of the architects of US strategic thought in the nuclear age, Albert Wohlstetter, was the central figure in the pathbreaking 'Basing Study' which raised the question of the survivability of US retaliatory forces to projected Soviet surprise attack capabilities: Wohlstetter, et al., *Selection and Use of Strategic Air Bases* (Santa Monica, Ca. April, 1954), Rand Corporation, R-266. His subsequent and seminal *Foreign Affairs* article ('The delicate balance of terror', vol. 37, no. 2, January, 1959) was among the earliest detailed expositions of the logic of deterrence via assured second-strike capabilities.

29 I am indebted for this insight to the anonymous reviewer of an earlier draft of this essay.

30 Thomas W. Wolfe and William R. Van Cleave, among others, share this view; see, for example, the citation from Wolfe in Van Cleave, op. cit., p. 47.

31 A remarkable group of analysts and scholars, whose paths intersected at the Rand Corporation; the principal figures, in my view, are Bernard Brodie, Herman Kahn, William W. Kaufmann, Thomas C. Schelling and Albert Wohlstetter. On this point, see the brief essay by Michael Howard, 'The classical strategists', *Problems of Modern Strategy*, Institute for Strategic Studies, 1970.

32 Frye, op. cit.

33 This is my interpretation, but it is consistent with the view, among others, of Raymond L. Garthoff, a long-time and highly regarded observer of Soviet military affairs and a participant in SALT I; see Garthoff, 'SALT and the Soviet military', *Problems of Communism*, January–February, 1975. On this point also, Pipes is in fundamental agreement (op. cit., p. 33), though his cryptic comments about the ABM treaty ('certain imprecisely defined limitations') and its connection to Soviet air defenses suggest once again a strategic perspective quite at variance with the US consensus described above.

34 My thinking, in pursuing this analysis, was clarified, though perhaps despite himself, by exposure to Dr Mikhail Milstein (Lt General-retired) of the Institute for the Study of the USA and Canada of the Soviet Academy of Sciences, in several seminars at Harvard and MIT during April of 1977.

5

Mutual Deterrence, Parity and Strategic Arms Limitation in Soviet Policy

RAYMOND L. GARTHOFF

One of the most controversial – and important – questions under-lying debate on Soviet intentions, détente, and strategic arms limitations (SALT) in particular, has concerned the Soviet view on mutual deterrence. Do the political and military leaders in Moscow accept mutual deterrence? Do they see it as a basis on which to negotiate strategic arms limitation? Or do they hold a fundamentally different view of the strategic relationship between the two superpowers, and have they been 'taking us for a ride' in SALT? Although some decision-makers and commen-tators have expressed judgment on this matter as though there were no doubt as to the answer, many others have been unsure and concerned. In particular, the continuing Soviet military build-up, and the continued expressions in published Soviet military writings of a war-waging military doctrine, have con-vinced some – and troubled others – as to Soviet views on mutual deterrence, and as to Soviet aims.

This chapter seeks to illuminate Soviet thinking on the subject, with consideration of the inter-relationship of Soviet ideological beliefs, political imperatives and calculation, military views and doctrine, and their intersection and reconciliation in Soviet policy.

The central conclusion of this analysis is that since the late 1960s, when SALT was launched, the Soviet political and mili-tary leadership has recognized that under contemporary condi-tions there is a strategic 'balance' between the two superpowers and, as a result, mutual deterrence; that the nuclear strategic balance is not transitory, but also not necessarily enduring, and that continuing military efforts are required to assure its stability and continuation; that agreed strategic arms limitations can make a contribution, possibly a significant one, to reducing these otherwise necessary reciprocal military efforts; but, finally, that in recent years US readiness to accept parity and strategic arms limitations reflecting and perpetuating parity has become increasingly doubtful.

More broadly, the Soviet leaders believe that peaceful co-existence – with continued political and ideological competition – *is* the preferable alternative to an unrestrained arms race and to recurring high-risk political-military confrontation; they realize that detente and a relaxation of tensions is in the interests of the USSR, and that nuclear war would not be. This does not mean that Soviet foreign policy is passive or rests on satisfaction with the *status quo*. But Soviet leaders believe that the need to avoid a nuclear war can best be served by prudent actions within a framework of mutual strategic deterrence between the Soviet Union and the United States.

Military Views

Lenin embraced the observation of Clausewitz that 'war is a continuation of policy by other means', and this indeed represents a natural Marxist-Leninist conception.[1] Remarkably, some Soviet writers (mainly but not exclusively civilians) have over the past two decades been so impressed by the inexpediency and enormous dangers of any nuclear world war (or indeed any war which could escalate into such a war) that they have seemed to challenge this view. They, in turn, have been criticized and refuted by other spokesmen, mainly military. Yet the question keeps arising. Why? Mainly because the two sides are not engaged in a theoretical disputation, but in a political argument with considerable potential importance for military programs and policy. In fact, both sides accept the basic premise that war is a matter of policy or political motivation; both sides also accept the fact that resort to nuclear war would not be expedient as a matter of policy. The real underlying debate is whether war is recognized as so unpromising and dangerous that it can never occur. Such a question has profound implications for military requirements. Is a force dedicated to deterrence enough? And if war were to occur, is a war-waging capability needed to seek a pyrrhic 'victory'?

In the early and mid-1960s, after general acceptance of the theses on the non-inevitability, non-necessity and non-expediency of nuclear war, Khrushchev and others began to argue further that nuclear war would spell the end of world civilization, and was therefore not only unacceptable but unthinkable.[2] One civilian commentator on political-military subjects carried this argument to the point of paraphrasing Clausewitz (and Lenin) to say 'War can only be the continuation of madness'.[3] This statement, along with a number of others, was made in the context of ideological-political Soviet polemics with the Chinese communists. The more orthodox Soviet military line was, while agreeing that nuclear war precisely as a continuation of politics made no sense *as a policy option for the USSR*, to insist on the risks that such a war could occur and on the need for powerful Soviet military forces to deter such a war.[4] Thus, military spokesmen distinguished between war as a continuation of policy, which was reaffirmed, and war as a useful instrument of policy, which it was found not to be;[5] and many stressed the need to be able to wage and seek to win a war if it could not be averted.

In 1965, the late Major General Nikolai Talensky, former editor of the military theoretical journal *Military Thought* (at the time of military doctrinal rejuvenation after Stalin's death in the mid-1950s) and an outspoken 'revisionist', argued: 'In our days there is no more dangerous illusion than the idea that thermo-nuclear war can still serve as an instrument of politics, that it is possible to achieve political aims by using nuclear weapons and still survive.'[6] Several Soviet military writers subsequently attacked General Talensky's position (and criticized him by name), arguing not that his position was theoretically wrong, but that it was practically dangerous because it undercut the rationale for maintaining necessary large military forces.[7]

Some of the discussions in the 1960s, especially non-public military writings, made clear that the military were taking issue not with the assessment of the catastrophic consequences of a nuclear war or the need to avoid such a war, but with discussions which made war 'unthinkable' and therefore cast doubt on the need for Soviet military programs and requirements; war was seen as deterred (by Soviet military strength) and therefore unlikely, but not inconceivable, and hence requiring Soviet strategic planning, force requirements and morale-sustaining statements of confidence in victory if war should come.[8]

The debate was renewed in the early and mid-1970s – during and after SALT I and the rise of détente. Other civilian writers, some with positions close to political leaders, again stressed the cataclysmic nature of a nuclear world war, and clearly indicated there would be no meaningful 'victor' in such a war.[9] And again there were a number of counterarguments, usually by military–

theoretical writers, mainly challenging implications of these discussions for Soviet military strength as a deterrent, but also as a
war-waging and war-winning force if a world nuclear war should
ever occur.[10] (More recently, however, as we shall note later,
some of these military writers have made a rather sharp turn
toward accepting views which they previously criticized.)

Some discussions have sought to reconcile the two opposing
views. Dr Trofimenko, for example, has cited 'the Leninist thesis
on the fact that war is a continuation of policy ... by forcible
means', but one which is no longer 'in practice a usable instrument of policy when an aggressor in the course of struggle for
"victory" can himself be annihilated'. He finds the chief reason
for the abandonment of war as an expedient, usable instrument
not in the destructive nature of the weapons themselves, arguing
that 'imperialism would not hesitate to resort to any weapon to
realize its designs'; but rather in the fact that 'the other side has
analogous means at its disposal in a potential conflict',[11] thus
justifying the need to maintain a strong (and perhaps even war-
waging) military force as a deterrent in order to buttress mutual
deterrence.[12]

Soviet military doctrine continues to be predicated on the
assumption that if a general nuclear war should occur, all elements of the armed forces would contribute to waging a decisive
struggle aimed at defeating world imperialism. Soviet military
power, and the constant enhancement of its capability and readiness, is thus justified primarily for deterrence, as well as to wage a
war if one should come despite Soviet efforts to prevent it. This
view is consistently held by the Soviet military and political
leaders. It is not accurate, as some Western commentators have
done, to counterpose Soviet military interest in a 'war-fighting'
and hopefully 'war-winning' posture to a 'deterrent' one; the
Soviets see the former capability as providing the most credible
deterrent, as well as serving as a contingent resort in the event of
war.

The three editions of the basic Soviet work on military doctrine, *Military Strategy*, edited by a commission headed by the late
Marshal Sokolovsky, show Soviet military recognition of the
emergence of mutual deterrence (as well as an equivocal and
changing view on its public embrace). In the first edition, which
appeared in 1962, there is a passage which not only attributes the
concept to Western strategists and leaders, but also endorses
it.[13] In discussion of 'Contemporary means of armed combat and
their effect on the nature of war', all three editions stress the colossal and unacceptable consequences of a world nuclear war. In

addition to citing US and other sources on tens of millions of casualties, the second edition added a quotation from Khrushchev (made in the interval after publication of the first edition), stating that at the beginning of 1963 the USA had more than 40,000 nuclear weapons, and 'the USSR also has more than enough of these means', so that 'scientists have calculated that 700–800 million people would die as a result of the initial strikes alone, and all the large cities of many countries'.[14] In the third edition this (as well as all the other references to or statements by Khrushchev) was deleted. But a new passage was added which, while less graphic, is even more explicit on the *unacceptability* of a world nuclear war to the USSR.[15] Thus, the most authoritative Soviet open military publication of the 1960s, with changing shadings, was quite forthright in recognizing the fact of mutual deterrence, despite some reticence to endorse the concept as formulated in the West.

One of the discussants in the 'debate' of the mid-1970s over the proper interpretation of the application of Clausewitz's thesis returned to this point in 1979. Aleksandr Bovin, political observer for *Izvestia*, noted that the dictum, 'War is a continuation of policy by other means, by means of force', has two meanings. One meaning, which is unaffected by such things as changes in military technology, is that every war is a continuation of the policy of the state that pursues it. The other meaning is that war represents a choice of conducting a policy by one or another means, including the possible choice of use of military force. As to this latter sense, Bovin states that while such a choice sometimes made sense in Clausewitz's day, it no longer does:

> Now take the present situation. Can one consider a general nuclear-missile war as a normal, sensible means of pursuing some particular political aim? Obviously one cannot do this because the consequences of such a war would be a catastrophe for mankind, and in the current situation the one to risk making a first nuclear strike would inevitably be doomed to destruction by the forces available for a retaliatory strike. This is in fact what is called the balance of terror, and although this position is far from ideal . . . it does nonetheless exist.[16]

There is still a 'debate' on the theme of Clausewitz's dictum, as seen in the following rather different (although not contradictory) way of saying essentially the same thing. Possibly related to the above statement by Bovin in later 1979, General Sidel'nikov (who as a colonel had taken issue with Bovin by name on the same issue in 1973!) wrote in *Red Star* in early 1980 a rebuttal to the

'Western' notion that 'the thesis on war as the continuation of policy by means of force has allegedly outlived its usefulness'. His argument is that 'a new world war can and must be prevented and that it must not – precisely, must not – arise as a continuation of policy, must not be chosen as a means of achieving political aims'. He is clear that war is no longer a rational *choice*. But what if the other side initiates war? Indeed, Sidel'nikov states his concern that the USA might unleash such a war in pursuit of an anti-Soviet policy. 'And if imperialist aggressive forces again [he had cited Hitler's attack] try to test our strength and foist a war on us, on the part of the Soviet Union that war would be a continuation of the policy the sole aim of which is to defend the socialist Fatherland and the achievements of socialism.[17]

The most important aspect of this particular question is the unfounded contention of some Western commentators, such as Professor Richard Pipes, that 'as long as the Russians persist in adhering to the Clausewitzian maxim on the function of war, mutual deterrence does not really exist'.[18] On the contrary the Soviet literature clearly shows that there is no contradiction between being 'Clausewitzian' and recognizing the validity of mutual deterrence.[19]

Mutual deterrence in Soviet writings is usually expressed in terms of assured retaliatory capability which would devastate the aggressor, because this formulation (rather than 'mutual assured destruction' capability) is more responsive to ideological sensitivity over the idea that the USSR could be considered a potential aggressor and thus needs to be deterred. (Only adversaries – the USA, more broadly the imperialists, and also the Chinese communists – are described as potential aggressors.) In addition, this formulation avoids identification with the specific content of the US concept of 'mutual assured destruction', often expressed in terms of a countervalue capability for destroying a specified percentage of the opponent's industry and population. This US interpretation is more limited than the Soviet recognition of mutual deterrence, which rests on mutual capability for devastating retaliation unacceptable to a rational potential initiator of war, without resting on calculations of arbitrary industrial and population losses which theoretically would be acceptable costs.

Some observers have posited a possible Soviet conception of 'deterrence by denial', as contrasted with the US conception of 'deterrence by punishment'. (Neither of course is a Soviet, or for that matter an official US, expression.) 'Deterrence by denial' is conceived as seeking to deter by maintaining a capability for thwarting and defeating a potential attack; 'deterrence by punishment' seeks to deter by relying instead on a capability for devastating punitive retaliation. Soviet force posture and 'war-waging' military doctrine does suggest the possible applicability of this idea, but Soviet statements on deterrence are usually couched in terms of retaliatory punishment, and it is not clear that such a distinction reflects a Soviet way of thinking.

The political leaders in their programmatic statements endorse the idea that deterrence requires strong and ready combat capability, but do not go on to discuss meeting requirements for waging and winning a war. Brezhnev, for example, states simply: 'Any potential aggressor is well aware that any attempt to launch a nuclear missile attack on our country would be met by devastating retaliation.'[20]

It is of interest to note that the action to be deterred is limited to any nuclear missile attack (or sometimes, any attack) on the USSR itself (sometimes broadened to include the socialist commonwealth, meaning the countries of the Warsaw Pact, but not such countries as Vietnam or Cuba).

Mutual Deterrence and the Initial Soviet SALT Decision

There is reason to believe that the US proposals in 1967 and 1968 to hold bilateral strategic arms limitations talks (SALT), and in particular the emphasis on avoiding an arms race in ABM systems, coincided with internal Soviet consideration of the implications for their own security, and for their future military programs, of the emerging attainment of mutual deterrence. While the transition to *mutual* deterrence had been long antici-pated in the USA, it nevertheless meant a shift from previous US superiority and an unmatched American assured retaliatory capability. For the Soviets, however, it meant the achievement for the first time of a real second-strike capability, and in their view greatly enchanced security not only against a possible American first strike, but also against diplomatic-military pressures sup-ported by the superior US 'position of strength' based on its monopoly of a secure second-strike capacity.

In the exchanges in 1967–9 leading up to the SALT talks and in their critical opening phase, the Soviet leadership showed an increasingly clear acceptance of, and commitment to, mutual deterrence, and an awareness of the role strategic arms limita-tions could play in reinforcing mutual deterrence and dampening the arms race.

In the first Soviet response to the US SALT proposal, in 1967, the discourse was primarily in traditional disarmament terms. By the time the Soviets were prepared to meet, in 1968, both sides had expressed interest in a wider dialogue on the strategic relationship, and in confidential exchanges had agreed that a main objective of the strategic arms talks would be to achieve and maintain stable strategic deterrence between the USA and USSR through agreed limitations on the deployment of strategic offensive and defensive arms, balanced so that neither side could obtain any military advantage and so that equal security should be assured for both sides.[21]

In the very first business meeting of the two SALT delegations in Helsinki (on 18 November 1969), both sides – and not by prearrangement – stated that mutual deterrence was the underpinning of strategic arms limitation. The Soviet delegation, in a prepared statement cleared by the highest political and military leaders in Moscow, expressed the Soviet view that:

> Even in the event that one of the sides were the first to be subjected to attack, it would undoubtedly retain the ability to inflict a retaliatory strike of crushing power. Thus, evidently, we all agree that war between our two countries would be disastrous for both sides. And it would be tantamount to suicide for the one who decided to start such a war.[22]

The Soviets prior to SALT had often described their own posture as one of deterrence, and had in their open military publications described deterrence, avoidance of war and readiness to rebuff any aggressor as the main objectives of their defense policy and posture.[23] But the above-cited explicit formulation of mutual deterrence had never before been so clearly expressed by authoritative Soviet spokesmen. The public military press, in particular, avoided positive references to *mutual* deterrence and *mutual* assured destruction, for reasons discussed earlier.

It is, therefore, of considerable interest and significance that during the key formative period of Soviet policy toward negotiations on strategic arms limitation there were very clear and explicit endorsements by influential Soviet *military* leaders of the concepts of mutual assured retaliation and mutual deterrence in *Military Thought*, the important confidential Soviet military journal.

At the very time the decision on whether to enter SALT talks was still being debated and decided in Moscow, although without reference to that fact, Marshal Nikolai I Krylov, Commander in Chief of the Strategic Missile Forces, wrote in *Military Thought* in November 1967:

Under contemporary circumstances, with the existence of a system for detecting missile launches, an attempt by an aggressor to inflict a surprise preemptive strike cannot give him a decisive advantage for the achievement of victory in war, and moreover will not save him from great destruction and human losses.[24]

Later, in mid-1968, General Vasendin and Colonel Kuznetsov stated:

Everyone knows that in contemporary conditions in an armed conflict of adversaries comparatively equal in power (in number and especially in quality of weapons) an immediate retaliatory strike of enormous destructive power is inevitable.[25]

These professional discussions, soberly stated in terms clearly applying to *both* sides, are quite different from the tone of articles in the public military press with their political purposes and stress on deterring the *other* side. Similarly, in May 1969, General of the Army Semyon P. Ivanov, commandant of the prestigious Military Academy of the General Staff, and previously Deputy Chief of the General Staff and Chief of its Operations Division, wrote:

With the existing level of development of nuclear missile weapons and their reliable cover below ground and under water it is impossible in practice to destroy them completely, and consequently it is also impossible to prevent an annihilating retaliatory strike.[26]

In the same May 1969 issue of *Military Thought*, its chief editor, Major General (now Lt General) V. I. Zemskov, after citing US sources (including Secretary McNamara) that 'the Soviet Union would be in a position to destroy all America after having withstood the first powerful strike on the part of the United States', goes on to cite the build-up of US strategic forces in the 1960s. He then makes an interesting transition from attribution of concepts of a 'nuclear balance', parity, and mutual deterrence to Western sources, to the Soviet and other communist parties' declaration of the devastation that would be caused by a world nuclear war, and from that to the Soviet policy aim of prevention of a world nuclear war. [27] Later in the article, in discussing Soviet military policy, he states:

The degree of probability of a particular type of war does not, of course, remain the same for each historical period, and changes under the influence of a number of political and military-technical factors. Of special importance in this connection can be the disruption of the 'nuclear balance'. It is possible, for example, in case of further sharp increase of nuclear potential or *the creation by one of the sides of highly effective means of anti-ballistic missile defense while the other side lags considerably in solution of these tasks. A change of the 'nuclear balance' in favor of the countries of imperialism would increase greatly the danger of a nuclear war.*[28]

It is clear from these passages that General Zemskov believed in 1969 that there was a 'nuclear balance' providing mutual potential destruction and therefore mutual deterrence, but that it was at least at that time a somewhat precarious balance from the *Soviet* standpoint, and particularly if the USA, which was well ahead of the USSR in developing antiballistic missile technology, should deploy an effective ABM defense. There is a clear relationship between this discussion and the Soviet decision, taken by that time and soon to become evident in SALT, that ballistic missile defenses of the two sides should if possible be sharply limited through a strategic arms limitation agreement so as not to risk restoring the USA to a position of superiority that could imperil the still reversible state of mutual assured retaliation and mutual deterrence.

A related point of considerable interest was made explicit in these same confidential discussions in *Military Thought*. The reader may have noted the reference by Marshal Krylov to 'the existence of a system for detecting missile launches' as one element in his conclusion on mutual deterrence. In his discussion, he explains further that he has in mind, and that the USSR had under at least some unspecified contingency guidance, a policy of 'launch on warning' or 'launch under attack' (though he does not use either Western expression):

> It must be stressed that under present conditions, when the Soviet Armed Forces are in constant combat readiness, any aggressor who initiates a nuclear war will not remain unpunished, a severe and inevitable retribution awaits him. With the presence in the armament of the troops of launchers and missiles completely ready for operation, as well as of systems for detecting enemy missile launches and other types of reconnaissance, *an aggressor is no longer able suddenly to destroy the missiles before their launch on the territory of the country against which the aggression is committed. They will have time during the flight of the missiles of the aggressor to leave their launchers and inflict a retaliatory strike against the enemy.*[29] (emphasis added)

During the SALT I negotiations, in 1970, the Soviet delegation referred in passing to the existence and continuous improvement of early-warning systems, owing to which ICBM silos might be empty by the time they were hit by an attacker's strike, the ICBMs having been launched by that time. The US delegation commented on this statement and expressed the hope that no government would launch its ICBM force solely on the possibly fallible reading of signals from its early-warning systems. It expressed the view that such a strategic doctrine seemed inconsistent with a proper concern for the problems of accidental or unauthorized launches or provocative third-party attack, which both delegations had been discussing. The Soviet delegation clearly was not authorized to enter a discussion of this subject, and had not intended in its initial statement to do so. Accordingly, it replied with an attempt to disassociate the question from accidental, unauthorized or provocative attacks, and referred awkwardly to unofficial *American* statements (not made in SALT) about possible launch on warning. The US delegation then provided an official US disavowal of the concept by Secretary of Defense Laird, with further criticism of the idea as potentially dangerous for automatic escalation or for starting a war by accident.[30] But efforts to elicit a statement on Soviet policy with respect to the concept met with silence, and in an unofficial comment General (now Marshal) Ogarkov, the senior Soviet military representative, remarked to his US counterpart that such operational matters went beyond the proper purview of SALT, and that military men understand the matter.[31]

These indications in *Military Thought* and in the exchanges in SALT that the Soviet authorities consider seriously a launch on warning concept helps to explain their relatively less excited concern over ICBM silo vulnerability. It raises the further question whether a concept which evidently arose at a time of relative Soviet inferiority may have continued since as a justification for keeping such a large ensiloed ICBM force (still today constituting 70 percent of Soviet strategic force capability) after the USA has deployed considerable counterforce capacity and is further developing and planning to deploy highly effective counterforce capabilities which could threaten the entire Soviet ICBM force – *if* it remained in its silos and tried to 'ride out' a US attack. The US pursuit of such a capability with the MK-12A warhead for Minuteman III, the MX missile, Pershing II, and Trident II, thus, may serve to increase Soviet reliance on a launch on warning concept.

It should be noted that in the mid-1950s the Soviet military had developed a concept of pre-emptive action in response to an imminent and irrevocable enemy decision to attack.[32] It was explicitly not a euphemism for a surprise first strike, but represented a last-minute seizure of the initiative to forestall an enemy attack. This concept, developed in the premissile age, and explicitly discussed only in *Military Thought* in the 1950s, was evidently modified, if not superseded, in the 1960s by the launch on warning concept. From this standpoint, launch on warning may be a step toward stability from pre-emption, but it remains a potentially destabilizing and dangerous possibility and the USA should seek ways to discourage the Soviets from any degree of reliance on it. Inherently, the *possibility* of launch on warning (or launch on first impact, or on multiple impacts, etc.) *does* contribute to the uncertainties any potential attacker must consider and that is good, but it would be dangerous if in fact resorted to in defense against anything except a proven assault.

In April 1969, an article by Anatoly A. Gromyko (son of the Foreign Minister and a distinguished 'American expert' in the Soviet Ministry of Foreign Affairs, then at the Academy of Sciences Institute of USA Studies) appeared in *Military Thought*. Articles in this journal by non-military contributors are uncommon; clearly the purpose of Gromyko's contribution was to present a rationale for SALT in terms appealing to its select military readership. The thrust of his argument was that US reaction to the build-up in Soviet strategic power (ICBMs were specifically noted) had led not only to the need for the USA to shift from 'massive retaliation' to 'flexible response' concepts and to accepting 'mutual assured destruction', but also had compelled the USA to seek strategic arms limitations and to curb the strategic arms race. (Incidentally, he suggested that Secretary McNamara had been forced out of his position as Secretary of Defense because of hard-line opposition by 'the military–industrial complex' and others to his 'realism' in recognizing the emergence of mutual deterrence.) More broadly, he argued in terms of differentiation among various elements of the US policy-making and policy-influencing elite which – by implication – should be recognized by the military readers, rather than assuming that all are single-mindedly hostile to any improvement of relations with the USSR.[33]

Soviet military theorists and leaders, including those we have cited above, continue to discuss ways and means of waging and seeking to win a general nuclear war should one occur. For reasons discussed earlier, they see no inconsistency in recognizing that such war would be an unprecedented disaster endangering all mankind, and therefore in supporting mutual deterrence based on mutual retaliatory capability, while also preparing to attempt to cope with the eventuality of war if it should come and to seek to emerge from it 'victorious', that is, less totally destroyed than 'capitalism'.

Accordingly, too, the Soviet military have had an active interest and role in SALT.[34] The strong endorsement of mutual deterrence made by the Soviet side from the very outset of the SALT talks, including by senior Soviet military representatives at SALT, has been noted. This was backed up by further concrete signals, including above all the Soviet indications (also from the very outset of SALT in late 1969) that they were opposed to a nationwide ABM deployment which not only could fuel the competition in strategic offensive arms, but also could upset mutual assured retaliation. The explicit prohibition on such nationwide ABM deployments contained in Article I of the ABM treaty was, in fact, included on Soviet initiative.[35]

In sum, we see that far from having to *infer* from such things as the Soviet acceptance of the ABM treaty that there is a Soviet interest in mutual deterrence based on assured mutual retaliatory capability, there is a clear case for it in confidential Soviet military discussions preceding (and, as we shall see, following) SALT I, and from the SALT negotiating history as well.

Parity and the Renunciation of Superiority

In the Soviet view – shared by military and civilian leaders – just as in the mainstream of US thinking in the 1970s, overall 'parity' has existed for about a decade. There are those – again, both in Moscow and in Washington – who are apprehensive as to whether this parity will be upset by some successful effort of the other side. But successive US Secretaries of Defense and chairmen of the Joint Chiefs of Staff have agreed, even when sounding such an alarm for the future (fortunately, one that seems each few years to recede to a few years hence), that 'at present' there is an overall strategic parity – that while each side has certain areas of superiority they balance out to yield parity overall.

Parity was, of course, for the Soviet side an improvement over the previous US unilateral superiority. Soviet political leaders from the ebullient Khrushchev of the late 1950s on had been claiming various partial superiorities, and overall parity. But only in the early 1970s did the Soviet military leaders admit that an assured retaliatory capability for the USSR had come about in the 1960s – actually, the late 1960s. And the Soviet military have acknowledged throughout the 1970s, as have the American, that while each side has certain areas of superiority, these balance out to yield an overall parity. Nevertheless, uncertainties remain as to the future.

In an interesting article on 'Military strategy and military technology' in *Military Thought* in April 1973, Major General Mikhail I. Cherednichenko, a well-known Soviet military theoretician and collaborator of the late Marshal Sokolovsky, described the evolution of mutual deterrence as a product of the 1960s – implicitly admitting that previously only the USA had had an assured retaliatory capability. General Cherednichenko saw mutual deterrence mainly as a product of advances in military technology permitting the USSR to match the long-standing US retaliatory capability. With reference to SALT I, signed a year earlier, he specifically comments that 'Definite successes have been achieved in strategic arms limitation negotiations'. But in seeking 'to prevent military superiority by aggressive [Western] forces', he also argues implicitly for the need to maintain Soviet military efforts to that end. SALT I was seen not as central, but as contributing to mutual deterrence by reducing the uncertainties generated by unlimited strategic technological competition – a contribution to preventing 'the possibility of unexpected major technological achievements' by the USA which could give it military superiority.[36]

Recent years have seen hopeful developments in Soviet acceptance of the implications of mutual deterrence for strategic and political objectives. This may in time facilitate strategic arms limitation, or at least mute and stabilize the competition.

Soviet military and political leaders ceased to call for strategic superiority as an objective after the 24th Party Congress in April 1971 (which also marked a turning point in SALT). Instead, mutual deterrence, a balance, parity and equal security are advocated. To be sure, this is often expressed in terms of implying that it is only the West which has aggressive aims which are restrained by mutual deterrence. But it is none the less an important advance. Brezhnev stated the general Soviet political view in 1975 in these words:

> International détente has become possible because a new relation of forces has been established in the world arena. Now the leaders of the bourgeois world can no longer entertain serious intentions of resolving the historic dispute between capitalism and socialism by force of arms. The senselessness and extreme danger of further tension are becoming increasingly obvious under conditions where both sides possess weapons of colossal destructive power.[37]

Notwithstanding the fact that each side sees only a need to deter the other, both recognize the fact of mutual strategic 'sufficiency' and assured retaliatory capability and the resulting mutual deterrence.

On the eve of the Carter administration, in a major policy address at Tula, Brezhnev authoritatively disavowed the aim of military superiority aimed at a first strike, reaffirming the aim of deterrence:

> Of course, Comrades, we are improving our defenses. It cannot be otherwise. We have never neglected and will never neglect the security of our country and the security of our allies. But the allegations that the Soviet Union is going beyond what is sufficient for defense, that it is striving for superiority in arms, with the aim of delivering a 'first strike,' are absurd and utterly unfounded ... Our efforts are aimed at preventing both first and second strikes and at preventing nuclear war altogether ... The Soviet Union's defense potential must be sufficient to deter anyone from disturbing our peaceful life. Not a course aimed at superiority in arms, but a course aimed at their reduction, at lessening military confrontation – that is our policy.[38]

The Soviet position was spelled out more fully in *Pravda* shortly after the Tula speech by the American affairs expert, Academician Arbatov. He vigorously refuted arguments that the USSR was seeking superiority, and accurately described in some detail areas of the strategic balance in which the USSR leads (the overall number of ICBM and SLBM missile launchers; strategic missile 'throw-weight') and in which the USA leads (numbers of strategic bombers and bomber 'throw-weight'; numbers of missile warheads; forward submarine bases; 'and much else'). Thus, he notes, that 'while enjoying an approximate equality (parity) in general, the two countries have within this parity considerable differences (asymmetries) in various components of their armed forces, connected with differences in geographic situations, the nature of possible threats to their security, technical characteristics of individual weapons systems, and even in traditions of military organization'. The main thing, though, is 'the existence of an approximate balance, that is, a parity in the relation of forces about which the USSR and the United States came to agreement with the signing of the principle of equal rights to security'.[39] Again on the occasion of the sixtieth anniversary of the Bolshevik Revolution, Brezhnev returned to this theme, stating:

> The Soviet Union is effectively looking after its own defense, but it

does not and will not seek military superiority over the other side. We do not want to upset the approximate balance of military strength existing at present ... between the USSR and the United States. But in return we insist that no one else should seek to upset it in his favor.[40]

This was a more far-reaching statement than his earlier one at Tula, denying an aim of superiority 'with the aim of a first strike': it denies superiority as a current or future aim for *any* purpose, as have many subsequent authoritative Soviet statements. Similarly, Marshal Kulikov wrote in 1978:

> The Soviet state, effectively looking after its defense, is not seeking to achieve military superiority over the other side, but at the same time, it cannot permit the approximate balance which has taken shape ... between the USSR and the US to be upset, to the disadvantage of our security.[41]

Soviet assertions that their strategic aims and programs are in pursuit of parity and not superiority must of course be judged on the merits of an objective evaluation of actual developments, rather than being accepted on faith. But such assertions are not without significance. Numerous authoritative commentators since 1977 have echoed these themes of Soviet acceptance of parity, equal security and the non-pursuit of superiority.

Especially interesting have been a number of commentaries and discussions in the open military press. Even before Brezhnev's Tula speech, in early 1977, *Red Star* carried two commentaries observing that 'parity' was a reality and had been the basis for US-Soviet relations 'in recent years', and that the military power of the USA and the USSR was said to be regarded by 'unbiased experts' as 'about equal'.[42]

Appearing about the same time as the Tula speech, although signed to press a month earlier (17 December 1976) was an interesting article in the *Military-Historical Journal* by Colonel Ye. Rybkin, long regarded in the West as a 'Red Hawk'. Colonel Rybkin, a professor on the Lenin Military-Political Academy staff, and later at the institute of Military History, citing Lenin that 'war is a continuation of policy', but in almost direct refutation of Rybkin's own earlier expressed views, noted the essential need for the possibility of peaceful coexistence and the prevention of war. [43] The point of particular interest to the present discussion is not only Rybkin's conclusion that 'Rejection of a nuclear war ... is dictated by the new realities of the era', but that 'nuclear parity', as it is called, has been established between the

USSR and the United States, that is, a certain balance of power, which was officially recognized at the Soviet-American [Summit] talks in 1972–4, with a mutual agreement not to disrupt this balance.[44] Moreover, in arguing that there is 'an objective need to end the arms race', Rybkin states that 'the quantity of nuclear weapons has reached such a level that a futher increase would in practice make no change', and he cites Brezhnev's statement of July 1974 that 'a sufficient quantity of arms has been amassed to destroy everything alive on earth several times over'.[45] (Brezhnev, incidentally, had echoed his own 1974 remarks a few weeks earlier in a speech in Bucharest.)[46]

In addition to numerous authoritative Soviet political and military renunciations of the objective of military superiority, and reaffirmation of the existence of parity and of the aim of preserving that parity, [47] the official US-USSR communiqué issued in Vienna on 18 June 1979, at the conclusion of the summit at which the SALT II treaty was signed, included a commitment by both sides that each 'is not striving and will not strive for military superiority, since that can only result in dangerous instability, generating higher levels of armaments with no benefit to the security of either side'.[48] This statement has often since been cited by Soviet writers. For example, General Sidel'nikov cites it approvingly in his article earlier quoted for his defense of Clausewitz's maxim. He strongly endorses maintaining the existing 'approximate balance' and 'parity' in military forces between the USA and the USSR. In addition to restating the now familiar position that 'the Soviet Union has not set itself the task of achieving military superiority', he questions the very meaningfulness of the concept.[49]

Another prominent Soviet military writer, Major General Rair Simonyan, a professor at the Frunze Academy, also argues:

> Given the priority of strategic forces, when both sides possess weapons capable of destroying many times over all life on earth, neither the addition of new armaments nor an increase in their destructive power can bring any substantial military – and still less political – advantage.[50]

He also cites and explicitly agrees with a US statement that: 'In the contemporary world it is impossible to insure security by means of an arms buildup.'[51] An editorial in *Red Star* in 1977, in arguing the need not to be complacent in the quest for peace, commented: 'After all, it is a case of the fate of world civilization and the future of all mankind'.[52] We thus see a new readiness by military as well as civilian commentators to accept strategic parity, mutual deterrence and the inadmissibility of nuclear war.

It is of some interest and significance that there is now also a campaign to go *beyond* codification of a nuclear balance on the basis of parity at the very high levels currently existing. This criticism from 'the left' so to speak is more noticeable with the quieting of reservations from 'the right' so sharply dramatized by Colonel Rybkin's 'conversion'. A writer in *Pravda* in late 1976 argued:

> Trying to justify the arms race, certain political circles in Western countries propagandize some sort of balance of terror which is supposedly necessary to maintain peace and to insure the security of peoples. But such a balance is an unreliable foundation for security. The real way to achieve security is to observe the principle of the non-use of force.[53]

This argument does not *oppose* a nuclear balance based on parity; it argues for a need to go beyond it. Others arguing this point usually stress the need to proceed to disarmament:

> The accumulated means of mass destruction are such that an exchange of nuclear strikes contradicts even the most narrowly construed national security interests and seriously threatens the lives of peoples . . .
> The 'balance of terror' cannot guarantee security . . . There is a danger of their [the accumulated weapons] accidental or unsanctioned use. The numbers of these weapons are constantly growing . . .
> In other words, if one wants to live in security, struggle to resolve the problems of disarmament.[54]

Even Brezhnev's speech on the sixtieth anniversary of the Bolshevik Revolution, after renouncing an aim of superiority and stating that the Soviets 'did not want to upset the approximate balance of military strength that now exists', went on to state:

> Needless to say, maintaining the existing balance is not an end in itself. We are in favor of starting a downward turn in the curve of the arms race and of gradually reducing the level of the military confrontation. We want to reduce substantially, and then to eliminate, the threat of nuclear war – the most formidable danger for mankind.[55]

Perhaps the most sophisticated argument along this line was made several years ago by two retired military men now with the Institute of the USA and Canada, General Mil'shtein and Colonel Semeyko. They stressed the importance of the Soviet-

American agreements of 1972 and the Prevention of Nuclear War Agreement of 1973, which they said were made possible only by 'proceeding from their mutual recognition of the fact that nuclear war would have devastating consequences for mankind and from the need to reduce and in the final analysis to eliminate the danger of nuclear war.[56] Mil'shtein and Semeyko are realistic in their criticism of nuclear deterrence as not being an 'ideal solution':

> Of course, the concept of 'nuclear deterrence,' which presupposes the existence of enormous nuclear forces capable of 'assured destruction' is not an ideal solution to the problem of peace and the prevention of nuclear conflict.[57]

They argue that some influential elements in the USA have tried to escape mutual deterrence by pursuing 'acceptable' limited nuclear options, 'selective targeting' concepts and the like. This course they reject, while endorsing the effort to move from mutual deterrence on the path of détente, arms limitation, disarmament and peaceful coexistence. 'Preventing nuclear war in any of its forms, large or small, and the limitation of the arms race, are the central problems of Soviet-American relations'.[58]

Another analyst at the USA Institute, Dr Trofimenko, has argued that the USA was led into SALT only by 'a realization of the impossibility of the United States achieving a position of strategic military superiority over the Soviet Union' and readiness to accept parity, and by recognition of 'the inevitability of a crushing counterstrike if the United States delivered a nuclear missile strike on the USSR'.[59] But he was led by consideration of military developments over the period 1972–6 to conclude:

> Indeed, the matter of preventing nuclear war is not a policy of passive temporizing based on a presumption that a certain formal codification of the Soviet-American nuclear balance carried out in recent years is necessary and sufficient to maintain military stability, but only major new constructive steps in the sphere of military détente are able really to prevent a gradual slide toward nuclear catastrophe.[60]

Growing Soviet Concern Over US Intentions

A number of discussions since 1977 have reflected disappointment and concern with the US position. As Brezhnev put it in a speech in May 1977:

I am convinced that not a single statesman, or public figure, or thinking person can avoid his share of responsibility in the struggle against the threat of war, for this means responsibility for the very future of mankind itself. I shall not conceal the fact that our concern over the continuing arms race, including the strategic arms race, has grown in connection with the positions adopted in these matters by the new American Administration.[61]

The Soviet military leaders, and other Soviet leaders and commentators, display considerable suspicion of US intentions, and concern not only over growing US capabilities, but also as to *why* this continued increase in capabilities is sought. To be sure, some of these expressions of concern doubtless serve other purposes, such as argument to support requested Soviet military programs. But many have the ring of sincerity about them and many cite incontrovertible evidence to support their arguments on capabilities, as well as 'evidence' which to the Soviets may seem convincing in allegations of nefarious US objectives and intentions.

Much of this may sound familiar to a US reader as a description of the obverse *American* suspicions of Soviet military build-up and hostile designs. A description of an adversary in terms of a 'mirror image' of oneself (either as equally benign *or* belligerent) based on unverified assumptions, often unconscious ones, must be eschewed; when, however, there *is* a parallel perception of the other side it is important to recognize that fact.

In the Soviet perception, the USA has continued, notwithstanding SALT and détente, to seek military superiority. Although some highly placed US leaders and others are considered to have 'soberly' evaluated the strategic situation and given up pursuit of supremacy, powerful forces are believed to continue to seek advantage and superiority in order to compel Soviet acquiescence in US policy preferences. Moreover, actual US military policy and programs are seen as seeking to upset or to circumvent the nuclear mutual deterrence balance.

A series of developments since the SALT I agreements were signed in 1972 are seen in this light, above all the open pursuit of counterforce capabilities through increasingly accurate and numerous MIRV systems. At the outset of SALT II in late 1972, the Soviet side did probe for reciprocal restraints on MIRV (and MARV) as well as more generally on new strategic programs of both sides. These efforts were swamped by the tough overall initial Soviet position in SALT II, the lack of synchronization of MIRV technology (with the USA unwilling to restrain its advantages for early deployment, particularly given erroneous intelligence estimates in the early 1970s exaggerating when the Soviets would develop and deploy MIRVs and concern over the greater MIRV potential of their larger throw-weight missiles), and the US priority given in the negotiations to attempts to move toward equalization of missile throw-weight.

The existing 1046 Poseidon and Minuteman III missiles with their 6000–7000 independently targetable warheads (to say nothing of the vastly superior American strategic bomber force, the hundreds of non-MIRVed ICBMs and SLBMs, and US theater nuclear forces capable of striking the USSR) provide a powerful counterforce capability against the overall Soviet ICBM force, bomber force and submarine force, since the latter two are not kept on the same degree of airfield alert or deployment at sea as are their US counterparts. While Americans focus on growing Minuteman vulnerability, the Soviets recognize that ICBMs are only about one fourth of the US strategic force, while the Soviet ICBM force will be vulnerable by the late 1980s – this is far more ominous for the Soviet side, because far more Soviet than US strategic eggs are in the fixed land-based ICBM force basket; about 70–75 percent of their total strategic force. Also, as noted above, other Soviet intercontinental forces are less numerous, less capable and more vulnerable. Given the concerns in the USA over the Soviet threat to US ICBMs, is it any wonder that conservative Soviet military planners and responsive political leaders would be concerned over the existing and growing US capabilities? The full currently planned and announced US programs for the mark 12A warhead for Minuteman III, the MX ICBM, and the Trident I and II systems – to say nothing of strategic cruise missiles and theater nuclear forces (TNF) in Europe – would result in a still *greater* US overall (and counterforce) advantage ten years from now than the US has today, *even* with all Soviet programs estimated to be deployed within that period! From the vantage-point of Moscow, while a general nuclear balance had come into being by the late 1960s, and parity was recognized and supported in the SALT accords, continued major Soviet military efforts are needed to keep up the balance.

Maintaining Mutual Deterrence

The Soviet leadership, like its US counterpart, continues to look in the first instance and in the final account to its own unilateral military strength as the guarantor of deterrence of the other side and, hence, of mutual deterrence. In both cases, the professional military leadership in particular remains somewhat skeptical of the role that arms control – especially bilateral (or multilateral) negotiated commitments to strategic arms limitations – can play in securing such deterrence. At the same time, there is good evidence that national leaderships, including at least some senior professional military men, have increasingly come to accept negotiated strategic arms limitations as a contributing element in providing more stable and less costly deterrent military forces. As one of the few established Soviet civilian commentators on strategic matters put it (in 1976): 'Under contemporary circumstances a real possibility to find a common interest with a potential adversary is to be found in the area of . . . the stabilization of the military balance by means of limiting the arms race.'[62]

Soviet generals often cite a statement made by General Secretary Brezhnev in 1970:

> We have created strategic forces which constitute a reliable means of deterring any aggressor. We shall respond to any and all attempts from any quarter to obtain military superiority over the USSR with a suitable increase in military strength to guarantee our defense. We cannot do otherwise.[63]

This, of course, remains a postulate of Soviet policy (as, indeed, of parallel US policy).

What effect has SALT had on the applicability of this postulate, and what is the potential role for SALT in the future? Let us recall the important discussion by General Zemskov in *Military Thought*, in 1969. He spoke of a 'nuclear balance' and of the particular importance of the possible 'disruption' of that balance in case of 'the creation by one of the sides of highly effective means of anti-ballistic missile defense while the other side lags considerably in solution of these tasks' and that it would 'increase greatly the danger of a nuclear war' if the West achieved such an advantage.[64] It is clear that this reflected a view held at the highest political and military levels, and the congruence of Soviet and US views and objectives led to the ABM treaty in SALT signed in May 1972.

Many Soviet writers have noted the effect of SALT in reflecting and supporting parity and the nuclear balance. Trofimenko expressed with particular precision the effect of the ABM treaty on mutual deterrence, as seen by the Soviets. He described 'a situation of equality of strategic capabilities of the USSR and the US stemming from the essential equality in the balance of strategic arms (in particular, since each of the sides under any circumstances retains the capability for a retaliatory strike on the vital centers of the other)'. While this situation had developed by the late 1960s, and was only implicitly codified in the SALT I agreements in 1972, Trofimenko does speak of 'the equalizing of the capabilities of the USSR and the US for a retaliatory strike (in particular as a result of the prohibition on the creation of nation-wide ABM systems through the 1972 Treaty),[65] and further:

> The conclusion of the ABM Treaty and its subsequent Protocol [reducing the number of permitted ABM defense areas from two to one for each side] for all practical purposes cast off the key link of 'offense – defense' in the field of strategic systems. By relinquishing deployment of nation-wide ABM systems, the two sides eliminated one of the main motivating stimuli to the further build-up of efforts in the field of offensive systems.[66]

This recognition of the key significance of the ABM treaty in 'preventing the emergence of a chain reaction of competition between offensive and defensive arms' was specifically cited by Marshal Grechko, then Minister of Defense, and General of the Army (now Marshal) Kulikov, then Chief of the General Staff, in endorsing the treaty when it was formally considered by the Supreme Soviet in the ratification process.[67] Aleksandr Bovin, following the signing of the SALT II treaty in 1979, similarly commented on the contribution of the SALT I ABM treaty.[68]

We should recall the second element in General Zemskov's analysis in 1969. In addition to noting the possibility of the disruption of the nuclear balance, if one side obtained an effective ABM capability and the other did not, he also had noted such a danger 'in case of a further sharp increase of nuclear [strike] potential' by one side.[69] And this is the risk Soviet military planners have seen in the qualitative and quantitative superiority of the USA in MIRVed systems throughout the 1970s.

There are many indications of this concern in Soviet discussions. Albeit without specific reference to MIRV, one worth citing is the statement by the now retired former General Staff Colonel Vasily M. Kulish, writing soon after the SALT I agreements had been reached:

> The appearance of new types of weapons could seriously affect the relation of military forces between the two world systems ... Far-reaching international consequences could arise in the event that one side possessed qualitatively new strategic weapons which could serve to neutralize the ability of the opposing side to carry out effective retaliatory operations ... even a relatively small and brief superiority by the United States over the Soviet Union in the

development of certain 'old' or 'new' types and systems of weapons that significantly increase the strategic effectiveness of American military power could exert a destabilizing influence on the international political situation throughout the entire world and present extremely unfavorable consequences for the cause of peace and socialism.[70]

The main concern of the Soviet leadership is US political-military strategic *intentions*. They are also concerned over growing US counterforce *capabilities* and parallel US advocacy of counterforce *concepts*, both because of threatened destabilization of the existing balance and because of what they suspect as to the underlying US intentions. Dr Trofimenko, for example, concludes that the 'genuine parity' reflected and bolstered by the SALT ABM treaty 'does not suit American theoreticians'. He argues that:

> the true nature of American strategic missile targeting is a most important state secret, and the American command can target its missiles in any way it wishes without speaking out publicly about it. Hence the public campaign of the Pentagon connected with the advertised 'retargeting' [of the Schlesinger Doctrine] is . . . a conscious effort to put psychological pressure on the other side.[71]

The reversal of US stated policy on the destabilizing nature of counterforce capabilities, and the open pursuit of such capabilities since 1974, has considerably raised Soviet suspicions, especially because it initially accompanied the failure in the latter half of the 1970s to reach a SALT agreement based on the Vladivostok accords.

The change of US policy on counterforce also illustrates a hazard of 'the SALT dialogue'. In the course of the SALT I discussions, the Soviet delegation evinced concern over apparent US programs for improving the accuracy of missiles to the extent of giving them counterforce capabilities. In accordance with authoritatively stated US policy at that time, the US delegation vigorously argued that it was *not* US policy to seek such accuracies, which would be destabilizing, and cited a publicly released letter from President Nixon to Senator Brooke which stated that the USA would *not* develop such capabilities. In 1974, Nixon reversed this policy, and programs were announced and pursued to attain the very capabilities previously denounced as destabilizing.

The deferral from further Senate consideration of the SALT II treaty by President Carter in January 1980 following the Soviet occupation of Afghanistan, and indeed the uncertain prospects for ratification of the treaty even prior to that development, raised a question as to whether the strategic arms limitation effort could proceed on the basis of the SALT II treaty. The advent of the Reagan Administration, and its decision not to ratify the treaty, makes the future of SALT even more uncertain. Meanwhile, the Soviet reaction to the general collapse of détente in 1980 was to reaffirm a need for détente, and for military parity and renunciation of attempts to gain superiority, but with strong attacks on US policy and alleged pursuit of superiority as major obstacles to détente. Thus, General Sidel'nikov in 1980 described 'President Carter's indefinite postponement of the examination of the SALT II Treaty in the Senate', and a series of US military actions, as 'being used by imperialist aggressive forces for the purpose of strengthening their military might and for achieving military superiority over the Soviet Union and its allies'. In the new climate, he went on to say that 'the fact that the United States and other states of the NATO bloc, despite their international commitments, have set on the course of achieving military superiority has never been doubted'. He cited in particular as 'further evidence' the NATO decision on deploying new theater nuclear systems and the five-year US military program of increasing expenditures. Numerous other commentaries have noted these and other recent developments, in addition to those cited in the late 1970s (the mark 12A warhead for Minuteman III, the MX, the Trident I and especially II, the cruise missiles) as indications that the USA is seeking to upset parity and reacquire military superiority. Some of these protestations may be inflated for propaganda effect, but it is highly likely that even before the collapse of the SALT II treaty, and with their own military programs set in train in the late 1970s, Soviet military men have been concerned over whether the USA could gain an advantage. One line of argument has focused on the development of superiority through qualitative advances. As Colonel Semeyko has put it:

> The correlation of strategic forces is very sensitive to disruption. There could be an equal number of means of delivering strategic nuclear weapons, but if one side insured superiority for itself in all or nearly all of the most important characteristics of these weapons, it would possess superiority.[73]

Semeyko himself, after the signing of the SALT II treaty, continued to argue that differences cancel out and form a rough strategic balance. He noted that this is often not recognized in the USA: 'for example, if the Soviet Union has more heavy missiles, then that is bad, it is a threat, but if the United States has more heavy bombers, then it is said to be of small significance.[74] Marshal Ogarkov is more blunt on depiction of the military balance in the USA. He writes:

> An analysis of such 'computations' shows that those who compile them either manipulate the data without any conscience, or simply dream it up. Certain American figures who know the state of the strategic offensive weapons of the sides deliberately and crudely distort the true balance of forces between the USSR and the United States.[75]

Soviet suspicions may sometimes be fed by 'mirror image' application of their own doctrines. Thus, General Simonyan, after listing the US strategic military programs they see as threatening the balance, and citing authoritative US sources on seeking a counterforce capability, observes:

> Indeed, a power which sets itself the aim of destroying the 'potential enemy's' [strategic] military facilities *must* [sic] be the first to deliver a strike, *because otherwise its nuclear charges will land on empty missile launch silos and airfields.*[76] (emphasis added)

Soviet launch on warning doctrine, documented earlier from *Military Thought*, thus, leads Soviet military men to infer from US open pursuit of counterforce capabilities a US first-strike intention, or at least to see in US doctrine 'confirmation' of a suspicion as to our intentions!

The process of 'hedging' on parity by seeking a margin of insurance is occasionally recognized by Soviet commentators, but without much sympathy and without admitting that it affects their own defense programming. Indeed, it is usually dismissed as a US pretext for seeking superiority. For example, one commentator speaks of:

> the concept of the need for so-called 'redundancy,' the quantitative and qualitative superiority of the US strategic forces 'as a counter to an unexpected Soviet threat' ... and only then to engage in talks with Moscow on arms limitations ... In fact, they fear not imaginary dangers of 'Soviet superiority' but precisely equality and parity, hoping to gain military superiority through new spurts in the arms race.[77]

Soviet commentators, in alleging a US quest for military superiority, also frequently affirm that the USSR will not permit the USA to attain such superiority.[78]

One additional aspect of the strains on prospects for strategic arms limitation, even if SALT II had eventually been ratified, is the problem caused by European theater nuclear forces (TNF). While the NATO decision of December 1979 to deploy 572 US Pershing II medium-range ballistic missiles (MRBMs) and cruise missiles (GLCMs) was seen in NATO as a move not only appropriate, but required to match growing Soviet theater nuclear capabilities (especially the SS-20), the Soviet objection that this new capability to strike targets deep in the USSR circumvents the equal SALT II limits on US-Soviet strategic weapons is not merely propaganda; it reflects a real perception and concern. We shall cite but one comment, from General of the Army Sergei F. Akhromeyev, First Deputy Chief of the General Staff:

> The Soviet Union is not setting for itself the task of striving for military superiority over the United States, but it cannot remain indifferent to the increase in US military potential and cannot permit the existing parity of forces to be upset.[79]

He notes that the Pershing II and theater cruise missiles will have ranges of 2,600 km and will be deployed so as to make it possible 'to destroy targets over a considerable part of Soviet territory – up to the Volga . . . The Soviet Union must regard them as weapons of strategic significance'. Finally, 'Such actions automatically call for reflection as to whether they accord with the aims of the negotiations and agreements on limiting strategic offensive arms'.[80]

A Soviet journal commented on US defense decisions in 1978–9 that 'A whole series of steps announced by the White House, which were presented as a kind of 'payment' for ratification of the SALT II Treaty, in effect meant the circumvention of its provisions'. It noted that 'all these measures were taken by the USA long before the events in Afghanistan. President Carter's decision (in January 1980) to suspend the treaty ratification process is only one link in a long chain of undercutting actions'.[81] More generally, Brezhnev personally commented after the US deferral of Senate consideration of SALT II, 'We cannot regard the American Administration's actions other than as an ill-considered attempt to use the events in Afghanistan to block international efforts to lessen the military danger, strengthen peace, and limit the arms race'.[82] The official Soviet reply to the 'Carter doctrine' proclaimed in January 1980 described it as 'clearly revealing Washington's course directed at overthrowing the existing approximate balance of forces between the USSR and the United States and at achieving American military superiority'.[83] In this connection it cited the President's statement that the USA should be prepared to pay any price that may be required to remain 'the strongest country in the world'. Several Soviet leaders referred in their Supreme Soviet 'election speeches' in February 1980 to the alleged US objective of upsetting the existing parity and balance of military power between the USA and the USSR in an attempt to gain military superiority (as Gromyko put it). And the then Prime Minister Kosygin pledged that: 'No one must be left in any doubt that the Soviet Union will not allow any disruption of the balance of forces which has come about in the world to the detriment of its security'.[84]

Many Soviet commentators have also referred to the alleged US attempt 'to destabilize global strategic parity in its own favor', and failure to recognize 'an axiom of contemporary international relations: security in the age of nuclear parity is based on stability, and stability is based on the mutual acknowledgement of equality and on abandoning the aspiration for superiority'.[85]

We do not need to accept at face value Soviet protestation of innocence on their own part for their share of responsibility for the arms race and deterioration of détente, nor their accusations of US culpability, in order to recognize that the Soviet *perception* of developments may indeed differ significantly from our own. Undoubtedly, there are now stronger pressures to ensure by unilateral Soviet military programs that the USA does not upset parity and achieve military superiority. The prospects for renewed strategic arms limitation (as of this writing, in early 1980) are dim. None the less, the Soviet acceptance of parity and mutual deterrence, renunciation of the goal of superiority, and professed support of negotiated strategic arms limitation, are now clearer than they were a decade ago. Problems in negotiation are formidable, as the SALT experience of the 1970s has shown. The continued and, indeed, intensified efforts of both sides to rely more upon unilateral military programs than on negotiated constraints to secure deterrence compounds the difficulty, as does the inexorable march of military technology. But a start has been made, and the opportunity to continue the effort at negotiated strategic arms limitation, if at present eclipsed, is not foreclosed. Maintaining mutual deterrence is not easy, even if mutual deterrence is recognized as preferable to the attainable alternatives; and negotiating agreed restraints is, while the best way to support it, also the most difficult.

Conclusion

A number of US commentators have argued that the Soviets, and in particular the Soviet military, reject mutual deterrence, and sometimes they have then questioned the basis for possible strategic arms limitation. These writers were not sufficiently aware of the record. It has sometimes been alleged that Soviet statements on such propositions as mutual deterrence and the unacceptability of general nuclear war are 'for export', and they are constrasted with selected open Soviet military discussions. The evidence from such sources as the confidential USSR Ministry of Defense organ *Military Thought* dispels such erroneous conclusions.

The record indicates that the Soviet political and military leadership accepts a strategic nuclear balance and parity between the USSR and the USA as a fact, and as the probable and desirable prospect for the foreseeable future. They are pursuing extensive military programs to ensure that they do not fail to maintain their side of the balance, which they see as in some jeopardy given US programs. They seek to stabilize and to maintain mutual deterrence.

In Marxist-Leninist eyes, military power is not and should not be the driving element in world politics. With 'imperialist' military power held in check, the decisive social-economic forces of history would determine the future of the world. In their view, the USA came to accept mutual deterrence, and some strategic arms limitations, not because it is our preference, but because we had no alternative given the general world 'correlation of forces', and Soviet military power in particular. Now they fear that the US thinks that it can regain superiority and that it is unprepared to accept parity.

Strategic arms limitation achieved one signal concrete success in the SALT I ABM treaty. The SALT II treaty, if ratified, would have helped to constrain and to delimit the strategic arms competition; but if it had gone into effect or if some of its provisions are tacitly accepted, the remaining non-limited opportunities for major new arms programs are great. The absence of success to date in limiting effectively strategic offensive arms has thus been seen in Moscow as requiring continuing unilateral efforts, even strenuous ones, to prevent our upsetting the strategic nuclear balance.

Much of what has been said in the preceding paragraphs could easily be turned around to describe US views of the situation. This is not owing to any careless resort to a 'mirror image'. There are, in fact, a number of parallel perceptions – and misperceptions – held by both sides. Despite greatly differing ultimate national goals, the principal problems in strategic arms control are *not* due to differing operative aims of the two sides, but to differing perceptions, to mutual suspicions, and to the difficulties of gearing very different military forces and programs into balanced and mutually acceptable strategic arms limitations. To illuminate Soviet thinking on this matter, is one step to understanding the problem and to finding its solution.

Notes: Chapter 5

1 See Raymond L. Garthoff, *Soviet Military Doctrine* (Glencoe, Il.: Free Press, 1953), pp. 9–19, 51–7.
2 In fact, this view began to be developed by some Soviet leaders even before Stalin's death, and was prematurely (in political terms) stated by Malenkov in 1954. See Raymond L. Garthoff, 'The death of Stalin and the birth of mutual deterrence', *Survey*, no. 111, 1980.
3 Boris Dmitriyev, 'Brass hats: Peking and Clausewitz', *Izvestia (News)*, 25 September, 1963. ('Boris Dmitriyev' is the pen-name of a Soviet diplomat and scholar specializing in American political-military affairs.)
4 For example, Marshal Sergei S. Biryuzov (then Chief of the General Staff), 'Politics and nuclear weapons', *Izvestia*, 11 December, 1963.
5 For example, Major General N. Sushko and Major T. Kondratkov, 'War and politics in the "nuclear age"', *Kommunist vooruzhennykh sil (Communist of the Armed Forces)*, no. 2, January, 1964, pp. 14–23. (Kondratkov, as a colonel, was to return to this theme in the late 1960s and 1970s.)
6 Major General N. A. Talensky, 'The late war: some reflections', *Mezhdunarodnaya zhizn (International Affairs)*, no. 5, May, 1965, p. 23.
7 Lt Colonel Ye. I. Rybkin, 'On the nature of nuclear missile war', *Kommunist vooruzhennykh sil*, no. 17, September, 1965; Colonel I. Sidel'nikov, 'V. I. Lenin on the class approach in determining the nature of wars', *Krasnaya zvezda (Red Star)*, 22 September, 1965; Colonel I. Grudinin, 'On the question of the essense of war', *Krasnaya zvezda*, 12 July, 1966; and Editorial, 'Theory, politics, and ideology: on the essense of war', *Krasnaya zvezda*, 24 January, 1967.
8 See the discussion in Raymond L. Garthoff, 'Mutual deterrence and strategic arms limitation in Soviet policy', *International Security*, vol. 3, no. 1, Summer, 1978, pp. 117–21.
9 In particular, Aleksandr Bovin, Georgy Arbatov and Veniamin Dolgin; see A. I. Krylov, 'October and the strategy of peace', *Voprosy filosofii (Problems of Philosophy)*, no. 3, March, 1968; G. A. Arbatov, 'The stalemate of the policy of force', *Problemy mira i sotsializma (Problems of Peace and Socialism)*, no. 2, February, 1974, and 'Soviet-American relations in a new stage', *Pravda*, 22 July, 1973; A. Bovin, Internationalism, and coexistence', *Novoye vremya (New Times)*, no. 30, July, 1973, and 'Peace and social progress', *Izvestia*, 11 July, 1973 (only in the first edition, substituting a *different* article, also by Bovin, in later editions!), and 'Socialist, class politics', *Molodoi kommunist (The Young Communist)*, no. 4, April, 1974; and V. G. Dolgin, 'Peaceful coexistence and the factors contributing to its deepening and development', *Voprosy filosofii*, no. 1, January, 1974. There have been many others, usually with the discussion not developed so fully as in these articles.
10 For example, see Major General K. Bochkarev, 'The question of the sociological aspect of the struggle against the forces of aggression and war', *Voyennaya mysl' (Military Thought)*, no. 9, September, 1968, pp. 3–16; Bochkarev, 'Nuclear arms and the fate of social progress', *Sovetskaya Kirgiziya (Soviet Kirgizia)*, 25 August, 1970; Major General A. Milovidov, 'A philosophical analysis of military thought', *Krasnaya zvezda (Red Star)*, 17 May, 1973; Colonel I. Sidel'nikov, 'Peaceful coexistence and the

people's security', *Krasnaya zvezda*, 14 August 1973; Colonel Ye. Rybkin, 'The Leninist conception of nuclear war and the present day', *Kommunist vooruzhennykh sil (Communist of the Armed Forces)*, no. 20, October, 1973; Rear Admiral V. Shelyag, 'Two world outlooks – two views on war', *Krasnaya zvezda*, 7 February, 1974; and Colonel T. Kondratkov, 'War as a continuation of policy', *Soviet Military Review*, no. 2, February, 1974.

11 G. A. Trofimenko, *SShA : Politika, voina, ideologiya (The USA: Politics, War and Ideology)* (Moscow: Mysl', 1976), pp. 292–3.

12 See also Colonel T. R. Kondratkov, 'Social-philosophical aspects of problems of war and peace', *Voprosy filosofii*, no. 4, April, 1975.

13 Marshal V. D. Sokolovsky (ed.), *Voyennaya strategiya (Military Strategy)* (Moscow: Voenizdat, 1962), pp. 74–5.

14 ibid, 2nd edition, 1963, p. 244.

15 ibid, 3rd edition, 1968, p. 239.

16 Aleksandr Bovin,'Détente: results of the 1970s' *Radio Moscow*, Domestic Service, 25 December, 1979.

17 Major General I. Sidel'nikov, 'Who needs military superiority and why', *Krasnaya zvezda*, 15 January, 1980.

18 Richard Pipes, 'Why the Soviet Union thinks it could fight and win a nuclear war', *Commentary*, July, 1977, p. 34.

19 For a very thorough review of Soviet sources and excellent discussion of the questions of nuclear war as an instrument of policy, and views on the consequences of nuclear war and 'victory', see Robert L. Arnett's unpublished doctoral dissertation 'Soviet attitudes toward nuclear war survival (1962–1977): has there been a change?' (Ohio State University, 1979), with key findings given in his articles 'Soviet views on nuclear war', in *Arms Control Today*, October, 1978, pp. 1–5, and 'Soviet attitudes towards nuclear war: do they really think they can win?', *Journal of Strategic Studies*, London, vol. 2, no. 2, September, 1979, pp. 172–91.

20 L. I. Brezhnev in *Materialy XXIV s'yezda KPSS (Materials of the Twenty-Fourth Congress of the CPSU)* (Moscow: Politizdat, 1971), p. 81, and see A. N. Kosygin, p. 186.

21 See Raymond L. Garthoff, 'SALT I: an evaluation', *World Politics*, October, 1978.

22 By happenstance, the initial Soviet statement can be cited, as it was the only one not stamped '*Sekretno*'; from that time on, copies of formal statements exchanged between the delegations were marked 'Secret' ('*Sekretno*'). (This, incidentally, escalated the level of shared 'security classification'; previous to SALT, exchanged US and Soviet messages or papers were normally marked 'Confidential', when specifically marked at all.)

23 For an example that coincided closely with the first Soviet response to the US proposal for SALT, see 'Theory, politics, and ideology: on the essence of war', *Krasnaya zvezda*, 24 January, 1967.

24 Marshal N. I. Krylov, 'The nuclear missile shield of the Soviet state', *Voyennaya mysl'*, no. 11, November, 1967, p. 20.

25 Major General N. Vasendin and Colonel N. Kuznetsov, 'Contemporary war and surprise', *Voyennaya mysl'*, no. 6, June, 1968, p. 42.

26 General of the Army S. P. Ivanov, 'Soviet military doctrine and strategy', *Voyennaya mysl'*, no. 5, May, 1969, p. 47.

27 Major General V. I. Zemskov, 'Wars of the contemporary era', *Voyennaya mysl'*, no. 5, May, 1969, p. 57.

28 ibid., p. 59; emphasis added.

29 Marshal Krylov, 'The nuclear missile shield', op. cit., p. 20; Krylov also indicated a 'fallback' reliance on hardening of missile launchers, 'even in the most unfavorable circumstances, if a portion of missiles is unable to be launched before the strike by the missiles of the aggressor'.

30 Secretary of Defense Harold Brown, each year since 1978, has been much more ambiguous in Congressional testimony as to conditions under which the USA might or might not launch its ICBMs before Soviet missiles struck ICBM silos in the US. See George C. Wilson, 'Brown cautious on response to attack', *Washington Post*, 24 October, 1977; and Brown's speech on 23 June, 1978, stating: 'The Soviets would have to consider the possibility that our Minuteman missiles would no longer be in their silos

when their ICBMs arrived. We have not adopted a doctrine of launch under attack but they surely would have to take such a possibility into consideration.' And see *Report of the Secretary of Defense Harold Brown to the Congress on the FY 1980 Budget*, 25 January, 1979, p. 15; and *Report of the Secretary of Defense Harold Brown to the Congress on the FY 1981 Budget*, 29 January, 1980, p. 86.

31 This comment is the one referred to somewhat inaccurately by John Newhouse, in *Cold Dawn: The Story of SALT* (New York: Holt, Rinehart & Winston, 1973), p. 192, and often cited. It did not refer to 'military hardware', but to military operational concepts, and Ogarkov did not refer to excluding *his* civilian colleagues, as this passage in the Newhouse account suggests.

32 See Raymond L. Garthoff, *Soviet Strategy in the Nuclear Age* (New York:Praeger, 1958), pp. 84–7.

33 Anatoly A. Gromyko, 'American theoreticians between "total war" and peace', *Voyennaya mysl*, no. 4, April, 1969, pp. 86–92.

34 See Raymond L. Garthoff, 'SALT and the Soviet military', *Problems of Communism*, January–February, 1975, pp. 21–37.

35 See Raymond L. Garthoff, 'Negotiating with the Russians: some lessons from SALT', *International Security*, vol. 1, no. 4, Spring, 1977, p. 17.

36 Major General M. I. Cherednichenko, 'Military strategy and military technology', *Voyennaya mysl*, no. 4, April, 1973, p. 42.

37 L. I. Brezhnev, 'In the name of peace and happiness for Soviet people', *Pravda*, 14 June, 1975. See also Brezhnev, *Pravda*, 22 July, 1974, and *Pravda*, 25 November, 1976.

38 L. I. Brezhnev, 'Outstanding exploit of the defenders of Tula', *Radio Moscow*, 18 January, 1977; and in *Pravda* and *Izvestia*, 19 January, 1977.

39 G. A. Arbatov, 'The great lie of the opponents of détente', *Pravda*, 5 February, 1977; Arbatov repeated this point in a broadcast interview on *Radio Moscow* on 12 February, 1977.

40 L. I. Brezhnev, 'The Great October Revolution and the progress of mankind', *Radio Moscow* (live), 2 November, 1977; also in *Pravda* and *Izvestia*, 3 November, 1977.

41 Marshal Viktor A. Kulikov, 'Sixty years on guard over the achievements of the October Revolution', *Partiinaya zhizn (Party Life)*, no. 3, February, 1978, p. 28.

42 TASS, 'Who sets the tone?', *Krasnaya zvezda*, 12 January, 1977, and Yury Kornilov, 'Myths and facts', *Krasnaya zvezda*, 14 January, 1977.

43 Colonel Ye. Rybkin, 'The 25th Congress of the CPSU and the problem of peaceful coexistence between socialism and capitalism', *Voyenno-istoricheskii zhurnal*, no. 1, January, 1977, p. 5 ff.

44 ibid., p. 8.

45 ibid., p. 8 (the original Brezhnev statement is in *Pravda*, 22 July,1974).

46 L. I. Brezhnev, *Radio Moscow* (TASS), 24 November, 1976.

47 To cite but a few: Marshal N. Ogarkov, *Pravda*, 2 August, 1979; Marshal D. Ustinov, *Pravda*, 25 October, 1979; Ogarkov, *Partiinaya zhizn'*, no. 2, February, 1979, p. 27; and Lt General (ret.) M. Mil'shtein, *SShA*, no. 10, October, 1978, p. 10.

48 *Vienna Summit, June 15-18, 1979* (Washington, DC: US Department of State, Selected Documents No. 13, 1979), p. 7.

49 General Sidel'nikov, *Krasnaya zvezda*, 15 January, 1980; see also V. Kuznetsov, *Novoye vremya*, no. 37, 7 September, 1979, p. 31, for a similar statement.

50 Major General R. Simonyan, 'Disarmament – demand of the times: concerning the risk of confrontation', *Pravda*, 14 June, 1977.

51 ibid.

52 Editorial, 'Vigilance must be raised higher!', *Krasnaya zvezda*, 22 June, 1977.

53 V. Larin, 'A topical proposal', *Pravda*, 27 October, 1976; see also A. Bovin, *Radio Moscow*, 19 June, 1979; B. Andrianov and V. Nekrasov, *Radio Moscow*, 18 June, 1979; G. Shakhnazarov, 'The arms race is a danger to the peoples', *Krasnaya zvezda*, 14 June, 1979; and Dr (Colonel) V. Kulish, 'A balance of trust and not a balance of terror', *Novoye vremya*, no. 22, May, 1979, pp. 4–6.

54 Yu. Nilov, 'The time has come to call a halt', *Novoye vremya*, no. 23, June, 1977, p. 6.

55 L. I. Brezhnev, *Radio Moscow*, 2 November, 1977; *Pravda* and *Izvestia*, 3 November, 1977; this passage was omitted in the speech as delivered live on Radio Moscow, but

was included in subsequent broadcasts in translation and in all printed versions of the speech.

56 Lt General M. A. Mil'shtein and Colonel L. S. Semeyko, 'The problem of the inadmissibility of a nuclear conflict (on new approaches in the United States)', *SShA*, no. 11, November, 1974, p. 4.
57 ibid., p. 9; see also Colonel D. Proektor, 'Two approaches to military policy', *Novoye vremya*, no. 48, November, 1978.
58 ibid., pp. 10–12.
59 G. A. Trofimenko, 'US foreign policy in the seventies: words and deeds', *SShA*, no. 12, December, 1976, pp. 15, 19.
60 ibid., p. 27.
61 L. I. Brezhnev, *Radio Moscow*, 29 May, 1977.
62 G. A. Trofimenko, *SShA: Politika, voina, ideologiya*, p. 324.
63 L. I. Brezhnev, *Leninskim kursom (The Leninist Course)*, Vol. 3 (Moscow: Politizdat, 1970), p. 541.
64 Zemskov, 'Wars of the contemporary era', p. 59.
65 Trofimenko, *SShA: Politika, voina, ideologiya*, pp. 317, 318.
66 ibid., pp. 324–5.
67 The quotation is from General of the Army Viktor G. Kulikov, cited in *Izvestia*, 24 August, 1972; a similar statement by Marshal Andrei A. Grechko appears in *Pravda*, 30 September, 1972.
68 Bovin, *Radio Moscow*, 19 June, 1979.
69 Zemskov, 'Wars of the contemporary era', p. 59.
70 Colonel V. M. Kulish, in *Voyennaya sila i mezhdunarodnye otnosheniya (Military Force and International Relations)* (Moscow: IMO, 1972), p. 226.
71 Trofimenko, *SShA: Politika, voina, ideologiya*, p. 319.
72 Major General I. Sidel'nikov, *Krasnaya zvezda*, 15 January, 1980.
73 Colonel L. Semeyko, 'Imperialism's strategic concepts: the course toward military superiority', *Krasnaya zvezda*, 24 March, 1979.
74 Colonel L. Semeyko, on the 'International Observers Roundtable', on *Radio Moscow*, Domestic Service, 5 August, 1979.
75 Marshal N. Ogarkov, 'The myth about the "Soviet military threat" and reality', *Pravda*, 2 August, 1979.
76 Major General (Dr of Military Science) R. Simonyan, 'In search of a new strategy', *Krasnaya zvezda*, 19 March, 1979.
77 V. Nekrasov, 'An absurd but dangerous myth', *Kommunist*, no. 12, August, 1979, p. 98.
78 Colonel L. Semeyko, *Krasnaya zvezda*, 24 March, 1979; see also Major General I. Sidel'nikov, *Krasnaya zvezda*, 15 January, 1980, and Marshal D. Ustinov, *Pravda*, 25 October, 1979.
79 General of the Army Sergei F. Akhromeyev, 'Dangerous US aspirations to nuclear supremacy', *Horizont* (East Germany), no. 3, January, 1980, p. 3, based on a *Novosti* interview originally issued 24 December, 1979, in Moscow.
80 ibid.; see also G. Dadyants, 'Operation Pershing II,' *Sotsialisticheskaya industriya*, 19 October, 1979; Lt General N. F. Chervov and V. Zagladin, on *Radio Moscow*, Domestic Service, 20 October, 1979; and Colonel L. Semeyko, 'Where "Eurostrategy" is aiming', *Krasnaya zvezda*, 28 October, 1979.
81 Editorial, 'Invariability of a principled course', *Za rubezhom*, no. 4, 17 January, 1980, p. 1.
82 L. I. Brezhnev, 'Replies to questions of a *Pravda* correspondent', *Pravda*, 13 January, 1980.
83 Editorial, 'On the US President's State of the Union message', *Pravda*, 29 January, 1980.
84 Andrei Gromyko, address (recorded), *Radio Moscow*, Domestic Service, 18 February, 1980; and Aleksei Kosygin, address (live), *Radio Moscow*, Domestic Service, 21 February, 1980; see also Mikhail Suslov, résumé of 20 February speech, *Radio Moscow*, Domestic Service, 20 February, 1980, for another reference to an alleged attempt to upset approximate parity and attain superiority.
85 Vladimir B. Lomeyko, 'International observers roundtable', *Radio Moscow*, Domestic Service, 10 February, 1980.

6

Soviet Naval Doctrine and Strategy

MICHAEL McGWIRE

The Soviet navy has become a significant factor in the debate
about intentions, détente and arms limitations, because its submarines carry a large part of the Soviet missile inventory, and
because of the navy's involvement in trouble spots around the
world. The West has encouraged this Soviet emphasis on sea-
based strategic strike systems but is deeply suspicious of the naval
activism, claiming that there is no legitimate requirement for the
USSR, a land power, to deploy such forces.

The Soviets acknowledge the asymmetry of interests when they
stress that the major change in the international situation after
World War II was that Russia's potential opponents were the
'traditional maritime powers'. On the other hand, they reject the
idea that because the USSR is primarily a land power, it does not
have important maritime interests, both purposive and preventive. The West, however, has found it hard to perceive the naval
requirements which flow from the USSR's geopolitical circumstances, or to comprehend the measures it has adopted to meet
these requirements. As long as the Soviet navy remained tied to
home waters and offered no direct threat to North America, this
lack of comprehension was not serious. But now that the Soviet
navy has become a factor in our diplomatic calculations, it is
necessary to appreciate what motivates these developments, and
to understand the different types of political commitment that
underlie various aspects of Soviet naval policy.

One way of achieving this is to review Soviet naval developments since World War II, tracing the evolution of policy as it
responded to changing perceptions of threat, technological innovations and shifts in national priorities.[1] But the Soviet navy is
also important as a case study that illuminates the wider debate
about the USSR's military posture and its willingness to wage
nuclear war. I have therefore approached this subject through a

discussion of Soviet naval doctrine, a term I use in its broad Western sense, which is closer in meaning to the Soviet term 'military (or naval) art'.[2]

The evidence for such doctrine comes from what the Soviets say and write, from how they deploy, operate and exercise their forces, and from the number and characteristics of their ships, submarines and aircraft. Taken together, these data provide a reasonable body of evidence, particularly when public pronouncements can be evaluated against the more concrete types of data, although the quality of understanding will always depend on the depth of hindsight. Warship building programs are particularly important in this context, since procurement decisions can often be dated with some confidence and ship characteristics give a fair idea of the then-prevailing force requirements and operational concepts.[3]

Background Factors

Doctrine is the product of an evolutionary process, and it is relevant that for the last 200 years or so the Russian navy has generally been the third or fourth largest in the world although its effectiveness has fluctuated widely. Russia used naval forces in the eighteenth century to gain control of her Baltic and Black Sea coasts, and four times between 1768 and 1827 she deployed sizable squadrons to the Mediterranean for a year or more. For three of these deployments, during the third, fifth and sixth wars with Turkey, ships were drawn from the Baltic Fleet and were used in operations against the southern side of the Black Sea exits.

Increasingly thereafter, Russia found herself confronting predominantly maritime powers. In the Black Sea, Britain used her naval strength to prevent or reverse Russian gains at the expense of the failing Ottoman Empire; Britain intervened directly in the seventh Turkish War (1853–6, Crimea) and the peace treaty forbade Russia a Black Sea Fleet; in the eighth Turkish war (1876–7), British pressure ensured that Russia would not gain control of the Straits. In the Far East, Russo-Japanese rivalry culminated in a disastrous war and the loss of two Russian fleets. In 1918, the Western navies provided vital support to the forces of counter-revolution. As a consequence, Russia's naval policy was increasingly dominated by the requirement to defend four widely separated fleet areas against maritime powers who could concentrate their forces at will.

It is, therefore, wrong to suggest that Russia has only

recently awoken to the significance of sea power. She used it in the past to her own advantage, and has more often seen its long arm used against her. Over the years she committed very substantial resources to naval construction, and the major warship building program which was initiated in 1945 was the fourth attempt in sixty-five years to build up a strong Russian fleet. But national strategy involves setting priorities and balancing competing claims for scarce resources. Russia was predominantly a land power; the only threats to her territorial existence had come by land; the army was the basis of security at home and influence abroad. Naval forces were, indeed, required to defend against assault from the sea and to counter the capability of maritime powers to dictate the outcome of events in areas adjacent to Russia. But these forces were seen as an expensive necessity rather than a preferred instrument of policy.

This ordering of priorities and the army's domination of military thought largely persist today,[4] and are enshrined in the concept of a combined arms approach to military problems. This bias was, if anything, accentuated by the reorganization of the armed forces into five branches. It is characterized by the fact that out of twenty Full Members on the Central Committee, fifteen come from the Ground Forces,[5] and that (until very recently) the naval share of the Soviet defense budget is estimated to be only 18 percent, and this includes the cost of the ballistic missile submarine force.

Certain tendencies in Russian naval doctrine can probably be ascribed to this persistent state of affairs. Limited resources and the relative imbalance of naval power have encouraged a spirit of technical and conceptual innovation, and a readiness to adopt new but unproven technological advances. This is exemplified by the destruction of the Turkish Fleet at Sinope using highly explosive shells in 1853, the daring use of torpedo boats in the eighth Turkish war in 1877, the very early emphasis on submarines, and in the mid-1950s, the application of cruise missiles to maritime platforms. Usually starting from behind in terms of conventional capabilities, and with little chance of overhauling from astern, the naval leadership has frequently sought to get ahead by taking a different (and unexpected) tack.

This tendency to innovate was reinforced by the post-revolutionary emphasis on original, 'proletarian' solutions to strategic problems, and by the more enduring ideological commitment to 'scientific objectivity'. Current writing stresses the need to assess naval requirements from first principles, and the fallacy of mirroring an opponent's capability. However, innovations are not always successful. And during the last twenty years this combination of restricted resources, a faith in objective assessment and a belief in innovation has sometimes led to the development of task- and scenario-specific capabilities which have lacked the flexibility to cope with changes in the nature of the threat. The mid-1950s decision to place primary reliance on long-range cruise missiles (which had yet to be developed), carried by surface ship and diesel submarine, had just that result. It is also an example of the army-oriented political leadership taking decisions against specific naval advice. Kuznetsov's objections to this ill-founded concept cost him his job as Commander in Chief of the Navy. Gorshkov, at 45, was brought in to implement the new policy

But it should not be assumed that the effect of this land forces orientation has been, or is, all bad. It can, of course, be argued that it has led to the hobbling of naval forces by army commanders, from the scuttling of the fleet before Sevastopol in 1854, to operations in the Baltic and Black Sea during World War II. But several of these examples lose their force when analyzed in terms of relative capabilities and practical objectives, rather than classical naval theory. It is also true that army dominance encouraged the centralization of command and a rather rigid approach to battle planning. But 'unified command' is now the fashion, and modern warfare demands close command and control. It so happens that Russia's traditional centralized command structure is well suited to contemporary requirements, in principle, if not always in practice. Its deficiencies lie more in its style of operation than its organizational structure.

A good case can be made that the emphasis on a 'combined arms' approach and the existence of an army-oriented political leadership did, in fact, have an invigorating effect on the development of Soviet naval doctrine, not least by saving it from the fallacy that naval strategy was a universal science, whose rules have been discovered by Colomb, Corbett and Mahan. A pragmatic approach, combined with strictly limited resources, introduced a healthy realism to naval planning and, for example, encouraged the emergence of the 'small war' doctrine in the early 1930s, based on the limited types of warship that could then be built. More pertinently, when it did become possible to plan for capital ship construction at the end of the 1930s, Stalin refused Kuznetsov's request for carriers, on the ground that the Red Fleet would not be operating off distant shores. Naval procurement was to be tailored to Russia's particular requirements, and not to some idealized perception of what 'a navy' should be.

The army-oriented leadership has required the navy to undertake tasks which have violated its traditional assumptions about naval operations, and forced the development of radical concepts. A particular example was the shift to forward deployment in the early 1960s, whereby ill-armed Soviet naval units were required to maintain close company with US forces in the Mediterranean, an area where the West enjoyed overwhelming maritime preponderance. This idea of relying on 'the protection of peace' to safeguard such exposed deployments was a daring concept, given the general tenor of the Western strategic debate at that time. The decision to ignore the survivability of such units and exploit the characteristics of nuclear-missile war was a major departure from traditional naval thought.

More specifically, ground force thinking can be seen in the concept of close-shadowing Sixth Fleet carriers with a gun-armed destroyer. In artillery terms, that unit was acting as a forward observation post, and in the event of war would call down fire from medium- or intermediate-range ballistic missiles emplaced in southwest Russia.[6] A similar concept was spelled out in Grechko's statement in December 1972, that the wartime mission of the strategic rocket forces (SRF) included the destruction of 'enemy means of nuclear attack, and troops and naval groupings in theaters of military operation on land and sea',[7] although by now, target data would be provided by satellite surveillance systems.

On balance, the injection of army concepts, the emphasis on combined arms, and the common development of weapon systems like missiles and aircraft have been fruitful in terms of capabilities and doctrine. Even when a new idea was initially unsuccessful, as was the long-range surface-to-surface missile (SSM), it often served the purpose of breaking with traditional concepts and opening new avenues for development. It is true that the leadership's perception of the navy as an expensive necessity has often led to the definition of naval requirements in narrow terms of countering specific threats, instead of more general capabilities, and that this has restricted the navy's flexibility. On the other hand, the sheer preponderance of ground force opinion engenders clearly defined priorities and a readiness to apply the resources of all relevant branches of the armed forces to meet any serious threat, including those that come from the sea.

Contingency Planning and the Reality of World War

Soviet military doctrine has evolved in response to what have been seen as a series of direct threats to the state's existence. The Soviet leadership has always taken the likelihood of war very seriously, and more importantly, it has been prepared to think through the implications and to take the measures necessary to secure ultimate victory should war come. This was demonstrated by the industrial relocation policies of the 1930s, and by the contingency plans for physically removing industrial plants from the path of the German advance, measures which between them enabled the post-invasion build-up of Soviet military strength. This same approach persists today, and Soviet military doctrine can only be understood within the context of contingency planning for worst-case situations.

The readiness to think through the implications of the nuclear arms race does not imply that the USSR would willingly embark on general nuclear war with the West. Very much the reverse. Marxist-Leninist theory asserts that the initiation[8] of war as a deliberate act of policy can only be justified if (1) the USSR is virtually certain of winning, and (2) the gains clearly outweigh the cost.[9] War with the West meets neither of these criteria. Communist theory and Soviet national interests coincide in this matter, and it is widely accepted by students of the USSR that the prevention and avoidance of world war is a prime objective of Soviet foreign policy. In fact, Malenkov and Khrushchev both expressed the opinion that there could be no winners in nuclear war, and at different times they both advocated some form of deterrence policy, as a means of reducing expenditure on defense. Neither of them was successful because the security-conscious collective leadership was unwilling to base the defense of the homeland on an unproven theoretical construct.

In his book *Military Strategy*, Sokolovskij did not discuss the Soviet strategic delivery capability in terms of 'deterrent forces', but in terms of war-fighting. He states that

> strategic operation of a future nuclear war will comprise the co-ordinated operation of the branches of the armed forces, and will be conducted according to a common concept or plan ... The main forces of such an operation will be strategic nuclear weapons.[10]

In discussing such nuclear missile attacks, he says that 'the basic aim of this type of operation is to undermine the military power of the enemy by eliminating the nuclear means of fighting and formations of the armed forces, and eliminating the military-economic potential by destroying the economic foundations of the war, and by disrupting governmental and military control'.[11] This is war-fighting with nuclear weapons.

Inevitably, such a war would be 'world war', which Marxist-Leninist theory defines as a fight to the finish between the socialist and capitalist systems; defeat would be synonymous with extinction, and victory with survival.[12] It is the catastrophic consequences of defeat which explains why, despite the admittedly low probability of such a war occurring, preparations to fight and win one are given such high priority within the USSR. But, for victory in such circumstances to have any meaning, it is necessary to ensure the continued existence of (1) some kind of governmental apparatus, and (2) a social and economic base on which to rebuild a socialist society. These minimum essential requirements, coupled with the concept of a fight to the finish, provide the framework for Soviet military doctrine.

On the evidence available, it seems likely that contingency plans to cover the possibility of world war provide for two equally important sets of objectives. The first set focuses on *extirpating the capitalist system*, the aims being to:

- destroy enemy forces-in-being;
- destroy the system's war-making potential;
- destroy the system's structure of governmental and social control.

The second set of objectives focuses on *preserving the socialist system*, the aims being to:

- protect the physical structure of government and secure its capacity for effective operation throughout the state;
- ensure the survival of a certain proportion of the working population and of the nation's industrial base;
- secure an alternative economic base which can contribute to the rebuilding of society.

It is clear that the measures required to destroy certain types of enemy forces-in-being will simultaneously further the second set of objectives, by limiting the enemy's capacity to wreak destruction on the Soviet homeland. Other implications of these dual sets of objectives are perhaps less obvious.

First, operations in NATO Europe. These come primarily under the second set of objectives, because of Western Europe's potential as an alternative economic base on which to help rebuild the socialist system. This has two corollaries: (1) Western Europe must be taken over,[13] and (2) battle damage must be kept to the minimum. While it will be necessary to destroy those NATO forces-in-being which can strike at Russia, and to establish effective control throughout the area, the strategy is to limit the extent of devastation through selective weapons policies, restricting military operations to essential areas, and using the diplomatic tools of bribery, blackmail and coercion to their fullest extent. The concept of operations, therefore, avoids 'meat-grinder' tactics except where essential to break through the main battle front. The emphasis is on high mobility and deep penetration, on the ability to seize and hold areas in the enemy's rear, and on the extensive use of chemical rather than explosive weapons.

Secondly, Western sea-based strategic delivery systems. When Polaris first became operational, its most vaunted characteristic was its invulnerability which (in deterrence theory) provided for an 'assured response'. But from the Soviet point of view, the more important implication of this invulnerability was that these missiles could be held back from the initial nuclear exchange, with the fair certainty that they would remain available for use at a subsequent stage of the war. So, too, could carrier-based nuclear-strike aircraft.[14] What was more, the USA appeared to be shifting its emphasis from land- to sea-based systems; to quote Gorshkov, one-third of the West's nuclear inventory was seaborne in 1966, and by 1971 the proportion would have reached one-half.[15] These developments bore directly on the USSR's strategy of using Western Europe as an alternative economic base for the rebuilding of the socialist system. If Western sea-based systems were withheld from the initial exchange, they would be available to deny the USSR this use of Europe.

Thirdly, strategic reserves. Largely ignored by nuclear deterrence theory, the requirement for strategic reserves is integral to the concept of war-fighting with nuclear weapons. No one can foretell the course of such a conflict, but Soviet strategy must assume that the availability of nuclear weapons may be critical at certain stages. It must also assume that sole possession of a substantial capability is likely to determine the final outcome of the war and the political structure of the postwar world. The West has sea-based systems which can be withheld from the initial exchange, and the USSR must at least match this capability for deferred strikes. But the Soviet requirement for strategic reserves goes beyond this basic requirement. By definition, world war is a struggle between social *systems* and the USSR's potential opponents are not limited to members of the NATO alliance, but extend throughout the world, at least to include the OECD countries and the USA's military protectorates. Although there is no direct equivalent to the targets which an occupied Europe would offer the USA,[16] Soviet strategy must allow that the conflict will become global[17] and provide against the emergence of capitalist power bases outside the NATO area.

Fourthly, China. The USSR may hope that in a fight to the finish between capitalism and socialism, China would take its side. Nevertheless, Soviet contingency planners must assume that world war may also mean war with China. If the USSR is to avoid being irrevocably committed to automatically devastating China at the outbreak of a world war[18] and thereby forfeiting the possibility of an alliance, then the nuclear weapons required to cover the contingency of war with China (or to compel its neutrality), must be of a kind that can survive nuclear strikes by the West.

And fifthly, strategic infrastructure. A world war will be fought mainly with the weapons and material that exist at the outset, and combat endurance will depend heavily on prepositioned stockpiles. Most of these need to be readily available to the main engagement zones,[19] but in view of the global scale of conflict, stockpiles are also required in distant parts of the world. One way of achieving this is to supply a client state with more arms than it can absorb;[20] another is to acquire base and storage areas overseas.[21] The strategic infrastructure includes the existence of the physical facilities which will be required to gain access to distant areas and to sustain wartime operations there. Control of such facilities is not essential prior to the outbreak of the war, and where key pieces are missing from the strategic map (ports, airfields, roads), these can be provided in peacetime under the guise of economic aid.[22] Meanwhile, the growing possibility of war with China adds another dimension to the requirement.

The Navy as a Branch of the Armed Forces

It is fair to say that since the early 1920s, the Soviet leadership has demonstrated a sustained awareness of the requirement for maritime defense. Stalin and Khrushchev both took a personal interest in naval matters, and given the geostrategic circumstances and the scale of competing priorities, the navy appears to have had at least its fair share of scarce resources. The basic procurement and strategic policies have been well founded, if not always fully successful.

Stalin recognized the need for four operationally independent fleets and established the Pacific Fleet in 1932 and the Northern

Fleet in 1933;[23] he sought to ensure their self-sufficiency by providing each with its own naval construction facilities, located at some distance from the open sea to be safe from enemy seizure. These two shipyards at Komsomol'sk, on the Amur, and Severodvinsk, on the White Sea, are now the two premier nuclear submarine building yards. He also set out to link the three Western fleets by inland waterway and established a submarine building yard at Gor'kij on the Volga, which was able to continue production throughout World War II. Curvatures on the Trans-Siberian Railway were calculated to allow the shipment of submarines (whole and in sections) to the Pacific by rail.

After the war, when the USSR was faced by the 'traditional maritime powers', the leadership responded with mass-production warship building programs to cover the threat of invasion, and the allocation of nuclear reactors to submarines intended for strategic delivery. It is true that when the threat of seaborne invasion was downgraded in 1954, there were savage cuts in conventional warship construction, but this was partly justified by the availability of long-range surface-to-surface missiles (SSM). And, when a new threat to the homeland emerged in the shape of seaborne nuclear strike systems, the leadership responded by doubling the production of nuclear submarines. Military publications acknowledge the importance of the navy's role. The 1962 edition of *Military Strategy* emphasized the great changes in maritime warfare since World War II, and stressed that in future war the navy's primary theater of operations would be the open ocean and that it must not be tied to ground force theaters of operations. Writing in 1971, Marshal Grechko noted that maritime combat was achieving a special significance and that navies could have an enormous impact on the entire course of a future war.[24]

Of course, there is a difference between what the navy thinks it ought to have and what the national leadership finds 'reasonable' in the face of competing priorities. We have seen that the naval establishment lost its case in 1954–5, but it appears to have been more successful in 1960–64, during the debate which stemmed from the introduction of the new defense policy in January 1960, and its subsequent modification in the wake of the Kennedy initiatives. Disagreement seems to have focused on the navy's role in nuclear war,[25] with an extreme faction arguing that a fleet was no longer necessary, even in its traditional role of supporting the army ashore, and that land-based missiles could deal with enemy surface groups, and even with submerged submarines.[26] From its side, the navy was arguing that the threat from Polaris was being underestimated, that the role of surface ships was being under-emphasized, and that undue reliance had been placed on ground and rocket forces to the neglect of other means of warfare.[27] However, by mid-1964 the threat from Polaris had been acknowledged as being the navy's first priority,[28] and the warship building programs provided explicit recognition of the surface ship's role, if perhaps not as generously as the navy might have wished.

Naval interests were again heavily engaged during 1969–73, in the wide-ranging debate about foreign and domestic policy, and about the dangers of war and the future roles of the armed services.[29] The initial evidence of naval involvement came from the series of eleven articles published during 1972–3 over Gorshkov's name in *Morskoj sbornik* under the title 'Navies in war and peace'.[30] These articles were rich in information and contained a strong element of 'educating the fleet', but the dominant tone was one of advocacy and justification, which extended beyond the contention that the USSR needed a powerful navy for use in both peace and war, to criticisms of the formulation of naval policy and the composition of the fleet. Halfway through the series *Morskoj sbornik* began to encounter unprecedented delays in being released to the press by the army-controlled military censors (delays which extended into 1974), and during the same period there were major turnovers of the journal's editorial board, which were again unprecedented.[31] These concrete reactions, reinforced by other circumstantial evidence, confirmed the strong textual indicators that a major debate was underway, with powerful coalitions on either side.[32]

Gorshkov presented a strong argument. Using selective historical analysis, his central theme was the increasing importance of naval forces as an instrument of state policy in peacetime and as a means of influencing the course and outcome of wars of all kinds. Seapower was a necessary adjunct to great power status, which could not be sustained without a powerful fleet. But naval forces had to be shaped in response to specific requirements, and this demanded a conscious policy concerning the role of seapower in each nation's plans. Gorshkov asserted that the USSR lacked such a policy. In consequence, the USSR had an unbalanced fleet that was deficient in surface ships, both as to numbers and range of types, and the navy had been shaped too closely to a single, restrictive and largely defensive mission. If the USSR was to exploit the potential of seapower as an instrument of policy, it must have a greatly improved worldwide capability. It certainly had the economic and industrial capacity to build and sustain such a fleet.[33]

On a more specific note, Gorshkov, writing at the end of 1971, strongly opposed any weakening of the USSR's position in the eastern Mediterranean, whether through some kind of mutual agreement with the USA, or by withdrawing Soviet forces from Egypt, which would imperil the navy's access to Egyptian ports and airfields. The growing probability of such a withdrawal may well have been the precipitating cause of the series' publication.[34]

The Gorshkov series provided a valuable insight to Soviet naval requirements and to the perceived deficiency in surface forces in particular. But the 54,000 words of sustained argument also provided a window on the wider debate and allowed certain inferences as to how opinion divided on particular issues, mainly in terms of attitudes but sometimes in terms of institutions and interests.[35] It is relevant to this discussion that among the inferred opponents to Gorshkov's advocacy were those who believed that the probability of world war continued to be high, that military power had limited utility as an instrument of state policy outside the Soviet bloc, and that Soviet-US confrontation risked escalation. The Merchant Fleet was inferred as an opposing institution and Grechko was one of two individuals identified in the analysis by name.[36]

Grechko's opposition was inferred from his article 'The fleet of the homeland', published in the 1971 Navy Day issue of *Morskoj sbornik*, following the 24th Party Congress.[37] Grechko does not play down the USSR's very real requirement for a navy, or its vital role in the country's defense. But his initial discussion covers all branches of the armed forces, the nuclear submarines being bracketed with the SRF. The emphasis is on the navy in war and on deterring attack on Russia. An article in *Morskoj sbornik* by the Minister of Defense on this occasion was itself unusual, but more importantly, the tone and substance read very differently from what appeared subsequently in the Gorshkov series. Further evidence that Gorshkov and Grechko had divergent viewpoints was provided by the latter's booklet, *On Guard for Peace and the Building of Communism*, which claims a direct link with the decisions of the 24th Party Congress.[38] It placed primary emphasis on combat readiness and discussed the USSR's international commitments only in terms of other socialist states. This approach was poles apart from the argument in the Gorshkov series (which was written in the wake of the Party Congress but did *not* claim direct links with its decisions), for an assertive overseas policy based on military power, and for the navy's unique qualifications as an instrument of state policy in peacetime. Lying somewhere between the two viewpoints is

Military Force and International Relations, edited by Kulish. This book is linked explicitly to the Party Congress and would seem to reflect most accurately the Congress' endorsement of an expansion of the 'internationalist function' of the Soviet armed forces. It discusses the increasing importance of a 'Soviet military presence' in distant regions, but while it gives due attention to the navy's role (including mention of the Mediterranean squadron), it is concerned with the problem of strategic mobility and the more general requirement for 'mobile and well trained and well equipped forces'.[39] In contrast, Gorshkov places all his emphasis on the navy's unique qualifications and is at pains to point out the inherent limitations of other forms of military force in this role.

It seems possible that Gorshkov's opponents intended to rebut his arguments through a series of articles on military theoretical problems in *Krasnaya zvezda*. The series was announced in April 1973 under the general title 'The defense of socialism: questions of theory', but ceased without explanation after the second article in May 1973.[40] This coincided with the temporary lifting of censorship delays on *Morskoj sbornik* and can be seen as an imposed truce, which may have been connected with the appointment of Grechko to the Politburo in late April.[41]

A compromise biased in the navy's favor seems to have been reached by mid-1974. In an article published in May, Grechko acknowledged that the 'historic function of the Soviet armed forces is not restricted merely to ... defending the homeland and other socialist states' and that their external function had now been 'expanded and enriched with new content'.[42] This brought him into line with the policies endorsed by the 24th Party Congress.[43] In July, Gorshkov acknowledged that the main naval mission in war was coming to be operations against targets on land, rather than combating the enemy fleet.[44] He thus accepted the formal prioritization of missions which the military leadership appears to have been trying to enforce since 1966–7. However, a significant increase in the future allocation of resources to the navy had been approved and the preparation of a book to be entitled *The Seapower of the State* was authorized. The latter would reflect the interests of those involved in the wider-ranging debate which prompted (and enabled) the publication of the Gorshkov series.

Although the book originally was not scheduled for publication until the second quarter of 1976, it appeared without warning in February, just two weeks before the 25th Party Congress.[45] The underlying message was much the same as the Gorshkov series, but the book's scope and structure differed considerably. It was

almost three times as long, with significant additions and deletions to the original material, it was much more carefully written
and the style was less polemical .The historical analysis, which
made up 80 percent of the articles and provided the basis for
Gorshkov's original argument, reappeared as the second chapter
of the book, although with substantial amendments. Of the
remaining two-thirds of the book, 85 percent was essentially new
material, and fell into two categories. The first chapter was
devoted to an extensive discussion of the importance of the ocean
of the non-military aspects of seapower, subjects which had been
treated very cursorily in the articles and, unlike the latter, the
chapter read as if the different sections had been written by
specialists. For example, the book had almost 11,000 words on
maritime transportation (compared to only 75 in the articles),
and a former Minister of the Merchant Fleet was a contributing
author to the book.[46] The other two chapters, making up some 45
percent of the book, focused on naval matters and comprised a
not very interesting review of naval developments since World
War II (Chapter 3) and a discussion of contemporary problems in
naval warfare (Chapter 4).

Compromise does not, of course, mean the end of disagreement. With this in mind, we can turn to consider the implications
of three new and important sections in the final chapter of
Gorshkov's book, which are headed 'Fleet against fleet and fleet
against shore', 'Problems of balancing navies' and 'Command of
the sea'. There is unlikely to have been any dispute over the
absolute (as opposed to relative) importance of the fleet-against-
shore mission. The Soviet navy had led the world in developing
submarine-launched ballistic missiles, and it was the navy which
had argued within the defense establishment that the threat from
Polaris was being underestimated. Throughout the 1960s, naval
writing emphasized the fundamental nature of these technological developments and discussed their implications in terms of
naval warfare.

Disagreement appears to have been (and continues to be)
centered on the relevance to modern war of the navy's traditional
role and of general-purpose naval forces. Evidence of attempts by
the military establishment to downgrade this role can be seen in
the 1968 edition of *Military Strategy*, which placed the SSBN
force on a par with the SRF.[47] For navies in general, it added to
the mission of 'nuclear strikes against objects on the continents
... and the active search for enemy naval forces, and their destruction', but *deleted* from the section on structuring the armed
forces the sentence: 'Hence, the principal mission of our navy in

modern war will be combat with enemy forces at sea and in their bases.'

While the primary importance of the navy's strike and counter-strike missions is always acknowledged, this downgrading of the traditional role was not matched in contemporary naval publications.[48] Indeed, *The Combat Path of the Soviet Navy*, a book that went to typesetting the month after Gorshkov's final article, asserts that the navy must carry out 'active operations' against enemy sea lines of communications, and goes on to say: 'Nor will such tasks as the destruction of enemy surface groups, and cooperation with the ground forces on the maritime axes, by means of amphibious landings and other operations, be taken away from the navy.'[49] The Gorshkov series only makes very brief reference to the navy's contribution to strategic strike and to its role in countering Western sea-based systems.[50] The great bulk of his descriptive analysis focuses on the use of general-purpose surface forces in both peacetime and war. He spends a substantial part of the articles demonstrating (by historical analogy) the importance of the traditional wartime role. Some 20 percent of the series is devoted to analyzing non-Russian worldwide naval operations in the two World Wars, and concerning the second one, he concludes that although the war was won in the continental theaters (primarily on the Russian front), naval operations had a significant effect on the general course of the war, and Western operations made an important contribution to the final outcome.

In his last article, Gorshkov does list the three tasks which comprise the navy's basic wartime mission:[51] (1) contributing to strategic strike, (2) blunting strategic strikes by enemy units, and (3) 'participating in the operations conducted by ground forces in the continental theaters of military operations'. Apart from their order, Gorshkov does not distinguish between the tasks in importance, but he adds that the third one involves 'a large number of complex and major missions'. Within the context of the series as a whole, one can infer that he envisages a wide range of operations, comparable to those discharged by navies in World War II. It should also be noted that in *Combat Path of the Soviet Navy* (which was under preparation at the time of Gorshkov's series), the tasks of strategic delivery and countering the enemy's naval strike forces are quite specifically assigned equal importance.[52]

These well-entrenched positions, coupled with the concept of *Seapower of the State* as a compromise, help to explain why the section in that book entitled 'Fleet against fleet and fleet against shore' pays lip service to the newly agreed priority, but devotes most of its space to illustrating the importance of the traditional naval role. This is achieved first, by extending the definition of fleet-against-shore to include landing operations: the 'pure' form, intended to gain and maintain command of the sea (352/5, 353/4);[53] and those operations which are 'tied to the simultaneous accomplishment of other missions' (352/4). It is then shown that this second category of fleet-against-fleet (which comprises the vast bulk of naval operations – 354/2) is, in fact, supporting operations against the shore. This allows the navy's main objective to be defined as 'securing the fulfillment of all missions *related* [emphasis added] to operations against enemy land targets, and to the protection of one's own territory from the attacks of his navy' (354/3). This clearly places attacks on the shore and defense against such attacks on the same level; a later formulation is less explicit, but the full context yields a similar interpretation (360/3–4).[54]

Under the guise of exceptions to the general rule, the book smuggles in numerous examples of traditional naval operations which have had strategic significance (351/2), or have been *more* important than the battle on land (349/3). The extensive definition of fleet-against-shore operations allows discussion of the traditional roles played by navies in World War II, including the importance of carriers as general-purpose forces.

Apparently, Gorshkov is able (with suitable obfuscation) to maintain his advocacy of the navy's wartime role and the continued importance of its traditional mission. It is, therefore, all the more striking that, in the book, he chose to mute his criticisms of the navy's structural characteristics.

It is true that the section entitled 'Problems of balancing navies' provides a critical analysis of great power fleet structures since 1905 in terms of their capacity to handle the unforeseen demands of war, and it can be inferred from his invariable condemnations that Gorshkov favors maximum flexibility. It is also true that his analysis provides examples that could be used to support almost any argument, and certainly Gorshkov stresses that a future war will be fought with forces-in-being (413/4, 439/5). And, as in his articles, he points to the limiting effect of Germany's concentration on submarines, which was exacerbated by its failure to provide antiASW forces for their support (429/1–2). He also puts in a good word for the carrier (443/3). But the more significant aspect is Gorshkov's retreat on what is implied by the term 'balanced'.

In the articles, the question of balance is touched on briefly, but to some purpose. When analyzing the main types of naval operations in World War II, Gorshkov points out that the task-specific fleets were severely handicapped in comparison with those which had a broad and more balanced capability, capable of carrying out large-scale and strategic-type missions. As unfavorable examples, he cites the German navy, which was virtually limited to attacking sea communications, and the Japanese navy, which had almost no ASW capability. By contrast, the British and US navies were able to carry out 'broad strategic missions'.[55] However, in the book, Gorshkov castigates the British and Americans along with the Germans and Japanese, and reverts to the restrictive definition of a 'balanced fleet' (413/2), which was publicized in 1967.[56] In that version 'balance' denotes the capability to carry out assigned missions in differing circumstances, but says nothing about the mission structure. The meaning which Gorshkov developed in his articles sees 'balance' as stemming from the *choice* of mission, which must be defined in as general terms as possible, in order to exploit the navy's inherent versatility and to allow for unforeseen eventualities. Unquestionably, the definition in the book represents a retreat, but the choice of mission is now less important, given Gorshkov's ability to redefine its meaning in terms which suit the navy's purposes, as he did with 'fleet against shore'. In any case, the importance of the surface-ship role had been acknowledged by the authorization of two additional classes, a shift in official attitudes which was reflected in the difference in tone between what he wrote in his final article,[57] and the comparable statement in the book. The latter notes that 'the priority given to the development of the submarine and aircraft ... presupposes a matching developing of the other arms of naval forces', without which no mission can be successfully completed, and among which surface ships will play the most important role (412/6).

And finally, the section entitled 'Command of the sea'. This was the first substantial discussion of the subject in recent years,[58] and Gorshkov was concerned to demonstrate the continuing validity of the concept, rather than how to achieve it. He stresses its uniqueness to the maritime environment (unlike most theoretical categories such as mass, maneuver, etc., which are common to all aspects of military art), and asserts that it is the most 'vital concept' in the art of naval warfare. The discussion provides powerful support to the arguments advanced in the other two sections for the continued relevance of the fleet-against-fleet role, and for the importance of general-purpose forces, particularly the antiASW–proSSBN element.

The central theme of Gorshkov's discussion is that developments in nuclear missile war have increased the importance of ensuring local command of the sea in key areas for particular periods of time. The strategic significance of sea-based nuclear delivery systems makes it all the more essential to ensure a 'favorable operating regime' for one's own forces. He argues that local command of the sea is essential to the successful discharge of the navy's primary mission (379/2), and that, undoubtedly, the imperialists will seek to wrest such command for themselves at the very outset of war (380/2). Furthermore, gaining command of the sea has always depended on the necessary measures having been taken in time of peace (371/1) and (by implication), the suddenness of nuclear missile war makes these preparatory measures all the more essential.

The book brings out all the classical advantages of gaining command of the sea, including the fact that the effect of a single engagement on the balance of naval strength will endure for the whole war, and he comes close to explicitly advocating the 'pure form' of fleet-against-fleet operations. But two points are of particular interest in terms of Soviet contingency plans. Drawing on Soviet experience in World War II, Gorshkov observes that the occupation of coastal regions by the ground forces greatly facilitated establishing command of adjacent sea areas (379/3). Bearing in mind the significance of the Barents and Norwegian seas to the security of the Soviet SSBN force, plus the reference in his articles to the invasion of Norway by Germany in World War II,[59] the relevance of this observation to Svalbard, Iceland and key stretches of the Norwegian coast is striking.

The second point concerns the necessity of 'establishing the conditions for gaining command of the sea (at the outset of war) ... while still at peace' (371/1). The measures he lists include 'forming groupings of forces and so disposing them in a theater that they have local superiority over the enemy, and also providing the appropriate organization of forces in the maritime theaters of operation (sea and ocean), and a system of basing, command and control, etc., as required by their missions'. These requirements could well be used to describe the pattern of Soviet activity since 1964, when the navy first began to establish significant forces in distant sea areas, a process which is still in progress today.

The book, then, is not just a simple exposé of the role of seapower in the contemporary world, but part of a continuing argument about the navy's role and the resources being allocated to it. The nub of the argument is summed up rather nicely in the 'Fleet against fleet' section, where Gorshkov criticizes Napoleon for blaming his admirals for repeated failure, whereas the fault really lay in his own 'inability to make a timely analysis of the French navy's capabilities, and to use it in the struggle with the enemy' (356/3). Napoleon's failure to invade England in 1805 was not due primarily to Britain's unchallenged maritime superiority, but in his 'one-sided strategy, which stemmed from his preoccupation with operations in the land theaters and his lack of understanding of the navy, his disregard for its capabilities in war, and as a result, his inability to use it in a struggle with a naval power, such as England was at the time' (355/4). The analogy with present circumstances is striking.[60] In Gorshkov's view, the failure of the Soviet military leadership to understand or even to analyze properly the navy's role, coupled with its prejudices concerning particular weapons and platforms, has meant that on the one hand the fleet has been configured for a relatively narrow span of specific missions, and on the other hand it lacks the full range of forces with which to discharge these missions effectively. In peacetime, this inability to comprehend the navy's potential leads to its underutilization as an instrument of overseas policy. In a war with maritime powers, it could lead to national disaster.

This critical tone, including the pointed reference to Napoleon's failures, is preserved in the second (amended) edition of the book, which appeared in November 1979. It is about 12·5 percent longer, the more significant increases being in the sections on Western military doctrine (which includes a discussion on cruise missiles) and operations against the shore, plus a new ten-page section which is somewhat misleadingly entitled 'The strategic employment of the fleet'. This turns out to be an argument in favor of a truly unified military strategy covering operations on land and sea, and it mainly consists of an historical critique of the traditional tendency toward separate continental and maritime strategies. Gorshkov notes that the USSR does have a unified strategy but it becomes clear that he is dissatisfied with its overall structure and method of application, and considers that the maritime aspects of the strategy are neither properly integrated, nor given sufficient attention. Gorshkov reminds the reader that there is now no sphere of armed conflict where any one branch of service can exercise absolute sovereignty and that all military operations now involve the employment of several branches of service to achieve a common goal. Using circumlocutory language and rather obscure argumentation, he goes on to make two related proposals which can be read as criticism of the existing situation.

In one (317/2), I understand him to say that, since naval operations are becoming increasingly important and since they rely on support from other branches of service, it is therefore desirable, when considering strategic missions in oceanic theaters, to review the ways of employing all the armed forces and not just the navy. From his full argument, I infer that Gorshkov considers that the other four branches of service give insufficient priority to naval missions when shaping their strategic concepts and employment policies, and perhaps are reluctant to subordinate themselves to naval requirements when supporting operations in the oceanic theaters.

In the other (317/3), I understand him to say that, given the continuing growth in the role of the Soviet navy (which stems from the increasing importance of sea-based strategic nuclear systems), it is necessary to formulate a multifaceted military strategy which will provide for the most expedient employment of all branches of service, while allowing that the relative importance of the continental and oceanic theaters may vary during the course of a war. This last point is particularly significant and, while Gorshkov is unlikely to be challenging the over-riding priority accorded to the European land battle in the initial stages of war with the Western maritime alliance, I infer that he is arguing that in other circumstances the oceanic theaters may be more important. Two come readily to mind: the initial phases of such a war in the Pacific theater; and the subsequent phases of such a war in the Atlantic theater. Gorshkov is flouting one of the armed forces' most basic dogmas by questioning the perennial primacy of the continental theaters of operation.

In summing up the source and substance of naval dissatisfaction, we are drawn back to my earlier comment that traditionally the navy has been seen as an expensive necessity, rather than a flexible instrument of state policy. Although changes may be afoot, it would seem that much of this attitude persists today and the upshot of the navy's complaint against the military leadership is summed up by Gorshkov in his indictment of Napoleon. The Soviet leadership's preoccupation with land operations, combined with a lack of understanding of the navy and a disregard for its capabilities (which it has failed to analyze properly), has resulted in a one-sided national strategy and an inability to make effective use of the navy in the struggle with its opponent, a maritime power (355/4, 356/3).

The dissatisfaction is over the unwillingness to recognize the navy's potentialities in peace and importance in war, and the inability to grasp the complexities of maritime warfare. The failure of the military leadership to understand or even to analyze properly the navy's role, coupled with its prejudices concerning particular weapons and platforms, has meant that on the one hand the fleet has been configured for a relatively narrow span of specific missions, and on the other hand that it lacks the full range of forces with which to discharge these missions effectively. The most persistent criticism (which reaches back into the 1950s), is of the army-dominated leadership's inability to grasp that task-specific naval forces, however deadly in themselves, require the support of general-purpose forces (particularly surface ships) if they are able to accomplish their tasks. The need for support to the SSBN force is the most frequently argued example. In peacetime, this lack of comprehension leads to the underutilization of the navy as an instrument of overseas policy. In a war with maritime powers, it could lead to national disaster.

The debate continues, but if we consider where the navy started from, it has made remarkable political gains. Albeit addressed to a wider audience, the navy's case was first deployed in its 'own' journal during 1972–3, as some 54,000 words spread over eleven issues and thirteen months. Three years later, the argument was extended, improved and restated in a book of 151,000 words, which had an unusually large printing of 60,000 copies, and was brought out ahead of schedule to meet a political deadline. Within four years a second 60,000 copy edition had been published, which is one-eighth longer and included a new section which extends naval claims even further. The military publishers categorized the first edition of the book as being for 'the military reader'; the second edition is specifically for 'admirals, generals and officers of the Soviet Army and Navy'. The argument evolved from defensive advocacy of the navy role, to a more rounded discussion of the importance of the ocean and of seapower in its broader sense, to challenging the primacy of the continental theaters in war. And as a final mark of approval, three of the contributing authors were promoted between the first and second editions, two to Vice-Admiral and one to Rear Admiral.

In the wake of the original series of articles, the navy was accorded an out-of-plan addition to its surface building program. But the more persuasive evidence that Soviet attitudes to the navy's role may be changing comes from the reviews of the first edition of *The Seapower of the State*.[61] These are exemplified by Marshal of the Soviet Union Bagramyan's comment in *Izvestia* that 'for the first time in Soviet literature, the author formulates the concept of seapower as a scientific category'. This judgment was echoed by other reviews, all of which stressed the book's contribution to military science and noted that the role of maritime power had, for the first time, been given a scientific formulation. This does not mean that all the ideas in the book have been fully accepted, but it does imply that the concept is now established in the mainstream of Soviet analytic discourse and (to quote Admiral of the Fleet Lobov), 'the book will be an important source for developing a correct viewpoint of the seapower of the state'. This is significant, because up to now Soviet theorists have had an ideological aversion to the concept, which they equated with Mahan, capitalism and colonialism. Just as Keynes's 'General Theory' legitimized the idea of deficit financing and induced a shift in national economic policies, so may this 'scientific formulation' engender a shift in Soviet perceptions of the navy's role in war and peace.

Naval Mission Structure

The Russian navy's traditional objective has been 'to defend the homeland', from which were derived its two main missions of (1) supporting army operations on land, and (2) repulsing attacks from the sea. These twin missions could be discharged most effectively by maintaining command of contiguous waters, but this was frequently not possible. In times of duress, the second mission was collapsed into the first, with operations on land having over-riding priority. In more favorable circumstances, the second mission was extended to carrying the war to the enemy, and the navy has a record of daring interdiction attacks on enemy forces in their ports and home waters.

In essence, this basic mission structure persists today, but in the years following World War II, the Soviet navy was faced with three major developments. First, her most likely opponents were now the traditional maritime powers, who had just demonstrated their capability to project and support continental-scale armies across vast distances at sea. Secondly, a series of quantum jumps in the range, accuracy and payload of maritime weapons introduced the capability of devastating one's opponents' territory with sea-based systems. And thirdly, China joined the ranks of the USSR's likely opponents. These developments increased the relative importance of the maritime components of warfare, requiring greater differentiation within the mission structure. At the same time, the development of a new range of land- and space-based weapon and surveillance systems for use against maritime targets meant that account had to be taken of the contribution to these missions by other branches of service.

On the basis of public pronouncements and other evidence,

there is a fair measure of agreement in the West on Soviet naval missions in war, although there is some dispute about their relative priority. These missions can be labeled:

- strike against shore;
- destruction of enemy naval forces;
- interdiction of enemy sea lines of communications;
- direct support of ground force operations;
- protection of own sea lines of communications.

Before discussing these missions, we must focus on the concept of area defense, which is fundamental to Soviet naval operations. The concept is based on two main zones: an inner one, where superiority of force allows local command of the sea to be secured, and the outer zone, where command is actively contested.[62] The greater part of Soviet naval policy and procurement since the 1920s can be explained in terms of their attempts to extend this maritime defense perimeter and, within it, the zone of effective command.

If the four widely separated fleets were to be ensured the superiority of force necessary to establish command in their respective areas, they would need to deny the enemy the opportunity to concentrate his forces against any one fleet. This objective could most economically be achieved by denying him physical access to the fleet areas. In this respect, Russia was favored by her geography. Three of these areas comprised semi-enclosed seas, and access to the Northern Fleet was canalized by ice during much of the year; only Petropavlovsk, the naval base on Kamchatka, lacked any geographical advantage of this kind. Until 1961, therefore, the navy's primary concern was to extend the inner zone of effective command to the natural defensive barriers, which would be seized by Soviet forces in the event of war. The outer zones did not extend very far beyond these geographic constrictions and were primarily seen as areas for interdicting the reinforcement of the enemy who already occupied these natural barriers.

But after 1961, the outer zone was extended to take account of the qualitatively new threat to the USSR posed by the Polaris submarine, as well as the continuing threat from carrier strike aircraft. In the Far East, the maritime defense perimeter was pushed out into the Philippine Sea and the northwest Pacific. To the west, the outer zones were extended to take in the Norwegian and North seas and the eastern Mediterranean, and the Soviet navy progressively contested the West's erstwhile maritime domination of these sea areas.

Maintaining command of contiguous waters, and contesting command of adjacent seas, is the precondition for discharging the majority of other naval missions, including the most important ones. Area defense will, therefore, be treated as a mission in its own right.

Strike against Shore

The mission of strategic strike was first laid on the navy in the immediate postwar years, when the submarine torpedo was the only available means of bringing an atomic weapon to bear on the continental USA. Soviet strategic delivery submarines were given top priority in nuclear propulsion, warheads and ballistic missiles. But despite these efforts, advances in US antisubmarine capabilities, coupled with Soviet technological inadequacies, meant that the first generation of series production units (comprising two diesel and two nuclear classes, one of each being armed with nuclear torpedoes, the other being armed with a surface-launched ballistic missile) were unable to meet the planned operational requirements. The mission was, therefore, taken away from the navy toward the end of the 1950s.

This decision was reversed in the 1960s, to match the shift in US emphasis from land- to sea-based strategic delivery systems, and the 1968 edition of *Military Strategy* placed the SSBN on a par with the SRF.[63] The SSBN force now has three overlapping roles, in that it can contribute:

- intercontinental strikes against targets in North America;
- continental strikes against targets on the Eurasian landmass;
- the national strategic reserve.

The Delta SSBN can carry out *intercontinental* strikes from home waters. If Yankees are targeted in this role, they need to be within 1,500 nm of the US coastline. Only three or four units are kept forward deployed, so the remainder would have to transit Western antisubmarine barriers to come within range.

The Yankee SSBN can cover a wide range of *continental* targets from Soviet home water, and for Northern Fleet units this includes 'shore facilities which support the operations of the Western SSBN force, and those ASW forces and systems which constrain the free egress and open-ocean operations of the Soviet submarine force'.[64] Six Golf II SSB were transferred to the Baltic in 1976, from where they can cover most naval facilities in NATO Europe.

In the event of world war, the ballistic missile submarines represent an important component of the *national strategic reserve*, because of their relative invulnerability. While it is clear that the Soviets do in fact think in these terms, there are no means of knowing their exact intentions in this respect. But one must assume that their operational plans provide for the greatest flexibility in the use or withholding of these systems, as best to influence the progress and outcome of the conflict.

Endless permutations of targeting, deployment and timing in these overlapping roles are possible, but they all raise the same two requirements:

1 Until such time as the missile submarines have fired all their weapons, or deployed to the open ocean, they must be kept secure against attack. This has led to the concept of defended ocean bastions.
2 If the submarines are deployed, they must be able to transit Western antisubmarine barriers in reasonable safety, and to survive attempts to find them in the open ocean. This raises a requirement for support forces.

This mission, therefore, involves both the ballistic missile submarines and the maritime forces assigned to their protection and support, and in seeking to discharge this mission, the Soviet navy has adopted an operational concept with inherent strategic advantages. If war appears imminent, the majority of SSBN will proceed to ocean bastions located in waters which are close to Soviet bases and far removed from the main strength of Western ASW. A policy of active defense has been adopted and, by deploying their SSBN in bastions, the Soviets obtain the benefits of defense in depth and concentration of force. This provides for the great majority of the Deltas and those of the Yankees which are assigned continental targets. Those Yankees which have to transit within range of intercontinental targets can wait until Western ASW defenses have been weakened during the initial stages of the war.

This pro-SSBN mission, demanding that enemy forces be countered at sea, is a force-consuming task and is an important function of the navy's submarine, air and surface components. The implications in terms of force requirements are discussed below in the context of the Area Defense Mission.

Destruction of Enemy Forces

The enemy's sea-based strategic nuclear strike systems present the primary maritime threat to the Russian homeland, and the task of countering these forces is on a par with the Soviet navy's own strategic mission.

In striving to counter this threat, the Soviets have been driven by two rather different concerns. The most immediate is damage limitation, both as it affects the Soviet homeland, and their ability to fight the landbattle. But more important is the withholding of these systems as tactical and strategic reserves. In the short run, they could then be used to deny the USSR the use of Western Europe as an alternative economic base for rebuilding the socialist system. In the longer run, the sole possession of a residual nuclear capacity is likely to determine the final outcome of a world war, and hence the political structure of the postwar world. It was this potential as a tactical and strategic reserve which required that Soviet forces be within weapon-range contact at the onset of war, and necessitated the navy's shift to forward deployment.

Countering the Ballistic Missile Submarine

By 1964, the Polaris submarine had replaced the carrier as the most dangerous component of this threat and overlapping concern for damage limitation and withholding focused attention on different aspects of the weapon system. To prevent their being withheld for use at a later stage, the SSBN must themselves be disabled, and this requires one to know their location. But damage limitation only requires that (preferably) all or (at least) some of the missiles should not reach their targets. The importance of this distinction is twofold: (1) once the submarine launches a missile, it reveals its position and renders itself liable to attack, and (2) the missile itself is vulnerable in its early stages.

Although the Soviets have been addressing the SSBN problem for over fifteen years, the final shape of their response is still not certain. However, we do know that from the start they recognized that the complexity of the problem would require the application of all available resources, including the involvement of other branches of service besides the navy. We can also assume, on the basis of established practice, that they would have pursued all available lines of attack, of which there were three: exclusion, trailing and area search–surveillance. Hindsight allows us to identify the traditional pattern of interim measures being applied (following an initial 'don't just sit there, do something' type of response), while the USSR sought to develop some kind of final, long-term answer to the problem of countering the submarine-launched ballistic missile.

The only line of attack which lent itself to interim measures was the exclusion of Polaris from those sea areas which were particularly favorable for targeting the USSR with sea-based strategic systems. If the USSR could make the likelihood of SSBN detection in those areas unacceptably high, the USA would have little choice but to deploy the submarines elsewhere. It seems probable that the Soviets thought this could be achieved by an extension and elaboration of the tactical concepts which had been successfully developed for the defense of the offshore zone, allowing that additional, purpose-designed ASW forces would be made available.

The *initial* response (lasting five years) was to extend the outer defense zone to the 1500 nm circle from Moscow, which covered the range of the early Polaris missile systems as well as the continuing strategic threat from carrierborne strike aircraft. In the Far East, the maritime defense perimeter was pushed out into the East China Sea and the Pacific. In the European theater, the outer defense zones were extended to take in the Norwegian and North seas and the eastern Mediterranean. Somewhat tentatively, the Soviet navy began to contest the West's domination of these sea areas, although they lacked the forces to make an effective challenge. Meanwhile, the major emphasis in surface-ship capabilities was switched from antisurface to antisubmarine systems, in part by starting on the major conversion of two existing classes, and in part by modifying the design of new construction programs, one currently building and the others projected.

In 1967–8 we see the shift from *initial* to *interim* response, as the specialized surface-ship ASW capability begins to enter service and the second (full) generation of nuclear submarine begins delivery. The first requirement was to turn the newly extended outer defense zones into something more than lines on a chart, and there was a noticeable increase in the navigational assertiveness of Soviet naval units operating in zones. The second requirement was to extend the area of naval concern to take in the 2500 nm circle of threat, which included the eastern half of the North Atlantic and the northern half of the Arabian Sea. There was a progressive build-up in the number of ships on forward deployment and extension of their areas of operation. Ship-days deployed rose steadily until 1972–3, at which stage they leveled off, as if having reached some previously determined level.

While many of these deployments were directed at excluding Polaris–Poseidon from the more favorable launch areas, the rest were probably intended to provide the operational experience and infrastructure, which would be needed to support the other two lines of attack. As originally planned, it was probably hoped that ten years would be sufficient to develop a range of measures which, beginning in 1972–3, would allow some kind of *final* response along each of the three lines of attack, even if they needed further improvement.

Considering 'exclusion' first, it was probably intended to start consolidating the ASW capability in the newly extended outer defense zones. By 1972–3, the build-up of specialized ASW forces would be significant, with the 1970s family of new-construction surface units beginning to augment the capability provided by the major conversions and design modifications. New fixed-wing ASW aircraft would be entering service, and improved ASW variants of the second-generation nuclear-powered attack submarines would be nearing delivery. It may also have been planned that the WIG-type vehicle, with its capacity for high-speed low-level search would be available by this date, which would add an important new dimension to what would be essentially conventional capabilities. It was probably assumed that these measures, supplemented by those developed for the other lines of attack, would so threaten the security of the Polaris–Poseidon that the USA would choose to redeploy their SSBN to more distant sea areas.

Turning to the second possible line of attack, it was practicable to use active sonar to trail a Polaris SSBN with another nuclear submarine. Given the state of the ASW art in the early 1960s, this probably seemed the most readily available and certain means of providing continuous target-location data on Polaris units, since it only required the refinement of existing technologies, rather than seeking to achieve a breakthrough in unfamiliar fields. It seems probable that the Alpha SSN was originally designed with this role in mind. The lead unit was delivered in 1970–71, and the considerable increase in speed and diving depth probably reflects the natural if incorrect assumption that any successor to the Polaris classes would have a significantly improved performance.

The third line of attack was an area search–surveillance. Russia's geographic situation, coupled with its technological disadvantage in acoustic detection methods, virtually forced the Soviets to place their major emphasis on discovering other ways of detecting a submerged submarine and developing those means of doing so. If successful, this line of attack would yield the best results in terms of flexibility and cost-effectiveness, since it would not be tied to separate ocean basins, nor would it be dependent upon the number of US SSBN, but would have a worldwide application against all types of submarine.

There is now sufficient evidence to be certain that the Soviets did indeed take this unconventional route (while not neglecting the acoustic aspects of ASW), although the level of success is hard to identify. It seems unlikely that they expected to develop a fully functioning space-based surface-anomaly system within ten years, although certain of the components might well be operational by 1972–3. However, in terms of their original timetable it may be relevant that by late 1972 the Soviets claimed the capability of using land-based ballistic missiles against targets in remote sea areas, and that a sea-based tactical ballistic missile system (SS-NX-13) was being tested in 1973 and was expected to enter service in 1974.

That things did not work out as originally planned, is hardly a matter for surprise. A consistent feature of Soviet naval developments since the war has been, on the one hand, a marked capacity to devise innovative solutions to complex operational problems, and on the other hand, a limited ability to move from imaginative concepts to their practical application.

It seems likely that the development of the high-speed deep-diving Alpha proved more difficult than had been forseen, delaying series production of this class. The adoption in the early 1970s of the 'defended bastion' concept for SSBN, would have placed an increased emphasis on the outer defense zones in the Norwegian Sea and the northwest Pacific, to the detriment of plans for the eastern Mediterranean and the Arabian Sea. And it is possible that the SS-NX-13 became a casualty of the SALT process.

However, another consistent feature of Soviet naval policy has been its persistence in the face of daunting technological odds, which is well exemplified by the fifteen years it took to develop an effective counter to the strike carrier. Therefore, although it is difficult to know the present level of achievement, there is every reason to assume that the Soviets are still striving to develop an effective counter to the SSBN, and are probably still pursuing all three lines of attack. Although these have been discussed separately, they are in fact mutually supportive and of course the results of research into non-accoustic methods of detection will increase the effectiveness of all three approaches. Confined waters lend themselves to some variant of the area defense concept, whereas the open ocean is more suitable for satellite surveillance. Surface surveillance satellites have now been in service a dozen years or more, and one must assume that a missile-launch detection capability has already been developed, if not actually deployed. Some analysts believe that non-accoustic methods of submarine detection are already operational in space.[65] In addition to any such space-based surface-anomaly detectors, one would also expect to see new developments in the passive trailing of submerged submarines, in high-speed low-altitude airborne search, and in the detection of wake-related surface phenomena by ship- and land-based sensors.

Assuming that the problem of location can be solved, the problem of attacking the submarine is comparatively simple. When Soviet forces are in direct contact, they will have available an array of long-range weapons. In the ocean expanses, it seems probable that the USSR intended to develop a common system for antisurface and antisubmarine strike, using terminally guided ballistic missiles, as described below.

If it is not possible to locate the SSBN until it launches a missile, the threat from those that are withheld for later use can be reduced if they are deprived of targeting, navigation and command and control information by disrupting communication links and attacking the sources of such information. High priority is, therefore, given to the destruction of SSBN base and operational support facilities at the onset of war.

Countering the Carrier

It appears that the Soviets feel they have developed an effective counter to the strike carrier, although it took them more than fifteen years to achieve this. The two components of this mission (target location and strike) are handled somewhat differently in each of the three main types of scenario, namely, continuous company, meeting engagement and distant targeting.

'Continuous company' describes the situation in the eastern Mediterranean, an outer defense zone. When carriers operate within this area, primary responsibility for providing target-location data lies with the surface units, which remain in close company. They also provide local command and control and a secure communications link with headquarters ashore, and are therefore likely to continue in this role, despite their vulnerability. The main strike arm is now the cruise missile-armed submarine, probably backed by IR/MRBM. Aircraft based in the USSR lack the rapid response time essential to this scenario, and while they remain a threat to Western forces they are not critical to the operational concept.

The 'meeting engagement' is best exemplified by the deployment of carriers from US east-coast ports to launch strikes against the USSR from the south Norwegian Sea. In such circumstances, target-location data are provided by a mix of forward pickets (AGIs, etc.), and aircraft and satellite surveillance. The force will be harassed by air and submarine attacks *en route*, but the main engagement will take place in the encounter zone. Here, the force will be subjected to successive, heavy attacks by air- and submarine-launched missiles at the same time that it is transiting a torpedo-attack submarine barrier. If the carrier force is configured for nuclear strike against the USSR, the encounter zone is located to the west of the probable launch area; but should it be configured for operations in the Norwegian Sea (e.g. in support of counter-SSBN operations or flank reinforcement), the main encounter is likely to be north of the Gap. SSM-armed surface ships will probably be used in the latter case but will be held back in the former. It seems likely that the large antisubmarine ships will be deployed to hinder attempts by Western ASW forces to prevent the missile-armed submarines from launching their weapons. Variations of this concept apply in the Pacific, and in the Mediterranean when US forces are not already deployed in the eastern basin.

The 'distant-targeting' scenario covers those carriers that do not immediately threaten the USSR at the outbreak of war but, if not disposed of, will contribute to the US reserve. In these circumstances, target-location information is provided by air and satellite reconnaissance. It appears likely that it was originally planned that strike would rely primarily on two different types of terminally guided ballistic missile systems, one land-based and the other submarine-based. The SRF's capability to strike surface groupings was explicitly claimed in 1972 and, despite time-of-flight problems, there appear to be no insuperable reasons why ICBM should not be used against high-value naval targets. A submarine-based system would require the unit to remain within strike range of its target(s). A 400 nm tactical SLBM (SS-NX-13) was undergoing trials in 1972; it appears to have been shelved for reasons that remain unclear (although it may have been to do with SALT I), and the present status of this system is uncertain.

The first two of these scenarios depend heavily on the concept of a defense perimeter and area defense. All three are applicable to high-value surface targets other than carriers.

Surface Warfare

The mission of 'destroying enemy forces' is not restricted in time to the early days of war, nor limited in targets to Western strike forces. The general thrust of Gorshkov's writings suggests that the navy, at least, has thought through the implications of a fight to the finish with a capitalist maritime coalition. Gorshkov's most recent argument (in the second edition of his book), that in different phases of a world war the oceanic theaters may become more important than the continental one, combined with his long-standing emphasis on the flexibility of general-purpose surface ships and the ability of naval forces to survive the nuclear exchange, suggest that the navy may be thinking of wide-ranging operations in the latter stages of a nuclear war. While it is hard to envisage detailed scenarios with any confidence, the mobility and firepower embodied in warships could have a critical impact on a protracted conflict in what may well be a largely preindustrial world.

Area Defense

Area defense is central to certain of the missions which have already been discussed. It is the way to secure the safety of home waters as SSBN bastions, and to prevent enemy carriers and missile submarines from closing the USSR to launch their strikes. The success of these and several other missions will depend on the extent to which the Soviets can establish command of the sea in those areas. This is best discussed in terms of the inner and outer defense zones.

The Baltic, Black and Barents seas are *inner* defense zones and it can be assumed that the Soviets count on establishing effective command of these waters at the onset of war.[66] This will involve seizure of the Baltic and Black Sea exits and parts of arctic Norway. Command of these sea areas will automatically:

- secure the close support of army operations, including tactical landings and naval bombardment;
- secure coastal communications, including logistic support of the landbattle;
- prevent the enemy from carrying out amphibious assaults and from providing close support to army operations ashore.

The concept of an inner defense zone also applies in the Pacific, although operational requirements will be modulated by diplomatic considerations such as keeping Japan neutral. However, one can assume that effective command will be sought in the

Pacific off Kamchatka and over at least part of the Sea of Japan, and it seems likely that SSBN bastions will be located in the Sea of Okhotsk, where the Kuril chain provides a defensive barrier to seaward. In such circumstances, the two straits bordered by Soviet and Japanese territory acquire new significance. Nemuro Strait, between the eastern corner of Hokkaido and the disputed islands of Kunashiri and Shikotan, provides access to the Sea of Okhotsk, as does Kunashiri Strait which separates Etorofu Island to the northeast. The importance of being able to close off such access to its SSBN bastion in the event of world war may underlie the regarrisoning of these islands by the USSR in 1978. Soya (or La Perouse) Strait, between the northern end of Hokkaido and Sakhalin, gives similar access from the Sea of Japan, but it also provides the most secure route between the naval base at Vladivostok and the Pacific Ocean. In order to control this twenty-mile strait effectively, the Soviets may consider it necessary to occupy the tip of Hokkaido at the outbreak of war. Although less obvious, a similar requirement could arise with Namuro Strait, some 300 miles to the east, and might be extended to occupying the whole of Hokkaido's northeastern shore, which serves as the southern limit to the Sea of Okhotsk.

The combined *outer* defense zone of the Northern and Baltic Fleet areas takes in the Norwegian and North seas, with the outer defense perimeter running from Greenland through Iceland and the UK. This outer defense zone is of considerable strategic importance to the USSR. The Norwegian Sea provides defense in depth to the SSBN bastions located in the Greenland and Barents seas; the main NATO antisubmarine barrier is located across the Greenland–Iceland–UK gap; seaborne reinforcements and supplies for Western forces in Denmark and northwest Germany have to cross the North Sea, which also provides access for Soviet amphibious hooks and flank support. Gaining command of this area has high priority, with command of the Norwegian Sea now being seen as a necessity rather than a convenience. Maintaining command will be facilitated by seizing key stretches of the Norwegian coast, and if Iceland and the Faeroes cannot be secured for Soviet use, they must at least be denied to the West. As a way of tilting the balance in their favor, the Soviets will seek to pin down Western forces by mining, and draw others away by diversionary attacks. It will still be a costly struggle and the Soviets must assume that the destruction of their air bases will deny them the use of shore-based air support.

The eastern Mediterranean is designated by the Soviets as an Ocean Theater of Military Operations (OTVD) and in considering its importance as an outer defense zone, we must distinguish between peace and war. Its importance in peacetime derives from its use as a deployment area by Western strike systems targeted on the USSR. This spurs the development of location and strike systems appropriate to the geographical conditions, and these would be used at the onset of war. Thereafter, there would seem to be no great urgency for the USSR to gain command of the eastern Mediterranean. In practical terms, the Black Sea Fleet's outer defense zone is probably coterminous with the Aegean, which provides a defensible perimeter and a haven for submarines operating against NATO communications.

The outer defense zone in the Pacific has importance as a shield both to the SSBN bastions and against US sea-based strike systems. However, if the bastions are located in the Sea of Okhotsk, the Kuriles chain provides a natural defensive barrier. Meanwhile, there are no clearly defined geographical areas comparable to the North and Norwegian seas and the Iceland–Faeroes gap, nor will the landbattle have the same relevance. In such circumstances, effective command throughout the outer defense zone is unlikely to have a high priority.

There would seem to be a latent outer defense zone in the northwest quadrant of the Indian Ocean, covering the seaward approaches to the Persian Gulf, and the Arabian Sea is designated as an OTVD. In the event of world war, the USSR is likely to move south to control the Gulf, and will need naval forces on the far side of the Straits of Hormuz to fend off assaults by US strike carriers and amphibious groups. It may also have trouble from the regional navies.

Within the area-defense concept, antisurface operations had over-riding priority for the first ten to fifteen years after the war, but thereafter antisubmarine warfare became increasingly important, and until very recently it had the highest priority in terms of force characteristics and research and development. The progressive improvement in the Soviet navy's ASW capability largely matched the seaward extension of the antisubmarine defense zones, and the Soviet approach to the problem continued to reflect the concepts developed when the zones were comparatively narrow. At the initial stage, shore-based systems played the major role, with the various sensors operated by the observations and communications service providing detection data to shore-based helicopters carrying sonobuoys. The solution was still a combined arms one, with offshore defense units being vectored to join the hunt and to prosecute enemy contacts, while a proportion of the torpedo-armed diesel submarines (which had originally been intended to provide defense in depth against surface groups) were switched to the antisubmarine role. All these operations were controlled by the naval headquarters ashore, and procedures were developed for coordinating operations by the various types of units.

When it became necessary to extend the seaward limit of the defense zone beyond the effective radius of shore-based helicopters, it was natural to think in terms of placing them on a seagoing platform; hence the Moskva class of helicopter-carrying antisubmarine cruiser. Meanwhile, the demise of large surface ships as executors of the countercarrier mission released destroyers to antisubmarine area defense, and methods of coordinating the various airborne, surface, subsurface and land-based systems continued to evolve.

While the concept of an antisubmarine defense zone is most effective in waters directly contiguous to one's coastline, similar procedures have been adopted in the outer zones, including the eastern Mediterranean. Area defense *per se* is not possible in such areas, hence greater emphasis was placed on various types of detection barriers and on a Soviet variant of hunter–killer groups that involves surface ships and submarines working together. However, by the end of the 1960s, priority in the employment of conventional ASW forces has been shifted from counter-SSBN operations in forward areas such as the eastern Mediterranean and Arabian Sea, to reinforcing the security of the Soviet SSBN bastions in the north and Pacific.

There appear to have been two main reasons for this shift in emphasis. The most significant was Western press reports in 1967–8 that the US was intending to develop two new classes of submarine for service in 1973–4, one very fast and the other very silent, the latter being specifically designed to operate against Soviet SSBN. This, of course, had major implications in terms of the Soviet decision to embody a substantial part of the nation's strategic reserve in ballistic missile submarines, and served to focus attention on their security. The Deltas were due to begin entering service at the same period, and they would require an active defense system to protect them from these purpose-designed hunter–killer submarines. Meanwhile, as more antisubmarine systems became available, mounted in surface ships, submarines and aircraft, it must have become increasingly clear to the Soviets that however innovative, these traditional ASW methods had inherent limitations, and an effective solution to the Polaris–Poseidon problem would have to wait for the results of research and development still in progress.

Hence, the shift in emphasis to extending the inner defense zones in the Northern Fleet area and in the Pacific off Kamchatka, and to providing them with watertight ASW defenses. It was recognised that the latter would need more than a reallocation of existing assets, and the ninth five-year plan approved by the 24th Party Congress in 1971, provided for a substantial increase in the resources allocated to surface warship construction, reflecting a significant change in operational requirements. Formerly, it was accepted that distant water surface units would be unlikely to survive the initial stages of a war and, since the size of the different surface types was severely constrained, their design focused on the capability to weather a pre-emptive attack just long enough to discharge their primary mission, a limited objective which was in tune with the prevailing perception that war with the West would be brutal but short. However, the shift in operational emphasis was decided shortly after Soviet military doctrine had accepted that a protracted war was possible, and this new requirement to protect the SSBN bastions for however long such a war might last, necessitated a radical change in naval design criteria. Surface ships now had to be capable of the sustained operations needed to gain and maintain command of a large sea area, such as the Norwegian Sea, and this required long endurance, large magazine loads and an underway replenishment capability.

This meant a significant increase in the size of individual ships. The ninth five-year plan, therefore, provided that the follow-on classes, planned to begin delivery in 1980, would be scaled up one type-size, with a cruiser-sized ship of about 12,000 tons, a destroyer-size of about 8,000 tons and an ocean escort or frigate size of about 4,000 tons.[67] In addition, the plan authorized a class of heavily armed nuclear-powered battle cruisers, which would serve as command ships.[68] A similar scaling-up process was applied to amphibious vessels, reflecting the new requirement for a long-range heavy-assault lift, suitable for seizing key islands and/or stretches of the Norwegian coast.[69]

Despite these substantial increases, the navy considered that it would still have insufficient forces to discharge the new mission effectively and, as we have seen, Gorshkov went public with the navy's case. Within the context of this particular mission, the argument would have focused on the specifics of the threat to Soviet SSBN. The direct threat would come from US attack submarines, but the latter's success would depend on Soviet ASW defenses being suppressed by supporting surface forces. The Soviet navy would have to assume that US carrier groups would be deployed in support of US SSN, whereas Soviet shore-based air would cease to be available after the initial exchange. Without the air component, there could be no certainty that the Soviets would be able to prevent the carrier groups from penetrating the outer defense zones. It could be assumed that the US carriers would seek to establish command of the surface and the air, denying their use to Soviet ASW forces, that they would harry the defending SSN, and they might even become directly involved in hunting down Soviet SSBN.[70] If the Soviet navy was to prevail against this kind of force, it would need a comparable capability, including effective sea-based air.[71] I presume it was the inherent plausibility of this scenario which allowed the navy to win its case, resulting in the addition of a second large destroyer class to the existing program (allowing each to be optimized for a different aspect of maritime warfare)[72] and authority to go ahead with the design of a large air-superiority carrier.[73]

Interdicting Enemy Sea Communications

The interdiction of enemy sea lines of communication is a traditional mission, although its importance has fluctuated with changing perceptions of the likely nature and duration of an East–West war. Recently, the possibility of protracted nuclear conflict or of conventional war has increased its relative importance, which is currently stressed by the Soviet navy. While attack on sea lines of communication would appear less urgent than some other missions, they have the great advantage of tying down Western ASW forces and diverting them from posing a threat to the SSBN strategic reserve. It therefore seems certain that although the anti-SLOC mission could in principle be deferred, sufficient forces will be allocated to ensure the diversion of Western ASW forces from areas of primary Soviet concern such as the Norwegian Sea.

In the initial stages of a war, intratheater shipping (which will be particularly vulnerable to mining) will almost certainly be more important than transoceanic convoys, unless the latter are already closing their destination. It should, however, be stressed that the mission of interdicting enemy sea communications is viewed in its broadest sense and includes destruction of terminal facilities and distribution networks by air or missile strike, the mining of ports and assembly areas, and attacks on all types of escort force.

In the subsequent phases of a war, the Soviet navy's ability to disrupt the sea communications of the opposing maritime coalition could be critical to the outcome of the fight to the finish which their doctrine envisages. It seems likely that both sides' ocean surveillance capability would be largely out of action by then, in which circumstances Soviet surface units could play a major role in the battle of sea communications.

Protecting Own Sea Communications

Traditionally, Russian sea communications have been limited to coastal shipping and this came within the general concept of area defense, although escorts were provided. Soviet forces were barely involved in the protection of the ocean convoys which brought supplies to the USSR during World War II. However, in the event of a future war with China, the USSR must be prepared to supply its Far Eastern Front by sea, and to protect such shipments against attacks by Chinese naval forces, which include the world's third largest submarine force. This threat to shipping reaches back to the northwestern parts of the Indian Ocean, where it could be posed by Chinese forces using friendly bases (e.g. Pakistan or, in the early 1970s, South Yemen), by US forces, or even by regional navies. The timely arrival of military supplies would be critical to the landbattle in the Far East and, if circumstances prevented their shipment via the Red Sea, the Soviets would have to exploit the route used by the Allies in the two world wars, shipping down across Iran and out through the Persian Gulf.

The Navy's Peacetime Role.

We can say with some certainty that the navy's shift to forward deployment in 1961 was prompted by the requirements for strategic defense against sea-based nuclear delivery systems, a conclusion that is evidenced by the timing of the change of polity, the areas chosen for deployment and the operational employment of the forces within these areas.[74] Although the original rationale remains valid and continues to underlie the main pattern of Soviet naval activity, some of the specific reasons for the shift to forward deployment have been eroded or overlaid with new ones, and among the latter we find the emergence of the navy's peacetime role.

The presence of naval forces in distant sea areas provided opportunities for their political exploitation, and this coincided with a hardening of Soviet attitudes toward the USA and its overseas involvements, and a progressive shift toward a more assertive Soviet global policy. This was probably outlined at the

23rd Party Congress in 1966.[75] The 24th Party Congress in 1971 appears to have extended the trend by addressing directly the role of a Soviet military presence, and Grechko's recantation in 1974 would seem to confirm the general direction.

The long-term prognosis is, however, still unclear. It seems likely that the decision to commit Soviet forces to the air defense of Egypt in 1970 was finely balanced and, even if there had not already been a reversal of opinion, the eviction of these forces in 1972 must have given pause for thought. It is true that the long-drawn-out SALT negotiations are likely to have engendered a progressive but fundamental shift in Soviet threat perceptions, including a downward re-evaluation of the dangers of escalation from Soviet-US confrontations in the third world. But while some in the USSR would have argued that this, coupled with the improving correlation of forces, required a more assertive global policy, there would have been others who argued for shifting scarce resources to the domestic economy. Meanwhile, there would remain the unconvinced. The latter might well make up the great majority of the military establishment, who would doubt whether the threat had in fact changed and would continue to press priority for the direct defense of the USSR and to argue the dangers of overseas adventure, unless they were intended to strengthen the strategic infrastructure for wartime missions.

It seems likely that some compromise was reached by early 1973, whereby it was decided that direct Soviet involvement overseas would be limited to the provision of advisers, weapons and strategic logistic support, the combat role being delegated to the Soviet-equipped forces of 'revolutionary' states such as North Korea, Vietnam and Cuba. It can be argued that this policy ensures the USSR the best of all worlds; namely, being able to affect the outcome of an overseas conflict with direct battlefield support, while ensuring that political commitment and liability remain strictly limited. This is achieved by facilitating the arrangements and providing the lift to bring cobelligerents to the zone of conflict; by ensuring that the client state receives adequate military supplies in the course of battle; and by remaining relatively silent about Soviet involvement until after the event.

A result of these decisions has been the increasing readiness to use a 'Soviet military presence' in support of overseas objectives. Between 1967–72, as warship-days in distant waters rose year by year, so too did the trend in the political exploitation of this naval presence. And since 1973, Soviet naval forces have been used in a number of ways including crisis management, latent interposition, logistic support, political pressure and peacetime assistance.

In a major study of the employment of Soviet naval forces in peacetime,[76] Dismukes and McConnell concluded that they have been widely used for political purposes and that a significant proportion of their operations are driven by political considerations, rather than war-related requirements. However, questions still remain as to the level of political commitment behind those operations and as to the extent to which the navy's potential as a flexible instrument of overseas policy will come to determine future force requirements.

Soviet pronouncements refer to the navy's peacetime role in general terms such as 'defending (or securing) state interests', a nebulous formulation, whose scope has yet to be systematically researched. They also speak of the navy's 'international duty', of 'increasing Soviet prestige and influence' and of 'rebuffing imperialism'. While not losing sight of the all-encompassing scope of 'securing state interests', it is useful to distinguish between four types of objectives which underlie this peacetime employment, because each type involves a different level of risk and degree of political commitment.

At the low end of the scale of commitment, we have 'protecting Soviet lives and property'. This objective is referred to but has received little priority to date. There is one clear example where a naval demonstration in February 1969 appears to have secured the release of Soviet trawlers from Ghanaian custody, but the more usual form is to have landing ships standing by to evacuate key equipment from conflict zones.

At the high end of the scale we have 'establishing a strategic infrastructure to support war-related missions', which embraces the physical, political and operational aspects. This objective is not referred to directly, but can be inferred from the pattern of overseas military involvement during the last twenty years, and is implied in some of the more recent Soviet writings. I believe this task has provided the primary motive for a broad span of decisions, ranging from promoting a coup in a client state; to acquiring base rights by barely concealed coercion. The pressure on Egypt (1961–7) for naval support facilities[77] provides a good example of this objective, although the original impulse became obscured by wider involvements as the policy acquired its own momentum ... and complications. Somalia is another example, with the initial interest in 1968–9 stemming from the Arabian Sea's potential as a patrol area for Poseidon submarines, but being overtaken in 1971–2 by the broader concerns of conflict with China and protracted world war. Because the task of establishing a strategic infrastructure concerns the security of the homeland, it is likely to be backed by a high level of political commitment, and the pattern suggests a willingness to incur high political costs in pursuit of this objective. However, so far the Soviets have not used military force to maintain their position when the host country has withdrawn its agreement to their presence, although on at least two occasions they have sought to engineer a coup to bring a more sympathetic regime to power.[78] Of course, once such an infrastructure has been established, it can also serve peacetime policies, as we see most clearly in the case of Soviet-built airfields in Africa.

In between these extremes we have the general objectives of 'Increasing Soviet prestige and influence'. Showing-the-flag increased sharply after 1968, but since 1972 the task has assumed new dimensions, extending to port clearance and minesweeping, and to providing support for revolutionary forces or to regimes threatened by secessionist elements. The Soviets are prepared to commit substantial resources to this objective but, although the propensity for risk-taking has risen steadily, the underlying political commitment is strictly limited.

Overlapping this general influence-building objective is the more restricted one of 'Countering imperialist aggression'. Despite much bombast in declaiming this task, I believe that in terms of risking a major confrontation with the West, Soviet political commitment is low. The first clearcut example was the establishment of the Guinea Patrol in December 1970, since when we have the deployments to the Bay of Bengal in 1971, to the South China Sea in 1972, and to Angola in 1975, as well as the three Middle East crises in 1967, 1970 and 1973, and most recently the increased deployment to the Indian Ocean to balance the build-up of US naval forces in the wake of the Iranian hostage crisis and the Soviet takeover of Afghanistan. The series of three crises in the Middle East did show a shift from a narrow concern with the strike carriers toward a more general concern for the overall capability of the Sixth Fleet.[79] But none of these examples provides evidence of Soviet readiness to actually engage Western naval forces, in order to prevent them from intervening against a Soviet client state. Indeed, it is a moot point whether the reactive deployment of a Soviet detachment during the Indo-Pakistan war in December 1971 achieved anything at all. For instance, was the force authorized to attack the US carrier group if it had launched its strike aircraft toward some unknowable target? What purpose was served by rushing a force to the South China Sea in response to the mining of Haiphong (which just hung around for a few days and then returned home), or was this the result of an interservice argument in Moscow? And what of areas like the Mediterranean, where the urge to 'counter imperialist aggression' is tempered by the dangers of confrontation and escalation to nuclear war?

What we do see is progressively greater involvement by the Soviet navy in the provision of logistic support both prior to and during third-party conflicts. In 1973, Soviet landing ships carried Moroccan troops to Syria, with convoy escort. Landing ships were also used during the subsequent war to ferry military supplies from Black Sea ports to Syria. More significantly, SAM-armed naval units were stationed under the final approaches to the main resupply airfields in Syria and Egypt, as if to cover against Israeli air attack.[80] And most recently, we have the escorting of military supplies being ferried from Aden to Ethiopia.

The evidence suggests a policy of incrementalism, which explores opportunities as they occur or are created, a policy of probing Western responses and establishing precedents. The role of a 'Soviet military presence' in support of overseas objectives will, therefore, be shaped by the scale and style of the Western response to the various Soviet initiatives. In this context, the distinction which has just been drawn between the employment of Soviet naval forces to secure the safe arrival of logistic support and their employment to prevent Western intervention against a client state is important. So, too, is the distinction between the USSR's willingness to risk hostilities with a third-party state, and their continuing reluctance to engage US naval forces. Meanwhile we should bear in mind that the Soviet navy's role in this more assertive overseas policy is secondary. The primary instruments are the provision of arms, military advice and training; the transport of men, munitions and equipment by merchant ship and long-range air; and direct participation by the combat troops of revolutionary states. The primary role of the navy is to provide protection and support and to serve as an earnest of Soviet commitment.

This brings us to the question of whether there is some Soviet grand design driving a coordinated oceans policy in support of overseas objectives. The short answer is no, but we must distinguish here between the operational aspects and the setting of objectives. The military-style organization of the merchant, fishing and research fleets means that it is relatively simple to make use of their ships in peacetime for naval support tasks such as replenishment and forward picketing, and they all make some contribution to the generalized requirement for worldwide intelligence and information gathering. There are also the geostrategic advantages to be gained in terms of a worldwide infra-structure, actual or potential. The latter includes the provision of improved harbor facilities in locations which would assume great strategic significance for the USSR in the event of world war, as for example the fishing port at Gwardar in Baluchistan.

But when we turn to objectives, we see that the long-term interests of the three main ocean uses frequently diverge. The build-up of the fishing fleet stemmed from a decision in the late 1940s that fishery was a more cost-effective source of protein than collective farming. The build-up of the merchant fleet reflected the post-Stalin shift in the mid-1950s toward trade, aid and arms supply, and the consequential requirement to earn hard currency and avoid dependence on foreign bottoms. The navy's shift to forward deployment reflected the qualitatively new threat to the Soviet homeland from distant sea areas. Inevitably there is some conflict between these divergent interests, and at the Law of the Sea negotiations the narrow domestic concerns of the Soviet fishing industry ran counter to the foreign policy objective of increasing Soviet influence. Similarly, national security concerns and the concept of strategic infrastructure have led the USSR into political entanglements which would seem to be against its broader interests. Only the merchant fleet consistently serves these more general foreign policy goals, and I see it as the principal maritime instrument of Soviet overseas policy.

Of course, these judgments are based on past evidence, and we cannot be sure how things will develop in the future. It is clear that a policy toward the employment of forces in peacetime has been evolved progressively and, although the navy's political role stemmed from the presence in distant seas of warships which had been deployed forward in 'strategic' defense, changes in threat perception, risk and opportunities meant that this role has become increasingly important. This brings us back to the question of whether the Soviet navy is still perceived as an expensive necessity, whose forces are procured exclusively for war-related tasks, or whether it is coming to be seen as a preferred instrument of policy for pursuing overseas objectives in peacetime. This is hard to answer, not least because the Soviets do not seem to have made up their minds on the matter.

We are not even certain of where Gorshkov stands in this matter. Until the publication of the series of articles over his name in 1972, there were few indications that Gorshkov was a long-standing advocate of far-flung, balanced fleets; one could well argue the reverse. Twenty-five years ago he was brought to Moscow by Khrushchev to implement decisions which were primarily designed to release resources from naval use to the civilian economy. If they had been carried through, they would have resulted in a task-specific, defensively oriented navy, more firmly tied to home waters than at any time in its history. The 1957–8 decisions (which were prompted by Western technological advances rather than any change in Soviet objectives) would have partially broken these ties, but only to end up with an unbalanced fleet, depending wholly on submarines and aircraft for distant operations. While it can be argued that these particular procurement decisions derived directly from the political leadership, no such defense can be offered where combat capabilities and operational readiness were concerned. Yet the shift to forward deployment seems to have come as an unwelcome surprise to the Soviet navy, which was operationally ill-prepared for the move. As late as February 1963,[81] seven years after he had taken over as Commander in Chief of the navy, Gorshkov had to lecture the fleet on the need to get to sea and stay there, so as to develop an ocean-going all-weather capability. Writing in 1968,[82] Gorshkov noted there had been a need to 'meet the qualitatively new requirements' which had involved the 'organic restructuring of the navy and the reorienting of traditional naval policy'. This is hardly the picture of a navy straining at some political leash which was thwarting its peacetime aspirations. It also gives the lie to self-serving claims that contemporary Soviet naval policy stems from the mid-1950s, when Gorshkov took over.

It is true that in his articles, Gorshkov was clearly arguing for an assertive foreign policy and for the importance of navies as an instrument of state policy in peacetime. But we have seen that he went well beyond the 'party line' as expounded by Kulish, and we must remember that one of the main purposes of his articles was to release more resources to naval construction and all arguments were grist to that mill. Nor do we know the exact makeup of the powerful coalition of interests which emboldened Gorshkov to make what was a very untypical stand against agreed policy. There was, however, a major cleavage of opinion within the Soviet leadership at this period over foreign and defense policy questions and their impact on the domestic economy, and Gorshkov could only hope to draw support for the navy's case from the 'harder' side of that debate. It may, therefore, be that he angled his argument regarding the navy's peacetime role in that direction. And when we compare the articles with the subsequent book, we do indeed find a different emphasis. The navy's peacetime role is much less prominent, and the material from the article which discusses this subject is reproduced in heavily amended form. A new section has been added, which looks at Western naval involvement in 'Local wars of imperialism', but these two sections make up less than 7 percent of the whole. The bulk of the book is devoted to war-related subjects or to the non-military aspects of seapower.

Turning to shipbuilding evidence, we see that there are clearly defined war-fighting requirements for all classes which are currently building or forecast. The long-range amphibious ships are configured for opposed assault in hostile waters, which argues against them having been built primarily for a peacetime role. We also have evidence which indicates that the new large carrier was justified in terms of defending the SSBN bastions and not for peacetime intervention. Writing in February 1967,[83] Gorshkov gave the standard line of disparaging the carrier's vulnerability and reaffirming the correctness of the Soviet decision to rely on missiles. At this date, the Soviet navy had three years' experience in the Mediterranean and in less than a year would be moving to the second phase of its shift to forward deployment and the greater political exploitation of naval forces in distant sea areas; but Gorshkov did not argue for a proper aircraft carrier. However, writing in 1972, he makes no reference to the carrier's vulnerability although he was also silent about its contemporary tasks and capabilities; however, he did deploy a rarely quoted Leninist principle which argued (by implication) that since the enemy had carriers, so must the USSR.[84] And this was part of his larger argument for general-purpose surface forces which were needed to defend the SSBN bastions.

Lastly, we need to consider the USSR's geostrategic circumstances. It stretches from Western Europe to Japan, borders twelve states and another seven are directly accessible across short stretches of sea. The country spans 170° of longitude (a full 180° if we include the Warsaw Pact), and thus looks south at half the globe. About 85 percent of the world's population lives within 3,000 miles of Soviet territory, although China blocks immediate access to Southeast Asia. Western Europe, North Africa, the Middle East and the Indian subcontinent are all within 2,000 miles of the USSR, while the territories of its national security zone are contiguous. In terms of strategic access, the USSR is Mackinder's heartland, and the availability of strategic air lift backed by merchant shipping means that the navy's role in projecting Soviet military power is potentially less important.

To sum up, additional resources have been allocated to naval construction and there are clear indications that the Soviet leadership has accepted that the importance of the navy's role has increased significantly, both absolutely and relative to the other branches of service, and this process may continue in the future. Meanwhile, a policy for the employment of Soviet naval forces in pursuit of peacetime objectives has evolved progressively, but there is yet no evidence that this is seen as a primary (as opposed to supporting) means of projecting Soviet power in distant parts of the globe. However, the concept of seapower has now been accepted as relevant to the USSR's circumstances, and while the theoretical implications are probably still being worked out, one of the upshots in the future may be a new willingness to use Soviet naval forces to counter Western military intervention. We know from Gorshkov's definition of a balanced fleet that the navy is prepared to 'secure state interests in peacetime'. Since an early reference to this task gave it as the particular responsibility of the submarine force,[85] one must assume that combat operations are not excluded.

Overview

In drawing together the discussion, we need to distinguish between the Soviet navy as it is today and as it will be in a decade or so. We know that for the past ten years or more, Admiral Gorshkov and his supporters have been dissatisfied with the strength and structure of the fleet, in relation to the requirements being levied on it. The failure of the military leadership to appreciate fully the navy's role, coupled with prejudices concerning particular weapons and platforms, had meant that on the one hand, the fleet had been configured for a relatively narrow span of specific missions, with a consequential loss of flexibility, and on the other hand it lacked the full range of forces to discharge these missions effectively. Gorshkov's judgment paralleled official US assessments, which noted that the Soviet navy's mission was limited to sea denial, whereas Western navies had the broader strategic mission of securing the use of the sea for a wide range of purposes.

Gorshkov's most persistent criticism has been of the military leadership's inability to grasp the fact that task-specific naval forces, however deadly in themselves, require the support of general-purpose forces (particularly surface ships), if they are to be able to accomplish their task.[86] He continues to argue that army dominance has meant that the importance of seapower in a struggle with maritime states has been de-emphasized and a relatively low priority has been given to traditional naval roles in war and in peace. Again, this would seem fair comment, and is supported by official US assessments which continue to credit an overall margin of superiority to the US navy, while making no allowance for the other forces that the Soviet navy would have to face in the event of world war.

It is difficult, therefore, to agree with Western assertions that the USSR, as a land power, now has more naval forces than it 'needs'. Any attempt to allocate existing Soviet forces among the various missions that have to be discharged at the onset of world war show that there is certainly no surplus of Soviet capability over what are seen as essential requirements.[87] What constitutes 'enough' is more difficult to determine, but it is relevant that when the procurement of present-day Soviet forces was originally decided in the 1961–4 period, the US navy was substantially larger than it is today. It is, therefore, largely fortuitous that the Soviet deficit is not greater. What is more, over the last twenty years, the West (i.e. NATO, including France, plus Australia, New Zealand and Japan) has taken delivery of two to three times as many distant water surface ships as the Soviet bloc, and the imbalance is even greater when account is taken of ship size and capability.[88] Until 1967, the West was even building more nuclear submarines than the USSR; after that time the Soviet delivery rate doubled. But the subsequent disparity was concentrated in SSBN, and the production rate of attack boats remained roughly in balance. Meanwhile, the USSR must take account of other countries, including Sweden, Spain, South Korea and Taiwan. Although both the USA and USSR must be wary of the large Chinese submarine force, the threat to Soviet interests is more direct. Indeed, a Soviet contingency planner has to allow that, with few exceptions, all the significant navies in the world are at best neutral and most of them must be included in the list of potential adversaries.

This is not to underestimate the very real strength of the Soviet navy, or the threat that it could pose to Western interests. But when we divide these forces between the four widely separated fleet areas, Soviet naval strength falls into perspective, particularly when we take account of the demanding requirements for area defense, and consider the scale of forces that can be assembled against them.[89] Certainly, the West has had cause to be concerned, and the large submarine force was especially worrying. Nevertheless, Gorshkov was justified in his complaints about the serious limitations on the navy's capabilities . . . which flowed from its narrow mission structure, its task-specific characteristics, and the paucity of general-purpose forces.

However, when we turn to the future, several separate

developments combine to create a rather different picture. First, there is the original 1969–70 planning decision to increase substantially the size of the follow-on classes of the three major surface warship types and to build a class of battlecruisers to serve as command ships; these ships began delivery in 1980. Secondly, there is the navy's successful battle to add a second large destroyer-size class to the existing program and to undertake the design of a large carrier. Thirdly, the Yankee conversion program (from SSBN to SSN)[90] means that seven attack units will now join the nuclear submarine force each year, compared to about four a year during the previous decade. Fourthly, the Backfire strike aircraft continues to replace Badger, and a new ASW aircraft is expected.

These programs mean that by 1995, allowing a twenty-five-year life cycle and using the new scaled-up categorization of types, we could expect about 15 cruiser-size ships (of some 12,000 tons), 65 destroyer-size (including Kara and Kresta II), and 55 frigate-size ships (Krivak and successor). There would also be 5 battlecruiser/command ships and perhaps 7-8 air capable ships, comprising 2 Moskva, 4 Kiev and 1–2 new-type large carriers. To put it another way, every three years the Soviet navy will acquire a powerful new battle group comprising a heavily armed battlecruiser, 3 cruisers and about 10 large destroyers. The first three or four of these battle groups will rely on a Kiev to provide a modicum of sea-based air support, but thereafter we might expect to see one fully capable air-superiority carrier for every two battle groups. On the submarine side, current building rates (assuming they persist) will boost the attack force to about 135 nuclear-powered units by the end of 1987, declining thereafter to stabilize at about 100 SSN by the end of 1992. By the end of 1987, the SSBN force will still stand at about 60 units carrying some 950 missiles but could rise thereafter to stabilize at 75 units carrying 1,200 missiles by the end of 1992.

But this greatly improved surface capability and the increased number of submarines is only half the story. The new Alpha class SSN, which can go faster and dive deeper than its US counterparts, represents the first real end product of the 1957–8 decision which singled out the submarine as the key component of the Soviet navy, with all that implies in terms of priority for research and development resources. The Alpha may well presage a series of advances that could challenge the West's technological lead in the submarine ASW field. A separate problem is presented by the tactical employment of ballistic missiles. It is clear that important elements of the military leadership have always been attracted to the concept of 'calling down fire' from land-based systems on naval targets, using satellite surveillance systems, or ships and submarines as forward observers. Even if the Soviets have yet to develop the capability they already claim, there is every reason to suppose they will persist in their efforts. And lastly, there is the matter of strategic ASW and Soviet efforts to develop a space-based area-search system. The latter may not be successful, but undoubtedly they will yield fruits in related fields which may surprise the West.

An interesting aspect of these different naval developments is that the great majority are the outcome of the regular planning process, where the army-dominated military leadership formulates requirements in response to prevailing military doctrine and changing perceptions of the threat. The concepts of sea-based strategic reserves and of protracted nuclear war combined to generate a range of new military requirements which, among other things, justified a one-third increase in the annual new-construction surface tonnage. This causal chain is in no way exceptional and a striking feature of Soviet naval policy since the war is the extent to which warship building programs and other forms of weapons procurement can be unambiguously tied to changes in the Soviet perception of the maritime threat. The evidence includes the cancellation as well as the initiation of programs, the cutting back process as well as the allocation of additional resources.[91] Given that the USSR has been in a position of overall maritime inferiority and is geographically disadvantaged, this was only to be expected. More surprising at times has been the relatively niggardly response to what have been correctly perceived requirements, reflecting the army's dominance of the defense decision-making process. This is not just a matter of relative priorities, but (as Gorshkov has argued) reflects an exaggerated respect for innovative technology in a field the military leadership does not properly understand.

However, in the last twenty-five years, the navy has progressively achieved a greater voice in how maritime requirements are to be met and, most recently, in formulating their content. There is a world of difference between the way in which the 'cruise missile solution' was imposed on the navy in the mid-1950s and the successful argument about naval requirements in the mid-1970s. This progressive change is a byproduct of the steadily increasing importance of the maritime component of the USSR's defense posture, initially because of the threat of nuclear attack from distant sea areas, and subsequently because of the sea-based national strategic reserve. The military leadership has readily acknowledged this growing importance but appears to be less happy with the increased autonomy this importance has provided the navy; an autonomy which is probably bolstered by the support the navy gets for its 'internationalist mission' from certain factions in the political leadership.

Meanwhile, in the second edition of his book, Gorshkov has moved beyond the question of naval requirements to challenge the Soviet dogma that military operations in the continental theaters will be decisive throughout a future war, and to argue that at certain stages the oceanic theaters will inevitably take precedence, with all that implies in terms of tasking the other branches of service. In doing so, it would seem that he has deliberately left the confines of 'military science' and entered the domain of 'military doctrine' in its formal Soviet sense, once again appealing over the military's head to the party leadership.

Whether Gorshkov will be fully successful remains to be seen, and certainly there are strong institutional interests which must feel threatened by this steady rise in the navy's relative importance. However, the outcome may depend as much on the progress of the internal debate over war-fighting *versus* deterrence-through-punishment policies, and the scale of resources the Soviets are prepared to commit to covering the contingency of a world war, fought to the finish. Gorshkov's assertion that the oceanic theaters will become more important than the continental ones, presupposes an extended struggle with the capitalist maritime coalition. The institutional implications of carrying a war-fighting doctrine to its logical conclusion may encourage members of the military leadership to consider more carefully the wider advantages of a policy of mutual deterrence based on MAD.

This, however, all lies in the future, if anywhere. For the present, we can conclude from this analysis of Soviet military doctrine that their military planners take the possibility of nuclear war very seriously. The existence of a strategic reserve implies that the USSR is prepared to wage war should deterrence fail. The concept of SSBN bastions and the allocation of substantial numbers of submarine and surface units to their protection is not itself sufficient evidence of such a mission, since this could be intended to protect the SSBN force from US interdiction during the conventional phase of a war. However, the fact that these pro-SSBN forces are now being provided with an organic air capability, although this breaches the principle of cost effectiveness that underlies the combined arms approach, argues that the forces are required to be fully effective in the postexchange phase, when shore-based air support will no longer be available. A second body of evidence is provided by the efforts to develop the means of countering Western ballistic missile submarines. This cannot be explained solely in terms of damage limitation, since the USSR has no defense against the more substantial ICBM force and, notwithstanding US declaratory policy, it must allow that in the heat of crisis, these missiles would be launched 'on warning'. An earlier example is provided by the allocation of resources to counter the strike carrier (including doubling the building rate of nuclear submarines), despite the establishment of the air defense force of the country (PVO) as a separate branch of the service to defend the USSR against nuclear strike aircraft. Efforts to counter the sea-based element of the US strategic inventory must, therefore, be related to its war-fighting and reserve potential.

The scale of resources which the Soviets have allocated to the two main naval missions of strategic strike and counterstrike is a good indication of the priority given to being able to fight a nuclear war should deterrence fail. The very attempt to develop a counter to the US SSBN serves to validate the thesis, since the apparent insolubility of the problem led Western analysts to dismiss the possibility that the Soviets would even try.[92]

Further evidence is provided by the Soviet willingness to incur the political costs involved in prepositioning their forces in key strategic areas, costs that undermine the influence-building thesis. An early and unambiguous example was the basing of submarines in Albania, giving access to the far side of the Turkish Straits. Following their eviction in 1961, the Soviets brought sustained pressure on Egypt for access to their facilities which would allow them to develop a counter to the US strategic strike capability in the Mediterranean.[93] However, we have also seen that the political commitment to establish the strategic infrastructure for waging global war clearly has its limits, and these appear to be related mainly to military operations in the continental theaters.

In terms of operational activity, the present naval posture is one of being on guard against the possibility of war, rather than preparing for its inevitability; of being prepositioned rather than poised. Training follows a regular annual cycle and operational readiness is relatively low, both in the home fleet areas and when forward deployed. Nor does the pattern of Soviet warship construction give the impression of an urge to war, despite the recent increase in the allocation of resources to naval shipbuilding. It seems designed to meet the immediate requirements generated by the existing balance of forces and respective military postures, and to have the capacity for a surge response should a new challenge emerge.

However, whatever the underlying rationale, the emergence during the next ten years of a powerful Soviet fleet with a true worldwide capability, will provide the leadership with an important new instrument of overseas policy in peacetime. At the same time, the concept of seapower has acquired a new respectability in Soviet military thought. These developments, combined with the lowered expectation that confrontation will escalate to world war, favor the emergence of a more assertive Soviet naval policy, designed to counter the projection of Western military power around the globe.

Notes: Chapter 6

1 For such an approach, see my 'The rationale for the development of Soviet sea power', in *US Naval Institute Proceedings*, May, 1980.
2 Military art represents a body of thinking about methods of waging war in accordance with military doctrine. Military art derives from military doctrine and military science, and encompasses strategy, operations and tactics. Little of interest can be said about military doctrine in a purely naval context.
3 For a summary description of this analytical method, see my 'Turning points in Soviet naval policy', in *Soviet Naval Developments: Context and Capability* (henceforth SND), M. MccGwire (ed.) (New York: Praeger, 1973), pp. 176–209.
4 There was only one naval title among fifteen books in the 'Officers Library' series announced in 1957, and not a single naval title in the seventeen books of the new series announced in 1964. There were probably only two naval titles among fifty important military books published 1960–9. See H. F. Scott, *Soviet Military Doctrine: Its Formulation and Dissemination*, Stanford Research Institute, June, 1971, pp. 81–92. The Naval Academy is only one among fifteen arm-of-service academies at the Command and Staff level. During the period 1965–70, the navy achieved its proportionate share of Candidates of Science from the Lenin Military-Political Academy (i.e. at the Commander level) but achieved no Doctors of Science (ibid., pp. 120–4).
5 The other four branches and the Main Political Administration rate one apiece: see John McDonnell, 'The Soviet defense industry as a pressure group', in *Soviet Naval Policy: Objectives and Constraints* (henceforth *SNP*), M. MccGwire, K. Booth and J. McDonnell (eds) (New York: Praeger), p. 104; those figures apply to the 1971–6 period, but there was no change in the committee elected at the 25th Party Congress.
6 Although there was no firm evidence of such targeting, this was inferred at the time from the persistence of close shadowing, whether or not there was any seaborne countercarrier capability present; such a capability was not achieved on a sustained basis until the end of the 1960s. Russia-based aircraft were not suitable for this strike role, since their response time was too long, and they first had to breach the NATO air defense barrier. There were, however, sufficient land-based missiles to cover this requirement, and the task was technically feasible. The existence of such a concept is supported by the subsequent claim for a more extensive capability of this type.
7 A.A. Grechko, 'A socialist multinational army', *Krasnaya zvezda*, 17 December, 1972.
8 This term does not cover launching a pre-emptive attack to weaken or prevent an inevitable enemy assault.
9 P. Vigor, *The Soviet View of War, Peace and Neutrality* (London: Routledge & Kegan Paul, 1975); for a summary version, see 'The Soviet View of War', *SND*, pp. 17-18.

10 V. D. Sokolovskij, *Voennaya Strategiva* (New York: Crane, Russak, 1968), pp. 346–7; explicit statements concerning the targets of strategic systems remained unchanged in the 1962, 1963 and 1968 editions.

11 ibid., p. 349.

12 P. Vigor, op. cit., *SND*, p. 22.

13 In strict war-fighting terms, it would be simpler, more certain and more cost-effective to ravage Europe with nuclear weapons, as is clearly planned for the USA. However, the Soviet military posture in Eastern Europe, Warsaw Pact exercise scenarios, and Soviet military pronouncements, all indicate a rapid advance into NATO Europe. Planning to seize this area only makes military sense, if it is intended to make subsequent use of the territory and its resources. Those who argue that the present Soviet military posture indicates an intention to seize Europe in circumstances other than in a world war, ignore their Marxist-Leninist theory and the importance of the cost–benefit calculus. The occupation of Europe can only be expected to yield benefits in the surreal circumstances of a world war, which the Soviet leadership has been unable to avoid.

14 This was not just Soviet paranoia. A senior NATO commander gave this as his policy in 1961.

15 *Morskoj sbornik* (henceforth *Msh*), May, 1966, p. 9; February, 1967, p. 16.

16 Europe only becomes a US target zone once it has been occupied by the Soviets. Canada (and perhaps parts of Mexico) would be included in the Soviets' initial strike plan.

17 Gorshkov stresses the global character of a future world war, but his statements can be read as referring to SSBN operating areas, rather than their targets on land. S. G. Gorshkov, *Morskaya Mosch' gosudarstva* (Moscow: Voenizaat, 1976), p. 363.

18 This could well be present policy, as the only way of ensuring that China does not emerge from the war stronger than Russia.

19 Leonard Sullivan observes that this would explain the stockpiling of superseded weapons and equipment in forward areas, after units have been re-equipped with more modern arms.

20 This idea was prompted by Avigdor Haselkorn, *The Evolution of Soviet Security, Strategy 1965—75* (New York: Crane, Russak, 1978); however, he sees such arms as being intended for redeployment to other client states in 'peacetime' conflict situations.

21 The facilities established in Somalia were capable of supporting a much larger Soviet force than has operated in the Indian Ocean so far.

22 Development of the fishing port at Gwadar in Baluchistan, 100 miles from the Pakistan-Iranian border could be an example of such a strategy.

23 The Pacific Fleet was called 'Far East Naval Forces' until January, 1935; the Northern Fleet was called 'Northern Naval Flotilla' until May, 1937.

24 A.A. Grechko, 'The fleet of our homeland', *Msb*, July, 1971.

25 For a summary of this debate, see H. Ullman, 'The counter Polaris task', in *SNP* pp. 586–90; also D. Cox 'Sea power and Soviet foreign policy', US Naval Institute Proceedings, June, 1969, p. 59.

26 S. G. Gorshkov, 'Razvitie Sovetskogo Voenno Morskogo Isskusstva', *Msb*, February, 1967, pp. 19–20. Gorshkov places this controversy in the mid-1950s; but so too does he place the decisions which underlie the present structure of the navy, which clearly originate from a later period, although he would like to tie them to his appointment as Commander in Chief. This kind of argument is likely to have persisted throughout the later 1950s, until resolved in the early 1960s.

27 For a clear exposition of the navy viewpoint, see V. A. Alafuzov, 'On the appearance of the work *Military Strategy*', *Msb*, January, 1963, pp. 88–96; Admiral Alafuzov had been Chief of the Main Naval Staff during the war.

28 V. D. Sokolovskij and M. I. Cheredruchenko, *Krasnaya zvezda*, 25 and 28 August, 1964.

29 For evidence of this wider debate, see Marshal Shulman, 'Trends in Soviet foreign policy', *SNP*, pp. 8–10 (also published at greater length as 'Towards a Western philosophy of coexistence', in *Foreign Affairs*, October, 1973); also John Erickson, 'Soviet defence policy and naval interests', *SNP*, p. 60.

30 *Msb*, 1972, nos. 2–6, 8–12; 1973, no. 2.

31 Publication anomalies were first identified by R. Weinland: see 'Analysis of Admiral

Gorshkov's navies in war and peace', *SNP*, pp. 558–65. This analysis was refined and extended by John McDonnell in his *Bibliographic Analysis of Morskoj sbornik 1963—75* (Halifax, Nova Scotia: Centre for Foreign Policy Studies, Dalhousie University, September, 1977). There is additional circumstantial evidence which points to this same conclusion; see *SNI*, p. 55.

32 Further confirmation of this assessment came in 1976 with the reviews of Gorshkov's subsequent book (see below) and in 1979 with the evidence of new surface warship building programs. There were, however, some analysts (notably James McConnell) who argued that Gorshkov was not engaged in advocacy, but was announcing a political decision to withhold submarine-launch missiles from the initial strikes. For McConnell's argument, see his 'Military-political tasks of the Soviet navy in war and peace', pp. 183–209 of *Soviet Oceans Development*, prepared by John Hardt for the Senate National Oceans Policy Study (henceforth *SOD*), US GPO, October, 1976. My 'Naval power and Soviet oceans policy', in the same publication, includes a rejoinder to the advocacy argument; see B. and C. Apps, pp. 167–82. For a later exposition of McConnell's analysis see 'The Gorshkov articles, the new Gorshkov book, and their relation to policy', in M. MccGwire and J. McDonnell (eds), *Soviet Naval Influence: Domestic and Foreign Dimensions* (henceforth *SNI*) (New York: Praeger, 1977), pp. 565–620.

33 For a convenient version of the analysis underlying this summary, see *SOD*, pp. 79–132. An edited version of my initial but more comprehensive analysis, May, 1973, appears in *Admiral Gorshkov on 'Navies in War and Peace'* (Washington, DC: Center for Naval Analyses, September, 1974), CRC 252, which also contains analyses by R. Weinland and J. McConnell.

34 Some 10 percent of the series is devoted to the Mediterranean and Black Sea. The second article (cleared for typesetting in January, 1972) includes a chapter, 'The Russians in the Mediterranean', which is nominally about the period prior to 1855, but speaks clearly and at length about the strategic importance and political legitimacy of the present-day Soviet naval presence in the area. Gorshkov returns to discuss the Mediterranean (and its contemporary significance) throughout the series, and it is the only area to have a chapter of its own.

35 This tabulation was prepared in May, 1973, on the basis of the initial analysis.

36 The other was Brezhnev; his opposition to certain aspects of the articles was inferred from the fact that Gorshkov not only ignored his June, 1971, proposal for mutual restrictions on naval operations, but advanced a contrary line of argument, particularly as regards the Mediterranean. However, Brezhnev's proposal was probably designed to limit the naval costs of a Soviet withdrawal from Egypt, which Gorshkov clearly opposed. Therefore, nothing can be inferred about where Brezhnev stood on Gorshkov's central argument.

37 *Msb*, July, 1971; exercise OKEAN '70 is described as demonstrating the navy's readiness to repel attacks on Russia and to launch its own strikes. Only submarines, naval aviation and the landings in the Arctic receive special mention, with submarines singled out for a paragraph on their own. The non-mention of surface ships, by far the most numerous component in the exercise, seems pointed. Reference to US imperialism is limited to Southeast Asia, Soviet support being limited to 'fraternal aid'.

38 A. A. Grechko, *Na Strache Mira: Stroitel' stva Kommunizma* (Moscow: Voenizaat, 1971). A 112- page booklet designed for a 'broad range of readers' that 'describes the great historical mission of the Soviet Armed Forces, and the increased tasks posed for them ... by the 24th CPSU Congress'.

39 V. V. Kulish, *Voennaya Sila: Mezhdunarodnye Otnoshenniya* (Moscow: Mevhdunarodnye Otnosheniia, 1972), pp. 135–7.

40 Lt General J. Zavyalov, 'The creative nature of Soviet military doctrine', 19 April, 1973; Major General A. Milovidov 'A philosophical analysis of military thought', 17 May, 1973. Neither article addressed Gorshkov's arguments directly but both took issue with some aspect of what he said. Zavyalov stressed the primacy of political factors and the fundamental position of the political content of military doctrine. Milovidov emphasized that you cannot take examples from one historical period to support arguments in the contemporary period, which is, of course, what Gorshkov did.

41 This was the first time since Zhukov's ouster in 1957 that a professional military officer was co-opted onto the highest party body. Gromyko (Foreign Affairs) and Adropov (KGB) joined the Politburo on the same date.

42 A. A. Grechko, 'The leading role of the CPSU in building the army of a developed Socialist Society', *Voprosy istorn KPSS*, May, 1974, pp. 38–9; Weinland has compared this with earlier pronouncements, including a comparable article in *Kommunist*, May, 1973, and concludes there was a distinct shift in emphasis; see SNP, p. 569.

43 J. McDonnell notes that Grechko's 1974 article followed the same general line as one by A. A. Yepishev (Chief of the Main Political Administration of the Armed forces) in *Moguchee Oruzhie Partn.*, which was released to the press at the end of 1972.

44 'Soviet national seapower', *Pravda*, 28 July, 1974. One is tempted to tie Admiral Kasatanov's retirement in October, 1974, to this compromise for the reasons given in my initial analysis, n. 33, above.

45 S. G. Gorshkov, *Morskaya Moshch' gosudarstva* (op. cit.); cleared for typesetting 1 August, 1975; released to the press 27 November, 1975.

46 V. G. Bakaev, in Gorshkov, op. cit.

47 This reflected the imminent availability of the Yankee SSBN; additions and deletions are by comparison with the 1963 edition; see Harriet Fast Scott, op. cit., pp. 235–40, 243, 308, 319, respectively. In the 1968 Russian edition, pp. 235, 240, 243, 308, 330.

48 For example, S. E. Zakharov, *Istoriya Voenno-Morskogo Iskusstva* (Moscow: Voenizdat, 1969), p. 561.

49 A. V. Bazov, *Boevoj put, Sovetskogo Voenno-Morskogo Flota* (Moscow: Voenizdat, 1974), p. 492.

50 These are listed and analyzed in Appendix B to my 'Naval power and Soviet oceans policy', in *SOD*, p. 167.

51 *Msb*, February, 1973, p. 21; hereafter, *Msb* references will show year/month/page/paragraph (73/2/21/3).

52 *Boevoj put*, op. cit., p. 491; the tasks are referred to as 'important' and 'no less important', respectively.

53 Numbers in brackets refer to page/paragraph of the Russian edition, op. cit., n. 45.

54 The glaring internal contradiction in para. 360/4 is explained by the earlier division of fleet-against-fleet operations into two categories. Use of the term '*borba*' (cf. 352/5) confirms that the final sentence in this paragraph is referring to the 'pure form', intended solely to gain and maintain command.

55 *Msb*, 72/11/32/5; 73/2/20/7.8

56 *Msb*, 67/2/20, n. 1: 'able to discharge assigned tasks in both nuclear-missile and conventional war and also to secure state interests at sea in peacetime'.

57 *Msb*, 73/2/20/7.8, 2/21/1; see *SOD*, pp. 116-18 for a discussion of these paragraphs, which read like advocacy.

58 This constitutes a subsection of 'Some theoretical questions of naval warfare', which, in other respects, reproduces verbatim the greater part of Gorshkov's December, 1974, *Msb* article. 'Command of the sea' is a substantial addition, which takes almost as much space as all the other seven categories together. For a discussion of earlier references to command of the sea, see P. Vigor, 'Soviet understanding of command of the sea', and my 'Command of the sea in Soviet naval strategy', in *SNP*, pp. 601-22, 623-36.

59 *Msb*, 72/9/16/6.

60 This analogy is comparable to (but much more pertinent than) the critical remarks in the Gorshkov series about those who fail to understand the significance of seapower (*Msb*, 72/3/20/2-21/2; 72/4/9/1-22/9).

61 These were analyzed by John McDonnell in a working paper presented at the fourth workshop on Soviet naval developments (1977). References: Bagramyan, *Izvestia*, 22 May, 1976, p. 5; Lobov, *Msb*, 76/4/99-105.

62 The Soviets speak in terms of three zones, but the third one is beyond the defense perimeter. Robert Herrick discusses these in his book, *Soviet Naval Strategy* (Annapolis, Md: United States Naval Institute, 1967), and his current research is throwing further light on this concept

63 See n. 24, above.

64 R. O. Welander, *et al.*, *The Soviet Navy Declaratory Doctrine for Theater Nuclear Warfare* (Washington, DC: BDM Corporation, 1977), Report No. DNA (Defense

Nuclear Agency) 4434T. 30 September, p. 41; this is a most useful study and I have drawn freely on the conclusions.

65 Especially K. J. Moore; see 'Developments in submarine systems' and 'Antisubmarine warfare', in *SNI*, pp. 151–84, 185–200. Moore highlights the Soviet emphasis on non-acoustic methods of submarine detection, the use of satellites in this and related roles, and the concept of the extended ASW team, which includes satellites, air, submarine, surface ships and shorebased missiles. He notes discussion in Soviet journals of new methods of submarine propulsion and the development of wing-in-ground effect vehicles, suitable for high-speed area search.

66 The concept of area defense is part and parcel of maritime theaters of military operation (MTVD). In a 1979 (unpublished) paper, James Westwood draws attention to the latter concept and its derivation from the army's land-based equivalent (TVD), and he itemized the various types of zone which can be found in such theaters. He notes that the concept of MTVDs is related to the defense of a few delimited geographical regions. He identifies five MTVDs, three of which are referred to as closed (Baltic, Black Sea and Sea of Japan), while the other two look out onto great oceans (Northern Sea and Kamchatka). There are also two ocean theaters of military operations (OTVD), one comprising the Eastern Mediterranean and the other the Arabian Sea.

67 *Aviation Week and Space Technology*, 24 September, 1979, p. 139: *Milwaukee Journal*, 31 December, 1979.

68 This class is building at Baltic Yard, Leningrad, and will have taken over the 'battleship slip' on which the nuclear icebreakers Arktika and Sibir were built. The lead ship of this class, named Kirov, was delivered to the navy in 1980; *Aviation Week and Space Technology*, 18 February, 1980, p. 21.

69 The Polnochny size was dropped from the inventory, the Alligator size carried on (Ropuchka), and a much larger ship, the Ivan Rogov class, was added.

70 Bradford Dismukes was the first to draw attention to Soviet concerns in this direction; see 'The Soviet naval general purpose force: roles and missions in wartime', *SNP*, pp. 573–84.

71 For a summary of the evidence that the Gorshkov series was, *inter alia*, arguing for carriers, see my 'Naval power and Soviet oceans policy', in *SOD*, pp.118–19.

72 See article by Admirals Zumwalt and Bagley in the *Milwaukee Sentinel*, 31 December, 1979; also *New York Times*, 17 December, 1979.

73 In December 1979, press reports quoted US defense officials as saying that Admiral Gorshkov had acknowledged that a carrier was under construction. It is expected to be about 78,000 tons, carrying about eighty-five aircraft; *New York Times*, 17 December, 1979; see also *Aviation Week and Space Technology*, 20 August and 24 September, 1979, pp. 14 and 142, 146, respectively, and *New York Times*, 17 March, 1979.

74 See my 'The Soviet navy in the seventies', Appendix, *SNI*, pp. 653-7.

75 I am indebted to James McConnell for this point.

76 B. N. Dismukes and J. M. McConnell (eds), *Soviet Naval Diplomacy* (Oxford; Pergamon Press, 1979). This book has been prepared by seven members of the Center for Naval Analyses, Washington, DC, and comprises a comprehensive survey and analysis of the peacetime employment of Soviet naval forces. This whole article reflects my debt to the analysts at CNA, although I would not claim that we agree on all points.

77 See G. Dragnich, 'The Soviet Union's quest for access to naval facilities in Egypt prior to the June war of 1967; *SNP*, 237-77.

78 Albania and Egypt.

79 See R. G. Weinland, *Superpower Naval Diplomacy in the October 1973 Arab–Israeli War* (Washington, DC: Center for Naval Analyses, 1979), Professional Paper No. 221, June.

80 ibid.

81 *Krasnaya zvezda*, 5 February, 1963.

82 *Krasnaya zvezda*, 11 February, 1968.

83 *Msb*, 67/2/19/2-3.

84 *Msb*, 72/6/12/7; see n. 48, above.

85 S. Gorshkov, *Krasnaya zvezda*, 30 October, 1962.

86 Gorshkov alluded to this problem when talking with Western naval officers in late 1971 – early 1972. In the course of a discussion on 'balanced forces', Gorshkov commented

that while it was easy to defend the requirement for submarines, it was much harder to justify the need for surface ships.

87 I make such an attempt in ch. 4 in Paul Nitze and Leonard Sullivan, *Securing the Seas* (Boulder Co.: Westview Press, 1979).

88 It must be stressed that this is *not* the same as comparing naval strengths, but it does help one to appreciate the Soviet perception of Western naval programs.

89 See Nitze and Sullivan, op. cit., ch. 9, 'Comparative force levels ... ' by Leonard Sullivan for an extended discussion of these points.

90 *Time Magazine*, 14 January, 1980; US statements indicate that nuclear construction has dropped from ten to seven units a year. This suggests that SSBN production is running at 3 p.a. and in measure as Deltas join the fleet, Yankees are being converted to SSN.

91 I address this whole question of primary determinants of naval policy, and in the process, cover my flank against accusations of 'monocausal explanations' or 'rational actor models' in 'The turning points of Soviet naval policy', *SND*, pp. 176–209.

92 Throughout the 1960s, the hypothesis that the Soviet navy's first priority was to develop a counter to the Polaris submarine was ridiculed on the ground of the mission's impracticability.

93 See G.S. Dragnich's 'The Soviet Union's quest for access to naval facilities in Egypt prior to the June war of 1967', in M. MccGwire *et al.*, *Soviet Naval Policy: Objectives and Constraints* (New York: Praeger, 1975) *(SNP)*, pp. 237–77; Dragnich's analysis highlights the persistence of Soviet efforts and the costs they were willing to shoulder to obtain this access.

PART THREE

The Non-Strategic Dimension

7

The Soviet Style of War

NATHAN LEITES

This chapter contributes to discussions about how the Soviets –
particularly the ground forces – would fight, by a study of mostly
Soviet words and writings about war, as well as about the armed
forces in peacetime. I have not examined words related to 'ideology', limiting myself to statements about military events, both in
the present and recent past (the era of Brezhnev) as well as in
1941–5. Hence my main sources, apart from books of military
analysis, are *Red Star* (the armed forces' daily), The *Military
Herald* (the ground forces' monthly), *Communist of the Armed
Forces* (the political department's fortnightly); memoirs of Soviet
and German commanders in World War II, and the *Military-
Historical Journal* (monthly). Even when articles in these publications are signed by persons of modest military rank, I presume
them to have been screened for conformity with the preferences
of the High Command ('the Authorities').

How pertinent are the 1940s for the 1980s? The authorities'
insistence on the current relevance of the 'front experience' is, in
my surmise, far from sham:

> To study the experience of the Great Fatherland War means to
> prepare oneself in the most serious manner ... I should like to
> advise officers ... to have at home a small library [*'bibliotechka'*] of
> [War] memoirs.[1]

The only *series* of books on military matters published in the
1970s is a set of volumes called *Tactics in Combat Examples*
examples from the war. In many cases below, points about simulated combat parallel those about real battle. In other cases, I
have no direct evidence of the persistence of traits documented
for the war. Nevertheless, I shall even then use the present tense,
expressing the conjecture that what was important a third of a
century ago has not ceased to be significant.

I treat reactions attributed to Stalin as I do those of other commanders in the war. Where he exaggerates traits shown by others in less extreme fashion, he illuminates by this very fact. Characteristics shown by armed forces in peacetime are not apt to remain unchanged when war comes. However, wartime behaviour will be related to them. Preferences expressed in peacetime for certain calculations and modes of conduct in war are not apt to be fully realized when war comes. But, again, conduct in war will be related to such antecedents.

Nuclear weapons rarely appear in the military world evoked below. Officers – the only ones who speak *in public* about details of war in the USSR – never discuss strategic nuclear war and rarely theater nuclear operations. The latter are mostly treated, during the period studied, in a small set of books on 'operational art' and 'tactics' published in the later 1960s and early 1970s. There, theater nuclear weapons were largely presented simply as more powerful conventional arms.

What inferences, if any, can be drawn from the portrait developed below with regard to *real* Soviet propensities on nuclear weapons; e.g. with regard to pre-emption? If it be true that the High Command is drawn to this concept, I would expect (a) that they will be intent on procuring evidence which would make pre-emption seem indicated, but also (b) that they would stop short of disregarding contrary evidence or of dispensing with evidence.

In sum, my purpose is not to offer conclusions about questions such as the most effective defense against a Warsaw Pact assault. This debate has been joined authoritatively by others, notably Steven L. Canby in his writings about rethinking the NATO military problem. The Alliance's adherence to a doctrine concentrating on superior firepower is well known. This contrasts markedly with a Soviet armored doctrine that is maneuver-oriented. The Soviet perspective, however, has often been misconstrued in the West. My purpose is not to adjudicate between different approaches to an optimum NATO defense, but rather to present through the writings of Soviet authorities themselves their own views on pursuing conflict. I call this the Soviet style of war.

The Single, Brief, Big Strike

As the ratio of force over target rises, it is affirmed that the average yield of a resource unit employed rises too. The upper

bounds to this relation are no doubt perceived, but hardly mentioned. 'The concentration of *all* means on *one* ... operation', an
early analyst already advances,

> may yield a big economy of force. An enemy front capable of
> enduring dozens of small strikes may be broken by one big strike.
> In certain conditions, a certain mass [*massivnost*] of operation is
> necessary in order to obtain even minimal results.[2]

It is 'particularly with small units' that, according to an analyst,
counterattacks 'will not always be useful': the 'important' ones
are 'strong', involving 'large forces of armored troops in combination with ... troops landed from the air'.[3] The Soviets have yet to
be touched by the sense that anything but the big may be beauti-
ful. How is 'the quickest restoration of faulty machines' obtained?
Well, 'by massing mechanics'.[4]

As we already know, there are according to the Authorities
economies from compressing the application of a given amount of
'forces and means' in time. For one thing, it is held, losses inflicted
within a short time exercise a greater moral impact on personnel
than losses occurring during a protracted period. Hence, the
massing of artillery must attain a sufficient expenditure of
ammunition on target during a unit of time. Thus, a military
leader recalls that during the third phase of World War II, 'the
basic tendencies in the perfecting of artillery preparation were the
shortening of its duration, the increase in density'.[5] The point is
still today 'to bring down short but powerful fire raids on the
enemy'.[6] For operations at sea, Admiral Gorshkov demands a
'further reduction in the duration of impact on the enemy with a
simultaneous increase in the power ... of strikes'. [7]

It is high power per time unit which is believed to raise the
probability of achieving what Soviet planners cherish: producing
a temporary cessation of the enemy's 'capacity for combat' – a
period during which he has become unable to 'put up resistance',
while he is not yet even working on the 'reestablishment' of his
capacity for combat; or is already making efforts to this end, but
has not yet succeeded; a period which one can and must, on the
one hand, prolong by continued striking, and on the other hand,
'utilize' to 'complete the crushing of the enemy'. 'The same
degree of losses', affirms an analyst of the 1930s quoted in the
1970s, 'can either ruin a unit if it is inflicted in the course of a short
... assault, or it can be endured almost without any notice if
members of the unit are eliminated from battle in the course of a
long time'.[8]

The higher one's ability to concentrate in both time and space –

such is the traditional assertion of the High Command – the greater one's assurance of victory over *superior* forces. 'When opposing forces are roughly comparable in equipment and training', the U.S. Defense Department explained in 1976, 'it is generally believed that the attacker must have an overall superiority all along the front in order to advance towards his objectives'.[9] The Soviets seem to disagree. The experience of war, they will say, shows that final results of combat action depend not only on the relationship of forces and means of the fighting sides, but also on the selection of the direction of the main blow. Thus, in the years of the Civil War, when the enemy was superior in forces and means, the determination, among numerous fronts, of the main one was the basic task of strategy. It is affirmed that the Central Committee of the Party solved this task. Soviet military strategy, taking account of the overall insufficiency of its forces and particularly of technical means, boldly proceeded to mass them against the main enemy. It is said that examples of this approach are the concentration of the basic forces of the Red Army on the Eastern Front against Kolchak, and on the Southern Front again Denikin.

To the extent to which a high ratio of impact over target depends on the 'massing' ('*massirovanie*') in space of 'forces and means', it is important to hide such massing from the enemy long enough to disable him from counteracting it by strike or change in his deployment. Having always been aware of this requirement, the Authorities are equally conscious of how much more stringent nuclear weapons have made it. But here as elsewhere they seem – or affect – to be impressed by the continuity between prenuclear and nuclear fighting.

The beliefs sketched above tend toward recommending an early employment of a large fraction of one's resources. This is to be done quickly, against a small fraction of the enemy's force. Correspondingly, the 'initial strike is to be exalted.

'Earlier', Tukhachevskii observed already in the 1930s, 'one began by defeating the secondary forces of the adversary, and finished . . . with his definitive crushing. Now one begins . . . with a basic decisive strike and defers until later the . . . defeat of the weaker echeloned units of the enemy'.[10]

In 1977, a general officer expressed 'the striving to throw oneself on [*obrushit'sya na*] the enemy with one's full might from the first minute'.[11] Indeed, if there is something to the adage that 'success in battle is born as the first shot rings out',[12] then that shot should be as loud as one can make it. Maximum combat power should be placed in the forward assault wave. If 'as they say, a good beginning is half of the whole business',[13] it is important to make it as good as one can. 'One of the most important conditions for achieving success in a meeting engagement' is – 'as is known' – 'the initial attack'.[14] 'Delivering a strong initial strike plays', another officer confirms, 'an important role in obtaining success in a meeting engagement'.[15] Thus, a general officer can affirm that 'the initial strike must always be the strongest'.[16]

When one senses that a succession of strikes cannot be avoided if one wants to defeat the enemy rather than enjoy an illusion of might, one is apt to discover benefits in keeping within the constraints of reality. Striking in succession reduces the enemy's chance of 'divining' one's 'design' (*'razgadat zamysel'*).

Strikes in succession are multiple; and there seems to be a peculiar force to 'one strike following the other', particularly when each of them is mightier than its predecessor (*'narashchivanie'*). 'The offensive', an analyst advanced already in the 1930s 'must consist of a whole series of waves which run towards the shore with ever-increased force';[17] and even in the 1920s Tukhachevskii had recommended 'an uninterruptedly increasing strike'.[18]

During the artillery preparation of the attack, fire strikes should be 'mounting': this is an 'uninterruptedly mounting storm'.[19] Precisely because 'in the contemporary offensive the troops will even more often [than before] encounter the tendency toward the diminution of the strength of the strike', they should be imbued with 'the necessity of increasing it'.[20]

This uninterrupted mounting of attack is, of course, critical, since the enemy may use the time of which one is making him a gift so as to increase his 'forces and means'. 'The experience of the last war has shown', to an analyst, 'that often troops having been highly successful at night, encountered on the morning of the following day an organized resistance by the enemy'. This, of course, 'is explained by the fact that the interruptions ... had permitted the enemy to accomplish a maneuver with reserves and units from other directions'.[21]

Above all, introducing a pause is to risk permitting the opponent to undo all the work one may already have done towards 'depriving the enemy of his capacity for combat'. It is only uninterrupted actions which deprive the enemy of the time and the possibility for establishing order in his troops, once we have succeeded in striking him with disarray. 'Even a small pause gives the enemy a breathing spell, allows him to collect his forces ... to organize counteraction'[22] It is not only 'the withdrawing enemy' who 'must not be allowed any breathing spell',[23] but the enemy pure and simply. It is indeed 'the main thing' 'not to give the enemy any breathing spell'.[24] With such, his capacity for rapid 'recuperation' ('*vosstanovlenie*') is very high; without them, very low, as lack of time and increase of fatigue are combined.

Uninterruptedness which avoids the damages of forgone time and procures such advantages as exhausting the enemy is insistently required by the Authorities. They perceive the dictum of uninterruptedness to be so uncongenial to their subordinates that incessant and stringent pressure toward it becomes the necessary condition for avoiding lapses from it: 'If you press on him [a subordinate officer], he attacks. If you leave him out of your sight, he stops.'[25]

If one, in a rare case, deviates from the dominant position, one may obscure this by first playing obeisance to it. 'One must not conceive of the uninterruptedness in the attack', an analyst for once advances, 'as a stopless [*bezostanovochnyi*] movement forward'. Also 'the transition from the attack to other forms of combat action ... is often connected with stopping [*ostanovka*]'. And 'when repelling the counterattack of superior forces of the enemy, it may be appropriate to strike him with fire from place'. With such boldness emerges a cardinal rule of Soviet warfare – 'Let there be fewer unjustified pauses'.[26]

For the key is 'one strike after the other'.[27] 'It is not permissible to stop.'[28] 'Let us not stop' ('*neostanovlivat'sya*')![29] Whatever you do in war, move (forward) while you do it; and do it while you move. 'The armed reconnaissance patrol', we read about a simulated battle, 'performed reconnaissance while moving'.[30] In fact, according to a Western analyst 'Soviet reconnaissance detachments do not operate like their British counterparts ... sit down and observe and report and observe again'. Rather, 'they observe what they can and report what they can while continuing with their advance'.[31] What is peculiar here, one may observe about the meeting engagement, is that the organization of the crushing of the enemy is realized during the march of the two sides toward each other.

Above all, as an analyst put it as early as the 1930s 'what is new in contemporary fire is ... firing while moving'[32] – in contrast to 'a company or a platoon which began with firing in place, then stopped fire and began to move, they made a halt again so as to fire and so forth'.[33]

There is an insistence on not allowing any adverse circumstances to slow one down, on acting in any conditions 'without decreasing one's tempo'.[34] Very near the beginning of a chapter, in a leading treatise on a subject as broad as 'The influence of science and techniques of the development of the means of warfighting', the author makes a demand as particular as that for 'the fulfillment of daytime norms at night'.[35] In this ever-pressing advance forward, there can be no time for rest, and night as well as day must be used to the end of decisively crushing the enemy. One of the several benefits from fighting also at night is the uninterruptedness of combat thus obtained. 'The offensive', so goes a prominent prescription' 'is going to be conducted uninterruptedly until the full crushing of the enemy, day and night and in any weather'.[36] There will be an 'around-the-clock conduct of the offensive'.[37] Not only 'can night not be a cause for ceasing combat operations',[38] even 'a pause between actions during the night and those during the day is inadmissible'.[39]

Men and equipment are replaced which have reached the physical limit of endurance – after an employment which was, of course, 'uninterrupted' – by new persons and pieces. Then, these, in turn and without interruption, enter upon their (uninterrupted) tour of duty. 'The uninterruptedness of pursuit [in the War] was', an analyst recalls, 'attained ... above all by the periodic interchange of the pursuing troops by bringing second echelon and reserves into the battle'.[40] Thus, we are told, in the course of the Weichsel-Oder operation the advance detachments of some units of the 3rd Guards Tank Army were changed five times in the period from 14 January to 24 January 1945, and the advance detachments of some units of the 2nd Guards Tank Army six times in the period of 18 January through 30 January. The uninterrupted combat action of tanks in advance detachments rarely exceeded two to three days. 'Soviet night offensive plans', a Western analyst observes, 'include provision for replacement units from reserves and second echelons to continue the assault'. For 'Soviet planners are ... cognizant that night combat is a physically draining experience', and hence 'means are allotted ... so that the advance can continue without respite for their opponents'.[41]

Indeed, a third of a century later, portrayals of the war minimize pauses between those operations which took place. 'In 1945', a military leader affirms after thirty years, 'the length of the preparation of offensives become shorter'. In fact, 'in some cases there were ... no periods of preparation. The peculiarity here consisted in measures for the preparation of the next offensive being accomplished in the course of conducting offensive or defensive operations'. 'The Soviet forces', an editorial of the armed forces daily recalls, 'fought with the [German] enemy without so-called climatic pauses judged indispensable in bourgeois military science'.[42]

The Battle For Time

Why do the Soviets make such a fuss about swiftness? Does not the technology of war in general and contemporary battle in particular render its importance evident? Precisely because that is the case, Soviet commanders may sense themselves placed before an all the more harrowing difficulty. To Bolshevik sensibility – in what is felt as a matter of common sense rather than thought of as a theorem of Marxism–Leninism – human nature is prone to 'scorn' time. 'We do not value the minute,' observes an officer, 'and sometimes we do not even consider half an hour an important amount of time'.[43] There is, a colleague notes, an 'aimless waste of training time'.[44]

'For the Russians', a Western analyst observes about the High Command, 'time is not ... of *great* value, it is of the *utmost* value'.[45] 'Time', a leading Soviet analyst does, indeed, observe about 'the revolution in war', 'has come to play not simply an important, but a decisive role in determining ... the outcome of combat'.[46] 'Let us remember', another analyst exhorts, 'the precepts of A. V. Suvorov: "Procrastination is like death. An instant gives victory. One minutes decides the outcome of a battle, one hour the success of a campaign." '[47]

The worth of an action is, it may be advanced, dominated not by its content, but rather by its timing. 'Even the most exact forecast', an editorial of the military daily insists, 'is useless if made belatedly, even the most sensible measures will not bring success if they are realized in slow manner ... Unfortunately, some commanders are not aware of this'.[48] It is even possible to attain the maximum of apparent success, 'to destroy an enemy grouping fully and arrive at the intended line, and yet not to fulfill one's mission if one has accomplished all this ... while being late'.[49]

Human nature, the Authorities discern, justifies and facilitates neglect of time by assuming that it will be feasible to make up for lost time later; an assumption that, in reality, they argue has always been improbable and is even less practicable. 'In contemporary conditions', one will recall, 'it is even more difficult (and often even impossible) to compensate for time wasted [*upushchenno*].'[50]

The consequence of any degree of 'being late' is worse than failure; it is apt to be a severe setback. The smallest delay accordingly leads to the non-fulfillment of the mission, to large losses of troops and equipment. If neglect of even one of the requirements on which moving troops depend leads to 'late' fulfillment of the mission, this will 'in some cases' entail 'the *destruction* of the advance'.[51] In fact, behind any 'lateness', annihilation seems to lurk.

The belief that in battle time works for the enemy is hardly enunciated but constantly applied. This is in contrast to the Marxist-Leninist belief about history. 'Time', a rare civilian writing in the armed forces' daily on a New Year's day will say, 'works for us ... Time is ... our friend, our helper, our élan [*stikhiya*]'.[52] The contrary atmosphere prevails about combat: 'The fingers of the clock' in a submarine moving toward a simulated duel 'mark seconds, minutes. For whom does this time work? Whose victory does it secure?' The indeterminacy thinly masks a dread answer: 'Perhaps it is already too late, perhaps the appropriate moment has already been permitted to pass without action [*upushchit*]'.[53] Time works for us only on condition that we fully utilize it for action. Time works against us as we are impelled by our human nature to disregard it; our Bolshevik mastery of that nature is never sufficient.

Then gaining time is gaining the battle. 'Gaining time ... is all-important for achieving the objective of the march';[54] 'success comes to the side which knows ... how to take decisions ... and to deliver strikes ... more rapidly';[55] 'to win time is to win the battle'.[56] And carried to extremes: 'if you win seconds, you win the battle.'[57]

With the usual Soviet expressions of disregard for limits – which I would suspect to be less than fully serious, but still more than a shallow pretense – the Authorities insist that there are always 'unutilized reserves' of time, that it is always possible to be yet quicker than one has already made oneself. Recalling that 'according to some calculations a human being in the course of an average duration of life is capable of assimilating an enormous mass of information', an analyst observes, that 'something similar can be said about the psyche's reserve with regard to rapidity'. In fact, he notes, 'the possibilities of man to accelerate the speed of his activity' are nothing less than 'remarkable'.[58]

So valued is swiftness that the Authorities are willing – sometimes – to concede what is so uncongenial to them: that costs, often in casualties, should be assumed on its behalf. While 'it is universally known that one cannot attack machine guns frontally [*idti v lob na*]', declares an analyst, 'there may be a situation where this cannot be avoided, because only thus can one destroy them more quickly'.[59] The point, endlessly applied, is that any time which could have been saved in performing our own actions is a gift offered to the enemy, which he will use against us.

While we, for instance, attack, 'the enemy strives to counteract the offensive'. The less time we give him for that, the better for us. It is, 'therefore', that 'the main thing in maneuver is high speed, swiftness'. For 'one must strive to disrupt the "enemy's" design so that he is constantly too late in his . . . countermeasures': 'the speed of his maneuvers should be lower than that of the movements performed by our units.'[60] For example, 'it is very important for obtaining success in the whole operation to accomplish the breakthrough at the end of the very first day of the offensive'. For 'in the opposite case the enemy, utilizing the pause, can in the course of the night bring reserves into the region of the breakthrough'.[61] Similarly, if the accumulation of forces in an airborne landing is slow, this gives the enemy more of a possibility for concentrating his forces and means with the aim of annihilating them. 'The "enemy" ', notes a reporter of a simulated combat, 'did not fail to utilize the minutes and seconds with the gift of which he had been presented'.[62]

Time works for the enemy with particular force in the mode of combat preferred by the Soviets, the offensive. 'Every offensive operation', an analyst observed in the 1920s, 'offers advantages in the first half of its duration';[63] for 'the offense gradually loses the advantages deriving from surprise and preparation'; hence, 'one must not allow an offensive to drag on until its dying breath [*indykhanie*]',[64] or even as a 'slow gnawing-through [*progryzanie*]' of the defense.

Permitting an offensive to become 'dragged-out' rather than 'crushing the enemy rapidly [*v kratchaishii srok*]',[65] is, in particular, dooming it to failure because of the limited endurance of the preferred offensive weapon, the manned combat vehicle. 'It is disadvantageous', an analyst pointed out in the less inhibited 1930s,

> for a moto-mechanized unit to engage itself in a protracted [*zatyazhnyi*] combat. They cannot wait long for the arrival of replacements. A brief, decisive strike, and then either pursuit or leaving the battle – such is the . . . principle of any highly mobile unit.[66]

The aversion to frontal attack derives in part from the horror of protractedness: 'attacking from the front', a military leader recalls, 'is to entangle oneself into a protracted . . . battle'[67] 'a frontal [*v lob*] attack would inevitably have led to a protracted battle'.[68] The stress on bypassing the defense's strongpoints once its forward positions have been breached derives in part from the same dread: one should then move toward the enemy's 'depth', 'without drawing the main forces into protracted battle against stubbornly resisting groups'. By the same token, if the operation one is engaged in has been forced upon one by the enemy, it is urged to doom him by rendering the battle protracted. Defeating the Germans was, in a well-known theme, 'disrupting the German plan for a swift-flowing [*skototechnyi*] war'.

In contemporary conditions, it is essential to attack before the enemy has had time to deploy his anti-tank guided missiles (ATGMs).[69] In the 1930s, already a pioneer of the tank had demonstrated that 'the worth of a mechanized unit shows itself in the highest degree . . . when the enemy has not yet had time to . . . organize . . . antiarmor defense'.[70] The company commander, in one simulated combat, 'understood that success depended . . . on how quickly he would succeed in arriving at the river in order to utilize the unpreparedness of the "enemy," particularly of his system of antitank fire'.[71] The less you delay, the more probable that your time of attack will be earlier than that expected by the enemy. He will then be surprised, with the capital consequences that follow from that. 'For the attainment of surprise in a meeting engagement', an officer must 'attack the enemy earlier than he expected it'.[72] When, on one occasion during the war,

> at eight o'clock the artillery preparation began. The enemy soldiers, apparently assuming that preparation would be repeated [after having ceased] did not even leave their shelters. Not permitting them to come to their senses, the rifle unit broke into the first trench.[73]

And:

> a [German] NCO of the 313th Infantry Regiment taken prisoner the 23rd of June [1944, in the Belorussian operation] in the first enemy echelon indicated: '. . . We were deafened by the artillery fire of the Russians. I and two soldiers of my unit were sitting in the dugout . . . When I sent one of them to look . . . he immediately cried out: "Already! Already!" When we jumped outside, I saw that the Russians were already in the trench. The Russians broke into our position even before the end of the artillery fire.'[74]

– never mind at what casualties inflicted on themselves.

The underlying theme is to trade force for time. 'In a series of cases', an analyst observes, 'one must deliver a strike even before the complete readiness of one's troops', as 'one thus obtains a larger effect'.[75] 'Sometimes', another analyst elaborates, 'commanders of divisions, when deploying artillery in a meeting engagement, go slow with the opening of fire, waiting for all batteries to be ready'. Now, 'in a meeting engagement this is inadmissible': 'time here has decisive significance.' For

> an attack without any delay even by a few units which have already arrived at the enemy's defense line, may have a much larger effect than one with larger forces, but conducted after the enemy has been able to gain time for the organization of his defense.

Observing in the 1920s that 'many among our commanders, however strange and sad it may be, do not resolve upon ... bold envelopments', Tukhachevskii added that 'if they accomplish them at all, they perform them in the most dangerous fashion, that is ... slowly'.[76] 'In a number of units', observes an editorial of the military daily in 1977, 'slowness in the deployment into combat array and in striking from the march is still tolerated'.[77]

The belief that, in war, time works against them makes the Authorities keenly aware of time becoming less and less available as military technology advances. 'That which even in a recent past it took troops days to do, must now be done in half a day, in a few hours, even in tens of minutes.'[78] 'A deficit in time', in modern war, 'becomes the commander's permanent companion'.[79] It is even apt to be a 'sharp deficit',[80] if not 'the sharpest'.[81] 'High speeds', an officer attempts to persuade recalcitrant addicts of slowness, 'are not a subjective (i.e. arbitrary) demand, but the will of the times ... a requirement of contemporary combat which can be replaced by nothing else'.[82]

Rapidity – as any other favorable attribute, in the Bolshevik view – does not come by itself to humans whose spontaneity leads them in the opposite direction. Rather, as we have already seen, protracted work is necessary – and sufficient – for producing swiftness in operations. While opposing routine in the macro-aspects of a decision, the Authorities value it in the microfeatures of execution. Fighters commendably 'attempt to work on their conduct in battle until it becomes automatic'.[83] They 'develop their habits to the level of automatism',[84] creating in themselves 'the so-called "memory of the hands"'.[85] For it is 'automatism which permits, for instance, the artillerist in the moment of danger not to think of how to take a shell, which angle to adopt'.[86] And when 'every movement', say of the pilot, is 'worked up to having become automatic', then and only then can he 'give all his attention to the search for the target';[87] and (what is not made explicit, but presumably intended) spend less time on finding it.

Conversely, one object of surprise is to lengthen the victim's reaction time. 'The strike was so unexpected that the "enemy" was incapable of beginning organized resistance right away'. Therefore (presumably), 'the tankists succeeded in fragmenting his column'.[88]

The Costs of Swiftness

Commanders sharing the attitudes which I have described are apt to allow insufficient time for the missions they set, leaning over backward against the propensity to slowness which they perceive in others and, perhaps, in themselves. 'Sometimes orders are given when it is perfectly clear that it is impossible to fulfill them within the time indicated.'[89] 'In exercises it still happens', an anonymous authority observes, 'that commanders . . . ask of their artillery and aviation tasks which are clearly beyond their forces.' Thus,

> in a recent exercise the unit commanded by . . . E. Nikitin was stopped in the course of advance by the fire of the 'enemy's' anti-tank weapons from the slopes of a commanding height. The Commander ordered the artillery batteries to suppress them, and the Company to attack the strongpoint on the height after five minutes. He did not take account of the fact that the artillerists would be unable to fulfill their task within such a brief time.[90]

'In exercises', the same authority discerns:

> there are still cases where, for instance, a battalion commander, ordering the sappers allocated to him to create a passage through a minefield of the 'enemy', allows them much less time than is required for that. As a result, the attacking unit is arrested by the obstacle, the speed of the attack sinks.[91]

It becomes appropriate to insist that 'commanders are obliged to take meticulous account of the fact that personnel needs time for the locating of targets . . . and the opening of fire'.[92]

The Authorities have increasingly come to note 'a disregard', in the words of a Western analyst, 'of quality for the sake of speed',[93] or, in the formulation of a Soviet observer, 'chasing after rapidity at the expense of correctness'.[94] While they press for speed, the Authorities may discover that 'in the race for swiftness, thorough calculations are omitted'.[95] They discern (once more in the Bolshevik tradition) a penchant, in the words of an analyst, towards 'hasty decision, taken without a sufficient analysis of the situation . . . without the execution of the indispensable analysis of the calculations',[96] 'a striving to save time at the price of taking an insufficiently founded decision'.[97] 'Commanders of platoons were carried away [*uvlekat'sya*] by rapidity in working on norms for firing, and neglected precision'.[98]

The need for rapid decision is one of the factors which inspire misgivings about the disposition of commanders to depend highly on orders or at least guidance from above, a presumably massive factor barely acknowledged. 'If in the decisive moment the commander . . . waits for prompting "from above" and delays taking a decision, he will not', a general officer foresees, 'obtain success'.[99]

It is, as we would expect, but rarely admitted that it is 'the fear of . . . actions . . . without an order from above', which is 'one of the major causes of indecisiveness in critical moments';[100] that, in the words of a military leader, 'one still finds commanders . . . who delay decisions on questions which can be deferred out of a *fear* of responsibility'.[101]

Decision-time saved, however, is combat-time gained. 'To command in efficient fashion', an analyst points out, 'means . . . to spend as little time as possible on the processes of commanding, so as to put a maximum of time at the disposal of the troops, since it is precisely the troops which . . . inflict losses on the enemy'.[102] The more advanced the military technology, the shorter the available decision-time. 'The art of war at sea', Admiral Gorshkov observes, 'found itself faced with the necessity of resolving . . . tasks in shorter and shorter time spans'.[103] The shorter the actual decision-time, the higher the chance of forestalling the enemy, with the favorable consequences which follow from that.

Thus, the 'struggle' against slowness discussed in the present chapter is also in the service of another major orientation of the Authorities, their fight against the inclination to be passive toward the enemy.

The atmosphere around speed is such that it becomes appropriate to recall that 'high speed is not an end in itself'.[104] It is unusual to acknowledge that speed costs, as an analyst does when he discusses the exceptions made during the war concerning the rule that in an offensive the motorized riflemen go first: 'While tank armies breaking through the tactical zone of the enemy's defense bore definite losses . . . this procedure gained time.'[105]

But it is even more unusual to envisage sacrificing speed. 'Every maneuver', explain analysts stressing the role of that aspect of war, 'requires a certain amount of time for its preparation and execution, and it would seem that it will always be connected with . . . a reduction in the tempo of the offensive'. Hence, 'sometimes it is held that from the point of view of high speeds of the offensive what would be appropriate would be a . . .

stopless ... movement forward'[106] – which, the authors dare to imply, would cost more than would be gained. Even the most obvious sacrifices of rapidity for other advantages may be presented as exceptions which have to be strenuously argued:

> Naturally, one must not exclude that it will sometimes be necessary [*pridetsya*] to wait until levels of radiation sink ... To risk the health of personnel, the security of the unit in the name of high speed is not appropriate [*ne sleduet*], unless it is acutely indispensable to do so.[107]

Nothwithstanding, it is important to reaffirm that in Soviet military thinking, speed offers not only victory, but also economy beyond that of time: both of force and of loss, 'the attainment of success in minimal time and with little blood';[108] avoiding the dreaded 'dragged-out' campaign. During the war, an analyst observes, 'speeds of offensive and losses were inversely proportional'. In fact, 'with an offensive of 20 to 50 kilometers a day, casualties were more than three times less among tank personnel or only half as many with speeds of advance of 4–10 kilometers a day'.[109] In addition, 'a high speed of advance ... secures for the offense the fulfillment of its mission ... with smaller expenditure in ammunition and fuel'.[110]

On the other hand, the enemy's losses vary directly as a function of one's own speed: 'with high speeds of the offensive the losses of the defense ... increase.' Thus, 'in the Weichsel-Oder operation the Fourth Tank Army advancing with a daily tempo of 30–33 kilometers made twice the number of prisoners as with a tempo of 10–13 kilometers'. Also, 'with high speeds of the offensive usually the number of seized automobiles, artillery, and tanks rises'.[111]

Just how does speed promote victory? First, it facilitates surprise: 'There exists a direct relation between the speed of the offensive and surprise.' The transition of the offensive from the march secures the secrecy of preparations and, thus 'the surprise in the assault'.[112]

Secondly, speed reduces the enemy's efficacy even beyond the effects of surprise. As 'rapidly attacking tanks exercise a strong moral and psychic influence on the defenders', a general officer observes, 'the accuracy of their fire will be reduced'.[113]

Thirdly, once more, time works for the enemy, because it allows him to employ more countermeasures. 'The higher the speed of the offensive, the greater the possibility of ... victory', because 'with a low speed of the offensive, the enemy ... acquires the time for strengthening his defensive position, for ... transferring new forces and means to the menaced sector'.[114] Conversely, 'high speeds of attack ... deprive the enemy of the possibility of undertaking effective countermeasures'.[115] There is always the possibility that breaking through the enemy's 'tactical zone', while still feasible, will become slow and costly. In case the defense succeeds in regrouping its forces *earlier* than the attacker is able to utilize the results of his strikes for moving into the depth, the attempted breakthrough becomes a 'gnawing through' [*progrizanie*] of the defense, and then the losses of the attacker mount. Or, and even worse, 'since the concentration of reserves [for defense] in the threatened direction [of an enemy offensive] proceeded in a tempo more rapid than the enemy's offensive, his advance was arrested'.[116] So often, one recalls about war and simulated battle, that while the defense was being broken – but all too slowly – the enemy succeeded in moving up reserves and created a defense on a new line.

Fourthly, besides the gains from speed which I have described, there is the protection it affords against the enemy's actions: it maximizes the chances not only for victory, but also for survival (and thus again for victory).

In the atmosphere which I have described one may express any doubt in the great benefits of speed only in the most gingerly fashion. 'We must not forget', one will then say, 'that by themselves ... technical possibilities of speed do not secure success'. This is overlooked when 'simplifying his task, a battalion commander had not deemed it necessary to organize intelligence meticulously on his route of march so as to oppose the "enemy" in case of necessity'. Rather, 'all the efforts of the commander were directed towards obtaining maximum speed'. However, 'which basic criteria must the deployment of a column marching toward a meeting engagement satisfy?' While 'naturally, it must guarantee a high speed of movement, this ... is not all': 'the order of march must also correspond to the combat objectives of the unit, give it the capacity for rapid and independent actions, minimize its vulnerability ... and render it capable of quick changes in the direction of movements.'[117]

Planning and Flexibility

That the Authorities believe the disposition to skimp on preparations to be strong, seems to be indicated by their emphasis on the cost of doing so. Preparation is a virtue sufficiently respected by Soviet officers that it becomes appropriate for the High Command to spell out aspects of that activity which may seem obvious in the West. Thus, a military analyst formulates the 'rule' that 'the more complicated an exercise, the more thoroughly must one prepare for it'.[118] 'The exacting [*trebovatel'nyi*] commander does not allow vehicles to be mounted until he has convinced himself that they are all in good order.'[119]

Overcoming his subordinates' aversion to preparation then becomes a major objective of a commander. It is 'as a first priority [*v pervuyu ochered*]' that, according to a military leader, 'the commander must obtain that ... every officer and sergeant prepare himself well for exercises'.[120]

Thus emerges what a German commander called 'the typical Soviet determining of conduct in advance [*Vorausdisponieron*]', the wisdom of which it is rare to see doubted:

> Do you remember the pedantic German staff officer in Tolstoy's *War and Peace*? He displays everything on the shelf [*raskladyvat' po polochkim*]: 'The first column will march ... the second column will march ...' A century and a half has passed since those times, but the partisans of excessive detail [*punktual' nost'*] have not disappeared.[121]

What is apt to be insufficient in that preparation is the level of detail. In simulated combat it will apparently not be wholly surprising, if 'the fire means of the "enemy", the obstacles in front of his forward edge and in his near depth were not thoroughly studied'.[122] 'In one exercise', a military leader notes, 'the reports of Officers G. Eibenko and B. Shaplevskii ... did not contain indications about the time of action, the force and the design of the enemy'.[123] 'In how standardized a fashion', muses a junior officer,

> we often approach certain elements of combat! For instance, in the repulse of a counterattack. Is it really indifferent to the tankmen ... which type of vehicles the enemy has, which antitank weapons? If the enemy tanks are heavy, one must fight them in one fashion, if they are medium or light, quite differently.

Yet,

> we sometimes prefer to repulse a faceless counterattack. Often one can hear: if you would begin to impose nuances on the subordinates, you won't find time for the main things.[124]

Changing the Initial Plan

As war, like all of history, abounds in sharp turns, the commander – so the Authorities insist – should be capable of veering sharply in short order, in contrast to 'the crew [of a boat] which was set up only for one variant of fire'.[125] 'The Communist vanguard of the working class', a Soviet leader declares, 'creates in itself the readiness towards a rapid shift of the forms and means of class struggle in accord with changes in the situation'.[126] 'Marxism–Leninism', a theoretician observes in similar and equally familiar words, 'teaches that the revolutionary class must ... be ready for the quickest and most unexpected substitution of one form of struggle for another'.[127] Identically, to a military analyst 'high operational efficacy' is, 'above all', 'reacting in timely fashion to all changes in the situation',[128] being capable both of 'rapid transition from one mode of combat to the other' and of 'their simultaneous employment'.[129]

As in this case, one must be capable of 'suddenly changing the direction of movement',[130] 'transferring efforts in a new direction'.[131] 'A characteristic trait' of the third and concluding period of the War', according to a general officer:

> was the quick transfer of the efforts of aviation units from one direction to another, from one group of targets to another ... Thus, on June 24, 1944, the Commander of the First Air Army, General T. T. Khryukin, retargeted within a few minutes his air units from the direction of Orshan to that of Bodyshev.[132]

Similarly for *modes* of combat. 'In contemporary war', an analyst recalls, 'the situation can change so sharply that it is difficult to count on victory without the skill to pass quickly from one form of military action to another'.[133] 'In extremely difficult circumstances', recollects another, 'it was important' ('for the repelling of counterattacks') to make 'a quick and organized transition to the defense', to take 'a timely decision to go over to the defense'.[134]

In the official wisdom cited here, attention is averted from one aspect of what is recommended – the modification/abolition of previous decisions. For that is a difficulty.

When the Authorities consider their subordinates' propensity for improvisation, they demand a maximum of planning. But when they face unpredictability, they admit the cost of deciding before an operation what could be settled in its course, depending on that course.

When the Authorities are aware of the advantages in limiting advance planning, they are also apt to perceive the benefits which may depend on modifying an initial design, and displeased with a propensity of commanders to execute (if they execute at all) the decisions made before the start of an operation.

Of course, the Authorities pretend to be unaware of their own inclinations to such a stance, confessing only through their allegations about the enemy:

> From the interrogation of prisoners it became evident that the Germand Command and troops act to a high degree in routine fashion [*po shablonu*] ... merely fulfilling orders in blind fashion. Hence, as soon as the situation changed, the Germans lost their bearing, conducted themselves with extreme passivity, waiting for orders from the senior commander, orders which in the given situation could not always be received in good time.[135]

The Authorities discern, in the words of an analyst of the 1920s, the frequent presence of a 'fierce [*zhestokyi*], implacable [*neumolimyi*] striving for an objective which has been enshrined in a document [*zaprotokolirovat*]';[136] of, as one may say, stubbornness in realizing a mode of combat action which had been chosen earlier; of not taking account of a changed relationship of forces. A 'good decision' may 'in the course of combat' be 'blindly maintained', with 'no corrections' made in it 'despite sharp changes in the situation' – and 'victory missed'.[137] 'In conditions when basic changes in the situation have taken place', two analysts note, 'loss of time results habitually not from working out a new decision, but from overcoming doubts whether it is indispensable to change a plan elaborated earlier'.[138] 'It takes them', a German commander agrees about his Soviet counterparts, 'a lot of time to alter their plans, especially during an action'.[139] 'Russian officers in command', another German colleague goes further, 'strictly ... adhere ... to previous decisions. They disregard changes in the situation, the reactions of the enemy'.[140]

The aversion to modifying plans in the course of executing them is expressed in a number of ways in the very advocacy of such an act. That aversion may be acknowledged. 'To take the optimal decision', a senior officer observes, 'to render it more specific [*utochnit*] in good time, and *even* [*dazhe*] to change it if the interests of combat require that'.[141] Recalling that 'often a maneuver is hindered by the decision initially taken', a military leader declares that 'one must not be *afraid of changing it*'.[142] While, in the view of an analyst, 'it is useful that officers prior to going out to the terrain take decisions from the map', 'it is not a *disaster* [*beda*] if it subsequently becomes necessary ... to change them'.[143]

The emphasis on the modifiability of plans ('the art of leading a battle does not tolerate a stubborn attachment [*priverzhennost*] to a plan established beforehand')[144] is, in the surmise developed above, in good part a reaction to the opposite inclination, that of blindly going through with a plan once established.

That propensity, in its turn, is fostered by the sense of power that going through with one's plan in conditions which suggests its replacement may give: 'I want it, I have thus decided.' Such an attitude proves the unlimited reach of the pressures of one's will (*volevoi nazhim*), perhaps a major gratification derived from the 'stubbornness' (*'upryamstvo'*) of this stance.

There was, of course, also the opposite outcome. Soviet 'persistence', at whatever cost, attained its objective. As an analyst observes, 'breaking through the deeply echeloned defense of the enemy required a series of insistent [*nastoichivyi*], never-ceasing [*neprekrashchayushchyi*] attacks'.[145] A German commander perceives an 'accepted Russian principle – once "Ivan" makes up his mind to ... gain certain objectives, he throws in ... troops and continues to do so until he has secured his objective or exhausted his reserve'.[146]

That the Soviets will in such fashion secure their objective would seem even more probable to the Authorities if they attributed to their side, as they well may, an edge in endurance. To the defenders of Stalingrad, 'after each repelled attack it seemed that it was no more possible to endure the next assault'.[147] Still, they did, and the Authorities may count upon winning endurance races.

The requirement upon oneself and others to persist until success in the face of failure may, in addition, be a reaction (usually not a fully conscious one) against the suspicion that one is ready to give up at the first difficulty.

Offense, Defense and Retreat

The unconscious Bolshevik suspicion that soldiers will shrink in the face of adversity may be associated with the preference, vigorously advanced throughout the literature, for the offensive. Commanders and analysts alike exhort their followers to turn away from the inclination to defend, choosing instead the bold *attack* that alone will ensure the crushing of the enemy. In that large majority of stories about simulated combat in which the reporting officer puts himself into the place of one of the contending sides – the other then coming to be called 'the enemy' – it is almost always the attacking party which is thus favoured. And the attacker then usually wins.

The preference for the offensive is such that even when the side taking the offensive is called 'Westerners', as in Kafkaz, conducted in the presence of Marshal Grechko and foreign observers, the outcome of the battle is at least in doubt:

> The steel wedge of the 'Westerners' penetrates even more deeply into the deployment of 'Easterners.' But the latter, as also the 'Westerners,' have reserves. That means that stubborn combat is yet to come.[148]

Noting that 'in exercises it is not rare that one of the sides, usually the defense, essentially merely "plays into the hands [*podygryvat'*]" of the other', a senior officer insists that

> if, let us say, the attacker has prepared his attack badly or organized his actions insufficiently, while the defender performs well, then naturally he should be awarded success, and the offense forced to stop ... and to repeat the attack.

Alas, it happens in exercises that 'the unit on the offense moves forward independently of the degree to which the "enemy" has been defeated'.[149]

During the war, for an important current of military sensibility (not of doctrine), only the offensive was appropriate – a reaction which I would surmise to persist. For the very stance of attack expresses strength, since 'the very fact of taking the offensive reveals a stronger will'.[150] But superior 'will' is conducive to victory: 'in approximately equal conditions', we read, 'success in battle is attained by the one who ... foists his will on the enemy'.[151]

Superior *aktivnost'* (activeness) achieves that success – and is not offense more 'active' than defense? 'The role of battle *aktivnost'* in obtaining victory has in contemporary conditions grown to such an extent', an analyst judges, 'that one has begun to consider it one of the main principles of military art'.[152] 'In battle', an editorial of the military daily counsels, 'success invariably falls to the one who, other conditions being equal, acts more actively'[153] – is more on the offensive.

Navalit'sya (to fall on the enemy), and *obrushit'sya* (to come down on him), may be sensed as acts of irresistible power, whatever more tangible measurements of the relationship of forces may indicate. This faith in the near-magical power of bold will is, to be sure, not unopposed among Soviet commanders nor, I would surmise, insignificant. With such a sense, one may entertain the expectation that a new technology usable by both sides will benefit the offense.

The Authorities' intense preference for the offensive may do more than express the gratifications it provides and the confidence one places in it. The offensive may also be strenuously urged to the extent that it is so as to overcome reluctance toward it. 'It is not a secret', we hear in a rare lifting of silence on such a matter, which might seem obvious in the West,

> 'that on the ... [psychological] plane the offensive is a more difficult mode of action than, let us say, the defense. Here the soldiers ... believe in the ... protective force of their covers, in their system of fire. In the offensive, however, they are more vulnerable; with every step danger lurks. In these conditions fear may emerge.

Indeed,

> in the past War, the offensive sometimes petered out [*zakhlebyvat'sya*] because one did not succeed in the decisive moment to overcome, precisely, fear. Then the soldiers laid down under the fire of the enemy, the forward line of the defense was not reached.[154]

As we shall soon see, when reminiscing about the war, the Authorities show a propensity of commanders to indulge in the offensive to excess; but in current analyses and prescriptions as well as in accounts of simulated combat, the point hardly appears (with one exception, the 'frontal strike', as I shall show below).

Might the propensity for inappropriate offensives have declined to an extent such that it is not even worth warning against it anymore? That seems unlikely. I would rather surmise that there is a ban on dealing in public with a defect as grave and as detrimental to the image of the USSR as that of having offense-happy commanders.

If there is, as I have just tried to show, a Soviet inclination to indulge in the offensive to excess, an opposite disposition also seems to exist. When one does not act according to the maxim, 'a strike group must *only* strive forward, not look at its flank',[155] one may be *highly* preoccupied by threats to one's flanks which might result from advancing:

> German commanders have been puzzled by the Soviet refusal, in the winter of 1945, to press on from the Oder to Berlin – their decision to stop for two months so as to eliminate the threat from East Prussia, Pomerania, Silesia to the flanks of their force advancing westward.

When one does not act according to the maxim of *bypassing*

enemy strongpoints when moving into his depth after a break-through, one may be *highly* concerned with seizing them first, even at high cost of effort, loss and time.

Offensive actions, the Authorities point out, will be insufficient not only when one fears being encircled, but also when one does not aim at encircling and then annihilating the enemy, but is content merely to push him back (*vytalkivanie*) by a frontal strike – a mode of striking which is not only apt to fail and to cost dearly, but also to be of insufficient yield when it succeeds.

It is precisely the exclusive capacity of the offense to *annihilate* the enemy which renders it precious. 'The offensive always was and remains today the most decisive manner of action because only as a result of the offensive is the full annihilation of the forces and means of the enemy obtained.'[156] An officer may go out of his way to remark that 'with defense only, one cannot decide a combat task. One must annihilate the enemy'.[157]

But the offensive is only a necessary, not a sufficient condition for annihilating the enemy. For that to occur, it must, as we have already seen, not be misconstrued as a means of merely pushing him back. One must not even permit him to go back: 'The basic requirements of maneuvering tactics: not to push the enemy back [*vytesnit'*] from one line to the other, but to annihilate him.'[158]

These exhortations notwithstanding, there is among the Authorities the belief in a disposition to wait to be struck by the enemy before striking him. 'Instead of actively searching for the "enemy" ... he preferred to wait', we hear about a submarine commander in simulated combat. 'Perhaps the "enemy" will show himself', he says.[159] While the Authorities do not often talk about the disposition to wait for the enemy, they assign, in my guess, considerable strength to it, as one of the expressions of a penchant not only for delay, but also for 'passivity'. 'They', Stalin alleged about the Guard Units of the Soviet Army in the fall of 1941, 'did not *wait for the moment at which the enemy would strike them*' – exactly what the Soviet government had done two months earlier. 'One must ... strike first rather than "*respond* [*otvechat*] to fire'.[160]

It is precisely this ideal of denying the enemy the initiative of opening fire that allows the Soviet military to undertake even *defensive* operations without compromising its requirement for bold attack: 'When the "enemy" is preparing ... an attack', one must 'react to this at that very instant'.[161] 'The commander ... divining [*razgadat'*] the intentions of the enemy, forestalls in good time and effectively the surprise strike which he is preparing, paralyzes all his undertakings in their beginning (*zarodyshe*).'[162]

Aversion to Defense

It is a rarity in the literature to find it publicly argued that defense is interchangeable with offense according to conditions, that both are mere instruments in 'the battle for the alteration of the relationship of forces'.[163]

Accordingly, it is more commonly found that there is 'the rejection in Soviet military strategy of the legitimacy [*pravomernost'*] of defense on the strategic level'.[164] The reason is, of course, that defense lacks those characteristics of offense which render it appropriate, even mandatory on the highest of the three levels of war (strategic, operational, tactical) which Soviet analysts perceive.

That an aversion to defense extends through each of these 'planes' is visible in many ways, suggesting the Soviet view that for the duration of an entire war, only offensives would be conducted. In a simulated combat,

> the major had two paths available in trying to change the course of the duel. The first was to create a firm defense, to inflict significant losses on the 'enemy,' forcing him to renounce further active doings.

The Western reader might think that would be good enough, but no; for

> in such a case *the initiative* remained with the rival. Remembering the statement in the Regulations that the *crushing of the enemy* can be attained only by a decisive offensive, the battalion commander chose the other path ... forestalling the 'enemy,' the battalion unexpectedly went over to the offensive.[165]

This deep-seated aversion to defense disposes one, when recommending it, to justify it as one of the dark sides of military life, which realistically, one must recognize as inevitable. Loath to outlaw defense, the Authorities suggest that it is acceptable to turn to it in unfavourable circumstances. Deplorable though defense may be, they seem to say, it should be tolerated as one of the numerous unpleasant aspects of life. 'Wars which would from beginning to end contain only victorious offensives', recalls Lenin in words used as a motto for the part of a manual treating defense, 'did not occur in world history, or, if they occurred, only as exceptions'.[166]

Being squeamish – and even skeptical – about gains from defense, the Authorities are reluctant to envisage choosing it freely. True enough, they do observe that defense may be either 'forced' or, on the contrary, adopted 'in advance'; 'deliberately', 'not in immediate contact with the enemy'. There have even been cases, they admit, where defense bore this non-'forced' character. While, an officer recalls about the war, 'the majority of defensive operations were forced upon us, there were also those which were prepared in advance, whose design was worked out already before the beginning of the active doings of the enemy troops', notably, 'the operation of Kursk, of Lake Balaton and some others'.[167] 'As is well known', it is elaborated, 'in the battle of Kursk, the Soviet High Command deliberately renounced forestalling the enemy in the transition to the offensive, so as to give this possibility to the enemy, and in the course of defensive actions to grind up his strategic groupings, and then to inflict a crushing blow on him' – a 'decision all the more remarkable as our troops were fully capable of taking the offensive'.[168]

Yet emphasis on non-'forced' defense is exceptional. As a rule, that possibility is neglected in favor of the somber presentation of defense as 'forced': 'The ... War showed that defense is ... forced.'[169] So it was, so it will be: 'the transition of tanks to the defense', it is foreseen, 'is a forced reaction; they will go over to the defense, as a rule ... under the strikes of the enemy's superior forces'.[170]

Having thus put defense into its inferior place, the Authorities proceed to make that place habitable. Defense, they stress, is conducted on behalf of offense. Beyond being a means for offense, defense is presented as itself enjoying more and more of the latter's precious qualities. Defense is counteroffensive – indeed, more and more so. 'Modern defense', declares an editorial of the military daily, 'is based on combining stubbornness in holding positions' – the 'passivity' of 'holding' being alleviated by 'stubbornness' – 'with counteroffensives'.[171] With the advance in military technology, one is apt to affirm, the role of offensive action in defense rises: 'The highest expression of activity in defense is the conducting of counterattacks and counterstrikes.'[172] These glimpses of Soviet military wisdom, ostensibly favourable to defense, both mask and reveal an aversion to 'strict [*zhestkyi*] defense', without sweetening counterstrikes.

What, as we already know, makes sheer defense so obnoxious is succinctly expressed by a military leader when he demands that 'one must learn not to beat off [*otbivat'sya ot*] the enemy but ... to impose one's will on him'[173] for in defense it is the enemy who succeeds in 'fettering' the defender.[174]

In the judgment of many Western analysts, the advantages of

defense are not as fully stated by the Authorities as the benefits from offense. It has not always been thus. In the 1920s an analyst could envisage the situation in which 'one of the contestants in advance renounces the initiative and strives to utilize the strong properties [*sil'nyie svoistva*] of the defense'[175] – a sentence unpublishable at present. 'The strength [*sila*] of the defense', the Field Manual of 1936 declared, 'consists in the more advantageous utilization of fire, terrain, engineering works, and chemical means' (paragraph 224) – another pronouncement which has become unusual. It is rare to hear an officer, addressing himself to 'the strong sides of the defense', observe that 'fire from prepared positions significantly surpasses in effectiveness the fire of the attackers'.[176]

While the requirement is stressed that the offense in its sector must be sharply superior in mass to the defense, it is only in an earlier period that the converse could be argued, as it was in the Field Manual of 1936, that, 'in defense, victory can be attained with small forces also over a superior enemy' (p. 16). 'Defense', in the formulation of the Field Manual of 1944, 'is a form of combat in which troops, utilizing the advantageous conditions of terrain, its engineering reinforcement, and the force of contemporary fire, can hold positions occupied against superior forces of the enemy' (paragraph 474). Later it would become exceedingly rare to advance that 'the defenders are capable of stopping the attack of a superior enemy with smaller forces'.[177]

The Authorities, as I have already noted, are loath to acknowledge that, while in certain conditions it will be the offensive which optimizes the value of the force ratio between oneself and the enemy, in other circumstances it will be defense.

One of those circumstances favouring defense is related to the difference in losses entailed by offense and defense respectively. In an earlier theme, 'we do not need to fear partial setbacks [when on the defense] in our first echelon, as the attacking enemy in obtaining such advantages wears himself out [*istoshchat'sya*]'.[178] Indeed, 'the defense should be built in such a fashion that it exhausts [*izmatyvat'*] the enemy's forces in the zone of obstacles so as to ... annihilate the enemy when he arrives at the first edge'.[179] 'The Soviet troops', an analyst could still recall twenty years later about defense in the war's first period, 'in bitter battles ... inflicted heavy losses on the enemy, obtaining thereby a radical change of the situation'.[180] But by that time the *general* statement that defense may optimize force ratio had already for a long time been reduced to inconspicuousness.

A similar justification of the defensive argues that it may

optimize the force ratio by allowing a gain in time to be utilized for differential reinforcement – a perspective avoided by the Soviets, perhaps so as not to encourage the forecast that distressing aspects of the last war will recur in a future conflict.

Retreating into Flight

Prior to the war there was a substantial disposition to regard retreat as normal. 'If . . . the troops have to retreat [*otkhodit'*]', an analyst might then say in routine fashion, 'it is necessary to decide in advance on those lines on which it is possible to hold the enemy attack'.[181] Like defense, retreat was presented as the handmaiden of offense:

> Retreat is a concept which fully enters into that of the attack. I retreat over 100–200 kilometers so as to go over to the attack on a certain line at a certain moment decided by myself.[182]

'Retreat', simply, 'is one of the moments in the general course of offensive operations'.[183]

At present little of that attitude is visible in the public expressions of the Authorities. The classic Bolshevik rejection of any reluctance to retreat, with its standard complement of rationales, are now rare in public print. There are few recent companions to the statement authorized by Marshal Sokolovskii that, while 'always and in all armies there has been scorn for retreat, those armed forces which do not master . . . retreat . . . more often than not suffer defeat'.[184] It is bold of the marshal to further allow the truism that 'troops may be forced to retreat as a result of an unsuccessful defensive battle'[185] – as well as the inescapable admission that 'sometimes a retreat can be conducted *deliberately* with the aim of occupying a more favorable position for subsequent combat'.[186] It is exceptional to hear from a general officer that in the first phase of the war, 'retreat grew beyond the frame of maneuver and became a . . . mode of combat action'. Then 'it was essentially conducted with the aim of leading units out of impending strikes of the enemy or of occupying more advantageous lines of defense in one's depth'. There was retreat 'when it was only by the temporary abandonment of a part of the territory that one could change the unfavorable situation which had emerged'.[187]

Retreat in recent days has been largely expunged from the presentation of the war. Having described a certain pattern of deployment of the Soviet forces adopted at its beginning, an analyst becomes original when he adds that in these conditions it was 'with relative ease' that the enemy 'forced our troops to retreat'.[188] It is rare to recall the evident fact that 'in the first phase of the Great Fatherland War our units were forced to retreat under the strikes of the superior enemy'.[189]

In earlier days however, *retreat for gain* was presented as one of the normal modes of seeking military advantage. 'One must', an analyst proposed in the 1920s, 'look for a gain in time by *deliberate* [*prednamerennyi*] *retreat*'.[190] 'The enemy', Tukhachevskii pointed out in the 1930s, 'may turn out to be forced [*prinuzhden*] to draw supplementary resources towards those fronts where we, deliberately surrendering territory, do not place decisive strikes'.[191] 'There is', declared Frunze in the 1920s, 'strategic retreat caused by the striving ... to lure [*zavlekat'*] the enemy deeper so as to crush him better'.[192] In the official image of the first phase of the war during the late Stalin era, the Soviet army drew (*vytyagivat'*) the enemy into a strategic situation unfavorable to him. 'The ... past of our ... country', the Field Manual of 1944 observed,

> furnishes many examples when by retreat the enemy was lured [*zatyagivat'*], exhausted, and then a crushing strike inflicted on him. Thus it was in the days of the Fatherland War of 1812, thus it was many times also in the Civil War ... Retreat may be applied so as to create favorable conditions for the continuation of the ... struggle with the enemy and even for his defeat (Kutuzov in 1805 in the war with Napoleon, and in 1811 in the war with Turkey). (p. 11)

But after Stalin, 'luring' was banned, as least in public expression.

In the era during which a strategy of retreat enjoyed acceptability, one could declare the irrelevance of ground, the sole importance of force. 'The defender', an analyst observed in the 1920s,

> will ... not always be bound by a position in space [*mestnost'*]. Often space does not play a decisive role for him ... He may withdraw [*otkhodit*] under the pressure of the enemy until his and the enemy's forces are equalized.[193]

Later, this view was eliminated, at least from public utterance. The Field Manual of 1936 could envisage retreat so as to *render an unfavorable force ratio more propitious*: 'the enemy, rendered weak [*obessilennyi*] in overcoming the depth of the defense.' 'Retreating troops', one could observe in the 1920s, 'put

themselves in order through the path of gaining time and space
[*sic*]'[194] – just as 'the withdrawing enemy [may be] gaining in the
maneuver of retreat an operational situation advantageous to
him'.[195]

From the war to the end of Stalin's reign, the retreats in the first
phase of the conflict, difficult to deny, were justified as an application of Kutuzov's strategy in 1812, updated by the contrast drawn
between the temporary advantages enjoyed by the 'treacherous'
aggressor and the 'permanently operating factors' in which the
victim is, of course, superior. Such was the explanation of 'the
forced [*vynuzhdennyi*] retreat into the depth of the country', an
explanation accompanied by the creation of an Order of Kutuzov
for excellence in retreating. The need to put the least-bad face on
initial defeat by the Germans thus temporarily gave rise to a
public rejection of squeamishness toward retreat, as shown by
Lenin in the face of the hard German peace conditions of early
1918.

One might have thought that in the rehabilitation of Stalin as a
military leader during the later 1960s and 1970s, the Authorities
would have renewed recourse to what one might call 'the
Kutuzov Out'. Instead, they demonstrated their fear of retreat by
downplaying its occurrence during the war, a task rendered more
practicable by the passage of time. What happened during 'the
first period' of the war is now mostly just 'defense'. In the
mid-1970s an article by a prominent analyst on *'Tactics in the
years of the Great Fatherland War'*[196] does not include the word
'retreat' (which would presumably sully the anniversary being
celebrated) and in only one passage deals with events designated
by the avoided term. The general does, however, acknowledge
'defense' amply, at the same time turning the reader's attention
(perhaps even his own) away from the fact that much space was
given up when conducting it: 'In the first and most difficult period
of the war ... the Soviet Union essentially conducted strategic
defense.'[197]

There is in the final analysis only one kind of rearward movement that the Authorities seem able and willing to view as a
means, with no negative nature, to some greater end – namely,
that which has short-run deception as its aim. In this case, the
enemy wastes his resources in attacking what he believes to be
our forward line, from which we have secretly retreated.

Degrading the Enemy's Capacity to Calculate

Recommending, as we have seen, a reliance on 'massing' in

certain ways, the Authorities seem, on the other hand, disturbed by a disposition to aim at success by the *quantity* of men and weapons rather than by the *quality* of their physical capacities and tactical, 'operational', and strategic employment. This concern has found expression even on a high level in the past, as when Tukhachevskii in 1920 recommended that

> one must not rely on the heroism of the troops. *Strategy must furnish tactics with tasks easy to accomplish*. This is obtained in the first place by the concentration in the place of the main blow of forces many times superior to those of the enemy.[198]

'In some cases', a military leader observes,

> the attention to training officers in conducting battle with *superior* enemy forces has been weakened ... With whatever calculations in training you become acquainted, everywhere you see that the commander, for instance in attacking ... enjoys a manifold superiority in forces.

But 'this will not always be the case'. So, 'why not train our officers to win a battle by ... maneuver, secret envelopment of flanks and rear, deceiving the enemy ... forestalling him in deploying into battle order and opening fire?'[199] After all, 'contemporary war', it may be useful to recall, 'is also a contest of minds'.[200]

More particularly, there is among Soviet military elites an inclination to rely on area fire and the multiple coverage of targets to ensure victory in battle. 'If a given combat is considered in isolation from the development of the operation', Tukhachevskii pointed out as early as in the 1920s, 'one can come to the conclusion having buried [*zasypat'*] the enemy with ammunition without counting [*bez scheta*], but win the battle'. Indeed, it is 'indisputable' that unlimited expenditure of ammunition 'resolves the problem of combat tactically'. However, 'such conduct sometimes, even usually, leads to unavoidable difficulties in the entire dimension of the deep ... operation'.[201]

'Soviet artillery practices differ', a US analyst points out,

> from the U.S. in that the U.S. has a tradition of accurate aimed fire ... Very rarely has the U.S. used the kind of fire which the Soviets seem not at all averse to using: to lay a given number of rounds in an area and rely upon ... [this] pattern of fire to produce the desired effect.[202]

'The rules of engagement', another American observes about

Soviet firing practices, 'are for maximum rates of fire until destruction is achieved'. Thus, 'missile units are authorized to expend multiple rounds at attacking helicopters without waiting to see results of the first rounds'.[203] 'The Soviets', observes a Western analyst, 'have used overprogramming ... redundant actions to hedge against ... uncertainties'.[204] Thus, the Soviet strategy is to weaken the strength of any given attempt to cross the river in favor of trying at several points. In so doing, they accept as a worst case, failure at all of them but one.

In simulated air defense, 'calculations showed that for the destruction of the targets more forces were necessary than what the commander allocated'. The problem, of course, was that the commander displayed a frequently encountered 'tendency to an economy of means'. Now,

> of course the aspiration of the commander to a sniper-like [*snaiperskyi*] precision is worthy of approval. [That the Authorities' demand for such precision is apt to have been weighing on him is conveniently overlooked.] But in real battle ... the destruction of the target appears as far from a simple matter, and that must find expression in the decision.[205]

That is, 'for the sake of reliability' it is preferable that 'each target ... [be] suppressed ... by fire from several kinds of weapons'.[206] Such a recommendation may throw some light on the well-known Soviet penchant for procuring several types of missiles with similar characteristics, or contribute to explaining the fact noted by a German commander that 'Russian artillery ... sometimes fired heavily at zones in which German deployments were suspected with insufficient probability'.[207]

While thus themselves tending to rely on area fire and multiple targeting, the Authorities also oppose it, requiring precision (*tochnost'*) in locating targets as well as accuracy in firing: the very first shot should already allow one to take the target off one's list. 'The point is not merely to annihilate the target', in one of the many formulations of this theme, 'the point is to hit it with the first shot, the first burst, the first missile, the first salvo or strike'. The object is to obtain victory, in the standard phrase, 'not by numbers but by skill [*ne chislom a numeniiem*]'.[208]

Stunning

Relying on 'skill' is achieving in the enemy precisely what one aims at preventing in oneself: a reduction in the efficiency with which he will use undestroyed resources. 'In order to obtain success', a military leader observes, 'the regimental commander must know how to ... provoke *loss of bearings* and *panic* among the enemy'.[209]

It is rare, however, that the words emphasized, more often inviting application to oneself, be used for the enemy. Their place is taken by one term which recalls a physical impact – '*oshelomlyat*', to stun – and, for a lesser level of degradation, '*zameshat*', to confuse, or its synonyms:

> I remembered the principle of Suvorov: 'To astonish is to vanquish [*udivit'* — *znachit pobedit'*].' I did not count on victory in this case [the counteroffensive at Stalingrad, 14 September, 1942, but I hoped to cause confusion [*pereputat' karty*] in the Fascist command.[210]

Confused/stunned, the enemy will reduce/abandon '*organizovannost*' – to act with cohesion and in a manner conforming to regulations – a quality which, observe the Authorities, is very fragile, yet yields great rewards. It is standard to demand 'the ... utilization of such sequels to a surprise attack as confusion among the enemy, his ... loss of bearings'[211] For 'it is well known that the aim of surprise [*vnezapnost'*] is to stun the enemy, to carry panic into his ranks, to paralyze his will ... to break up his organized resistance':[212] the action of troops 'uninformed about their enemy' and, hence, in a position to 'be attacked suddenly from any direction, acquires a spontaneous [*stikhiinyi*], unorganized ... character'.[213] 'Commanders', it may be recalled about the war, 'always strove to attack the enemy with surprise' – so as to destroy more of him in the act of surprise itself? No, 'to deprive him of the possibility of offering organized resistance'.[214]

Degrading the enemy's efficiency by reducing the time available to him to act is an important design. It is, as shown above, accomplished mainly in the context of surprising him. 'Surprise', declares the Field Manual of 1936, 'stuns' (p. 10); 'the interceptor ... stuns the "enemy" by a novel combat procedure', an officer relates about simulated combat in 1977.[215]

Achieving the same effect by rendering his current design inapplicable is as strongly intended as one's own capacity to change plans in mid-operation is doubted. Advancing that 'those are wrong who believe that an attack does not exercise a depressing [*ugnetayushchyi*] impression on an enemy', Frunze recalls that 'every one of us knows from his personal experience how an opponent taking the initiative, though he be much weaker, confounds [*putat'*] all calculations of his enemy, destroys [*rasstraivat'*] his plans'.[216] In a rare and significant reference to the subject, it is noted that one of the numerous advantages offered by nuclear weapons is that they 'render fully real the possibility of disrupting the enemy's design'.[217]

But in order to 'disrupt the enemy's calculations', you have, of course, to uncover them in good time, which contributes to the emphasis placed on 'deep penetration into the enemy's intentions'.[218] One will then want to believe – or to make believe – that one is superior to the enemy in this regard. If 'the enemy did not succeed [in, say, a battle of the war], this happened because he was unable to ... uncover the Soviet command's calculations correctly and in good time'[219] – protecting its own all the while.

One way to reduce the surprised enemy's efficiency is to deprive him of intelligence about the new situation in which he has to counter the strike delivered upon him. Those surprised, an analyst elaborates, 'have ... to change their prior plans without having sufficient information about the state of their forces'[220] – and the Authorities are aware of how difficult this task is to their own forces.

Surprise also sharply increases *time pressure* on its victims; a factor to which, as we have seen above, the Authorities are sensitive. Delivering an unexpected strike produces a 'deficit of time' for the enemy to take a decision; this may lead him to make a mistake which one can then 'utilize'. 'Seized unawares', an analyst elaborates, 'the enemy is forced to change his measures in haste ... he will be forced to seek measures counteracting the surprise assault in haste, as a consequence of which they will often be ineffective'.[221] 'Without making precise estimates ... of the composition and emplacement of the sides', the surprised enemy, according to another analyst, 'will ... *in haste* have to introduce modifications into his previous plan, which will turn out not to correspond to the situation at all'. Countermeasures 'insufficiently thought through ... will very often turn out to be of low effectiveness'.[222]

Just when the enemy has less time available, he will *need more*: being surprised will slow him up. In other words, surprise 'deprives the enemy of the possibility of taking effective countermeasures *quickly*'.[223] 'The application of modes of action unexpected by the enemy ... as a rule deprived him of the possibility of adopting quick responses.'[224]

The enemy surprise may, in fact, take over the job of destroying himself. When, on one occasion, 'the Hitlerites lost their bearings, they began to throw bombs on their own troops'.[225] Or he may become inactive. 'When surprise is obtained', in the unsurprising words of an analyst, 'by striking the enemy at places and times where and when he does not expect it', it 'paralyzes the will to resist'.[226] 'We did not fire a single shot against the Russians', declared a Hitlerite officer taken prisoner. 'The appearance of the Russians was so unexpected that a[n] ... instant hypnosis took place.'[227]

One may, in the interests of surprising one's enemy, give up not only the maximization of the strength of one's strike, but also the minimization of obstacles offered by the terrain. Since 'the enemy usually fortifies those sectors of a water barrier convenient for crossing, and defends them with larger forces', an analyst shows, 'for obtaining surprise it often appears advantageous to cross at a *difficult* sector where the enemy's defense is weak, where he expects a crossing least of all and can be taken unawares'.[228]

What is appreciated in inflicting *high losses* on enemy units seems sometimes not so much the ensuing shortfall of their resources as the engendered degradation of the survivors' performance: a factor more discreetly dealt with – as 'combat capacity' preserved – with regard to one's own side:

> But our troops, though they bore heavy losses, were far from having lost [*utratit'*] their capacity for combat [*boesposobnost'*].[229]
> Despite heavy losses, the unit preserved its combat capacity.[230]

'Having discovered the beginning of the enemy's retreat', an officer will write in standard fashion, 'the attackers deliver on him a powerful fire strike'. So as to reduce his force? No – 'striving to disorganize his actions'.[231] Indeed, 'the enemy suffered large losses as a consequence of which he fell into confusion'.[232]

Overview

A detailed discussion of the Soviet style of war – somewhat akin to the specific national approach to military affairs reviewed in Chapter 1 – is especially timely. As NATO undertakes such efforts at force improvement as the Long-term Defense Program, it is important to understand again what type of threat the Alliance is defending. Looking at the same lessons and literature that the Soviet Authorities study, in turn, leads to better understandings of their plans and perceptions. Questions of technology, such as those concerning artillery or antitank weaponry, and of tactics, such as those of speed or command, offer insights into the opponent's priorities as well as his vulnerabilities.

Over 200 years ago the French military commander Guibert wrote that 'the enemy must see me march when he believes me shackled by calculations of subsistence; this new type of war must astonish him, leave him no time to draw breath anywhere'. Most recently and catastrophically this 'new type' of war was suffered by the USSR at the hands of the Germans. The 'lessons' of that war have since dominated Russian military writings and exercises. Today, comparisons are being drawn in the West between the German offensives of World War II and current Soviet capacities to 'astonish' NATO. (Indeed, a newly confident and modernized Soviet military is returning to the German-style armored tactics that they had tried but were unable to adopt successfully in the past.)

There are obvious conceptual differences in the European military balances of 1940–41 and 1980–81; armor, for example, is today an integral part of the defense. Nevertheless, the Soviets believe that there is much to learn from World War II. As the literature describes, modern decisions regarding training, deployment and an array of combat procedures are legitimized in the Soviet style of war, because of their proven success on the battlefields four decades ago. This does not suggest a rigidity of thought. On the contrary, Soviet practice leaves considerable opportunity for battlefield creativity. An appreciation for the Soviet style and tempo can lead to solving the existing and contradictory Western prognoses regarding a NATO–Warsaw Pact conflict.

The Soviet military precepts of speed, surprise, concentration, and the constant offensive, have implications for other Western defense problems in addition to the Central Front. How these dicta translate to strategic nuclear considerations, for example, is the topic of extensive debate, as other chapters indicate.

The previous discussion of Soviet style establishes a data base from which Western analysts can draw further conclusions as they please. Irrespective of their interpretations, the preceding Soviet words on war let us at least see how the Soviets themselves believe that they will fight.

Notes: Chapter 7

1 General of the Army I. Tret'yak, *Voennya vestnik (Military Herald*, hereafter cited as VV), no. 9, 1977, p. 35.
2 A. A. Svechin, 1927, in A. V. Kadishev (ed.), *Voprosy strategii i operatiznogo isskusstva v sovetskikh voennykh trudakh*. (1917-40 gg.) (Moscow: Voenizdat, 1965), p. 257.
3 V. G. Reznichenko (ed.), *Taktika* (Moscow: Voenizdat, 1966), p. 32.

4 D. F. Loza, *Marh i vstrechnyi boi* (Moscow: Voenizdat, 1968), p. 66.
5 General of the Army A. Radzievskii, *Voenno-Istoricheskii zhurnal (Military Historical Journal*, hereafter cited as *VIZh*), 1975, no. 5, p. 38.
6 Loza, p. 94.
7 S. G. Gorshkov, *Morskaya Moshch' gosudarstva* (Moscow: Voenizdat, 1976), p. 370.
8 V. Triandafillow, quoted by A. A. Sidorenko, in *Nastuplenie* (Moscow: Voenizdat, 1970), p. 24.
9 Annual Report, FY 1977, p. 92.
10 Tukhachevskii, 1937, in Kadishev, op. cit., p. 134.
11 Lt General S. Krivda, *Komunist Vooruzhenykh Sil (The Communist of the Armed Forces*, hereafter cited as *KVS*), no. 1, 1977, p. 60.
12 Colonel A. Vorov'ev, *Krasnaya zvezda (Red Star*, hereafter cited as *KZ*), 27 December, 1974.
13 Captain V. Basok, *KZ*, 21 December, 1975.
14 Loza, p. 137.
15 Lt Colonel A. Zhentukhov, *VV*, no. 8, 1974, p. 65.
16 Major General A. Ryazanskii, *VV*, no. 6, 1969, p. 35.
17 G. S. Isserson, 1937, in Kadishev, 1965, p. 399.
18 Tukhachevskii, 1924, op. cit., p. 86.
19 A. I. Radzievskii (ed.), *Taktika v boevykh primerakh* (Moscow: Voenizdat, 1974), p. 26.
20 A. S. Milovidov and V. G. Kozlov (eds), *Filosofskoe naslgdie V. I. Lenina i problemy sovremennoi voiny* (Moscow: Voenizdat, 1972), p. 147.
21 Sidorenko, op. cit., p. 150.
22 Radzievskii, 1974, p. 94.
23 Sidorenko, p. 168.
24 Reznichenko, op. cit., p. 316.
25 A division commander quoted by N. K. Popel', *Tanki povernuli na zapad* (Moscow: Voenizdat, 1960), p. 120.
26 Colonel V. Smirnov, *VV*, 1977, no. 9, pp. 58–60.
27 Heading of a chapter, in K. S. Moskalenko, *Na yugozapadnam napravlenii* (2 vols) (Moscow: Nauka, 1973), Vol. 2, p. 78.
28 Popel', op. cit., p. 208.
29 Heading of a chapter, in A. T. Stuchenko, *Zavidnaya nasha sud'ba* (Moscow: Voenizdat, 1968), p. 203.
30 *KZ*, 12 December, 1975.
31 P. M. Vigor, *RUSI*, no. 4, 1975, p. 44.
32 A. L. Egorov, 1933, in Kadishev, 1965, p. 386.
33 Colonel M. Skorovodkin, *VV*, no. 3, 1959, p. 11
34 Loza, p. 170.
35 Lomov, p. 37.
36 Sidorenko, p. 57.
37 V. E. Savkin, *Osnovnye printsipy operativnogo iskusstva i taktiki* (Moscow: Voenizdat, 1972), p. 264.
38 Loza, p. 167.
39 Sidorenko, p. 223.
40 Reznichenko, p. 317.
41 Captain E. D. Betit, *Military Review*, no. 8, 1975, p. 30.
42 *KZ*, 24 January, 1974.
43 Colonel E. Datsyuk, *DVS*, no. 19, 1969, p. 58.
44 Lt Colonel L. Muzyka, *KZ*, 22 October, 1976.
45 P. H. Vigor, *RUSI*, no. 4, 1975, p. 44; emphasis in the text.
46 N. A. Lomov (ed.) *Nauchno-technicheskii progress i revolutsiia v voennom dele* (Moscow: Voenizdat, 1973), pp. 167-8.
47 Colonel V. Savkin, *VV*, no. 4, 1971, p. 30.
48 *KZ*, 13 August, 1974.
49 Reznichenko, p. 258.
50 Colonel A. Kitov, *KVS*, no. 2, 1976, p. 53.
51 Loza, p. 14.

52 V. Zakharchenko, *KZ*, 1 January, 1973.
53 Lt Commander Yu. Timoshchuk, *KZ*, 7 December, 1973.
54 Loza, pp. 85–6.
55 Lomov, p. 168.
56 Reznichenko, p. 259.
57 Major General K. Babenko, *KZ*, 3 August, 1976.
58 Colonel A. Kitov, *KVS*, no. 2, 1976, p. 53.
59 Lt Colonel Sinchuk, *VV*, no. 4, 1973, p. 27.
60 Colonel I. Vorov'ev, *KZ*, 15 May, 1974.
61 Sidorenko, p. 75.
62 Navy Captain V. Poshivailov, *KV*, 28 July, 1976.
63 A. A. Svechin, 1927, in Kadishev, 1965, p. 258.
64 Op. cit., p. 254.
65 Major General V. Platov, *KVS*, no. 1, 1976, p. 57.
66 F. I. Kuznetsov, 1930, in Kadishev, 1965, p. 572; the last sentence is emphasized in the text.
67 Colonel General I. Pavlovskii, *VV*, no. 4, 1964, p. 5.
68 Lt Colonel I. Sinchuk, *VV*, no. 4, 1973, p. 27.
69 See Philip A. Karber, *Survival*, May–June, 1976, p. 111.
70 K. B. Kalinovskii, 1931, in Kadishev, p. 565.
71 Colonel I. Vorov'ev, *KZ*, 26 May, 1973.
72 Colonel I. Vorov'ev, *VV*, no. 8, 1972, p. 18.
73 A. M. Adgamov, A. I. Demin and A. I. Smetanin, *Taktika v boevykh primerakh* (Moscow: Voenizdat, 1974), p. 41.
74 Radzievskii, 1974, p. 92.
75 Colonel V. Savkin, *VV*, no. 4, 1971, p. 32.
76 Tukhachevskii, 1920, in Kadishev, 1965, p. 78.
77 Editorial, *KZ*, 31 March, 1977.
78 Colonel A. Kitov, *KVS*, no. 2, 1976, p. 52.
79 Colonel V. Savkin, *VV*, no. 4, 1971, p. 32.
80 *KZ*, 15 January, 1976.
81 *KZ*, 11 March, 1976.
82 Colonel I. Kirin, *VV*, no. 7, 1973, p. 39.
83 *KZ*, 22 October, 1975.
84 Admiral G. Egorov, *KVS*, no. 6, 1975, p. 36.
85 KZ, 28 February, 1975.
86 Admiral N. Smirnov, *KVS*, no. 11, 1974, p. 31.
87 *KZ*, 4 July, 1974.
88 Colonel I. Vorov'ev, *KZ*, 20 October, 1976.
89 Editorial, *KVS*, no. 4, 1966, p. 6.
90 Editorial, *VV*, no. 6, 1976, p. 3.
91 Editorial, *VV*, no. 6, 1967, p. 5.
92 Major I. Slyuserenko, *VV*, no. 5, 1977, p. 57.
93 H. Goldhamer, *The Soviet Soldier: Soviet Military Management at the Troop Level* (New York: Crane, Russak, 1975), p. 121.
94 Colonel R. Dukov, *VV*, no. 3, 1971, p. 41.
95 *KZ*, 14 October, 1975.
96 Lomov, p. 173.
97 Colonel R. Dukov, *KZ*, 23 November, 1972.
98 Major I. Chuguev, *VV*, no. 1, 1969, p. 69.
99 Major General L. Boldyrev, *KZ*, 13 November, 1976.
100 ibid.
101 Marshal P. Batitskii, *KZ*, 16 January, 1976.
102 Lomov, p. 165.
103 S. G. Gorshkov, *Morskaya Moshch' gosudarstva* (Moscow: Voenizdat, 1976), p. 371.
104 Colonel Y. Lobachev, *VV*, no. 2, 1977, p. 44.
105 A. J. Radzievskii, *Tankovyi udar* (Moscow: Voenizdat, 1977), p. 43.
106 Yu. Z. Novikov and F. D. Sverdlov, *Manevr v obshchevoiskom boyu* (Moscow: Voenizdat, 1967), p. 24.

107 Colonel General I. Pavlovskii, *VV*, no. 4, 1964, p. 6.
108 Colonel R. Dukov, *KZ*, 23 June, 1973.
109 Sidorenko, p. 67.
110 Colonel G. Lobachev, *VV*, no. 2, 1977, p. 44.
111 Savkin, pp. 181–2.
112 Sidorenko, p. 67.
113 Major General Skorodumov, *VV*, no. 5, 1973, pp. 12–13.
114 Savkin, p. 226.
115 A. J. Radzievskii, op. cit., p. 48.
116 Colonel V. Maramzin, *VIZh*, no. 5, 1974, p. 20.
117 Colonel R. Dukov, *KZ*, 30 July, 1976.
118 Colonel R. Dukov, *VV*, no. 3, 1971, p. 41.
119 Colonel D. Shapovalov, *VV*, no. 2, 1965, p. 33.
120 General of the Army I. Pavlovskii, *VV*, no. 1, 1971, p. 7.
121 Colonel R. Dukov, *VV*, no. 3, 1971. p. 41.
122 Editorial, *VV*, no. 5, 1976, p. 3.
123 General of the Army I. Pavlovskii, *VV*, no. 7, 1968, p. 8.
124 Captain V. Misyura, *KZ*, 16 April, 1976.
125 Navy Captain V. Velayev, *KZ*, 6 April, 1973.
126 B. Ponomarev, *Kommunist*, no. 6, 1976, p. 29.
127 A. I. Sobolev, *Voprosy istorii, KPSS*, no. 11, 1975, trans. in *FBIS*, 11 December, 1975, p. A15.
128 Lomov, p. 173.
129 ibid., p. 149.
130 *KZ*, 22 January, 1976.
131 Lomov, p. 148.
132 Colonel General N. Skorodumov, *VIZh*, no. 9, 1974, p. 36.
133 Lt General V. Reznichenko, *KZ*, 9 December 1975.
134 Colonel S. Gladysh, *VIZh*, no. 3, 1974, p.30.
135 G. K. Zhukov, *Vospominaniya i razmyshleniya, Tom 1* (Moscow: Voenizdat, 1975), Vol. 1, p. 390.
136 A. A. Svechin, 1927, in Kadishev, 1965, p. 254.
137 Major General R. Simonyan, *VV*, no. 4, 1964, p. 24.
138 Colonel General A. Dement'ev and Colonel S. Petrov, *VIZh*, no. 7, 1978, p. 36.
139 K. von Tippelskirch, quoted by B. H. Liddell Hart, *The Other Side of the Hill* (London: Cassell, 1951), p. 337.
140 F. W. v. Mellenthin, *Panzer Battles 1939–1945* (London: Cassell, 1955), p. 229.
141 Lt General V. Ivanov, *VV*, no. 1, 1976, p. 33.
142 General of the Army I. Pavlovskii, *VV*, no. 1, 1975, p. 6.
143 Colonel V. Vinnikov, *VV*, no. 6, 1964, p. 23.
144 K. N. Galitskii, *Gody surovykh ispytanii* (Moscow: Nauka, 1973), p. 323.
145 Radzievskii, 1974, p. 17.
146 Mellenthin, p. 159.
147 V. I. Chuikov, *Nachalo puti* (Moscow: Voenizdat, 1962), p. 157.
148 *KZ*, 3 February, 1976.
149 Colonel General Kh. Ambaryan, *VV*, no. 7, 1973, pp. 5–6.
150 Sidorenko, p. 4.
151 Reznichenko, p. 85.
152 Lt General V. Reznichenko, *KZ*, 5 June, 1974.
153 *KZ*, 12 July, 1975.
154 Colonel P. Galotskii, *VV*, no. 11, 1978, p. 39.
155 Marshal S. K. Timoshenko, quoted in Moskalenko, Vol. 1, p. 177.
156 S. N. Kozlov, M. V. Smirnov, I. S. Baz' and P. A. Sidorov, *O sovetskoi voennoi nauke* (Moscow: Voenizdat, 1964), p. 354.
157 Colonel V. Erofeev, *VV*, no. 9, 1965, p. 31.
158 I. S. Konev, *Zapiski komanduyushego frontom 1943–1944* (Moscow: Nauka, 1972), p. 214.
159 Vice-Admiral V. Belashev, *KZ*, 13 December, 1975.
160 Editorial, *VV*, no. 8, 1963, p. 9.

161 *KZ*, 14 September, 1975.
162 A. A. Bulatov and V. G. Prozorov, *Takticheskaya vnezapnost'* (Moscow: Voenizdat, 1965), p. 143.
163 ibid., p. 16.
164 V. D. Sokolovskii, *Voennaya strategiya* (Moscow: Voenizdat, 1968), p. 356.
165 Colonel R. Dukov, *KZ*, 23 June, 1973.
166 Radzievskii, 1974, p. 191.
167 Colonel V. Maramzin, *VIZh*, no. 10, 1970, p. 24.
168 Savkin, pp. 336–7.
169 Reznichenko, p. 320.
170 A. Kh. Babadzhanyan (ed.) *Tanki i tankovye voiska* (Moscow: Voenizdat, 1970), p. 273.
171 *KZ*, 24 January, 1974.
172 A. I. Eremenko, *Zapiski komanduyushego frontom* (Moscow: Voenizdat, 1961), p. 298.
173 General of the Army I. Pavlovskii, *KZ*, 19 January, 1976.
174 Reznichenko, p. 86.
175 A. I. Verkhovskii, 1924, in Kadishev, 1970, pp. 39–40.
176 Colonel V. Erofeev, *VV*, no. 9, 1965, p. 30.
177 Colonel V. Erofeev, *VV*, no. 9, 1965, p. 30.
178 S. M. Belitskii, 1930, in Kadishev, 1965, p. 360.
179 S. K. Timoshenko, in A. V. Kadishev (ed.), *Voprosy taktiki v sovetskikh voennykh trudakh* (1917–1940 gg.) (Moscow: Voenizdat, 1940), p. 125.
180 Reznichenko, p. 320.
181 S. M. Belitskii, 1930, in Kadishev, 1965, op. cit., p. 360.
182 Frunze, 1922, in Kadishev, op. cit., p. 58.
183 op. cit., p. 47.
184 Sokolovskii, p. 358.
185 ibid.
186 ibid.
187 Radzievskii, 1974, pp. 256–7.
188 Reznichenko, p. 332.
189 Radzievskii, 1974, p. 256.
190 A. I. Verkhovskii, 1928, in Kadishev, 1965, op. cit., p. 280. Emphasis in text.
191 M. N. Tukhachevskii, 1932, in Kadishev, 1965, p. 121.
192 Frunze, 1992, in Kadishev, op. cit., p. 51.
193 A. I. Verkhovskii, 1924, in Kadishev, 1970, p. 37.
194 M. N. Tukhachevskii, 1924, op. cit., p. 36.
195 G. S. Isserson, 1937, op. cit., p. 398.
196 Lt General V. Reznichenko, *VV*, no. 4, 1975.
197 Major General N. Shekhovtsov, *VIZh*, no. 3, 1974, p. 48.
198 Tukhachevskii, 1920, in Kadishev, 1965, p. 82.
199 General of the Army I. Pavlovskii, *VV*, no. 1, 1975, p. 5.
200 Lt Colonel V. Ivanov, *VV*, no. 1, 1976, p. 35.
201 Tukhachevskii, 1929, in Kadishev, 1965, pp. 108–9.
202 Rand working paper.
203 Major Peter M. Wargo, US Army *Military Review*, no. 11, November, 1975, p. 7.
204 Jasper A. Welch, Jr, 'A conceptual approach to countering invasion threats to NATO', June, 1976, p. 3. (mimeo.)
205 Major General K. Dzyza, *KZ*, 16 November, 1971.
206 E. T. Marchenko (ed.) *Taktika v boevykh primerakh. Batal' on* (Moscow: Voenizdat, 1974).
207 E. Middeldorf, *Taktik im Russlandfeldzug* (Darmstadt: Mittler, 1956), p. 92.
208 Colonel V. Grushets, *KVS*, no. 11, 1975, p. 31.
209 General of the Army I. Pavlovskii, *VV*, no. 1, 1971, p. 9.
210 Chuikov, V. I. *180 dnei v ogne srazhenii. Iz zapisk Komandira 62-i.* (Moscow: Dosaaf, 1962), p. 19.
211 Sr Lt R. Urazmatov, *VV*, no. 11, 1978, p. 44.
212 Colonel N. Shishkin, *VV*, no. 6, 1978, p. 24.

213 Reznichenko, p. 212.
214 Marchenko, 1974, pp. 250–1.
215 Major G. Shul'ga, *KZ*, 30 March, p. 19.
216 Frunze, 1922, in Kadishev, 1965, p. 47.
217 Lomov, p. 172.
218 Savkin, p. 301.
219 Colonel S. Petrov, *VIZh*, no. 7, 1974, pp. 34–5.
220 Bulatov and Prozorov, p. 6.
221 Reznichenko, p. 83.
222 Savkin, p. 306.
223 Colonel R. Dukov, *KZ*, 23 June, 1972.
224 Colonel General A. Dement'ev and Colonel S. Petrov, *VIZh*, no. 7, 1978, p. 36.
225 Colonel G. Arten'ev and B. Bachurin, *KZ*, 10 June, 1973.
226 Lomov, p. 153.
227 Colonel V. Galavzhev, *VV*, no. 10, 1968, p. 43.
228 Sidorenko, pp. 194–5.
229 M. I. Kazakov, *Nad kartoi bylykh srazhenii* (Moscow: Voenizdat, 1965), p. 112.
230 I. I. Fedyuninskii, *Podnyatye po trevoge* (Moscow: Voenizdat, 1961), p. 26.
231 Colonel N. Shishkin, *VV*, no. 2, 1966, p. 30.
232 Marchenko, 1974, p. 201.

8

Soviet Military Doctrine and Warsaw Pact Exercises

CHRISTOPHER JONES

In the Warsaw Pact the primary function of Soviet military doctrine is to prevent Bulgaria, Hungary, East Germany, Poland and Czechoslovakia from adopting military doctrines of territorial defense similar to those of Romania and Yugoslavia. The Soviets use their military doctrine as the basis for joint Pact activities, all of which prevent members of the Pact from acquiring the capability to wage war of territorial defense. The most important of these activities is the system of joint military exercises.

The Yugoslavs and the Romanians reject both the theory and practice of the principal military-technical components of Soviet doctrine in favor of doctrines of territorial defense. They assume that the likely aggressor will use conventional rather than nuclear weapons. The military art (strategy, operations and tactics) of each of these two states addresses the problem of ensuring the survival of national military forces and national political leadership in the event of occupation of either country by an enemy force estimated at 750,000–1,250,000 soldiers. The troop training of each country emphasizes the training of regular and paramilitary forces for 'people's war' actions adapted to the special conditions of each country. The military-economic policies of Yugoslavia and Romania emphasize domestic production of small and medium-sized arms and limited purchase of Western and Chinese weapons, and transport and reconnaissance equipment. Romania and Yugoslavia jointly produce a jet interceptor outfitted with British engines. During an occupation, the national defense system of each country is designed to maintain the continuity of national political authority over civilians and to supply them with economic, medical and other necessities.[1]

According to the Yugoslavs, the formulation of postwar Yugoslav doctrine on territorial defense began in 1958.[2] The Romanians developed their postwar territorial defense system sometime between 1958, when Soviet troops withdrew from

Romania, and 1968, when President Ceauşescu mobilized the system the day after the Soviet intervention in Czechoslovakia. Available evidence suggests that the critical years in the development of Romania's territorial defense system were the late 1950s and early 1960s.[3] A former Polish intelligence officer who emigrated to the West has written that in the late 1950s, General Zygmunt Dusynski headed a group of high-ranking Polish officers who unsuccessfully attempted to draw up plans for establishing within the Warsaw Pact 'a separate, compact, well-defined "Polish Front", intended as an exclusive theater of operations for the Polish armed forces'.[4] According to this account, Dusynski's plans called for the formulation of a specifically Polish military doctrine, a Polish national defense system, and an independent Polish armaments industry.[5] In the late 1950s the East German defense ministry faced the task of developing a national military doctrine for the newly formed (1956) National People's Army. At the same time the pro-Soviet remnants of the Hungarian officer corps were in need of a Hungarian military doctrine predicated on participation in the Warsaw Pact, rather than on Imre Nagy's policy of withdrawal.

To borrow a Soviet expression, perhaps it is not altogether accidental that in the late 1950s when one or more East European states was developing a national military doctrine of territorial defense, the Soviets also began a major reformulation of military doctrine.[6] There may also be a connection between the appearance of Marshal V. D. Sokolovskii's *Military Strategy* in 1962 and the introduction of the Warsaw Pact's system of multilateral exercises. The first of these, which took place in late 1961, was followed by four more in 1962. Sokolovskii's text specifically called for the incorporation of East European forces in joint theater actions under Soviet command;[7] it insisted that because the next war fought in Europe would be a nuclear war, a new military art must be developed.[8] Other authoritative Soviet texts point out directly that there is a connection between formulating Soviet military doctrine and maintaining Soviet military alliances.[9]

Soviet theorists claim that the military-political component is the more decisive component of military doctrine. In the case of the Warsaw Pact, this claim is completely justified. For the five loyal East European members of the Warsaw Treaty Organization (WTO) the prerequisite for accepting the Soviet conceptions of military art, troop training, military economics and the organization of a national defense system, is acceptance of a common set of military-political axioms. For Yugoslavia and Romania, the theoretical basis for rejection of the military-technical component of Soviet doctrine is rejection of the military-political component and the diplomatic policies linked to it.

Soviet theorists have produced a voluminous literature which traces the origins of the WTO's military-political axioms back to Lenin. The following axioms form a circular argument in which each axiom is defined as a basic element of the others: joint defense of the gains of socialism in each fraternal country against external and internal enemies; proletarian internationalism; socialist internationalism; defense of the socialist fatherland; the Marxist-Leninist teaching on war and military affairs; the Marxist-Leninist conception of the necessity of the military-political unity of the armed forces of the socialist states; the concept of the 'combat confederation' of the armed forces of the socialist states; the concept of joint defense of socialism and peace.[10]

The Soviets use their military-political axioms to justify Soviet domination of all aspects of joint Pact activity, including the system of joint military exercises. In elaborating on the axioms pertinent to the system of WTO exercises, Soviet theorists demonstrate a distinct preference for vague enemies, such as imperialism, reaction, forces opposed to socialism and peace. These hostile forces are not confined to Europe or even to capitalist states; they constitute a worldwide threat to socialism and, Soviet analysts hasten to point out, are invariably organized in a coalition. The threat posed by this hostile coalition has led Major General Samoilenko to a conclusion shared by all his Soviet colleagues: 'The military unity of the socialist states is a vital necessity because a new world war, if the enemies of peace and socialism unleash it, will be a coalition war.'[11]

The Soviets have not maintained a monopoly on this military-political axiom. According to General of the Army A. A. Epishev, Chief of the Main Political Administration of the Soviet Armed Forces: 'The military doctrines of the socialist confederation proceed from the fact that it is possible to prevent a new world war only by the joint efforts of the fraternal socialist countries'.[12] Despite Epishev's claim, the military doctrines of two East European socialist states do not proceed from the Soviet assumption of how to prevent a new world war. Since the formation of the Warsaw Pact, the Yugoslav government has maintained that the greatest threat to world peace comes from the competition between the military coalitions headed by the USA and the USSR. One spokesman for this view, Major General Dusan Dozet, wrote in 1970:

This state of 'peace armed to the teeth', the balancing on the edge
of peace or war, does not, of course, eliminate the danger of direct
confrontation between the superpowers ...

It is precisely this state ... that conceals the greatest danger to
small and medium-sized countries, both those states outside the
blocs and those inside ...

The small and medium-sized countries are the lasting objects of
intensive pressure, intervention and aggression, this applying
equally to non-aligned and bloc-aligned countries.

They are not in a position to achieve security in a bloc mechan-
ism or under its protection.

Security can be achieved only by relying on their own forces.[13]

As a Pact member, Romania has been much more cautious
than Yugoslavia in condemning military blocs. But the Romanians have firmly rejected Soviet military-political axioms concerning aggressive imperialist designs on Romania. Ceauşescu has
also stated repeatedly that Romania will respond to aggression by
NATO only according to the provisions of the Warsaw Treaty
and the provisions of Romania's bilateral treaties with WTO
states. (Each of these treaties leaves it to Romania to decide what
form of assistance Romania will provide if another WTO member
is attacked.)[14] When the Soviets pressed Ceauşescu, at the
November 1978 meeting of the Political Consultative Committee
of the WTO, to agree to higher levels of military spending and
tighter integration of the WTO command structure, Ceauşescu
refused.[15] In seeking endorsement from the Romanian Central
Committee for his decision, Ceauşescu reaffirmed, albeit somewhat nervously, his rejection of Soviet military-political axioms
and his endorsement of Titoist military-political policies. According to the English translation of his address to the Central Committee provided by the Romanian news agency, Ceauşescu
declared:

In the case of an aggression in Europe against a country in the
membership of the Warsaw Pact, we will fulfill our obligations
taken under the Pact and also under the bilateral pacts of mutual
assistance, according to the respective provisions.

Naturally, we declare and will do everything for the military
pacts – both the NATO and the Warsaw Pact – to be abolished the
soonest since we are firmly convinced that it is not the military
pacts that ensure the independence, sovereignty and peace, but on
the contrary, they only maintain the state of tension ...

But, why not say it, our relations with all the neighboring
countries, with the states in this part of Europe are very good ...
countries like Greece and Turkey are not concerned with

intensifying the arming ... So why should we choose such a way? ...

Practically speaking, we have good relations with all countries of Europe – I mean those not in the Warsaw Pact. We have good relations with all NATO member countries and even very good relations with some of them.[16]

Soviet military-political theorists insist that the socialist con-federation has taken up arms only as a last resort, because the forces of imperialism have consistently rejected Soviet proposals for general and complete disarmament. They also insist that no small or medium-sized state can stand alone against the hostile coalition of imperialist forces, because such states lack the economic resources necessary to fend off the imperialist armies preparing for nuclear war.[17] Soviet theorists proceed from their discussion of the imperialist threat to argue that socialist armies exist not only to defend socialism against its external enemies, but against its internal enemies as well. Colonel Timorin writes that the internal function of a socialist army has three aspects: (1) as a psychological deterrent against antisocialist forces; (2) as a backup for internal security forces; (3) as a combat force 'in those cases when the opposition of the enemies of socialism within a country acquires significant scale, intensity, duration and sharp-ness (a counterrevolutionary uprising, mutiny, banditry, the unleashing of civil war)'.[18]

The Soviet volume on the WTO, edited by the late Marshal Iakubovskii, former Commander of the Pact, points out that in executing its internal functions a socialist army should not have to rely on its own forces, but can count on fraternal assistance from other socialist armies. The Iakubovskii text declares that one of the missions of the WTO is 'joint defense of the gains of socialism in each fraternal country when these gains are threatened by danger from internal or external reaction'.[19] This volume specifi-cally cites Soviet actions in Hungary in 1956 and Czechoslovakia in 1968 as examples of such fraternal assistance,[20] as do virtually all other detailed Soviet discussions of the principle of joint defense of the gains of socialism. The Chief of the Main Political Adminstration of the Soviet Armed Forces has identified the principle of joint defense of the gains of socialism as 'a law of history'.[21]

The principal threat to the axiom of joint defense of the gains of socialism against internal and external enemies is the challenge posed by the military doctrines of Yugoslavia and Romania. These doctrines are standing invitations to the defense ministries of East Europe to adopt strategies of territorial defense. In April

1968 the commandant of the Gottwald Military-Political Academy in Prague and several of his subordinates jointly drafted a 100-page memorandum outlining three possible defense postures for Czechoslovakia outside the Warsaw Pact. One was disarmament in conjunction with a general European disarmament; another was alliance with other small socialist states in central Europe; the third option was territorial defense.[22] Within one month of the drafting of the 'Gottwald Memorandum', Soviet troops entered Czechoslovakia on WTO maneuvers. After the intervention of 21 August, the Gottwald Academy was closed down for several years and the officers responsible for the 'Memorandum' were cashiered.

Soviet theorists have chosen not to attack Yugoslav and Romanian military doctrines by name. Instead, they have contented themselves with vociferous denunciations of Maoist military doctrine as unsuitable for small socialist countries.[23] In its denunciation of territorial defense as a Maoist heresy, the Soviet volume on the WTO edited by Marshal Iakubovskii specifically calls attention to the function of common military-political axioms as the basis for the Pact's adoption of common views on military art, troop training, military economics and the organization of national defense systems.[24]

The Soviets do not rely on the intrinsic logic of their military-political axioms to persuade East European defense ministries to accept these axioms and their military-technical corollaries. The Soviets depend on the force of the bilateral treaties and party programs into which these axioms have been written. Reincarnated as articles of international treaties and sections of party programs, the military-political axioms of Soviet doctrine are binding on the officers of five East European WTO countries in their capacities as state officials and party members.[25]

The System of Joint Warsaw Pact Exercises

The military-political axioms shared by the armed forces of the USSR and the five loyal East European members of the WTO require a theory of military art that eschews 'reliance on one's own forces' and facilitates multilateral intervention in each other's territory in joint defense of the gains of socialism against internal and external enemies. Published Soviet discussions of the strategy, operations and tactics of waging a war in Europe offer such a theory of military art. Analysts of these Soviet discussions have documented an emphasis on the offensive use of very large conventional forces capable of waging a limited nuclear war with Soviet nuclear weapons.[26] The available evidence indicates that the published Soviet discussions of the conduct of large-scale offensive actions using Soviet nuclear weapons serves as the basis of the military art (strategy, operations and tactics) practiced in the joint WTO exercises. This chapter suggests that in the joint exercises the Soviets drill the armies of the Pact for nuclear offense against the West in order to render those armies incapable of conventional defense against the East. It further proposes that in the joint exercises the Soviets prepare East European conventional forces for massive multilateral interventions in the member states of the alliance.

The following factors support the analysis of the system of joint forces: (1) the pattern of location of the exercises in which the armed forces of individual Pact members participate; (2) the pattern of assigning command of the joint exercises; (3) the practice of offensive actions, including nuclear actions, which rule out preparation for territorial defense; (4) the nature of the organization of staff work for the exercises; (5) the assignment of individual missions in the exercises to multinational combined arms groupings of forces; (6) the impact of the joint exercises on the nature of the military training programs of individual Pact members; (7) the impact on the careers of East European officers of the command structure of the exercises and the military-education system that prepares East European officers for WTO exercises; and (8) the nature of the political activities that take place during joint exercises.

The present analysis does not deny the potential role of Pact exercises in preparing WTO armies for war with NATO: it only says that preparation for war with NATO is not the primary purpose of Pact exercises. This is not to deny that Soviet force groups in East Europe practice the conduct of offensive nuclear war against NATO; it is only to imply that such practice is intended for an exclusively Soviet offensive.

The Warsaw Pact system of frequent, large-scale joint maneuvers on both a multilateral basis and bilateral basis (Soviet–East European) began in the 'Buria' exercise of October–November 1961 under Marshal A. A. Grechko. Grechko assumed his duties as WTO Commander in Chief in July 1960 after having served as Commander of the Soviet Ground Forces (1957–60) and Commander of the Group of Soviet Forces in Germany (1953–7). According to the volume on the WTO edited by the next Pact commander, Marshal Iakubovskii, joint tactical exercises had taken place before

1961[27] but this paper can identify only two such exercises, both bilateral. In August 1957, Soviet and East German troops conducted a joint exercise[28] while Grechko was still the Soviet commander in Germany. From 18 July to 8 August, 1958, the Soviet air force and the Bulgarian ground forces, air force and navy conducted a joint exercise in Bulgaria under the command of Soviet Air Marshal N. S. Skripko.[29]

Grechko expanded the scope of WTO exercises from the tactical level to the operational and strategic levels. According to the US air force translation of the Soviets' *Dictionary of Basic Military Terms*, a tactical exercise can involve a battalion, regiment, division or corps and may include combined-arms actions.[30] Tactical exercises practice tactics, which the Soviet dictionary (in the American translation) defines as 'objective laws of combat ... Each service and branch has its own tactics'.[31] This dictionary defines operational art as 'the theory and practice of preparing for and conducting combined and independent operations by major field formations or major formations of the Services'. An action at the operational level is an 'operational-strategic maneuver' which the Soviet dictionary defines as 'an organised movement of large groupings of major field forces of the armed forces within theaters of military operations for the purpose of creating the most advantageous grouping of men and equipment for the completion of assigned missions'.[32] Finally, a 'strategic maneuver' is defined as an action designed 'to secure the rapid and complete destruction of major enemy groupings'.[33]

By developing a system of bilateral and multilateral exercises at the tactical, operational and strategic levels, Marshal Grechko transformed the military organizations and capabilities of the five East European armies that were permanently drawn into the system of joint exercises. Soviet and East European sources readily identify the system of joint exercises as the central focus of Pact activities but they are erratic in providing information about the number and nature of the exercises. Graham Turbiville, a former US army intelligence officer, published in a journal of the US army a list of 36 major WTO exercises in the period from 1961 to 1977, but carefully disclaimed that his list was complete.[34] My paper, drawing on Turbiville's list and a combing of Soviet and East European materials, presents a list of 71 major WTO exercises for the period from 1961 to 1979. This list of 71 is probably short of the true total of the larger tactical, operational and strategic level exercises and the high-level command staff exercises. But even if the Soviets supplied a complete listing of the more important WTO exercises, it might still not give an accurate picture of the extent of the activities that take place under the system of joint exercises. Both Soviet and East European sources suggest that the number of lower-level tactical and joint staff exercises without the participation of troops is greater than the number of large-scale tactical, operational and strategic maneuvers and high-level command staff exercises.[35]

The Helsinki accords of 1975 required both NATO and the WTO to report only those exercises involving more than 25,000 troops and encouraged the invitation of observers. Whatever the intentions of those who drafted the sections on confidence-building measures, the actual effect is that the Soviets have probably reduced the size of most tactical and operational-strategic exercises to a figure below 25,000 and have sharply reduced the publication of all information on the system of joint exercises. Information on the system of joint exercises is for all practical purposes limited to the period from 1961 to 1974. Most of this information comes from the period after the appointment of Marshal Iakubovskii as Pact Commander in the spring of 1967. During 1967, Pact sources reported six large-scale joint exercises; in 1968, seven; in 1969, eleven; in 1970, four; in 1971, six; in 1972, five; in 1973, six; and in 1974, six. But in 1975, the year of the Helsinki agreement, the Soviets reported no joint WTO exercises; in 1976, two; in 1977, one; in 1978, none; and in 1979, two. If, in fact, the WTO sharply reduced the number of joint exercises after 1975, then it has virtually ceased what had been until 1975 the most important activity in the Warsaw Pact.

The Joint Exercises: Patterns of Location and Patterns of Command

The system of joint exercises introduced by Marshal Grechko provided for the periodic re-entry of Soviet and other WTO troops into the territories of the three countries where Soviet troops were not stationed in 1961: Czechoslovakia, Romania and Bulgaria. As a reciprocal gesture, Grechko's program invited the armed forces of Czechoslovakia, Romania and Bulgaria to participate in joint exercises on the territory of other WTO states, including, in at least two cases, multilateral exercises on the territory of the USSR. In 1962 the WTO held exercises in Czechoslovakia and Romania and also an exercise in Hungary in which Romanian troops participated. The different histories of Soviet-Czechoslovak relations and Soviet-Romanian relations after 1962 correspond closely to the different decisions taken by these two East European states on continued participation in WTO exercises.

The periodic WTO maneuvers in Czechoslovakia established a Soviet capability for rapid and massive occupation of Czechoslovak soil while simultaneously pre-empting the possibility of the development of a Czechoslovak system of territorial defense. According to Turbiville's list, the September 1962 exercise in Czechoslovakia of Czechoslovak, Soviet and Polish troops was followed in June 1964 by another exercise in Czechoslovakia which involved the participation of Czechoslovak, Soviet and East German troops. *Krasnaya zvezda* reported exercises in Czechoslovakia during 7–15 July, 1964, (which Turbiville does not), involving the command staffs of Soviet and Czechoslovak troops. The Czechoslovak Minister of Defense, Bohomir Lomsky, conducted the exercise in the presence of the Chief of the WTO Staff, P. I. Batov of the Soviet army, and V. A. Sudets, Comander of the Soviet Antiaircraft Troops.[36]

In 1966, in the presence of Marshal Grechko, General Lomsky commanded Czechoslovak, Soviet, East German and Hungarian forces in the Vltava exercises in Czechoslovakia. This exercise involved more than twenty organs of administration, large formations and special units, including airborne troops. According to *Krasnaya zvezda*, the materiel used in this exercise could have formed a single column 850 km long,[37] a distance greater than the length of Czechoslovakia from east to west. As an operational exercise, Vltava served as preparation for even larger operational exercises in 1968.

During the Prague spring, the system of WTO exercises provided Soviet forces with quick and convenient access to Czechoslovak territory. On 29 May, 1968, at a plenum of the Czechoslovak Central Committee, the loose coalition of 'progressives' more or less united around Dubček proposed a resolution calling for the convocation of an extraordinary party congress two years ahead of schedule in order to elect a new central committee. If they could pass the resolution, the progressives hoped that they would be able to name a majority of the delegates to the congress. With Soviet backing, the 'conservatives' surprised the progressives by voting for the resolution, which easily obtained a majority.[38] The next day, Soviet airborne troops landed at the Prague airport, and Soviet troops from the group of Soviet forces in Germany crossed into Bohemia. Startled Czechs called the Ministry of Defense to find out what had happened. Eventually Defense Minister Martin Dzur informed the press that Warsaw Pact maneuvers had just begun. A spokesman for the Ministry later explained that even the participants in the 30 May exercises had not been informed until the last moment so that the exercises would be 'as close as possible to reality'.[39] At least one of the Soviet officers on maneuvers took time off to address a group of members of the Czechoslovak party. According to a liberal Czech journal, he told them that if 'anti-socialist forces' threatened their country, 'the honest Communists' had only to ask and they would have at their disposal 'the entire Soviet army'.[40] If a Soviet officer did make such an offer, he was only carrying out the obligations required by the military-political axioms of the WTO states.

Pravda's coverage of the May plenum gave the impression of a debate that the conservatives dominated. One adopted resolution called for action against an alleged rightist danger.[41] During the Husak era, the spokesmen for the conservatives publicly stated that the May plenum had called for an offensive against the rightist danger in order to bring the conservatives victory in the late June – early July elections to choose delegates to the extraordinary party congress scheduled for 9 September.[42] A *Pravda* editorial of 19 July, 1968, admitted that the attempt to use the elections to defeat the progressives had backfired:

> The facts have shown that the offensive proclaimed by the May plenum of the Czechoslovak Communist Party Central Committee against the rightist, anti-socialist forces was not supported either ideologically, politically or organizationally ...
> It simply did not take place ...[43]

However, the offensive proclaimed by the May plenum was supported by the combat confederation of the armed forces of the Warsaw Pact. From 20–30 June, the Soviet troops in Czechoslovakia conducted a joint exercise with Czechoslovak troops and with Polish, German, Hungarian and Soviet troops who maneuvered on their home territories. Marshal Iakubovskii conducted these forces in the 'Shumava' exercise, which involved more than thirty organs of administration, including communications and logistics forces and special troops assigned to mark highways and other access routes.[44] After the 'conservatives' in the Czechoslovak party suffered a sharp setback in the contest for selection of delegates to the party congress, the Soviets issued repeated demands that the Czechoslovak Presidium meet with the Soviet leadership to discuss threats to the gains of socialism in Czechoslovakia.

After failing to get the Czechoslovak Presidium to attend a bilateral meeting, Brezhnev assembled his East European allies in Warsaw on 14 July. The five fraternal parties wrote the 'Warsaw Letter' addressed to the Central Commitee (not the Presidium) of the Czechoslovak party for the purpose of rallying the conservatives in the Central Committee to postpone the congress and purge the progressives on the Presidium. Noting that the Presidium of the Czechoslovak party had failed to respond to Brezhnev's request for a meeting, the five warned the Central Committee members about the growing threats of 'imperialism' and 'reaction', the two enemies identified by the military-political axioms of the WTO:

> The forces of reaction ... abusing the slogan of 'democratization', unleashed a campaign against the Czechoslovak Communist Party and its honest and devoted cadres, with the clear intention of liquidating the party's leading role, undermining the socialist system and putting Czechoslovakia against other socialist countries.[45]

Grim as the situation was, the authors of the Warsaw Letter did not give up hope:

> We know that there are forces in Czechoslovakia that are capable of upholding the socialist system and defeating the anti-socialist elements ...
> The tasks today are to give these healthy forces a clear perspective, rally them to action and mobilize them against the forces of counterrevolution.[46]

From Moscow's perspective, the healthy forces should not be discouraged by a mere electoral defeat. As the *Pravda* editorial of 19 July observed: 'Needless to say, the forces of socialism in Czechoslovakia, objectively measured, are far greater than those now striking at the revolutionary gains of the Czechoslovak people'.[47] At this time, the Soviet troops which had participated in the 'Shumava' exercise were still on Czechoslovak soil.

Dubček finally gave in and agreed to form an *ad hoc* delegation of the Czechoslovak leadership, drawn partly from the Presidium and partly from the Central Committee, to meet with the Soviet Politburo on 29 July in the Slovak town of Cierna. On 24 July General S. S. Mariakhin, Commander of the Rear Services of the Soviet Armed Forces, began conducting 'Neman', a massive logistical exercise. On 31 July, after the conclusion of the Cierna talks, *Krasnaya zvezda* revealed that the 'Neman' exercises had been shifted to Poland and East Germany under Mariakhin's command. These exercises ended on 9 August with the establishment of a joint Soviet-Polish-East German headquarters.[48]

Two days later, General S. M. Shtemenko, who had been named Chief of the WTO Staff in August, began directing an exercise of communications troops in the West Ukraine, Poland and East Germany. The exercise ended 20 August.[49] A British analyst reported that an exercise of Soviet and Hungarian communications troops took place in Hungary during 17–20 August.[50] On the night of 20–21 August, the armed forces of the USSR, East Germany, Poland, Hungary and Bulgaria occupied Czechoslovakia.[51] Soviet justification for the intervention drew upon the military-political axioms shared by the loyal WTO armies. According to *Pravda*, the fraternal armies had responded to a request from a group of party and state leaders for military assistance. 'The reason for this appeal', *Pravda* explained,

> is the threat posed to the socialist system existing in Czechoslovakia and the constitutionally-established state system by counterrevolutionary forces that have entered into collusion with external forces hostile to socialism.[52]

In 1962, Romania, like Czechoslovakia, agreed to the conduct of joint WTO exercises on its territory. As in most of the larger WTO exercises, the host defense minister commanded the exercise, but in this exercise[53] as in all Pact exercises,[54] central WTO agencies did the planning for the maneuvers, Marshal Grechko attended the 19 October exercise as did defense ministers from several WTO members and other high-ranking East European and Soviet military officers. Unidentified forces from Romania, the USSR and Bulgaria participated under the command of General Salajin of Romania. Judging by the fact that all the political activities of the exercises (parades, speeches, meetings, etc.) were held in the Romanian port of Constanta, it is possible that some naval forces participated in the exercises. According to translations of the classified journal *Voennaya mysl'* released to the public by the Central Intelligence Agency, General Salajin also commanded an exercise of Romanian, Soviet and Bulgarian forces in Romania sometime during the fall of 1963.[55]

After the 1963 exercises, Romania never again permitted WTO maneuvers on Romanian soil, although it has sent to other WTO exercises personnel whom the Romanians have described as observers and the Soviets have described as participants. The Romanians have agreed on at least two occasions, and probably three, to have Soviet and Bulgarian officers sit in a map room of the Romanian Defense Ministry and conduct with Romanian officers what both sides have described on two occasions as 'command-staff map maneuvers'.[56]

It might be possible to understand Romania's refusal to permit continued WTO exercises on Romanian soil if the exercises of 1962 and 1963 were similar to those held in 1964 and 1967 in Bulgaria, another Pact state without a Soviet garrison which also happened to have a coast on the Black Sea and extensive mountain and forest areas. *Krasnaya zvezda* claimed that Soviet, Bulgarian and Romanian forces participated in the 1964 exercise in Bulgaria, which included naval and airborne landings.[57] A Soviet-Bulgarian text, which claims that Romania joined the Soviets and Bulgarians in the 1967 Rodopy exercise in Bulgaria, reports that during this exercise, ground forces, air forces, naval forces and airborne troops conducted 'a defensive battle for the seizure of the sea coast and also for the conduct of actions in mountains and forest areas'.[58] If the 1962 and 1963 exercises in Romania also included naval and airborne landings for defensive seizure of the sea coast and mountain and forest areas, it is possible that the Romanians concluded that WTO exercises on their territory were not intended primarily as preparation for battles with NATO.

The Soviet-Bulgarian discussion of the Rodopy exercise revealed a style of organization which, if practiced in exercises on Romanian soil, might have preempted Romania's ability to determine the capabilities of its own forces. According to this study,

> For raising the effectiveness of the administration of troops in the [Rodopy] exercises there were mutual exchanges of groups and representatives among units and formations of various countries.
>
> This method of work was widely practiced: Bulgarian and Soviet officers [note the omission of any reference to Romanian officers] jointly worked out documents or participated in practical measures.
>
> As a result, the operational capabilities of staffs [i.e. the capabilities of staffs to organize movements of major field formations] was raised and the possibility was achieved of broadly and openly exchanging opinions in the questions decided.[59]

There are common patterns in the location of exercises and assignment of command in the WTO ground forces/combined arms exercises of the armed forces of the German Democratic Republic (GDR), Poland and Hungary, the three states in which Soviet garrisons were stationed prior to the introduction of the system of joint exercises. These patterns recur in the exercises of the Czechoslovak armed forces after the establishment of the Soviet Central Force Group in Czechoslovakia in 1968.

Documentation of these patterns is based on information from my list of seventy-one exercises.

For each of the national armed forces of the GDR, Poland and Hungary in the period from 1961 to 1979, about one-third of the ground forces–combined-arms exercises in which they participated were conducted exclusively on their own territory, about one-third were conducted entirely on foreign soil. The remainder of the exercises were conducted jointly on home and foreign territory. This pattern in the location of ground forces–combined-arms exercises reduces the opportunity for national defense ministries to develop a capability for the conduct of a war in defense of national territory.

For the national armed forces of the GDR, Poland and Hungary in the period from 1961 to 1979, at the very most only one-third of the WTO ground forces–combined-arms exercises in which they participated were exercises in which the national armed forces were commanded by their own officers. At least two-thirds of the ground forces–combined-arms exercises of any one of these national armed forces took place under the command of a foreign officer, both on home territory and on foreign soil. This pattern in the assignment of command reduces the possibility that the officers of a given state will acquire the experience necessary to conduct combined-arms actions in defense of their national territory, and also accustoms national military forces to accept commands from foreign officers.

The armed forces of the GDR participated in at least twenty-seven ground forces–combined-arms exercises in the period from 1961 to 1979 and probably many more.[60] Of these twenty-seven, seven took place exclusively on German soil; nine were held completely outside the GDR; and eleven took place jointly on the territory of East Germany, Poland or Czechoslovakia. Of these twenty-seven exercises, commanders can be identified for twenty-two: three had East German commanders, and twelve of the nineteen foreign commanders were Soviet officers.

The armed forces of Poland participated in at least twenty-five ground forces–combined-arms exercises in the period from 1961 to 1969, and probably more.[61] Of these twenty-five, seven were conducted entirely in Poland; seven were held completely outside Poland; and eleven were conducted jointly on the territory of Poland and the territory of the GDR or Czechoslovakia. Commanders can be identified for twenty-one of these exercises: six had Polish commanders, and ten of the fifteen foreign commanders were Soviet officers.

The same patterns appear in the ground forces–combined-arms exercises in which Hungary took part in the period from 1961 to 1979, although Hungary did not really begin to participate in the system of WTO exercises until 1966. The exercise of 1962 was probably held in order to invite Romanian troops to Hungary in return for the Romanian invitation to Soviet and Bulgarian troops to participate in the exercises of 1962. Another peculiarity of Hungary's participation in the joint exercises is that no large multilateral exercise took place in Hungary until 1979.[62] In the period from 1961 to 1979, the armed forces of Hungary participated in at least eighteen ground forces–combined-arms exercises, and probably more.[63] Of these eighteen, seven were conducted exclusively in Hungary; seven were conducted entirely outside Hungary; and four took place jointly on Hungarian and Czechoslovak territory. Commanders can be identified for only ten of these exercises; two had Hungarian commanders and five of the eight foreign commanders were Soviet officers.

The pattern of the participation of the Czechoslovak armed forces in ground forces–combined-arms exercises for the period from 1961 to 1979 deviates from the GDR, Polish and Hungarian patterns because of the high frequency of WTO maneuvers on Czechoslovak soil from 1961 to 1968, before the establishment of the Central Force Group. But for the period from 1969 to 1979, the patterns of exercises of the Czechoslovak armed forces conform to the patterns of the exercises of the GDR, Polish and Hungarian armed forces. For the period 1961 to 1979, the armed forces of Czechoslovakia participated in at least twenty-five ground forces–combined-arms exercises;[64] nine took place exclusively in Czechoslovakia; six were held on foreign soil; and ten were conducted jointly on the territory of Czechoslovakia and the GDR, Poland or Hungary. For the period 1961 to 1979, commanders can be identified for eighteen of the twenty-five exercises; five had Czechoslovak commanders, and six of the thirteen foreign commanders were Soviet officers.

For the period 1969 to 1979, the armed forces of Czechoslovakia participated in at least sixteen ground forces–combined-arms exercises; of which five were conducted exclusively in Czechoslovakia, four took place completely outside Czechoslovakia and seven were conducted jointly on the territory of Czechoslovakia and Hungary, the GDR, or Poland. Commanders can be identified for eleven of these sixteen exercises; three had Czechoslokav commanders and of the eight foreign commanders during this period after the 1968 invasion, only two were Soviet commanders.

The pattern of Bulgaria's participation in joint ground

forces–combined-arms exercises deviates from the patterns of the GDR, Poland, Hungary and Czechoslovakia (after 1968), because there is no Soviet garrison in Bulgaria and because Romania, the only WTO state on which Bulgaria borders, refuses to allow exercises held jointly on the territory of Bulgaria and Romania. For the period from 1961 to 1979, the armed forces of Bulgaria participated in four ground forces–combined-arms exercises held exclusively in Bulgaria, nine exercises conducted completely outside Bulgaria and one logistics exercise which the Soviets claim was held jointly on Bulgarian and Romanian soil.[65] Of these fourteen exercises, commanders can be identified for twelve. Of these twelve exercises, three had Bulgarian commanders, and five of the nine foreign commanders were Soviet officers.

The Iakubovskii text on the WTO says that joint WTO exercises regularly take place among the Pact antiaircraft troops, air forces, navies and special troops,[66] but Pact sources reveal very little about such exercises. For the seventeen that can be documented, commanders can be identified for fifteen. Of these, fourteen were Soviet officers, either the WTO Commander in Chief, the WTO Chief of Staff, or the Commanders of the Soviet Antiaircraft Troops, the Soviet air force, the Soviet navy or the Soviet Rear Services. Because Soviet sources occasionally identify the commander of the Soviet Antiaircraft Troops as *ex officio* commander of the WTO antiaircraft troops, it is possible that the commanders of the other Soviet service branches serve as *ex officio* commanders of the non-ground forces service branches of the WTO.[67] In any case, the pattern of the assignment of command in WTO exercises suggests that the antiaircraft troops, air forces, navies and rear services of the loyal Warsaw Pact states do not have an opportunity to practice the support of their sister national service branches in the defense of national territory.

Other Aspects of WTO Exercises: Offense and Nuclear Weapons; Planning and Conduct of Staff Work; Assignment of Missions to Multinational Groupings; Impact on the Training Programs of National Armed Forces; Impact on the Careers of East European Officers

Pact and Western sources agree that the larger WTO exercises often simulate the use of nuclear weapons in combat.[68] If these sources provided more detailed information about the specific kinds of weapons used in WTO exercises and the kinds of actions practiced, it might be possible to determine if the WTO exercises trained soldiers only for offensive actions and mainly for nuclear offense, as required by the published Soviet treatises on military art. Pact sources usually do not specify whether the actions conducted in joint exercises are offensive or defensive in character. They rarely mention the conduct of extensive defensive actions, but they occasionally discuss the conduct of extensive offensive actions in response to a NATO attack.[69] Evidence concerning other aspects of Pact exercises suggest that even if WTO exercises do practice defense using conventional weapons, they none the less rule out the practice of the synchronized defense of national territory by national service branches under national command.

One of these aspects is the organization of staff work for the exercises. Of the forty-nine WTO exercises from 1961 to 1979 for which commanders can be identified, twenty-one had East European commanders. But even though East European officers have regularly commanded WTO exercises, they do not appear to have the major responsibilities for planning the exercises. Their principal functions appear to be those of demonstrating regular national command of national armed forces and of accustoming other Pact armies to the principle of foreign command while sparing these armies the humiliation of maneuvering under the command of foreign officers drawn only from the Soviet armed forces. WTO communiqués invariably describe Pact exercises as being conducted not according to the plan of the national defense ministry of the commander of the exercise but 'according to the plan of the United Command' or 'according to the plan of the United Armed Forces' or 'according to the training program of the United Armed Forces'. The Iakubovskii text on the WTO says that the Staff of the United Armed Forces (UAF) has the responsibility for 'planning and conduct of joint maneuvers, exercises and military games of diverse scale – from the operational-strategic exercises to troop exercises and exercises of special troops'.[70] (In Soviet usage, 'special troops' include engineering, chemical, radio-technical, railway construction, road construction and automotive troops.) A Soviet-Polish text echoes the Iakubovskii volume on the role of central Pact agencies in planning the exercises: 'troop, naval, command-staff and special troop exercises, joint war games and maneuvers are regularly conducted according to the plan of the United Command of the armed forces of the Warsaw Pact members.'[71]

There is no information available on who serves as chief of staff for a given exercise. Nor is there any information as to whether exercise staffs are assembled on an *ad hoc* basis or are drawn from the WTO Staff. The Iakubovskii text says that the WTO Staff has participated in the conduct of five joint exercises and that the WTO Staff is multinational in composition.[72] Whenever *Krasnaya zvezda* mentions the staff of a particular WTO exercise, it points out that the staff is multinational.[73] In any case, there is no possibility that national general staffs are charged with the exclusive preparation or conduct of joint WTO exercises at any level.

The limited information available on the composition of the forces participating in the joint exercises suggests that missions are not assigned exclusively to the armed forces of one state, but are always shared by units drawn from the military forces of at least two states. Official communiqués almost always state that the purpose of a given exercise was to improve the interaction of the allied forces (rather than to prepare separate national armed forces for distinct missions). Pact discussions of the WTO often make the same point.[74] In its discussion of the 1965 October Storm exercise, the Iakubovskii text says that one purpose of the exercise was to check 'capabilities for organizing interaction in coalition groupings'.[75] This volume also noted in its discussion of the 1969 Oder-Neisse exercise, which it identified as at the time the largest WTO exercise ever held, 'In all stages there was widely carried out interaction and mutual aid among the sub-units and units of the allied armies in carrying out common tasks'.[76] According to the US air force translation of the Soviet *Dictionary of Basic Military Terms*, a Soviet 'unit' can be a grouping no bigger than a regiment and often smaller. This text identifies a Soviet 'sub-unit' as either a battalion, battery, company, platoon or squadron.[77]

During the Oder-Neisse exercises, *Krasnaya zvezda* mentioned a joint action carried out by East German armored forces, Czechoslovak airborne troops and the Polish and Soviet air forces; it also mentioned a joint action by naval infantry from the USSR, Poland and East Germany.[78] During the Brotherhood in Arms exercise of 1970, the Soviet army newspaper discussed a joint action executed by a German tank company and a Soviet tank company.[79] In a discussion of the Shield 72 exercises in Czechoslovakia, a joint Soviet-Czechoslovak study reported an action in which Hungarian artillery began shelling an enemy position after which unspecified Polish and Czechoslovak forces fought 'shoulder to shoulder', while being supported by Soviet mechanized infantry. When the enemy brought up reserves, Soviet tank, artillery and air forces went into action and annihilated the enemy.[80] The mutual interdependence of WTO armed forces in carrying out missions in joint exercises, or, probably more accurately, the dependence of East European armies on Soviet forces, may be characteristic of even low-level tactical exercises. According to a Czechoslovak officer writing in *Krasnya zvezda*, in a low-level tactical exercise of troops from the Central Force Group and the Czechoslovak army, two Czechoslovak officers declared that they could not have completed their mission 'were it not for the aid of Soviet officers'.[81]

Pact sources make it clear that there is a close connection between the system of joint exercises and the system of training the armed forces of the five loyal WTO members. The joint exercises serve as an evaluation of the results of troop training in a given year and as the basis for planning the training programs of the following year. The Iakubovskii text declares that 'according to the results of the exercises theoretical conclusions are reached and practical recommendations are made for introduction into the practice of troop training'.[82]

In 1963 Pact officers began meeting annually to review the exercises of the summer and fall, and to plan training programs and exercises for the coming year.[83] Since the creation of the Military Council of the Warsaw Pact in 1969, these sessions have been held jointly with sessions of the Military Council. The Iakubovskii text confirms that these joint sessions examine the results of combat and operational training for the preceding year and plan the training and exercise programs for the coming year.[84]

The Chairman of the Military Council is the WTO Commander in Chief; all of its members are his Soviet deputies[85] and his East European deputies, including a Romanian officer. The Iakubovskii volume notes that the recommendations of the Military Council have only a 'consultative' character but that 'as a rule' WTO members abide by them.[86] This arrangement probably suits the Soviets and the Romanians equally well: the Soviets can avoid Romanian vetoes and the Romanians can ignore the recommendations that as a rule are carried out by the other members of the Pact. The Chairman of the Military Council does not rely only on his East European deputies to carry out the recommendations of the Council. He also relies on a group of senior Soviet officers who serve as his liaison representatives to the armed forces of each member state.[87] According to the Iakubovskii study, one of the tasks of these liaison officers is 'to give aid to the national commands in the training of troops'.[88] Colonel Semin, a Soviet journalist specializing on the WTO, states:

Troop contingents assigned to the United Armed Forces daily carry out combat and political training according to the plans of the national commands, but the working out of the basic questions of the joint actions of these troops is carried out according to the plans of the United Command.[89]

Linking the organization of the Pact training programs to the joint exercise system enables the Soviets to control the training programs of the national armed forces assigned to the Warsaw Pact. The training programs, in turn, determine the capabilities of these national armed forces for specific kinds of military actions. This link is not a purely fortuitous result of the introduction of the system of joint exercises by Marshal Grechko; the theory of troop training and the theory of military art (strategy, operations and tactics) are both subtheories of the military-technical component of the military doctrines of the Warsaw Pact states. The five loyal East European members of the Pact have found that to embrace one subtheory of Soviet doctrine for the conduct of the joint exercises is to be embraced by the other subtheories.

The system of Warsaw Pact exercises affords Soviet officers the opportunity to evaluate the East European officers participating in the exercises. The Soviets may use such evaluations as one device for ensuring that national defense ministries will promote only those officers who have demonstrated loyalty to the military-political and military–technical concepts on which the Warsaw Pact is based. The opportunity for Soviet officers to evaluate the performances of East European officers arises from the role of the WTO Commander in Chief and the UAF Staff in evaluating the exercises. A 1973 diplomatic convention ratified by the five loyal East European members of the Pact insures Soviet domination of the Staff and the other central agencies of the Pact.[90] In addition, Soviet officers have directly commanded twenty-eight of the forty-nine WTO exercises for which commanders can be identified. Of these twenty-eight, Marshal Iakubovskii commanded twelve; General S. M. Shtemenko, former Chief of the WTO Staff, commanded three; the heads of the Soviet antiaircraft troops, the Soviet air force and the Soviet navy have together commanded a total of nine. The present WTO Commander, Marshal V. G. Kulikov, has been identified as the commander of only one exercise, but Kulikov's low profile is almost certainly the result of the post-Helsinki hiatus in reporting Pact maneuvers.

WTO sources frequently identify the joint exercises as critical examinations of troops, commanders and staffs. According to the Iakubovskii text, one purpose of the first multilateral WTO exercises, the 1961 'Buria' maneuvers under Marshal Grechko, was 'checking the preparation of operational staffs to carry out the administration of allied groupings of forces in the complex conditions of a combat situation'.[91] Just prior to a WTO exercise of 1970, a *Krasnaya zvezda* editorial noted, 'The personnel of the allied armies have come well-prepared to their autumn examinations (and an exercise is always a rigorous examination)'.[92] Following the completion of this exercise, *Krasnaya zvezda* quoted Marshal Iakubovskii as saying, 'the exercises which have taken place were a serious examination for the fraternal armies and indicate ... the skills of commanders and staffs in resolving tasks in complex, swiftly-changing circumstances'.[93]

A factor which may affect Soviet evaluations of the skills of East European commanders and staffs is the old-school tie. East European officers at the level of army captain have the option of pursuing the three to four years of postgraduate education necessary for promotion to command responsibilities at either an East European military academy or a Soviet academy.[94] The subject of instruction at all East European and Soviet postgraduate military academies is 'military doctrine' in the broad Soviet sense; often it is almost entirely a study of Soviet texts on the subfields of military doctrine.[95] Judging by the limited evidence available, the East European graduates of Soviet mid-career academies appear to do well in their subsequent careers.[96] Their success may be due to one or more of the following factors: the superior academic quality of Soviet military academies; 'old-boy' friendships with Soviet officers in central WTO agencies; the possible existence of a *'nomenklatura'* system that for all practical purposes reserves certain East European commands for graduates of Soviet military academies. According to a Western study, such a *'nomenklatura'* system exists in the Soviet Armed Forces for the graduates of the Soviet mid-career academies.[97]

The Voroshilov General Staff Academy in Moscow may have secured such a monopoly on the training of East European officers for command and staff positions in the joint WTO exercises. The Voroshilov Academy accepts Soviet and East European colonels and generals who have completed mid-career academies and trains them for command responsibilities in defense ministries, general staffs, service branches, military districts and naval fleets. A Soviet history of the Academy says that 'in response to the desire of the governments of the socialist states ... the Soviet government organized the training and improvement of the leading command staff of the fraternal armies in the Academy of the General Staff'.[98] This volume also suggests that the Voroshilov Academy alone is qualified to train WTO officers for the conduct of large-scale exercises: 'The designation of the Academy of the General Staff as the highest military-educational institution of the operational-strategic type determines the course of study and training of the generals and officers of the friendly socialist countries'.[99] This study notes that in the 1961–2 academic year, the Academy revised its program for foreign officers by placing them in a joint program with Soviet officers.[100] This revision coincided with the introduction of the system of joint exercises. In a brief discussion of the achievements of Voroshilov graduates, the text noted that Voroshilov graduates held 'high posts' in their national armed forces and played a prominent role in WTO exercises. For instance, in 1976, of the five East European states that send officers to the Voroshilov Academy, four had Voroshilov alumni as defense ministers, and all five had Voroshilov graduates as chiefs of staff.[101]

Krasnaya zvezda's accounts of individual WTO exercises[102] often identify East European officers in the exercises who are alumni of Soviet academies. *Krasnaya zvezda* occasionally quotes them as saying that their Soviet education prepared them well for the exercises and that it is very useful in the exercises to have a fluent command of Russian military terminology. These accounts of the interactions of WTO officers in joint exercises often note the friendships of Soviet and East European alumni of Soviet academies. *Krasnaya zvezda* reported during the 1970 Brotherhood in Arms exercises in the GDR, that Lt Colonel Wolfgang Chernig of the East German army was assigned to work with a group of Soviet officers among whom were graduates of an unidentified Soviet military academy in Leningrad where Chernig had also studied. Chernig told a *Krasnaya zvezda* correspondent that both he and his wife had warm memories of their years in Leningrad. The correspondent reported that Soviet officers had laughed after Chernig told *Krasnaya zvezda* about his wife's reaction to the news that her husband had been assigned to work with Soviet officers during Brotherhood in Arms. According to the front page story in *Krasnaya zvezda*, Frau Chernig had begged her husband, 'Take me with you as your driver. I would really like to meet some Russians again'.[103]

Political Activities in the Joint Exercises

Judging by accounts in *Krasnaya zvezda*, Warsaw Pact exercises seek to simulate a conflict in which a series of rapid, dispersed troop movements and tactical nuclear strikes take place, alternating those maneuvers with a series of political rallies, friendship meetings, concerts and visits to sites of historical and cultural interest. Soviet and East European sources pay far more attention to the military-political aspects of the joint exercises than they do to the military-technical aspects. Western observers of Pact exercises either ignore the political aspects of Pact exercises[104] or mention them only in passing.[105] The primary purpose of the political activities in the joint exercises is legitimizing the military-political axioms of joint defense of the gains of socialism against external and internal enemies. In practice, this means justifying a system of military exercises which preempts national capabilities for territorial defense and prepares Pact armies for intervention in each other's territories.

The themes of the political activities of the exercises come from the shared military-political axioms of the WTO and the military histories of each alliance member which are jointly written by Soviet and East European military historians. The military-historical literature of the Pact includes a thirty-five volume *Library of Victory* written by Soviet and East European authors. This series examines the joint struggle against fascism by the Soviet army, and civilian and military personnel from Poland, Czechoslovakia, Romania, Bulgaria, Hungary and Yugoslavia. The military-political literature of the WTO also includes several studies of the history of military cooperation between the USSR and individual East European Pact members.[106]

Pact sources began reporting political activities in the joint exercises in the fall of 1962.[107] The publicity given to the political aspects of the 1962 exercises coincides with the appointment in May 1962 of A. A. Epishev as Chief of the Main Political Administration of the Soviet Armed Forces. During General Epishev's tenure in office, the Soviet force groups in East Europe, the four western military districts of the USSR and the Soviet Black Sea and Baltic Sea Fleets have developed an extensive network of joint political activities directed by the main political administrations of the Warsaw Pact states. (Romania disbanded its main political administration in 1964.) The Soviet forces involved in the conduct of joint political activities with the WTO armed forces probably constitute about half of all Soviet military personnel. The joint political activities seek to cultivate feelings of proletarian internationalism among the multinational personnel of the Soviet Armed Forces and among the multinational personnel of the Warsaw Pact.

Some Western analysts have suggested that the officer corps of the USSR objects to the existence of the political administration of the Soviet armed forces, because this system impedes the development of Soviet military-technical capabilities.[108] Any Soviet officer with experience in the Soviet force groups in Europe, the Baltic or Black Sea Fleets or the four western military districts of the USSR probably finds that Soviet domination of the Warsaw Pact would not be possible in its present form without the WTO network of political administrations dedicated to the strengthening of proletarian internationalism and to the justification of the organizational structures of the WTO.[109]

General Epishev's background suggests that he was well-prepared to supervise the development of the military-political activities designed to safeguard Warsaw Pact forces from Romanian and Yugoslav military-political conceptions of 'reliance on one's own forces'. Before World War II, he was in charge of the cadre department of a Soviet division and received a mid-career degree from the Academy of Mechanization and Motorization. During the war, he served as a political officer with the Soviet forces that liberated Poland and Czechoslovakia. After the war, he served in the KGB and then worked in the Ukraine as a party secretary in charge of cadres. From 1955 to 1961, he was Soviet ambassador to Romania, and from 1961 to May 1962, he served as Soviet ambassador to Yugoslavia.[110]

Colonel Semin, a Soviet military journalist specializing in the WTO, presents the following outline of the conduct of political activities in joint exercises: representatives of the main political administrations of the participating armies form a united operational group. This group organizes meetings among the fraternal troops, meetings of the soldiers with the local population and plans programs of 'agitation-propaganda' and 'cultural enlightenment'. This group also supervises a joint press center, a joint multilingual newspaper published during the exercises, joint multilingual radio broadcasts for the participating soldiers and a joint cinematography group.[111] The film group probably submits entries for the annual Warsaw Pact Film Festival, which began in 1966.[112]

According to Colonel Semin, the main political administration of the officer under whose command the exercise is taking place 'as a rule' is responsible for the formation of the united operational group.[113] According to the Iakubovskii text, the united operational group has its representatives in the staff directing the exercise and in the political departments of the participating armed forces.[114] Colonel Semin notes, and Pact sources confirm, that the highest-ranking party, state and military officials of the host country participate in political meetings with the soldiers and in joint meetings of soldiers and civilians in factories, farms and towns. When the fraternal soldiers meet, they discuss ways of improving combat readiness, military mastery and their dedication to the principles of socialist internationalism. In addition to their meetings with the local population, the WTO personnel also visit war memorials and historical exhibits connected with the working-class movement of the host country. According to Colonel Semin, the political-education activities 'as a rule' take place during pauses in military actions. 'When the situation permits', the joint operational group organizes discussions and seminars on 'military-political and theoretical themes', speeches by propagandists, and the exchange of assemblies and films. The meetings of soldiers and civilians often include performances by choral and dance groups, orchestras and artists participating in the exercises.[115]

A joint Polish-Soviet study reports that during the Brotherhood in Arms exercises of 1970 in the GDR there were more than 40 meetings of allied military units, more than 200 political rallies involving soldiers and civilians and about 300 cultural programs.[116] According to a Soviet-Czechoslovak volume, during an unidentified exercise between the Soviet Central Force Group and the Czechoslovak People's Army, there were five meetings of commanders and political officers, six meetings of outstanding enlisted military personnel, four large political rallies and fifty joint excursions.[117] Political activities appear to take place even during low-level tactical exercises. *Krasnaya zvezda* reported, in 1971, that after jointly laying a pontoon bridge across the Danube, Soviet and Hungarian soldiers advanced to a concert given by the orchestra of the staff of the Southern Force Group.[118]

Krasnaya zvezda gave particularly detailed coverage to the political activities of the 1970 Brotherhood in Arms exercises, perhaps because, as the Soviet army newspaper noted, the fraternal armed forces were simultaneously observing the 15th anniversary of the WTO, the 100th birthday of Lenin, the 21st anniversary of the GDR and the 26th anniversary of the Czechoslovak People's Army.[119] *Krasnaya zvezda* recounted the visit to a Soviet tank regiment of Erich Muchlenburg, a full member of the East German Politburo. Muchlenburg gave a speech on the contribution of the exercises to the peace and security of the socialist confederation and then presented the regiment with a bust of Karl Marx. After having been reminded of the German origins of Soviet communism, the officers of the regiment then reminded Muchlenburg of the Soviet origins of German communism:

they ushered him into the regimental room of combat glory where they recounted the history of their regiment, including its participation in the conquest of Germany. A German officer accompanying Muchlenburg replied that in 1945 he had been a child in Swedt, one of the towns captured by this very regiment. *Krasnaya zvezda* pointed out that Swedt was now one of the terminals for the Friendship Oil Pipeline from the USSR.[120]

The political activities of the joint exercises focus on demonstrating the necessity of a multinational military alliance and on justifying multinational maneuvers on the soil of individual Pact members. During one of the most recent publicized exercises, the 'Friendship-79' exercises of Soviet and Czechoslovak troops in Czechoslovakia, *Krasnaya zvezda* reported the visit of a joint delegation of the fraternal armies to local villages and factories. *Krasnaya zvezda* specifically pointed out the multinational composition of the delegation: it included two Czechs, a Ukrainian, a Georgian, a Dagestani and a Tatar.[121] A *Krasnaya zvezda* editorial during the Brotherhood in Arms exercises explained the central role of Soviet forces in this multinational alliance:

> Yes, the soldiers of the fraternal armies speak in different languages, but they think in the same way. In this regard they are like brothers in one big family.
> Yes, and they understand and recognize that the older brother in this family is the Soviet soldier who defended his Fatherland, who brought freedom to the peoples of Europe and who in his military victory was always true to the international proletariat and struggled for the happiness of mankind.[122]

There are, however, historical reasons[123] for suggesting that Czechs, Ukrainians, Georgians, Dagestanis, Tatars and the other nationalities of the Warsaw Pact also have other, less fond memories of big brother. The goal of the political activities is to arm the soldiers of the WTO against such memories and against attacks on the military-political axiom of the necessity for joint defense of the gains of socialism against internal and external enemies. 'In bourgeois military sociology', warns General Epishev,

> there is often an attempt to portray the principles of the international defense of socialism as 'an attack on national sovereignty' as 'diktat' and 'the hegemony of certain countries'.[124]

According to the Chief of the Main Political Adminstration of the Soviet Armed Forces,

It is not difficult to see that the basic direction of the attack of bourgeois propaganda on the consciousness of the personnel of the armies of the socialist countries sets the goal of emphasizing national differences and opposing some socialist states to others.

All this is done to loosen the unbreakable moral-political unity of the socialist countries and their armed forces and to disrupt the fraternal relations which exist among them.[125]

M. S. Kirichenko, the author of a Soviet study of the Warsaw Pact, identifies some of the slanders used to loosen the unbreakable unity of the armed forces of the socialist states: (1) the Soviet army exported socialist revolutions to Eastern Europe; (2) the Soviet forces stationed in East Europe are occupation troops; (3) Soviet military specialists interfere in the internal affairs of East European armed forces; (4) Soviet troops crushed 'liberalization' in Hungary in 1956 and in Czechoslovakia in 1968.[126] Kirichenko calls for 'a sharp class struggle with the forces which propagandize various theories of "neutralism", "non-alignment", "an inter-bloc position" and "reliance on one's own forces" '.[127]

Several Soviet sources testify to the utility of political activities in preparing WTO soldiers for the moral-political strains of occupying a Warsaw Pact member. *Krasnaya zvezda's* coverage of the events in Czechoslovakia following the intervention of 20–21 August mentioned friendly meetings of the fraternal soldiers with Czechoslovak civilians in factories, farms and towns. The Soviet army newspaper often noted the concern of Soviet military personnel for the welfare of their colleagues in the Czechoslovak army, as demonstrated by the Soviet pilot who took it upon himself to fly a seriously-ill Czech soldier direct to Prague for medical treatment unavailable in Slovakia.[128] On his return from Czechoslovakia in 1968, Lt Christo Radulov of the Bulgarian People's Army and his unit stopped in the Odessa Military District to discuss the intervention with the soldiers of the district. At a political meeting he declared,

> It was difficult for us in the first days. The counterrevolutionaries and their chorus ranted and raved. It was necessary to have iron nerves in order not to succumb to the provocations.
>
> But for us the example was always the Soviet soldier, who demonstrated obvious control and self-mastery.[129]

At the same meeting, another Bulgarian officer, Parashkev Palukov, said,

> The joint entry of our troops into Czechoslovakia strengthened our friendship even more. We lived in one big family. And as in every family, we all shared.

Each of us is bringing back a great many addresses from the USSR, Hungary, Poland and the GDR. We are going to write and keep each other informed.

You know, we are more than friends. We are brothers in spirit, brothers in arms.[130]

For the Bulgarian soldiers who were not able to participate in the invasion of Czechoslovakia, subsequent joint WTO exercises provided opportunities to meet penpals from the fraternal armies.

In conclusion, the organization of both the military and political aspects of the WTO exercises is directed at justifying WTO policies which preempt the development of East European capabilities for territorial defense and at preparing Soviet and East European forces militarily and politically for intervention in East Europe. Soviet military doctrine serves not as the inspiration for the joint Warsaw Pact exercises – it is then justified. In turn, the exercises provide the Soviets with the means to enforce conformity to the military-political and military-technical components of Soviet doctrine.

Notes: Chapter 8

1 Both Yugoslavia and Romania have presented their military doctrines in a large number of publications; two English language presentations are: Major General Aleksandr Vukotic, *et al.* (eds), *The Yugoslav Concept of General People's Defense* (Belgrade: Medunarodna Politika, 1970); Colonel Iulian Cernat *et al.* (eds), *National Defense: The Romanian View* (Bucharest: Military Publishing House, 1976).

2 *The Yugoslav Concept of General People's Defense*, p. 61.

3 See my discussion in a forthcoming work, *Defending Socialism in East Europe* (Praeger). This volume will incorporate the study written for the National Council for Soviet and East European Research.

4 Michael Checinski, 'The postwar development of the Polish armed forces' (Rand, forthcoming), p. 17.

5 ibid.

6 Two authors date the reformation of Soviet doctrine to December, 1959; see Harriet Fast Scott and William F. Scott, *The Armed Forces of the USSR* (Boulder, Co.: Westview Press, 1979), pp. 41–2.

7 *Soviet Military Strategy* (in English) (Englewood Cliffs, NJ: Prentice Hall, 1963), p. 495.

8 ibid., ch. 6.

9 For instance, p. 229 of the discussion of military doctrine in Vol. 3 of *Sovetskaia voennaia entsiklopediia*: 'Soviet military doctrine accords paramount inportance (*pervostepennoe znachenie*) to close cooperation of the Soviet armed forces with the armed forces of the fraternal socialist countries.'

10 A typical circular definition of these terms appears in an article by the late WTO commander, Marshal I. I. Iakubovskii, 'XXV s"ezd KPSS i ukreplenie boevogo sodruzhestvo armii stran Varshavskogo dogovora' ('The 25th Congress of the CPSU and the strengthening of the combat confederation of the armed forces of the Warsaw Pact countries'), in *Voenno-istoricheskii zhurnal* no.8, 1976, p. 4 (*Military-history Journal*).

11 Major General V. F. Samoilenko, 'Voennoe sodruzhestvo stran sotsializma' ('The Military confederation of the socialist countries'), in S. A. Tiushkevich *et al.*, (eds), *Voina i armiia (War and Armed Forces)* (Moscow: Voenizdat, 1977), p. 366.

12 A. A. Epishev, *Ideologicheskaia bor'ba po voennym voprosam (Ideological Struggle in Military Questions)* (Moscow: Voenizdat, 1974), p. 91.

13 *The Yugoslav Concept of General People's Defense*, pp. 124–6.

14 See article 4 of the Warsaw Treaty; see article 8 of the Soviet Romanian Treaty of 1970.

15 The best account of the developments surrounding Ceauşescu's actions at the 1978 PCC meeting is Patrick Moore, 'The Ceauşescu Saga', Radio Free Europe Research: RAD Background Report, Romania/275, 20 December, 1978.

16 'Speech by Nicolae Ceauşescu ... at Plenary Meeting of the CC of the RCP', in Romania: Documents/Events, (Bucharest: Agerpress, November, 1978).

17 See I. I. Iakubovskii *et al.* (eds), *Boevoe sodruzhestvo narodov i armii stran Varshavskogo dogovora (The Combat Confederation of the Peoples and Armies of the Warsaw Pact Countries)* (Moscow: Voenizdat, 1975), ch. 4 and 5.

18 A. A. Timorin, 'Sotsialno-politicheskaia priroda i naznachenie sotsialisticheskik armii' (The Socio-Political Nature and Function of Socialist Armies'), in Tiushkevich, *et al.*, *Voina i armiia.*, pp. 352–3.

19 Iakubovskii, *Boevoe sodruzhestvo*, p. 30.

20 ibid., p. 133.

21 See Epishev, *Ideologicheskaia bor'ba*, pp. 71–2.

22 For a discussion of this document, see Christopher Jones, 'Dubček, Jan Palach and the Gottwald Memorandum: could Czechoslovakia have deterred the Soviet intervention?', *Soviet Armed Forces Review Annual*, vol. 3, 1979; for the Gottwald Academy's own summary of the 'Gottwald Memorandum', see *Osteuropa Archiv*, vol. 12, 1970.

23 For example, see Epishev, *Ideologicheskaia bor'ba*, pp. 83–90.

24 Iakubovskii, *Boevoe sodruzhestvo*, pp. 138–9.

25 Soviet texts on the WTO frequently call attention to the importance of the overlapping network of bilateral treaties and party programs in maintaining the cohesion of the WTO; for example, see Iakubovskii, *Boevoe sodruzhestvo*, p. 110; A. A. Epishev, *Partiia i armiia (The Party and the Armed Forces)* (Moscow: Politizdat, 1977), p. 321; A. A. Grechko, article in *Kommunist*, no.15, 1972, p. 41.

26 See two works by Joseph Douglass, *The Soviet Theater Nuclear Offensive* (Washington, DC: US Government Printing Office, 1976); and *Soviet Strategy for Nuclear War* (Stanford, Ca.: Hoover Institution Press, 1979); see also, Richard Pipes, 'Why the Soviet Union thinks it could fight and win a nuclear war', *Commentary*, July, 1977.

27 Iakubovskii (ed.), *Boevoe sodruzhestvo*, p. 151: 'In the first years joint exercises were conducted primarily on a tactical level, then beginning in 1961 they began to take place regularly on the operational and strategic scale, with the participation of almost all types of armed forces and types of troops.'

28 A. V. Antosiac (ed.), *Zarozhderie narodnikh armii stran-uchastnits Varshavskogo dogovora (The Birth of the Peoples' Armies of the Member States of the Warsaw Pact)* (Moscow: Voenizdat, 1975), p. 363.

29 A. A. Epishev (USSR), Velko Palin (Bulgaria) (eds.), *Naveki vmeste (Forever Together)* (Moscow: Voenizdat, 1969), p. 287.

30 *Dictionary of Basic Military Terms: A Soviet View* (Washington, DC: US Government Printing Office, n.d.), p. 219.

31 ibid., p. 218.

32 ibid., p. 144.

33 ibid., p. 213.

34 Graham H. Turbiville, Jr, 'Soviet bloc maneuvers', *Military Review*, August, 1978.

35 In the GDR *Volksarmee*, no. 25, 1969, Major General Fleisswehr of the GDR lists a total of forty joint exercises in the period 1964–8 conducted between the National People's Army of the GDR and the Group of Soviet Forces in Germany. Turbiville, who cites this article in his study, does not speculate how many, if any, of these forty are included in his list of thirty-six; I am not able to guess how many, if any, are included in my list of seventy-two. Fleisswehr, a GDR Deputy Minister of Defense in

1969, breaks down the forty as follows: ten joint command staff exercises for higher staffs; ten staff-and-command exercises using one German and one Soviet division; sixteen joint ground forces maneuvers and four joint naval and air exercises. My list of seventy-two indicates that for the period 1964–8 the service branches of the GDR participated in thirteen WTO exercises, but I cannot determine if the Soviet forces which participated in the ground forces exercises always included units from the Group of Soviet forces in Germany, as specified by Fleisswehr.

Naveki Vmeste, the joint Soviet-Bulgarian study which was published in 1969 reports (on p. 289) that 'in recent years' joint Soviet-Bulgarian exercises have been conducted 'on the most diverse scales with the participation of ground forces, air forces and navies'. But, apart from the 1958 Soviet-Bulgarian exercises in Bulgaria, the Soviets have reported only those in which they have claimed that Romania participated, a total of five. This total does not suggest exercise 'on the most diverse scales'.

A Soviet study of the Belorussian Military District noted that during the summer of 1967 one of its formations, the Irkutsk-Pinsk division, had participated in an exercise conducted on Polish soil with the Polish armed forces. This text also reported that 'formations' ['*soedinenie*'] and 'units' ['*chasti*'] of the Belorussian Military District and the Polish armed forces have 'more than once taken part in joint exercises and maneuvers'. (A. G. Ovchinnikov (ed.), *Krasnoznamennyi Belorusskkii voennyi okrug (The Red Banner Belorussian Military District)* (Minsk: Belarus, 1973), p. 501. This study did not indicate, however, how many times more than once. A 12 October, 1975, p. 2 article in *Krasnaya zvezda* mentioned in passing the conduct of a joint exercise of Soviet and Polish tank companies in the Silesian Military District of Poland but did not indicate whether such exercises had taken place more than once.

A Czech officer writing in the 10 October, 1972 issue of *Krasnaya zvezda* mentioned an incident in a Soviet Czechoslovak joint tactical exercise and then added, 'Frequently the sub-units (*podrazdelenie* – translation: a battalion or a company or a platoon or a squadron) of the two friendly armies act in combat actions, constituting a monolithic striking force'. On at least one other occasion (2 August, 1979), *Krasnaya zvezda* has mentioned joint Soviet-Czechoslovak exercises at the *podrazdelenie* level and on at least one occasion (14 July, 1971) has mentioned the conduct of low-level Soviet-Hungarian tactical exercises.

36 *Krasnaya zvezda*, 17 July, 1964.
37 *Krasnaya zvezda*, 21 September, 1966.
38 For a further discussion of this and related events, see my 'Autonomy and intervention: The CPSU and the struggle for the Czechoslovak Communist Party, 1968', *Orbis*, Summer, 1975.
39 Michel Tatu, 'Arrivee des premieres troupes sovietiques qui doivent participer aux "exercises du pacte de Varsovie" ', *Le Monde*, 31 May, 1968, in *L'Heresie Impossible* (Paris: Editions Bernard Grasset, 1968), p. 115.
40 ibid., Tatu quotes *Literarni Listy*.
41 'Plenum Tsentralnogo Komiteta ChSKP' ('Plenum of the Czechoslovak Communist Party Central Committee'), *Pravda*, 8 June, 1968, p. 4.
42 See the resolution adopted by the Husak Central Committee on the history of the 1968 events in Czechoslovakia, 'The Lessons of Crisis Development', published in *Pravda pobezdaet (The Truth Shall Prevail)* (Moscow: Politizdat, 1971).
43 *Pravda*, 19 July, 1968, p. 1.
44 Iakubovskii, *Boevoe sodruzhestvo*, p. 154.
45 *Pravda*, 15 July, 1968, p. 1.
46 ibid.
47 *Pravda*, 19 July, 1968.
48 *Krasnaya zvezda*, 24, 26, 31 July and 9 August, 1968.
49 ibid., 20 August, 1968.
50 Malcolm Mackintosh, 'The evolution of the Warsaw Pact', *Adelphi Papers*, no.58, June, 1969, p. 41.
51 For a further discussion of the role of WTO exercises in preparing for this invasion, see General James H. Polk, 'Reflections on the Czechoslovak invasion', *Strategic Review*, Winter, 1977.

52 *Pravda*, 22 August, 1968, p. 2; see also n.22 for General Epishev's discussion of how the military-political axioms of the combat confederation required a military response to the situation in Czechoslovakia.

53 *Krasnaya zvezda*, 19 October, 1962, wrote that the exercise was conducted 'according to the plan of preparation of the United Armed Forces of the Warsaw Pact'.

54 See p. 231-2 of this chapter and see also n.70.

55 Colonel D. Diev and Lt Colonel K. Spirov, 'Combat collaboration [better translation: 'The combat confederation . . .] of the armies of the Warsaw Pact States', *Voennaya mysl*, no.2, 1968, in CIA FBIS FPD 0049/69: 'Selected Translations from *Voennaya mysl*, 25 April, 1969', p. 64. It is possible that because of typographical or other errors in either the original Soviet edition or the CIA translation, the 1963 exercise referred to was in fact the 1962 exercise, which was not mentioned by Colonels Diev and Spirov, even though *Krasnaya zvezda* reported this exercise. However, the list presented by Colonels Diev and Spirov mentions selected exercises in chronological order; in this order the Romanian-Soviet-Bulgarian exercise of 1963 is listed *after* the September 1963 exercise in the GDR commanded by Heinz Hoffmann. Diev's list, like all other lists presented by WTO sources, is presented as a 'for example' citation. A given WTO source invariably omits exercises mentioned by other WTO sources.

56 Exercises of February 1972, as cited in Turbiville's list (no Pact sources confirm this); exercise of 12–21 February, 1973 in Iakubovskii, *Boevoe sodruzhestvo*, p. 292 (Turbiville does not report this); and exercise of 17–22 February, 1974, cited on p. 293 of Iakubovskii but not cited by Turbiville.

57 *Krasnaya zvezda*, 22 September, 1964.

58 Epishev and Palin (eds.), *Naveki Vmeste*, p. 290.

59 ibid., p. 290.

60 See n.35.

61 See n.35.

62 See my forthcoming *Defending Socialism in East Europe* for a possible explanation.

63 See n.35.

64 See n.35.

65 Exercises of 4-14 June, 1974.

66 Iakubovskii, *Boevoe sodruzhestvo*, p. 158.

67 For a further discussion of this possibility, see my forthcoming *Defending Socialism in East Europe*.

68 *Krasnaya zvezda* coverage of the October Storm exercise of 16–22 October, 1965, and of the Oder–Neisse exercise of 21–28 September, 1969; Mackintosh, 'The evolution of the Warsaw Pact', p. 8.

69 *Krasnaya zvezda*, 28 September, 1969; *Kommunist vooruzhennykh sil*, no. 13, 1973, p. 26.

70 Iakubovskii, *Boevoe sodruzhestvo*, p. 145.

71 P. A. Zhilin (USSR) and E. Jadziak (Poland) (eds), *Bratstvo po oruzhiiu (Brotherhood in Arms)* (Moscow: Voenizdat, 1975), p. 352.

72 Iakubovskii, *Boevoe sodruzhestvo*, p. 146 and pp. 290–3 for exercises of 24 June–2 July, 1971; 12–21 July, 1971; 28 February–4 March 1972; 4–16 September, 1972; 12–21 February, 1973.

73 *Krasnaya zvezda*, 29 September, 1969, and 10 September, 1976.

74 See Zhilin and Jadziak (eds), *Bratstvo po oruzhiiu*, pp. 353–5; and P. A. Zhilin (USSR) and F. Gerfurt (Czechoslovakia), *Na vechnye vremena (For Eternity)* (Moscow: Voenizdat, 1975), pp. 306-7.

75 Iakubovskii, *Boevoe sodruzhestvo*, p. 152.

76 ibid., p. 155.

77 *Dictionary of Basic Military Terms*, p. V.

78 *Krasnaya zvezda*, 26 September, 1969.

79 ibid., 7 October, 1979.

80 Zhilin and Gefurt (eds.), *Na vechnye vremena*, p. 307.

81 *Krasnaya zvezda*, 10 October, 1970.

82 Iakubovskii, *Boevoe sodruzhestvo*, p. 150.

83 The Iakubovskii text usually describes each of these meetings as assemblies of the 'leading staff of the WTO armies who meet to discuss combat and operational

training'. The wording used to describe these meetings from 1963 to 1969 is virtually identical with the wording used to describe joint sessions of the 'leading staff' of the WTO armies and the Military Council in the period beginning in 1969. These post-1969 sessions are specifically identified as discussions of the exercises of a given year for the purpose of preparing the training programs and exercises of the coming year.

84 ibid., p. 145.
85 See p.241 of this study.
86 ibid., p. 144.
87 ibid., p. 144; for indentification of these officers in 1978, see Central Intelligence Agency 'USSR's Organization of the Ministry of Defense', CR78-15257, December, 1978.
88 ibid.
89 Colonel V. Semin, in S. K. Il'in *et al*. (eds), *Partiino-politicheskaia rabota v Sovetskikh vooruzhennykh silakh (Party-Political Work in the Soviet Armed Forces)* (Moscow: Voenizdat, 1974), p. 591.
90 For a discussion of this document, see my article on the Warsaw Pact in the 1978 edition of *Soviet Armed Forces Review Annual*; and also in my forthcoming *Defending Socialism in East Europe*.
91 Iakubovskii, *Boevoe sodruzhestvo*, p. 151.
92 *Krasnaya zvezda*, 7 October, 1970.
93 ibid., 20 October, 1970; see also the editorial on 10 July, 1978: 'An exercise is the highest form of training and upbringing, and the most important means of raising field, air and naval mastery. It is difficult to overestimate their role in the improvement of the mastery of commanders and staffs in the administration of troops, the forces of the fleets and in the increase of the coordination of sub-units, units and ships and in the strengthening of discipline and organization.'
94 See my forthcoming *Defending Socialism in East Europe*.
95 ibid.
96 ibid.
97 H. F. and W. F. Scott, *The Armed Forces of the USSR*, 352: 'Once an officer has successfully completed work at a [post-graduate, mid-career] academy, he is assigned under a special *nomenklatura* or list of positions that can be filled only by officers who are graduates of military or naval academies or their equivalents.'
98 V. G. Kulikov (ed.), *Akademiia generalnogo shtaba (The General Staff Academy)* (Moscow: Voenizdat, 1976), p. 288.
99 ibid., p. 231.
100 ibid., p. 299.
101 ibid., p. 242.
102 See *Krasnaya zvezda*, 23 October, 1965 and its coverage of the Shield 76 exercises, the 1969 Oder-Neisse exercises and the 1970 Brotherhood in Arms exercises.
103 ibid., 7 October, 1970.
104 Turbiville, 'Soviet bloc maneuvers'.
105 Malcolm Mackintosh, 'The Warsaw Pact today', *Survival*, May–June, 1974, p. 122: 'From 1961 onwards the Pact organized a series of multi-lateral military exercises, many of which were well publicized ... most of them amounting in practice to large-scale politico-military demonstrations emphasizing the enthusiasm, interalliance solidarity and friendship of the component national armies.'
106 A. V. Antosiak *et al*. (eds), *Zarozhdenie narodnikh armii stran-uchastnits varshavskogo dogovora, 1941—1949 (The Birth of the Peoples' Armies of the Member States of the Warsaw Pact, 1941—1949)* (Moscow: Nauka, 1975); Epishev and Palin (eds), *Naveki vmeste*; Zhilin and Jadziac (eds), *Bratsvo po oruzhiiu*; Zhilin and Gefurt (eds), *Na vechnyi vremena*.
107 See *Krasnaya zvezda*, 10 October, 1962, for an account of the exercises in Poland; see ibid., 20 October, 1962, for an account of the exercises in Romania.
108 See Roman Kolkowicw, *The Soviet Military and the Communist Party* (Princeton University Press, 1967).
109 See my forthcoming, *Defending Socialism in East Europe*.
110 *Sovetskaia voennaia entsiklopediia*, Vol. 3, pp. 311–12.

111 Colonel V. Semin, in S.K. Il' in *et al*. (eds), *Partiino-politicheskaia rabota* . . ., p. 599.
112 P. I. Efimov (ed.), *Boevoe soiuz bratskikh armii (The Combat Union of the Fraternal Armies)* (Moscow: Voenizdat, 1974), p. 29.
113 Semin, in S.K. Il' in *Partiino-politicheskaia rabota* . . ., p. 599.
114 Iakubovskii, *Boevoe sodruzhestvo*, p. 263.
115 Semin in S.K. Il' in *Partiino-politicheskaia rabota*, pp. 600–601.
116 Zhilin and Jadziak (eds), *Bratstvo po oruzhiiu*, p. 355.
117 Zhilin and Gefurt (eds), *Na vechnye vremena*, p. 309.
118 *Krasnaya zvezda*, 14 July, 1971.
119 *Krasnaya zvezda*, 8 October, 1970.
120 ibid.
121 *Krasnaya zvezda*, 8 February, 1979.
122 *Krasnaya zvezda*, 8 October, 1970.
123 See Alexander M. Nekrich, *The Punished Peoples: The Deportation and Fate of Soviet Minorities at the End of the Second World War* (New York: W.W. Norton, 1978).
124 Epishev, *Ideologicheskaia bor'ba*, p. 104.
125 ibid., p. 110.
126 M. S. Kirichenko, *Na strazhe mira (Guarding the Peace)* (Minsk: Belarus, 1975), pp. 71–4.
127 ibid., p. 75.
128 'My stali lushche videt' ('We have begun to see better'), *Krasnaya zvezda*, 10 September, 1968.
129 N. T. Panferov *et al.* (eds), *Odesskii krasnoznamennyi (The Red Banner Odessa Military District)* (Kishinev: Kartia Moldoveniaske, 1975), p. 280.
130 ibid., p. 3.

9

Doctrine and Technology in Soviet Armaments Policy

DAVID HOLLOWAY

There is a widespread belief that the relationship which exists between military doctrine and military technology in the USSR is fundamentally different from that which exists in the USA. In the USSR, according to this belief, the development and procurement of new weapons are directed by, and responsive to, military doctrine; in the USA, on the other hand, military doctrine is only one of the factors determining weapons policies and has often to respond to technological innovations which derive from other sources. In an article on 'Technology and the military balance' Colonel Richard G. Head wrote that the Soviets reject 'the thesis that weapons should dictate military strategy'.[1] He argued that one of the significant differences between the USSR and the USA is that Soviet 'military doctrine is used to define requirements for new weapons' and 'is expected to produce weapons requirements to "pull" technology'.[2] These statements echo the widely held belief that in the USSR doctrine drives technology, while in the USA technology drives doctrine.

If this belief were true, it would have far-reaching consequences for our understanding of Soviet military policy, for it implies that Soviet doctrine is the key to Soviet weapons decisions and that by studying the doctrine we can tell what future Soviet weapons policies will be. It suggests also that Soviet weapons policies are rationally derived from a doctrinal blueprint, unhindered by the bureaucratic and industrial pressures which are so evident in the weapons policy-making of the Western powers. Because this belief is apparently widespread, and because its implications are significant, it is important to examine as carefully as possible the relationship between doctrine and technology in Soviet military policy.

The thesis that doctrine drives technology is by no means universally accepted by students of Soviet military affairs.

Matthew Gallagher, for example, writes that to interpret military doctrine as the key to Soviet strategic policy 'would be both to misread the doctrine and to underestimate the dynamics of the Soviet decision-making process'.[3] Gallagher argues that Soviet military doctrine is a 'highly generalized and ambiguous set of guidelines', in which each proposition is counterbalanced by a contradictory one.[4] He notes, for example, that according to Soviet doctrine a general nuclear war might be either short or long; that while strategic missiles would provide the main striking power, all forces would be required for victory; and that war with the NATO powers, while possibly nuclear, might also take a conventional form. Since Soviet doctrine is so permissive, it can hardly serve, in Gallagher's view, to provide detailed guidance for Soviet military policy.

In his study of Soviet procurement decision-making, Arthur Alexander takes a similar view, arguing that doctrine is a 'poor predictor of future capabilities'.[5] This is because doctrine is so 'elastic' that many different – and even contradictory – decisions could be compatible with it; consequently one cannot say from a study of doctrine which decisions will in fact be taken. Moreover, doctrine may merely serve to rationalize decisions which have already been taken for a variety of other reasons. If doctrine is out of line with existing forces, it may be impossible to say whether the doctrine will be adjusted to conform with the forces, or the forces developed to match the doctrine. Alexander pays little attention to doctrine in his study of decision-making in Soviet weapons procurement and goes so far as to assign a figure of 5–15 percent to its proportional influence in determining the level of overall defense expenditure.[6]

Neither Gallagher nor Alexander places much weight on doctrine as a factor in Soviet weapons decision-making, seeking the explanation for Soviet policies in other features of the USSR's system, in particular in the political and institutional context in which decisions are made. This is a very different approach from that which sees doctrine as providing general direction for policy and specific guidelines for weapons decisions.

The relationship between military doctrine and military science is particularly important to grasp. In the Soviet conception, doctrine embodies the fixed positions of the state on questions of war and military policy; military science, on the other hand, consists of the study of war and of the methods of waging it and is thus constantly developing. Doctrine has to take into account the economic and political conditions of the state, while military-scientific research is not constrained in this way. Doctrine is likely to remain stable for some time, being revised only in response to major political or military developments; military science, on the other hand, is constantly advancing as it tackles new problems. Doctrine is defined by the Party leadership, while military science is largely the prerogative of the General Staff and the military academies. Doctrine expresses the political character and purposes of the state, but draws on military science in the formulation of its military-technical side.[7]

The distinction between military doctrine and military science has been strongly emphasized by military writers in the post-Stalin period. There are two main reasons for this. The first is that the distinction is designed to prevent the imposition on military thought of a rigid doctrinal framework that would inhibit innovative thinking; such a framework was, in fact, imposed during the later years of Stalin's rule. The second is that the distinction helps to justify the influence of military thought on the policy of the state. Although it is accepted that military doctrine sets the general goals toward which military science should orient itself, it is also argued that a military doctrine which is divorced from military science – that is, from military advice – will be marked by subjectivism and voluntarism and thus prone to serious error.[8]

As Gallagher points out, Soviet statements of military doctrine are couched in very general terms.[9] This is perhaps to be expected in view of the political functions which the distinction between doctrine and military science performs. In practice that distinction is not always very sharp, but it is clear that the term 'doctrine' is used in a more restricted way in the USSR than in the UK or USA. Many elements of Soviet military science would be characterized as doctrine in the West. In this chapter, I shall use the term in this looser Western sense to refer to Soviet thinking on such general matters as the nature of Soviet policy and the character of war, as well as on such specific questions as the missions which are assigned to different forces in war. When 'doctrine' is used in its more restricted Soviet sense, this will be made clear.

When one turns to the other side of the relationship, it is evident that the term 'technology' is used in two different senses. The first refers to the creation of new systems in the research and development (R&D) process. Here the argument that doctrine drives technology implies that new weapons are created in response to military requirements that are derived from doctrine. The second sense refers to the quantities in which arms and equipment are procured. This sense can be extended to cover the norms of armament, that is, the quantities of arms which a particular military unit should have – for example, the number of tanks in a tank regiment.[10] Consequently, the thesis that doctrine is the key to Soviet armaments policy implies that both weapons innovations and the numbers of weapons procured are determined by doctrine, and not by other (bureaucratic, industrial or political) factors. It is the first of these arguments that is the more contentious and is examined here.

The relationship between doctrine and technology is too complex to be examined comprehensively in a single chapter. Three broad approaches are adopted here. First, the conception which Soviet writers have of the relationship is looked at. Then, the relationship between doctrine and technology in Soviet history is explored. Finally, the weapons acquisition process is analyzed to see what influences and pressures come into play in the creation of a new weapon.

Soviet Views of the Relationship between Doctrine and Technology.

In Marxist terms the ultimate dependence of armed forces and warfare on the material conditions of life is not in doubt. Engels, who had a greater interest in, and knowledge of, military affairs than Marx, put the matter very plainly:

> nothing is more dependent on economic conditions than the army and navy. Armament, military structure and organization, tactics and strategy depend primarily on the existing level of production and on communications. It is not the 'free creations of the intellect' of generals of genius that have revolutionized things here, but the invention of better weapons and changes in the human material, the soldiers; at the very most, the part played by generals of genius is limited to adapting methods of fighting to the new weapons and fighting men.[11]

In the same work Engels goes on to note that the advent of gunpowder and firearms revolutionized the methods of warfare and relationships of political power; yet these innovations, he writes, were 'a step forward in industry, that is, an economic advance', thus illustrating how warfare could be transformed by technological change:[12]

> From the history of infantry Engels drew the moral that 'the whole organization and method of warfare, and along with these victory and defeat, prove to be dependent on material, that is, economic

conditions; on the human material and the armaments material, and therefore on the quality and quantity of the population and on technical development'.[13]

Nor was Engels alone in this view, for Marx, after reading the article 'Army' which Engels had written for the *New American Cyclopedia*, wrote to him that the history of the army brought out more clearly than anything else the dependence of social relations on the productive forces.[14] And some years later, he exclaimed in a letter to Engels: 'Is our theory that the *organization of labor* is determined by the *means of production* confirmed anywhere more splendidly than in the man-slaughtering industry ?'[15] Later, Lenin was to write that 'military tactics depend on the level of military technology – Engels was the first to chew over this truth and put it in the mouths of Marxists'.[16]

All this amounts, in Marxist terms, to an authoritative statement of the determining influence of technological change on strategy and tactics. Soviet writers follow this line of argument, illustrating it with examples drawn from their own experience. Thus Babin, in his study of Engels as a military theorist, notes that the current scientific-technical revolution has affected the armed forces, and in particular their arms and equipment. The development of industry has provided the armed forces of the great powers with new types of military technology. And these, in their turn, have 'inevitably led to changes in the methods of waging war'.[17] Babin argues further that the appearance of nuclear-armed rockets has given the impact of modern technology on warfare its own specific character. Hitherto new weapons changed tactics first, then operational art and finally strategy. But now strategic missions can be carried out independently and not only through the cumulative effect of tactical and operational missions. Babin concludes that the development of armed forces since Engels's day has provided many examples of the dependence of changes in warfare on the advance of technology.[18]

Engels did not, however, hold the view that tactics changed only in response to technological advances; nor did he neglect the influence that tactics could exert on technology. In his history of the rifle, Engels pointed to the important effects which the new tactics introduced by the American and French revolutionary armies had on the development of the rifle in the nineteenth century. 'The combination of skirmishers with lines or columns became the essential characteristic of modern fighting', he wrote.[19] These changes were brought about, in Engels's view, not by technology but by the character of the soldiers mobilized by the American and French Revolutions – soldiers who were committed to the cause for which they were fighting, but who had not had extensive military training.[20] The new tactics created a demand for a gun which would combine the range and accuracy of the rifle with the speed and ease of loading, and the length of barrel, of the smooth-bore musket:

> Thus we see that with the very introduction of skirmishing into modern tactics, arose the demand for such an improved arm of war. In the nineteenth century, whenever a demand for a thing arises, and that demand is justified by the circumstances of the case, it is sure to be supplied. It was supplied in this case. Almost all improvements in small arms made since 1828 tended to supply it.[21]

Engels took the view that in the final instance military strategy and tactics were determined by the forces of production, including technology. At the same time, however, he acknowledged that the demands generated by changes in the methods of warfare could in turn exercise a powerful influence on the development of military technology.

Soviet writers follow Engels in pointing to the influence of tactics on military technology; indeed, they put rather more weight on it than Engels did. Babin, for example, claims that the twentieth century has provided many examples of weapons developed in response to the demands of tactics. The tank, he argues, made its appearance precisely because the tactics of the offensive required a weapon which would enable the attacking forces to overcome the enemy's firepower.[22] A more general statement of the same view is to be found in a Soviet work on scientific-technical progress and the revolution in military affairs:

> In considering the question of the influence of new weapons on the methods of armed combat, one should not forget the other side of the question. The developing methods of military operations place ever newer demands on armaments, on improving their tactical-technical characteristics and in so doing they give orders, as it were, for their further development ...
> Thus here we find the reverse influence of the methods of armed combat on weapons and military equipment. Perhaps this influence is less clearly expressed than the direct influence of weapons on tactics, operational art and strategy, but it – the reverse influence – does exist and must not be left out of account.[23]

It is clear that Soviet writers do not see doctrine as the driving force of technological progress, since they follow Engels in laying primary emphasis on the effects of such progress on the methods of warfare. At the same time, however, the prevailing Soviet view does not relegate doctrine to an insignificant role, but sees it as an important influence on the development of arms and equipment, and in particular on the ways in which they are employed.

Soviet military theorists do not, then, see the relationship between doctrine and technology as simple or unilinear. They point, rather, to an interaction between the two, in which the effects of technological change are dominant, but the influence of doctrine on technological development is also significant. The influence of doctrine can be either bad, in the sense of retarding technological advance, or good, in the sense of stimulating it and discerning its military implications at an early stage. Engels pointed out that 'in case after case' technological advances, once applied to warfare, had produced changes and even revolutions in its methods – 'often indeed against the will of the army high command'.[24] Soviet writers note that the methods of warfare almost always lag behind the capabilities of new weapons. It is important, therefore, for military policy that the laws and principles of the development of warfare should be understood so that the military implications of new technology can be assessed quickly and correctly.[25] A Polish study of the relationship between doctrine and armament in World War II argues that,

> the more correctly the military doctrine of a concrete state antici-
> pated the development of military technique, the more far-
> sightedly it appraised which elements of armament had vast
> perspectives of development and oriented itself precisely toward
> their development and utilization, the better it succeeded in play-
> ing the role of a stimulator of military technique.[26]

Thus, doctrine has more than the passive role of aiding adjustment to new technologies; it can also help to stimulate technological development.

This view lays a heavy responsibility on military doctrine, and on military thought in general. Bernard Brodie has argued that '*in the long run*, technology has transformed war pretty much in its own fashion'; the mistakes which men have made in assessing the military utility of new technologies have not ultimately affected the technological conditions of warfare.[27] But, as Brodie points out, '"the long run" can be a pretty long run indeed' and in the period of adjustment to new weapons, major conflicts can be decided by errors of judgment about the significance of new military technologies. Hence, to ascribe to technology the major role in determining the methods of warfare (as Soviet writers do) is not to deprive doctrine of its significant and responsible role in assessing the military utility of new technologies.

It is war that provides the ultimate severe and practical test of how well doctrine performs this role. It is only in armed combat that the final judgment can be passed on how well doctrine has stimulated technological advance and applied new technologies to warfare. Of course, performance in war does not depend only on doctrine and technology, but also, and more importantly, on how commanders and soldiers implement the doctrine and use the arms and equipment. Mastery of the art of war and commitment to the war effort are required if weapons are to be used to maximum effect. This is a lesson that the Soviet Armed Forces have learned by experience, and is a major preoccupation of Soviet military writing.

It is clear that the prevailing Soviet view of the relationship between doctrine and technology does not accord with either the position that assigns doctrine a central position in weapons decision-making or the alternative that relegates it to a subsidiary role. The relationship is seen as one of complex interdependence in which both elements are given considerable importance. Technological change exerts a determining influence on the methods of warfare, but doctrine has a significant role in adapting those methods to new weapons and in discerning at an early stage the military utility of new technologies.

Doctrine and Technology in Historical Perspective

The October Revolution brought about, in Bolshevik eyes, a fundamental change in the class character of the Russian state and hence of its military forces. In the early postrevolutionary years, intense arguments erupted about the practical implications of this political transformation. Many different issues were involved, among them the question of military doctrine. Frunze stressed the importance of a unified military doctrine, arguing that this alone could give direction to the development and training of the Red Army. Trotsky opposed this argument, on the ground that military doctrine had been appropriate for states of the old regime when a stable international system had existed; in a revolutionary period, he warned, doctrine, with its implication of set and fixed views, was inappropriate and might degenerate into doctrinairism. The tasks facing the Red Army were more prosaic ('to teach how to oil rifles and grease boots') than the abstractions of doctrine.[28]

Frunze also claimed that in the Civil War, Red military operations had exhibited special features – manoeuver and an offensive
spirit – which sprang from the class character of the Red Army.
These could, therefore, be taken as distinguishing marks of
proletarian, as opposed to bourgeois, military strategy. Here
too Trotsky took an opposing view, arguing that these features
followed not from the class character of the Red Army, but from
the nature of the war itself. Trotsky lost the argument (on political
rather than intellectual grounds) and Frunze's conception of the
nature and role of doctrine and of the character of Soviet military
strategy has remained an important element in Soviet military
thought.[29]

Soviet writers divide the history of their military doctrine and
military science into several periods.[30] The first major turning
point after the Revolution is seen to have come in 1929. It is from
that year that the transformation of the Red Army into a well-
equipped modern force is dated. The war with Germany did not
effect major changes in Soviet doctrine, in the Soviet sense of that
term, but it did have a profound influence on Soviet strategic and
tactical thought. 1953 was another important turning point in
Soviet doctrine, for in that year Stalin died and the Armed Forces
first received nuclear weapons.[31] The present period dates from
1960, when a new doctrine for the nuclear age was unveiled. Of
course, major changes have taken place within each of these
periods; there have been, for example, important developments
in Soviet military doctrine since 1960. Some of these turning
points are closely associated with technological change.

Although the Bolsheviks claimed that the revolution had created
in the Red Army an army of a new type, they realized that the
economic and technological basis of Soviet military power was
even weaker than that of the Imperial state before World War I.
The lack of modern armaments grew more worrisome as the
prospect of revolution in Europe receded and the idea of con-
structing socialism in one country gained ground. It became clear
that the USSR might have to fight alone against its enemies. In
January 1925, Frunze warned that a future war would not be like
the Civil War:

> Of course it will have the character of a class civil war in the sense
> that the White Guards will be on the enemy's side, while we, on the
> other hand, shall have allies in the camp of our enemies. But in
> equipment, in the methods of waging it, it will not be a war like our
> civil war. We shall have to deal with a splendid army, armed with
> all the latest technological advances, and if we do not have these

advances in our army then the prospects for us may prove very very unfavorable. This should be taken into account when we decide the question of the general preparation of the country for defense.[32]

As industrialization became an urgent objective of Soviet policy in the late 1920s, so too did the technological transformation of the Red Army.[33]

1929 was the year of the 'great break' in Soviet politics, when forced collectivization was launched and the industrialization drive was intensified. It was also a major turning point in Soviet military policy. In 1929 the Politburo decreed that the re-equipment of the Red Army be speeded up, calling for superiority in the decisive types of armament – aircraft, artillery and tanks.[34] In the same year, new Field Service Regulations were adopted. The Regulations Commission declared that,

> we have every reason to expect that [our] technological might will increase from year to year. We must not only refuse to accept a technological lag, but on the contrary, we must surpass our bourgeois neighbors in arms and equipment. This respect for material combat might and the material resources of war sharply distinguishes the new Field Service Regulations from the old ones [i.e. those of 1925].[35]

The new regulations stressed that a future war would be one of maneuver and that victory could be achieved only by a decisive offensive followed by relentless pursuit of the enemy into his own territory. They emphasized that the different arms should combine and interact, and provided instructions for the employment of tanks and aircraft.[36] In fact, the new regulations showed a commitment to modern weaponry that outstripped what the Red Army actually had at its disposal. During the 1930s a large defense industry was created to produce the weapons required by this conception of war.[37] The USSR accepted that military power rested upon industrial power, but it did not adopt the concept, which was popular with Western military theorists at the time, of small highly mechanized professional forces. The Soviet leaders sought instead to combine the mass army with modern military technology.[38]

The technological transformation of the Red Army was inspired by Soviet thinking about a future war and by the more general belief that the USSR, if it was to build socialism in isolation, needed a strong army. Here indeed military doctrine, which was so clearly linked to the Stalinist conception of Soviet development, provided general guidance for armaments policy. But many questions of strategy and tactics remained to be answered: how was the Red Army to employ the new weapons in the offensive operations to which doctrine was committed? During the 1930s, a great deal of thought and experiment was devoted to answering this question. Tukhachevskii and the officers close to him developed the concept of the 'operation in depth' as a way of using modern weapons in mobile offensive warfare.[39]

In his commentary on the temporary Field Service Regulations of 1936 Tukhachevskii wrote that,

> our technical means of combat with their great range make it possible to exert influence on the enemy not only directly at the front line, but to break through his position and attack him simultaneously in the whole depth of his order of battle. In operations with the previous technical means of combat only the forward edge of the enemy's position was destroyed, and a breach formed in the line of his front. Thanks to this the enemy had the opportunity of bringing up reserves in good time and liquidating the threat of a breakthrough. The modern means of combat make it possible to organize the attack in such a way that the enemy is struck in his whole depth, and his reserves can be delayed in their approach to the threatened sector. Now we have at our disposal such means as aviation and tank *desants*.[40]

Here was a new operational concept based on the most modern types of armament, and thus a clear example of the responsiveness of doctrine to technological change. In its turn, this concept helped to stimulate technological development, since it stressed the combination and interaction of different arms and was hostile to attempts to ascribe a decisive role to one weapon alone – for example, to Douhet's theory of air power.[41]

The military purge of 1937–8 had a profound effect on Soviet doctrine and technology. Most of the military innovators, notably Tukhachevskii himself, were eliminated and replaced with men of less ability and experience. Although military doctrine remained unchanged in its general outlines, many operational concepts – in particular that of the operation in depth – came under suspicion, because they were associated with those who had now been branded enemies of the people.[42] The mechanized corps – 'those shock forces of the operation in depth' – were disbanded at the end of 1939 as a result of a mistaken assessment of the lessons of the Spanish Civil War.[43] Military interest in long-range aviation declined sharply, while the parachute troops – a key element in the operation in depth – were broken up. Many of those engaged in developing and producing weapons were arrested, and work in such advanced fields as rocketry and radar was greatly set back.[44] By destroying so many men of talent the purge did incalculable harm to Soviet military power.

The war for which the USSR had prepared for so long began with the German attack on 22 June 1941. Paradoxically, Stalin was taken by surprise and the opening months of the war proved disastrous for the USSR.[45] In the late 1930s, the three basic principles of military doctrine (in the Soviet sense of the term) had been: constant readiness for a crushing repulse of any aggressor; defeat of the enemy on his own territory; attainment of victory with little bloodshed.[46] But the early stages of the war showed that the USSR had not been ready to meet an attack and saw the German armies penetrate deep into Soviet territory; victory seemed a long way off and much blood had already been spilt. Those who had warned against overemphasis on the offensive had been proved correct, for Soviet defensive operations had to be improvised in haste.[47] It was only as the German advance was held, and industry, re-established in the East, began to turn out weapons in large numbers, that the Red Army was able to reorganize itself for offensive operations. Tank armies, for example, could now be formed.[48]

The early months of the war had cast considerable doubt on Soviet military doctrine, but victory was taken as proof that the doctrine was sound. As long as Stalin lived, the early disasters could not be subjected to critical examination. The retreat of the Red Army was presented as 'active defense' – a bland description for so many blunders and losses. But even after Stalin's death, when the history of the war could be studied more freely, the conclusion was drawn that Soviet military doctrine had proved basically correct. General Lomov, one of the leading Soviet theorists, wrote that,

> of course, one cannot maintain that all these [doctrinal] positions proved correct in the Great Patriotic War. For example, the aim of achieving victory 'with little bloodshed' did not meet the peculiarities of modern war, and the possibility of enemy invasion of our territory was underestimated. However, in general our military doctrine and military art stood the test in the fire of war.[49]

The exceptions which Lomov notes are, of course, significant. (Indeed, it was General Svechin, who had seen a future war as one of attrition, who was proved most far-sighted; but his views had not been accepted by the High Command or the Party leadership.)[50]

Yet the failures of the early stages of the war have not been interpreted as failures of doctrine or military thought. General Kozlov, another theorist, has argued that,

> the failures which darkened the first period of the Great Patriotic War resulted not from errors in our doctrine, but from shortcomings in its application just before and during the war.[51]

The years 1938 to 1942 illustrate, in Soviet eyes, the gap that can exist between doctrine and its implementation. Policy does not spring automatically from doctrine; in order to understand policy one has to take account of the policy-making process.

But the war saw the beginnings of a revolution in military technology which was to have profound effects on Soviet military doctrine and institutions. Soviet physicists had been aware of the military potential of atomic energy before the war, and in 1940 had proposed to the government that the development of a uranium bomb be begun. It was only in 1943, however, that work on the atomic bomb was started, after information had been received about the German, British and American projects; the Soviet effort was intensified after Hiroshima and Nagasaki.[52] After 1938, Soviet rocket work had concentrated on boosters for aircraft and on rocket artillery. But German achievements reawakened Soviet interest, and soon after the end of the war a major program was under way in which Soviet rocket scientists and engineers drew heavily on German technology.[53] Nuclear weapons and long-range rockets were the most important, but not the only, elements in this military-technological revolution. Soviet work on radar had been cut short by the purge, but was restarted during the war. By the end of 1945 the USSR had launched a major research and development program in jet-engine technology.[54]

In some of these instances – notably rocketry and radar – the USSR could legitimately claim to have done pioneering work, but the immediate stimulus to the large-scale research and development program came from developments abroad. Military doctrine did not provide the initial impetus for these programs. Tukhachevskii had seen an important role for rockets in combat in depth, and for radar in air defense.[55] But between this conception and its realization in practice other factors intervened. In the event, it was the commitment by other governments to the new technologies that proved decisive in Soviet decision-making. The connection between doctrine and the new technologies was, therefore, loose to begin with. After Stalin's death, however, the postwar research and development programs were to lead to a fundamental re-evaluation of military doctrine.

In the last years of Stalin's life, Soviet military thought focused almost exclusively on the war. Lessons could be drawn only within the strict confines of 'Stalinist military science'. Stalin had declared that surprise was a 'transitory factor', not one of the 'permanently operating factors' in war, and this position could not be challenged.[56] Little attention was paid to the new weapons that were being developed; doctrine and technology were thus kept apart. Criticism of Soviet performance in the war became possible after Stalin's death, but by this time a revision of doctrine had been made necessary by the advances in weapons development. As General Povaly put it, the new weapons

> persistently demanded a fundamental reexamination of all fundamental principles of military doctrine and all military art, primarily strategy.[57]

One of the first fruits of this re-examination was the new emphasis which was now placed on surprise and the opening stages of war.[58]

The possibility of war between the socialist and capitalist camps has provided the main focus for Soviet military thought in the postwar period. Such a war would be, in the Soviet view, unprecedentedly intense and bitter because of the destructive power of modern weapons and because the survival of each social system would be at stake. In 1956, Khrushchev declared that the growing strength of the socialist camp meant that such a war was no longer fatally inevitable.[59] Since that time Soviet doctrine has stressed that the surest way of preventing war was to pursue peace by means of a foreign policy backed by military power.[60] Although the Party leaders have adopted a policy of peaceful coexistence, Soviet military thought has concentrated on the possibility of war with the Western powers. In 1957 the Ministry of Defense organized a major conference on military science. This was the first of a series of discussions on the nature of nuclear war. These discussions were followed closely by the Party leadership and served as the basis for the new military doctrine which Khrushchev unveiled in January 1960.[61]

Khrushchev opened the new phase of Soviet military doctrine with a speech in which he declared that a future war would be a rocket-nuclear war.[62] Such a war would begin with missile strikes deep into the enemy's rear. It was possible that a surprise attack would be launched against the USSR, but the Soviets would be able to retaliate and, because of the size of the country and the dispersion of the population, would suffer incomparably less than the West. The Soviet armed forces, said Khrushchev, had already gone over, to a considerable degree, to rocket-nuclear weapons; these weapons were being improved, and would continue to be improved until they were banned. Since the country's defense capability now depended not on manpower, but on firepower and the means of delivery, Khrushchev proposed a cut of one-third in the number of men in the armed forces.

Khrushchev's speech came one month after the establishment of the Strategic Rocket Forces as a separate branch of the armed forces, and represented the general conclusion reached in the discussions of the previous years.[63] The new doctrine was couched in extremely general terms. Khrushchev's speech indicated that rockets had already been chosen in preference to aircraft as the main delivery vehicle for nuclear weapons. This choice was made not for special doctrinal reasons, it seems, but because of the practical advantages of ballistic rockets over aircraft: they were invulnerable to air defenses and did not need in-flight refueling or bases outside the USSR in order to be able to strike targets anywhere in the world.[64] Khrushchev's speech marked the adaptation of doctrine to nuclear weapons and long-range ballistic rockets.

The new doctrine provided a framework for Soviet thinking about a future war, but it did not give specific guidelines for force planning or weapons procurement. During the 1960s there was considerable debate and discussion about the forces needed for nuclear war. It was accepted that rocket-nuclear weapons would provide the main striking force, but many open questions remained. The most contentious was the role of the ground forces: were they to be seen as occupation forces which would move into enemy territory in the wake of a nuclear strike, or would they have a major part to play in defeating enemy forces? This issue was further complicated by the argument that the non-nuclear variant of a war with the West had to be taken into account. These questions were finally settled by 1967. It was accepted that war with the West might be either long or short and that consequently the ground forces might have a major fighting role. It was accepted also that war, while possibly nuclear, might also be conventional. Since the late 1960s the ground forces have been expanded and adapted to meet these contingencies.[65]

The military discussions of the 1960s were complicated by

Khrushchev's apparent belief that war could be avoided, and political gains made, by virtue of the fact that the USSR possessed, for the first time, the ability to inflict widespread destruction on the continental USA. Deterrence through the threat of destruction seems to have been the object of Khrushchev's military policy, and he appears to have resisted military claims for the forces which the High Command thought necessary for waging and winning a nuclear war. Whatever disagreements there were in the High Command about the roles and missions of different forces in a nuclear war, there seems to have been overwhelming opposition to Khrushchev on this score.[66]

This difference of approach points to a crucial aspect of Soviet military doctrine. The political side of Soviet doctrine stresses the importance, and the possibility, of preventing a war between the socialist and capitalist camps. The military side attends to the question of waging and winning such a war, 'if the imperialists should unleash it' (to use the standard Soviet qualification). Consequently, deterrence is a political rather than a military concern, and receives almost no attention in Soviet military writings. Soviet doctrine sees the prevention of war as something to be achieved by means of a 'peace policy' – that is, a foreign policy which seeks to reduce the risks of war – backed by Soviet military might.[67] This may seem to be a quite logical and coherent position. But some members of the Soviet political leadership have wondered whether, if war with the West could be avoided, the costly preparation for such a war is necessary; they have doubted also whether it makes much sense to speak of victory in such a war. Malenkov in 1953 and Khrushchev in the early 1960s appear to have had doubts of this kind; both met with opposition from the military, who argued that preparation for war was necessary.[68]

When Khrushchev was removed from power in 1964, the USSR lagged very considerably behind the USA in strategic forces. The new Party leaders evidently accepted that, while war was to be avoided, it had to be prepared for. Strategic inferiority of any kind was rejected as unacceptable. But in the late 1960s, strategic parity with the USA and the prospect of intense competition in antiballistic missile (ABM) systems raised new questions of policy: in particular, was mutual vulnerability the only possible strategic relationship with the USA, or should the USSR strive for a significant strategic superiority? Raymond Garthoff has shown that in the late 1960s Soviet military thinking came to recognize the relationship of mutual vulnerability – and hence of mutual deterrence – as an objective fact.[69] From the Soviet point of view this has not been a question of the desirability of such a relationship – though, of course, it is better than US superiority. Rather, it has been acknowledged that actions by one side to break out of this relationship would be met by reactions from the other side, thus leading to new and costly spirals in strategic arms competition. It made sense, therefore, for the USSR to enter negotiations with the USA to stabilize the strategic relationship, while seeking whatever advantages might be gained in the process.[70] Soviet doctrine has not abandoned its belief that war should be prepared for: the civil defense effort tries to limit the damage a nuclear strike on the USSR would cause, while intensive research and development work on new ABM technologies shows that vulnerability is not accepted as something immutable, so that a technological breakthrough in this field might lead to another revision of doctrine. Yet, notwithstanding these qualifications, the military equilibrium with the USA has been recognized as an objective phenomenon of overwhelming significance.

The SALT I agreements were the practical result of this policy. They did not halt the strategic arms competition or put an end to Soviet efforts to ensure survival of the social system in the event of war. But they did provide matter for debate and discussion, in particular about the role of military power as an instrument of policy throughout the world. The attainment of parity had helped to neutralize US strategic power, and Soviet thinking could now turn to the problem of China and the restriction of Chinese and Western power outside the central military balances.[71] In other words, military power could now be used not only to safeguard the security of the USSR and its closest allies, but to support political change to Soviet advantage around the globe.

Both the projection of military power abroad and the acceptance of the military equilibrium with the USA have entered the canon of Soviet doctrine. In January 1977, for example, Brezhnev declared that,

> our efforts are aimed at preventing both first and second strikes and at preventing nuclear war altogether ... The Soviet Union's defense potential must be sufficient to deter anyone from disturbing our peaceful life. Not a course aimed at superiority in arms but a course aimed at their reduction – that is our policy.[72]

Such statements are undeniably general and it is difficult to see what precise practical consequences follow from them. Yet their significance should not be discounted for that reason alone. It was significant, for example, that the strategic debates of the 1960s led to permissive conclusions about the duration of a war with the

West and about the forces that would be needed for such a war. These conclusions provided, in turn, a permissive framework in which the different branches of the armed forces could press their claims for resources. If doctrine had pointed exclusively to the possibility of a short nuclear war with the West, this would have signified a rather different procurement policy. Similarly, if doctrine now stressed the need for overwhelming strategic superiority, this would indicate a rather different context for Soviet weapons policy-making.

This survey of the relationship between doctrine and technology has been unavoidably general. Yet it should be clear that the relationship is a complex one. Doctrine is not a function of technology alone, but is deeply rooted in political, cultural and economic conditions. Military technology, on the other hand, is not merely a function of doctrine, but rests on industrial and technological power. The defense industry was built up in the 1930s, because it was recognized that military power required modern weapons; the methods of warfare were, in turn, adapted to these weapons in the attempt to exploit them to greatest effect. The nuclear revolution in military affairs was precipitated by developments in science and technology and made a fundamental review of doctrine necessary. Once the new doctrine was formulated, it did provide a framework within which roles and missions could be assigned and weapons acquisition decisions made. But this, too, has been adapted to take account of technological changes and of the changing strategic relationship with the USA.

Doctrine and Technology in Weapons Acquisition

It is clear from the last section that the relationship between doctrine and technology cannot be examined in isolation from the Soviet policy-making system. Neither element can be seen only in relation to the other, and if, as has been suggested, the relationship between them is one of reciprocal influence, then it is important to ask how they relate to each other in the weapons acquisition process. Those who argue that doctrine drives technology imply that weapons acquisition is determined by the requirements of the armed forces, and that these requirements are derived from military doctrine. Those who play down the role of doctrine point to the influence which the institutional arrangements of the defense sector have on weapons development and production.[73]

The relationship between doctrine and technology can best be explored by examining the structure of the acquisition process and the various stages through which a system moves as it passes from conception to series production. The basic structure was created in the 1930s, although it has been modified to cope with the greatly expanded research and development effort of the postwar years. The two main elements in the process are the industrial ministries in the defense sector and the Ministry of Defense. These ministries work under the general direction of the Politburo, which exercises control over weapons acquisition through special central agencies.[74]

The ministries in the defense sector control production plants where weapons, subsystems and components are produced; research institutes engage in applied research in both weapons and production technology; and design bureaus design and develop weapons and major subsystems as well as production processes. The Ministry of Defense issues requirements, requests design proposals, concludes development contracts with the design bureaus, supervises development, conducts prototype trials, places orders for production and assimilates new equipment. The Ministry has the necessary technical and managerial competence for these tasks. Since 1947, there has been a Deputy Minister of Defense for either armament or electronics (from 1964 to 1970 a Deputy Chief of the General Staff); since 1978, there appear to be two such deputy ministers, one each for armament and electronics. These men are successors to Tukhachevskii, who was Chief of Armament from 1931 to 1936 and had a key role in the technological transformation of the Red Army. The postwar deputy ministers have played an important part in stimulating technological innovation and the development of new industries in the USSR.[75]

The different services of the armed forces have technical administrations (armaments directorates) which deal directly with the defense industry, issuing requirements, conducting tests and sending representatives to the design bureaus and production plants. Each service also has research establishments whose work is mainly related to the role of the armed forces in weapons acquisition: they help the services to decide on their operational requirements, to monitor scientific and technological developments, to test prototypes and to employ new equipment. These establishments may engage in some weapons development, but most of this work is done in the design bureaus of the defense industry ministries. The military academies also play an important role in military research and development, particularly in operational analysis and weapons design. There is no extensive class of civilian defense analysts in the USSR: analysis is done largely in military institutions.[76]

According to a study by Sarkisian and Minaev, the starting point for a new system is the recognition by the user that he faces new missions or that the missions he has to perform have changed in scope or character:

> The initial conditions for the conception of a new project are provided by radical changes in the character of the transport or combat operations which form the basic principles (the doctrine) in the sphere in which the aerospace vehicles function. Calculation of the country's economic potential and of scientific-technical progress provides the necessary conditions for a practicable project. Doctrine serves here as the organizing principle. Success in creating new systems and the appearance of types of systems which are new in principle influence, in their turn, the content of doctrine in a determining way. Thus in the process of creating systems there is an interaction between theory and practice: new missions – doctrine – conception of the system – the new system – doctrine.[77]

Here again the interaction of doctrine and technology is stressed, with technology seen as a determining influence on doctrine, and doctrine ascribed a key role as the 'organizing principle' in formulating requirements.

Several different elements are involved in the preliminary stages of a project. The customer does research into his operational requirements. The technical administration, which is responsible for procurement, must work closely with the staffs in charge of operational planning and combat training. In formulating the preliminary requirement the technical administration can draw on the work of the military academies and the Ministry of Defense's research establishments. According to Sarkisian and Minaev, the preliminary requirement should take account not only of the needs of the user, but also of the technology which will become available. In response to this requirement, several design bureaus, working closely with the industrial research institutes, prepare draft designs which show the appearance of the system, the basic design relationships, the main technical approaches and the resources needed to create and operate the system. These draft designs are analyzed and a set of proposals and recommendations is drawn up, specifying the system's characteristics, the resources needed, and the time required for development and production.[78]

A crucial aspect of this stage of the acquisition process is the adjustment that takes place between military requirements and

technological capabilities. One of the leading Soviet aerodynami-
cists, General Pyshnov of the Zhukovskii Air Force Engineering
Academy, has explained the process by which military aircraft are
conceived:

> Some people believe this process to be the following: military
> specialists in accordance with the demands of aviation draw up
> tactical and technical requirements for an aircraft, and the
> designer develops the aircraft according to them. In reality the
> history of the creation of new designs is more complex. The fact is
> that a new military aircraft is not set within the framework of
> well-established technical capabilities, but always represents a
> major step forward and is developed using means which have been
> relatively recently tested or have not been proved at all. Naturally
> the customers cannot give 'figures at will'. They independently
> study beforehand the present capabilities of aircraft construction
> and discuss with scientists, designers and flyers the advisability of
> creating the new vehicle. In addition they study what is being done
> in this field by the probable enemy and what he will have to
> counter the given aircraft. These are all difficult and complicated
> questions requiring the use of modern methods of research and a
> high level of training on the part of aviation specialists.[79]

This is an argument for the Ministry of Defence to have its own
'in-house' research establishments, so that military orders will be
based on sound analysis, not only of requirements, but also of
technological feasibility. Sarkisian and Minaev stress a rather
different point, arguing that as much freedom as possible should
be left to the designer in the choice of technical solutions; perhaps
disagreements do arise between customer and designer on this
issue.[80]

The design proposals will have to be evaluated and approved at
higher levels in the Ministry of Defense and in the industrial
ministry. By this time the less satisfactory designs will have been
weeded out, so that a smaller number – perhaps only one – will go
forward to the next stage. The basic document regulating design
and development is the Tactical-Technical Instruction ('*taktiko-
tekhnicheskoe zadanie*') which sets out the object and purpose of
the development; the operational cost and special requirements
of the prototype; the composition, and the stages of preparation
of the technical documentation.[81] Even at this stage, some give-
and-take may occur between requirements and technology. As
Sarkisian and Minaev comment,

> the appearance of new possibilities is not to be excluded. There-
> fore it is still necessary here to treat the customer's requirements as

indicating the directions of effort, although basically they ought to be regulating the work of those developing the system.[82]

Once the designs are completed, a decision is taken about the production of prototypes; at this stage too some designs may be dropped, although prototype competition does sometimes take place.

The building of prototypes may require more research and the development of new production technologies; it will certainly involve extensive laboratory and factory trials. The factory trials are conducted by representatives of the design bureau, the factory and the customer, to see whether the design meets the specifications in the Tactical-Technical Instruction. When they have been completed satisfactorily, the prototype is handed over for state trials. These are conducted by a special commission which is headed by an officer and consists of representatives of the various ministries involved. The state trials are intended to establish how the system will perform in operational conditions, and are normally conducted at the customer's testing ground. If these trials are successful, the customer accepts the system; if not, it may be sent back for modification. If more than one system has gone to the prototype stage, these trials may be competitive.[83]

The next major step is to put the system into series production. It is true that some systems are developed for experimental purposes only, but the general object of the research and development system is to develop systems that will be produced and deployed. Consequently, a decision in principle to produce the system is taken early in the life cycle, at the same time as the design decision.[84] If the state trials are successful, the chances that the system will be produced must be high. But the series production decision does not follow automatically from successful state trials. The first Soviet ICBM, the SS-6, passed its state trials in August 1957, but only four missiles were ever deployed.[85] In fact, the series production decision involves many considerations other than the performance of the system itself. Production of a new system has to be balanced against the production of other systems and incorporated into the overall procurement program. Besides, the conditions of the original decision may have altered: the system may have proved much more expensive than originally estimated, or the military requirement may have changed. Decisions about the production of major systems appear to be taken finally at the highest level, by the Defense Council or the Politburo. Here the widest considerations of foreign and defense policy will have to be taken into account.[86]

Once production is decided upon, work will be allocated to the series production plants. The basic document here is the Technical Conditions (*'tekhnicheskie usloviya'*) which sets out the purpose and sphere of application of the system, the basic tactical-technical data, the methods of quality control, and so on.[87] The Ministry of Defense has a team of representatives at the plant, whose main responsibility is to exercise quality control throughout the production process. This they appear to do quite strictly, thus ensuring that the armed forces do not receive defective equipment. Operational service is likely to generate requirements for modification, and the basic system may have to be adapted to new missions.[88]

There are two major features of the acquisition process which have an important bearing on the relationship between doctrine and technology. The first of these is the way in which military requirements are adjusted to technological feasibility. This happens in the early stages of creating a new system, but it takes place in a more general way too. In the 1930s, Soviet armaments policy was greatly influenced by foreign military technology. Much effort was devoted to acquiring foreign weapons and adapting them to Soviet requirements. This policy sprang naturally from the industrial backwardness of the USSR, but it did not result in mere imitation; in some cases – for example, that of the American Christie tank – it was the USSR and not the country of origin that saw the weapon's military potential.[89] But the state of Soviet industry and the level of technical skills in the population imposed major constraints on the development and production of armaments. The aircraft designer Tupolev argued that doctrine would have to adjust itself to the aircraft that could be produced, while designers should try to meet military requirements on the basis of available technology and production facilities. If this led to a lag in quality behind the West, then it could be compensated for by production in larger quantities.[90] Soviet industry was indeed suited to long production runs: the doctrinal emphasis on the quantity of weapons matched the quantitative targets of the early five-year plans. Soviet designers were encouraged to create designs that were suitable for mass production and simple enough to be operated and maintained by troops with a low level of technical skills. At their best Soviet designers met these requirements by designing very effective armaments such as the T-34 medium tank.

The value of such an approach to weapons design and development was confirmed in the war with Germany when mass production had to be organized in extremely difficult conditions.

That experience has remained an important influence on Soviet design philosophy, particularly in such areas as tank development.[91] It is sometimes argued that all Soviet weapons are marked by a distinctive design philosophy, which stresses simplicity, commonality and evolutionary development.[92] There is some truth in this argument, but two qualifications should be added. First, these features are to be found in US military research and development, too – though perhaps not to the same extent – so that it is wrong to lay too much emphasis on their distinctiveness.[93] Secondly, it is misleading to characterize all Soviet weapons development in this way, because there are some major exceptions and important differences between the different types of weapons.[94]

The patterns which have been discerned in Soviet weapons design and development can be explained in terms of the institutional arrangements of the defense industry. First, the funds for the research institutes do not depend directly on specific orders for equipment, although they will depend in a general way on the importance which a particular area is seen to have for weapons development. Similarly, military production seems not to fluctuate as much as in the USA. Hence the design bureaus, which are supported by a steady research effort, are in turn serving a steady production program.[95] This stability ensures a considerable degree of institutional continuity in the defense sector, and this continuity is likely to encourage evolutionary development, in as much as the design bureau will draw on its own experience in creating a new design.[96]

Secondly, the work of the design bureaus is constrained in a number of ways: by design procedures which the research institutes lay down in handbooks; by the norms which the ministry sets for the use of scarce materials and the control which it exercises over their allocation; and by the Ministry of Defense's representatives in the design bureaus. These constraints encourage standardized design procedures.[97] Thirdly, when the designer is faced with a new requirement, he is likely to try to meet it with what is at hand; he will wish to avoid dependence on other ministries for key elements of his design and he may regard the effort of removing the constraints imposed by other agencies as too troublesome. The separation of applied research from development suggests that the designer will turn to the research institute and take what is available rather than wait for something new; because development programs are not the way in which funds are acquired for applied research, there is no incentive to embark on exotic designs. These factors combine to encourage commonality in the use of subsystems and components; they also explain the practice of getting a new design into production and then modifying it as new components and subsystems become available. They might also be thought to encourage conservatism and evolutionary development; however, if a large applied research effort is underway, it may provide the basis for major intergenerational changes in design and technology.

The exceptions to these patterns spring from two sources. The first is the pressure which international competition has exerted on Soviet armaments policies. Rivalry with the advanced capitalist powers has justified a large research and development effort. More specifically, new paths of weapons development have been initiated in response to foreign innovations – whether in emulation (for example, atomic bomb development) or as a counter to foreign systems (for example, air and ballistic missile defense). In some cases the requirements generated by this competition have pushed Soviet designers to develop technologically over-ambitious systems; the Mya-4 (Bison) long-range bomber and the Galosh ABM system are cases in point. (Such systems refute the claim sometimes made that evolutionary development is a consequence of the predominance of requirements in the acquisition process.) The second source of innovation is the very large research effort in fundamental and applied science. Designers can draw on this in meeting military requirements. But this effort also provides discoveries which scientists or designers may wish to exploit for weapons development. The most notable instance of this kind was Kurchatov's proposal to develop a uranium bomb, but other initiatives too can be found.[98]

The second major feature of the weapons acquisition process to have an important bearing on the relationship between doctrine and technology is the role of the armed forces. They exercise considerable control over the acquisition process, and this control is backed by high political priority.[99] As a result, the armed forces enjoy a kind of consumer sovereignty which is unusual, if not unique, in the Soviet economy. Although they have to adapt their requirements to the defense sector's mode of operation, they control some of the most important decisions in the life cycle of a weapons system. For this reason doctrine does appear to have a major influence on the acquisition process; and this can be illustrated by reference to Soviet rocket development.

In the early 1930s, Soviet rocketry gained a new significance when Tukhachevskii saw that rockets could play an important role in the operation in depth by inflicting deep strikes on enemy forces. In 1932, he wrote to the Chief of the Military-Engineering Academy that,

special promise is held out by the GDL's [Gas Dynamics Laboratory, which at the time came under Tukhachevskii's Technical
Staff] experiments with a liquid-propellant rocket motor that has
recently been designed in the laboratory. In artillery and chemical
troops this motor will open up unlimited possibilities for firing
projectiles of any power and any range.[100]

Tukhachevskii was instrumental in setting up the RNII (*Reak-
tivnyi Nauchno-issledovatel'skii Institut* – Reaction Research
Institute) which was to play the major role in Soviet rocket
development after 1945.[101]

Soviet rocket work suffered from the purges but was revived
toward the end of the war with Germany, and by 1947 a major
research and development program was under way. Very soon a
basic choice had to be made between proceeding straight to the
development of an intercontinental rocket or building on the
German V-2 and moving step by step to the longer ranges. The
latter course was chosen, for a variety of reasons. One of the
reasons appears to have been that the artillerymen, who controlled the military side of rocket development, saw rockets as an
extension of artillery. It made sense, in that context, to extend
by gradual stages the ability to launch deep strikes against
the enemy. If rockets had been viewed as surrogate strategic
bombers, the pattern of development might well have been different. Thus, Soviet rocket development appears to have been
influenced strongly by military doctrine.[102]

This brief examination of the weapons acquisition process has
pointed to the importance both of the armed forces and their
doctrine and of the institutional arrangements for creating new
weapons. As General Pyshnov pointed out, the armed forces
cannot merely state their requirements and expect them to be
fulfilled. Weapons aquisition is more complex than that, and the
organization of the defense sector exercises a strong influence on
Soviet armaments policies. Moreover, the relationship between
doctrine and technology may vary from one period to another
within the same field. The history of Soviet rocket development
in the 1930s illustrates the point that doctrine can influence
technological progress by highlighting a particular field as being
of great potential. Rocket development in the 1940s showed that
doctrine could influence the way in which a new military technology was assimilated. The entry of rocket-nuclear weapons
into the arsenal in the 1950s caused a fundamental revision of
doctrine.

Finally, Soviet military thought recognizes that a large research
and development effort is needed to provide the basis for military

power. This effort is there not merely to respond to military requirements, but to provide new technologies with military significance. Consequently, it is important for military thought to direct its attention to these future possibilities. Two military writers have argued that scientific-technical progress

> is a guarantee that in future we can expect the appearance of new means of combat. Military strategy now has the task of developing in good time the methods of conducting military operations with the employment of these means, so that with the beginning of war we will not be forced, as Engels expressed it, gropingly to 'adapt' strategic concepts to the new weapons. It is no less important to learn to determine the directions of scientific-technical progress which will most facilitate a strengthening of the country's defenses and influence the changes and development of military strategy.[103]

In other words, as technological change becomes more rapid and more important for military power, so the role and responsibilities of military doctrine increase.

Conclusion

It has not been possible in this chapter to explore the relationship between doctrine and technology in all its complexity. But it has been suggested that complexity is an essential feature of the relationship. Contrary to one widespread view, Soviet military technology is not determined by military doctrine. Soviet theorists do not argue that doctrine does, or should, drive technology; they put more emphasis on the impact of technology on doctrine. Soviet history shows the influence of doctrine on technology, but indicates that technological advances have exercised an even more profound effect on doctrine. In the acquisition process the pull of military requirements is very powerful, but these requirements have to be adapted to the *modus operandi* of the defense sector.

All of this is not to say, however, that doctrine is unimportant or irrelevant for an understanding of Soviet policy. Soviet theorists ascribe doctrine a significant role in assessing the military utility of new technologies, in adapting the methods of warfare to new weapons, and in placing demands for the further development of armaments. Doctrine and discussions about doctrine have played a notable role in the history of Soviet defense policy. In the weapons acquisition process doctrine is regarded as the 'organising principle' in the formulation of a project. But doctrine is not seen by Soviet military writers as the key to making policy. Nor should it be seen by outside observers as the key to understanding Soviet policy. Doctrine has to be interpreted in its greater context.

Soviet doctrine is itself a complex phenomenon. The relationship between its political and military-technical sides is often neglected by Western studies. Yet this relationship, which appears at times to be ambiguous and tense, is crucial for an understanding of Soviet military thinking. Moreover, Soviet doctrine is neither monolithic, nor static. It is true that there are important elements of continuity which mark not only Soviet, but also Imperial Russian, military doctrine – the stress on the offensive being perhaps the most notable of these. But Soviet doctrine *has* changed. Even in the last years of Stalin's life, when strategic theory was constrained by the tenets of 'Stalinist military science', weapons were being developed which would have a revolutionary effect on strategy, and the pattern of their development was influenced by doctrine.

It is extremely important not to overlook the distinctive characteristics which Soviet doctrine derives from the economic, social, cultural and political conditions of Soviet life and history. But it is equally important not to exaggerate this distinctiveness. General Kozlov has written that,

> in the correlation between military science and doctrine, both in bourgeois states and here, there exist, no doubt, some common features. They are defined by a certain resemblance on the military-technical side, for more or less the same material conditions naturally give rise to similar views about the methods and forms of armed combat.[104]

Kozlov goes on to stress the basic political and philosophical differences that exist between Soviet and Western doctrine. But it is significant that, within the fundamentally different political contexts, he points to similarities in doctrine which follow from similarities in the material basis of military power.

Soviet military technology, it has been seen, possesses some specific features of its own. The Soviet economy has not proved particularly successful in generating technological advances. The defense sector, however, has performed better than civilian industry in this respect.[105] There are several reasons for this, but one of the most important is the power of the customer. Military requirements are backed by high political priority, while the armed forces exercise considerable control over the acquisition process. This suggests that requirements do play a key role in stimulating innovation and in giving direction to the military research and development effort. It may be, indeed, that requirements play a more important part in the Soviet acquisition process than in the US, as a consequence of the relative (though not absolute) weakness of innovation in Soviet industry. But two qualifications should be noted. First, the requirements have to be adapted to the pattern of operation of the defense sector. More importantly, Soviet requirements have to respond to the innovativeness of Western, and in particular of US, military technology; it is not only Soviet technology that exerts an influence on Soviet doctrine.

Soviet military thought sees both doctrine and technology as elements of military power: it is not only the arms, but the way in which men employ them, that affect the outcome of war. Soviet military thought gives considerable importance to doctrine and technology, but does not subscribe to either a purely doctrinal or a purely technological view of military power. The performance of the Soviet soldier, who uses the technology and puts the doctrine into practice, is a major preoccupation of Soviet writing. This is clear even in Soviet studies of military technology. Soviet theorists divide the modern revolution in military technology into three stages: the nuclear, rocket-nuclear and cybernetic. This last refers to the use of communications and computer technology in troop control (command and control) and more generally in military management. The object of Soviet interest in military cybernetics is to ensure that the destructive power embodied in the armed forces can be used in a controlled and effective way. The discussions of military cybernetics have inevitably merged with general questions about the performance of the Soviet soldier: the nature of command decisions, the bases of morale and discipline, the interaction of man and machine.[106] In looking at the relationship between doctrine and technology in Soviet policy, therefore, it should not be supposed that either the formulations of doctrine, or the progress of technology, have eliminated the human – the political, social and cultural – factor from Soviet thinking about war.

Notes: Chapter 9

1 *Foreign Affairs*, April, 1978, p. 548.
2 ibid., pp. 547, 548.
3 Matthew P. Gallagher, 'The military role in Soviet decision-making', in M. MccGwire, K. Booth and J. McDonnell (eds), *Soviet Naval Policy: Objectives and Constraints* (New York: Praeger, 1975), p. 56.
4 ibid.
5 Arthur J. Alexander, *Decision-making in Soviet Weapons Procurement*, Adelphi

Paper No. 147 and 148, International Institute for Strategic Studies, London, 1978-9, p. 54

6   ibid., p. 43.

7   For a discussion of the relationship between military doctrine and military science, see the entries in *Soryetskaya Voennaya Entsiklopedia* (hereafter *SVE*); see also S. N. Kozlov *et al.*, *O Sovyetskoi Voennoi Nauke*, 2nd ed. (Moscow: Voenizdat, 1964), pp. 379-91; Colonel General N. A. Lomov, 'O Sovyetskoi Voennoi Doktrine', and Major General S. N. Kozlov, 'Voennaya Doktrina i Voennaya Nauka', in *Problemy Revolyutsii v Voennom Dele* (Moscow: Voenizdat, 1965), pp. 40–56, 57–69.

8   Besides the references in n. 7, see *Spravochnik Ofitsera* (Moscow: Voenizdat, 1971), pp. 73–9.

9   Gallagher, op. cit., p. 56.

10 J. Erickson, 'Doctrine, technology and "style"', in J. Erickson and E. J. Feuchtwanger (eds), *Soviet Military Power and Performance* (London: Macmillan, 1979), p. 20.

11 F. Engels, *Anti-Dühring* (Moscow: Foreign Languages Press, 1962), p. 230.

12 ibid.

13 ibid., p. 236.

14 Marx to Engels, 25 September, 1857, Marx and Engels, *Selected Correspondence* (Moscow: Foreign Languages Press, n.d.), p. 118.

15 Marx to Engels, 7 July, 1866, ibid., p. 218.

16 Quoted in A.I. Babin, *F. Engels — vydayushchiisya voennyi teoretik rabochego klassa* (Moscow: Voenizdat, 1970), p. 180.

17 ibid., p. 190.

18 ibid., p. 191.

19 *Engels as a Military Critic*, with an introduction by W. H. Chaloner and W. O. Henderson (Manchester University Press, 1959), p. 45.

20 *Anti-Dühring*, pp. 232–3.

21 *Engels as a Military Critic*, p. 46.

22 Babin, op. cit., p. 196.

23 Colonel General N. A. Lomov (ed.), *Nauchno-tekhnicheskii progress i revolyutsiya v voennom dele* (Moscow: Voenizdat, 1973), p. 134.

24 *Anti-Dühring*, p. 236.

25 Lomov, op. cit., p. 134.

26 Andrzej Rzepniewski, 'Armaments development tendencies during the Second World War', in Witold Bieganski *et al.* (eds), *Military Technique Policy and Strategy in History* (Warsaw: Ministry of National Defence Publishing House, 1976), p. 208.

27 Bernard Brodie, 'Technological change, strategic doctrine and political outcomes', in Klaus Knorr (ed.), *Historical Dimensions of National Security Problems* (Lawrence; Manhattan; Wichita: University Press of Kansas, 1976), published for the National Security Education Program, p. 299.

28 M. V. Frunze, 'Vedinaya Voennaya Doktrina i Krasnaya Armiya', in *Izbrannye Proizvedeniya* (Moscow: Voenizda, 1977), pp. 29–46: this article was published in June, 1921; Leon Trotsky, 'Military doctrine or pseudo-military doctrinairism', in *Military Writings* (New York: Merit, 1969), pp. 31–69: this dates from December, 1921.

29 ibid; see also D. Fedotoff White, *The Growth of the Red Army* (Princeton University Press, 1944), chapter VI: 'The birth of a doctrine'; and John Erickson, *The Soviet High Command* (London: Macmillan, 1962), pp. 127–36.

30 Major General S. Kozlov, 'The formulation and development of Soviet military doctrine', *Voennaya mysl'*, no. 7, 1966, p. 48; all references to this journal are to the declassified English language version which is available in the Library of Congress; see also Army General S. Ivanov, 'Soviet military doctrine and strategy', *Voennaya mysl'*, no. 5, 1969, pp. 40–51.

31 Colonel General A. Radziyevskii, 'Thirty years of the Military Academy of the General Staff', *Voennaya mysl'*, no. 10, 1966, p. 8.

32 Quoted in *50 let Vooruzhennykh Sil SSSR* (Moscow: Voenizdat, 1968), p. 187.

33 Fedotoff White, op. cit., pp. 277–349; Erickson, op. cit., pp. 301–9.

34 *KPSS o Vooruzhennykh Silakh Sovyetskogo Soyuza* (Moscow: Voenizdat, 1969), pp. 264–6.

35 Quoted by Kozlov, loc. cit., *Voennaya mysl'*, p. 60.
36 *Voprosy strategii i operativnogo iskusstva v Sovyetskikh voennykh trudakh (1917–1941 gg.)* (Moscow: Voenizdat, 1965), p. 14.
37 Julian Cooper, *Defense Production and the Soviet Economy, 1929–41*, CREES Discussion Paper, University of Birmingham, 1976.
38 *Voprosy strategii ...*, op. cit., p. 17.
39 Vol. 2 (Moscow: Voenizdat, 1976), pp. 574–6.
40 M. N. Tukhachevskii, 'O Novom Polevom Ustave RKKA', in *Izbrannye Proizvedeniya*, Vol. 2 (Moscow: Voenizdat, 1964), pp. 255–6.
41 See Raymond Garthoff, *How Russia Makes War: Soviet Military Doctrine* (London: Allen & Unwin, 1954), pp. 171–82. But of course the principle of combined arms could not settle the question of which arms were to be combined and how, and thus left room for disagreement and argument. The role of strategic aviation was one of the contentious issues in the 1930s. It was the use of strategic bombers by the UK and the USA that finally resolved Soviet doubts. Early in 1945, it was decided to develop a long-range bomber; the initial design was later scrapped in favor of the Tu-4 copy of the US B-29; see B. V. Shavrov, *Istoriya konstruktsii samoletov v SSSR (1938–1950 gg)* (Moscow: Mashinostroeniye, 1978), pp. 354–5.
42 *Voprosy strategii ...*, op. cit., p. 22.
43 ibid.
44 Roy Medvedev, *Let History Judge* (Nottingham: Spokesman Books, 1976), pp. 226–9.
45 On this most important event, see, for example, A. M. Nekrich, *1941 22 iunya* (Moscow: Nauka, 1965); V. A. Anfilov, *Bessmertnyi Podvig* (Moscow: Nauka, 1971); John Erickson, *The Road to Stalingrad* (London: Weidenfeld & Nicholson, 1975).
46 Kozlov, loc. cit., *Voennaya mysl'*, p. 63.
47 A point made subsequently by Soviet historians; see Erickson, *The Soviet High Command*, op. cit., p. 582.
48 *50 let ...*, op. cit., pp. 333–7.
49 Lomov, loc. cit., p. 43.
50 Fedotoff White, op. cit., pp. 172–3.
51 Kozlov, loc. cit., *Voennaya mysl'*, p. 64.
52 David Holloway, *Entering the Nuclear Arms Race: The Soviet Decision to Build the Atomic Bomb, 1939–45*, Working Paper No. 9, International Security Studies Program, Woodrow Wilson International Center for Scholars, Washington, DC, 1979.
53 See, for example, Mitchell Sharpe and Frederick I. Ordway III, *The Rocket Team* (New York: Krowell, 1979).
54 Irina Radunskaya, *Askel' Berg — chelovek XX veka* (Moscow: Molodaya Gvardiya, 1971), pp. 167–237; A. Yakovlev, *Tsel' Zhizni* (Moscow: Politizdat, 1974), p. 420.
55 P. Ye. Khoroshilov, *Eto nachinalos'tak* (Moscow: Voenizdat, 1970), pp. 19–21; R. Bazurin, in *Aviatsiya i kosmonavtika*, no. 12, 1966, pp. 17–20.
56 Garthoff, op. cit., pp. 25–36.
57 Colonel General M. Povaly, 'Development of Soviet Military Strategy', *Voennaya mysl'*, no. 2, 1967, p. 64. General Povaly was Chief of the Operations Directorate of the General Staff when he wrote this article, and therefore in a good position to know about the effects of new weapons on doctrine.
58 Herbert S. Dinerstein, *War and the Soviet Union* (New York: Praeger, 1962) discusses these early post-Stalin debates; see also Matthew P. Gallagher, *The Soviet History of World War II* (New York: Praeger, 1963), pp. 128–33.
59 Lomov cites this as one of the theoretical underpinnings of Soviet military doctrine, loc. cit., pp. 40–1.
60 The Minister of Defense, D. F. Ustinov, has stated that 'in our doctrine the humane, profoundly just goals of peaceful Soviet foreign policy are organically combined with tireless concern for ensuring the security and defense capability of the country, for the reliable defense of the peaceful work of the Soviet people and of the peoples of the fraternal countries of socialism': *Izbrannye rechi i stat'i* (Moscow: Politizdat, 1979), p. 498.

61 *50 let...*, op. cit., p. 521; Harriet Fast Scott and William F. Scott, *The Armed Forces of the USSR* (Boulder, Col.: Westview Press, 1979), p. 41.
62 *Zasedaniya Verkhovnogo Sovyeta SSSR pyatogo sozyva (chetvyortaya sessiya). Steno-graficheskii otchet* (Moscow: Izdanie Verkhovnogo Sovyeta SSSR, 1960), pp. 10–59.
63 Scott and Scott, op. cit., p. 135.
64 *50 let...*, op. cit., p. 504.
65 On the debates of the early 1960s, see Thomas Wolfe, *Soviet Strategy at the Cross-roads* (Cambridge, Mass.:Harvard University Press, 1964); on the development of the ground forces, see chapter by John Erickson, in Lawrence L. Whetten (ed.), *The Future of Soviet Military Power* (New York: Crane, Russak, 1976).
66 Raymond L. Garthoff, *Soviet Military Policy* (London: Faber, 1966), p. 59.
67 See Ustinov's statement quoted in n. 61, above.
68 On Malenkov's position, see Gallagher, op. cit., p. 130.
69 See his chapter in this book.
70 'Every violation of this [strategic] equality, the supply of new systems of armament to armies, is fraught with serious consequences: it will provoke retaliatory measures and lead to a new spiral in the arms race, to a destabilization of the international situation, to new political difficulties': *Sovyetskie vooruzhennye Sily. Istoriya stroitel'stva* (Moscow: Voenizdat, 1978), p. 453.
71 Scott and Scott, op. cit., pp. 56–9.
72 *Pravda*, 19 January, 1977.
73 Alexander, op. cit., provides an extensive account of the institutional arrangements and organizational processes in the Soviet defense sector.
74 David Holloway, 'Innovation in the Defense Sector', in R. Amann and J. Cooper (eds), *Innovation in Soviet Industry* (forthcoming).
75 This is a very interesting group of men, about two of whom biographies have been written: Radunskaya, op. cit., about Engineer-Admiral Academician A. I. Berg; and Army General V. F. Tolubko, *Nedelin* (Moscow: Molodaya Gvardiya, 1979).
76 For an extensive analysis, see Holloway, loc. cit.
77 S. A. Sarkisian and E. S. Minaev, *Ekonomicheskaya otsenka letatel'nykh apparatov* (Moscow: Mashinostroeniye, 1972), pp. 27–9.
78 ibid.
79 Lt General of Engineering-Technical Service V. Pyshnov, 'Certain problems in the development of military aircraft', *Voennaya mysl'*, no. 10, 1963, p. 6.
80 op. cit., p. 29.
81 *SVE*, Vol. 3 (Moscow: Voenizdat, 1977), pp. 616–18. This article is signed by Colonel General N. N. Alekseev, Deputy Minister of Defence for Armament.
82 op. cit., p. 30.
83 ibid., pp. 27–30; Alekseev, loc. cit., pp. 616–17.
84 See Alexander, op. cit., pp. 31–5, for a discussion of the review process.
85 For a discussion of this decision, see Karl F. Spielmann, *Analyzing Soviet Strategic Decisions* (Boulder, Col.: Westview Press, 1979): N. A. Pilyugin, interview in *Pravda*, 17 May, 1978.
86 See David Holloway, 'Economics and the Soviet weapons acquisition process', to be published by the Joint Economic Committee, US Congress.
87 Alekseev, loc. cit., pp. 617–18.
88 Sarkisian and Minaev, op. cit., p. 28.
89 V. D. Mostovenko, *Tanki* (Moscow: Voenizdat, 1958), p. 95.
90 G. Ozerov, *Tupolevskaya Sharaga*, 2nd ed. (Frankfurt am Main, Possev Verlag, 1973), p. 57. According to Ozerov, Tupolev argued that to ensure 'that an irreparable gap does not open up between quantity and quality, it is essential: (1) to ensure the all-round development of experimental aircraft production, freeing it from worries about series production, and for this to create sufficiently strong series design bureaus at the factories; (2) to place two kinds of tasks before the experimental design bureaus: new models for series production, and long-term (perspective) machines which make a sharp advance in their characteristics': Alexander, op. cit., pp. 45–53, shows that the Mikoyan design bureau has followed a strategy of this kind.
91 One of those who worked in the tank industry during the war has written that 'the experience of the war shows that the design process ensures rapid introduction into

series production only when it is based on assemblies which have been mastered earlier. Consequently the continuous improvement of the basic assemblies is essential. To design a new tank, while at the same time creating new assemblies, means, as a rule, to pass on for series production an uncompleted tank': I. V.Yurasov, in P. N. Pospelov (ed.), *Sovyetskii Tyl v velikoi Otechestvennoi Voine. Kniga II. Trudovoi podvig naroda* (Moscow: Mysl', 1974), p. 113; contrast this with the statement by General Pyshnov (n. 80), who says that each new aircraft design will involve untested subsystems. It is a mistake to generalize about the design philosophy appropriate to different kinds of technology.

92 Alexander, op. cit., 31–5.

93 David Holloway, 'The Soviet style of military R&D', in F. A. Long and Judith Reppy (eds), *The Genesis of New Weapons: Decision-Making for Military R&D* (New York: Pergamon Press) (forthcoming).

94 The available figures on defense output seem to show a steady production rate, although this is conceivably a function of the way in which the figures are compiled; see, for example, Ministry of Defence (London) *Release on Soviet Weapons Production*, 1976. According to CIA estimates, the shares of Soviet defence outlays received by the different services have remained stable since the late 1960s; see *Estimated Soviet Defense Spending in Rubles, 1970–5*, CIA: SR 76-101210, May, 1976; *Estimated Soviet Defense Spending: Trends and Prospects*, CIA: SR 78-10121, June, 1978.

95 Holloway, 'The Soviet Style . . .', loc. cit.

96 ibid.

97 ibid.

98 See David Holloway, Soviet military R&D: managing the research-production cycle', in John Thomas and Ursula Kruse-Vaucienne (eds), *Soviet Science and Technology*, published by the George Washington University for the National Science Foundation, 1977, pp. 189–229.

99 V. P. Glushko, *Rocket-Engines GDL-OKB* (Moscow: Novosti Press Agency, 1975), p. 11.

100 ibid.

101 I. Chutko, in *Znamya*, no. 8, 1973, pp. 176–8.

102 See Sharpe and Ordway, op. cit., and Pilyugin, loc. cit., *SVE*, Vol. 2 (Moscow: Voenizdat, 1976), p. 578: Soviet artillery tactics seem to have influenced nuclear strategy in other ways, too. Soviet thinking about preemption is, for example, close to the idea of artillery *kontrpodgotovka* ('counterpreparation'); 'a pre-planned, brief, powerful, surprise burst of fire delivered by a defender against enemy groupings which are preparing for an offensive': *Slovar' osnovnykh voennykh terminov* (Moscow: Voenizdat, 1965), p. 111.

103 Lt General G. Semenov and Major General V. Prokhorov, 'Scientific-technical progress and some questions of strategy', *Voennaya mysl'*, no. 2, 1969, p. 23.

104 Kozlov, loc. cit., *Problemy . . .*, p. 67.

105 See ch. 2, Amann, Cooper, Davies (eds), op. cit.

106 See David Holloway, *Technology, Management and the Soviet Military Establishment*, Adelphi Paper No. 76, Institute for Strategic Studies, London, 1971; for a more general discussion, see Herbert Goldhamer, *The Soviet Soldier* (New York: Russak, 1975).

About the Contributors

ROBERT BATHURST is Adjunct Professor of National Security at the Naval Postgraduate School and was, during the 1979–80 academic year, an associate at the Russian Research Center, Harvard University. He is a former navy captain, who served as Assistant Naval Attaché to Moscow (1965–7), and later held the Layton Chair of Military Intelligence at the Naval War College. Dr Bathurst is the author of *Understanding the Soviet Navy* (Naval War College Press, 1980). The holder of a degree in Russian literature from Brown University, he is currently a writer, speaker and consultant.

FRITZ W. ERMARTH is Senior Technical Analyst at the Analysis Center, Northrop Corporation. He has been an analyst of Soviet and American strategic affairs at the Central Intelligence Agency and at the Rand Corporation, where he directed the latter's Strategic Studies Program. Since 1978, he has been a member of the National Security Council, working on US strategic and arms control policy.

RAYMOND L. GARTHOFF is a senior fellow at the Brookings Institution, having retired from the US Foreign Service, in which he last served as Ambassador to Bulgaria (1977–9). Dr Garthoff is the author of a number of books on Soviet political and military affairs, including *Soviet Military Policy* (New York: Praeger, 1966), *Soviet Strategy in the Nuclear Age* (New York: Praeger, 1958, 1962) and *Soviet Military Doctrine* (Glencoe, Il: Free Press, 1953). He was the Executive Secretary and Senior Adviser on the SALT I delegation (1969–72), and served as Deputy Director of the State Department's Bureau of Politico-Military Affairs from 1970 to 1973.

DAVID HOLLOWAY is lecturer in politics, University of Edinburgh. He has been a Research Associate at the International Institute for Strategic Studies in London, and during 1978–9, he was a fellow of the International Security Studies Program, Woodrow Wilson International Center for Scholars, Smithsonian Institution. He publishes frequently on the subject of technology in the Soviet Union, and is author of *Adelphi Paper 76*, published by the International Institute of Strategic Studies, entitled 'Technology, management, and the Soviet military establishment'.

CHRISTOPHER JONES has, since 1977, been working on a series of Soviet foreign–defense policy studies, supported by the American Council of Learned Societies, Harvard University's Russian Research Center, the National Council for Soviet and East European Research and the Ford Foundation. From 1975 to 1977, Dr Jones was an assistant professor of political science at Marquette University.

NATHAN LEITES is a member of the senior staff of the Rand Corporation, where he has had an ongoing affiliation with the Strategic Studies Center and has served on the faculty of the Rand Graduate Institute. From 1938 to 1941, he was a member of the faculty of the University of Chicago's department of political science, where he returned for the 1963–4 academic year. He is the author of *Operational Code of the Politburo* (1951) and *A Study of Bolshevism* (1953).

MICHAEL MCCGWIRE is a senior fellow at the Brookings Institution, and formerly Professor of Maritime and Strategic Studies at Dalhousie University's Center for Foreign Policy Studies, Halifax, Nova Scotia. He was editor (or coeditor) and major contributor to *Soviet Naval Developments* (1973), *Soviet Naval Policy* (1975) and *Soviet Naval Influence* (1977), all published by Praeger Press.

STANLEY SIENKIEWICZ is a Special Assistant to the US Under Secretary of State for Security Assistance. He has been a member of the Staff of the Senate Foreign Relations Committee, and formerly an analyst in the Department of Defense. He has been a foreign affairs fellow at the Council on Foreign Relations, and a research fellow at Harvard University's Center for Science and International Affairs.

About the Editor

DEREK LEEBAERT has been a Research Fellow, Center for Science and International Affairs at Harvard since 1975, and also serves as Managing Editor of *International Security* and Associate Editor of the *Journal of Policy Analysis and Management.* He was editor and CSIA work group leader for *European Security: Prospects for the 1980s* (Lexington, MA.: D. C. Heath, 1979).

Index